# Christian Anarchism

## A Political Commentary on the Gospel

## [Abridged edition]

Alexandre Christoyannopoulos

IMPRINT ACADEMIC

*Copyright © Alexandre Christoyannopoulos, 2011*

The moral rights of the author have been asserted.
No part of this publication may be reproduced in any form
without permission, except for the quotation of brief passages
in criticism and discussion.

Published in the UK by
Imprint Academic, PO Box 200, Exeter EX5 5YX, UK

Published in the USA by Imprint Academic,
Philosophy Documentation Center
PO Box 7147, Charlottesville, VA 22906-7147, USA

ISBN 978 184540247 1

A CIP catalogue record for this book is available from the
British Library and US Library of Congress

Christianity in its true sense puts an end to the State. It was so understood from its very beginning, and for that Christ was crucified.

— Leo Tolstoy

Where there is no love, put love and you will find love.

— St. John of the Cross

# Contents

**ACKNOWLEDGEMENTS** ........................................................................ VII

**INTRODUCTION – CHRISTIAN "ANARCHISM"?** ..................................... 1
   LOCATING CHRISTIAN ANARCHISM ................................................................ 1
      *In political theology* ............................................................................. 2
      *In political thought* .............................................................................. 4
   OUTLINING CHRISTIAN ANARCHISM ............................................................... 7
      *Aims, limits, and originality* ................................................................ 7
      *Technical issues* ................................................................................. 10
      *The structure of this book* ................................................................ 13
   CHRISTIAN ANARCHIST "THINKERS" ........................................................... 13
      *Leo Tolstoy* ........................................................................................ 14
      *Jacques Ellul* ..................................................................................... 16
      *Vernard Eller* ..................................................................................... 16
      *Michael C. Elliott* .............................................................................. 17
      *Dave Andrews* ................................................................................... 17
      *Key writers in the Catholic Worker movement* ................................ 18
      *Writers behind other Christian anarchist publications* ................... 21
      *William Lloyd Garrison* .................................................................... 22
      *Hugh O. Pentecost* ............................................................................ 23
      *Nicolas Berdyaev* .............................................................................. 23
      *William T. Cavanaugh* ..................................................................... 24
      *Jonathan Bartley* .............................................................................. 24
      *Christian anarcho-capitalists* ........................................................... 24
      *George Tarleton* ............................................................................... 25
      *Supportive thinkers* .......................................................................... 26

**PART I – THE CHRISTIAN ANARCHIST CRITIQUE OF THE STATE** . 29
**CHAPTER 1 – THE SERMON ON THE MOUNT: A MANIFESTO FOR CHRISTIAN ANARCHISM** ........................................................................ 30
   1.1 – RESIST NOT EVIL ................................................................................ 32
      *1.1.1 – Jesus' three illustrations* ..................................................... 32
      *1.1.2 – A purposeful reaction* ........................................................ 34
      *1.1.3 – Beyond lex talionis* ............................................................. 35
      *1.1.4 – The cycle of violence* .......................................................... 37
      *1.1.5 – Overcoming of the cycle of violence* ................................... 41
      *1.1.6 – Anarchist implications* ...................................................... 43
   1.2 – JUDGE NOT ........................................................................................ 47
   1.3 – LOVE YOUR ENEMIES ........................................................................ 49
   1.4 – SWEAR NOT AT ALL .......................................................................... 52
   1.5 – THE GOLDEN RULE ........................................................................... 55
   1.6 – REFLECTIONS ON OTHER PASSAGES IN THE SERMON ........................ 56

- 1.6.1 – Be not angry.................................................................................... 56
- 1.6.2 – Commit no adultery........................................................................ 59
- 1.6.3 – Seek no praise................................................................................. 59
- 1.6.4 – The Beatitudes ................................................................................ 59
- 1.6.5 – Worry not about security................................................................ 60
- 1.6.6 – Be the salt and the light.................................................................. 61
- 1.7 – FULFILLING THE OLD LAW ..................................................................... 61
- 1.8 – A MANIFESTO FOR CHRISTIAN ANARCHISM............................................ 65

## CHAPTER 2 – THE ANARCHISM IMPLIED IN JESUS' OTHER TEACHINGS AND EXAMPLE ..................................................................... 67

- 2.1 – THE OLD TESTAMENT ............................................................................ 68
  - 2.1.1 – 1 Samuel 8 .................................................................................... 68
  - 2.1.2 – Other Old Testament passages ..................................................... 72
- 2.2 – EXPECTATIONS OF A POLITICAL MESSIAH .............................................. 73
- 2.3 – JESUS' THIRD TEMPTATION IN THE WILDERNESS .................................... 75
- 2.4 – EXORCISMS AND MIRACLE HEALINGS .................................................... 77
- 2.5 – FORGIVE SEVENTY-SEVEN TIMES ........................................................... 78
- 2.6 – NOT JUDGING ONE ANOTHER ................................................................. 80
- 2.7 – BEING SERVANTS ................................................................................... 82
- 2.8 – THE TEMPLE CLEANSING ........................................................................ 83
- 2.9 – JESUS' ARREST ...................................................................................... 87
- 2.10 – JESUS' TRIAL ....................................................................................... 90
- 2.11 – JESUS' CRUCIFIXION ............................................................................ 93
  - 2.11.1 – Paul's "powers"........................................................................... 93
  - 2.11.2 – The defeat of the powers ............................................................. 95
  - 2.11.3 – The crucified "messiah" ............................................................. 96
  - 2.11.4 – The crux of Jesus' political teaching.......................................... 97
  - 2.11.5 – Taking up the cross .................................................................... 98
- 2.12 – JESUS' RESURRECTION....................................................................... 100
- 2.13 – REVELATION ..................................................................................... 102
- 2.14 – ALLEGEDLY VIOLENT PASSAGES........................................................ 104
- 2.15 – JESUS' ANARCHIST TEACHING AND EXAMPLE .................................... 106

## CHAPTER 3 – THE STATE'S WICKEDNESS AND THE CHURCH'S INFIDELITY ................................................................................................ 107

- 3.1 – THE HISTORY OF CHRISTENDOM .......................................................... 108
  - 3.1.1 – Constantine's temptation of the early church ............................ 108
  - 3.1.2 – Christendom and beyond............................................................ 112
- 3.2 – THE MODERN STATE AND ECONOMY ................................................... 113
  - 3.2.1 – The "state" ................................................................................. 113
  - 3.2.2 – State violence.............................................................................. 115
  - 3.2.3 – State deception........................................................................... 117
  - 3.2.4 – Economic exploitation................................................................ 121
  - 3.2.5 – The state as idolatry ................................................................... 125
- 3.3 – CHURCH DOCTRINE IN SUPPORT OF THE STATE.................................... 127
  - 3.3.1 – Reinterpretations of Jesus' commandments in the Sermon on the Mount . 128
  - 3.3.2 – Reinterpretations of non-resistance........................................... 130
  - 3.3.3 – Support for political authority ................................................... 135
- 3.4 – DECEPTIVE DOGMAS............................................................................ 136
  - 3.4.1 – Sanctimonious self-righteousness.............................................. 137

3.4.2 – *Obscure rituals and beliefs* ................................................................. *139*
3.4.3 – *Institutional religion*.......................................................................... *143*
3.5 – AWAKENING TO TRUE CHRISTIANITY ............................................................ 144


# PART II – THE CHRISTIAN ANARCHIST RESPONSE .................... 146

# CHAPTER 4 – RESPONDING TO THE STATE .................................. 147

4.1 – PAUL'S LETTER TO ROMAN CHRISTIANS, CHAPTER 13 ................................. 148
    4.1.1 – *Paul's weaknesses* ............................................................................ *149*
    4.1.2 – *The Christian anarchist exegesis: subversive subjection* ............... *150*
    4.1.3 – *Similar passages in the New Testament* ....................................... *156*
4.2 – JESUS' ADVICE ON TAXES ........................................................................... 157
    4.2.1 – *Caesar's things and God's things*................................................... *158*
    4.2.2 – *The temple tax and fish episode* .................................................... *160*
4.3 – PONDERING THE ROLE OF CIVIL DISOBEDIENCE............................................ 161
    4.3.1 – *Against civil disobedience*............................................................. *161*
    4.3.2 – *For (non-violent) civil disobedience*............................................. *162*
    4.3.3 – *Obedience to God*.......................................................................... *164*
4.4 – DISREGARDING THE ORGANS OF THE STATE ................................................ 165
    4.4.1 – *Holding office and voting*.............................................................. *165*
    4.4.2 – *Paying taxes*................................................................................... *166*
    4.4.3 – *Conscription and war*.................................................................... *166*
    4.4.4 – *Other state services* ....................................................................... *167*
4.5 – ON REVOLUTIONARY METHODS .................................................................. 167
    4.5.1 – *No compromise with violence* ....................................................... *168*
    4.5.2 – *Revolution by example* .................................................................. *171*

# CHAPTER 5 – COLLECTIVE WITNESS AS THE TRUE CHURCH ..... 174

5.1 – "A NEW SOCIETY WITHIN THE SHELL OF THE OLD"........................................ 175
    5.1.1 – *Repenting and joining the church*................................................. *175*
    5.1.2 – *An economy of care and sacrifice*................................................. *177*
    5.1.3 – *Subversive organisation*................................................................ *180*
5.2 – A DIFFICULT MISSION ................................................................................. 183
    5.2.1 – *Dealing with evil in the community* .............................................. *183*
    5.2.2 – *Heroic sacrifices by church members*........................................... *188*
5.3 – TRUST IN GOD............................................................................................ 191
    5.3.1 – *A beacon of faith* ........................................................................... *191*
    5.3.2 – *The mysterious growth of a mustard seed* .................................... *193*

# CHAPTER 6 – EXAMPLES OF CHRISTIAN ANARCHIST WITNESS . 196

6.1 – PRE-MODERN EXAMPLES ............................................................................ 197
    6.1.1 – *Early Christians* ............................................................................ *197*
    6.1.2 – *The Middle Ages and the Reformation* ......................................... *199*
6.2 – MODERN EXAMPLES ................................................................................... 202
    6.2.1 – *Garrison and his followers* ........................................................... *202*
    6.2.2 – *Ballou and the Hopedale community*........................................... *202*
    6.2.3 – *Tolstoy's personal example*........................................................... *203*
    6.2.4 – *Tolstoyism and Tolstoyan colonies*............................................... *204*
    6.2.5 – *Gandhi: a leader by example*........................................................ *207*
    6.2.6 – *The Catholic Worker movement* ................................................... *209*

    6.2.7 – *A Pinch of Salt and The Digger and Christian Anarchist* .......................... 210
    6.2.8 – *Online communities* ................................................................. 211
    6.2.9 – *Andrews' community work* ....................................................... 212
  6.3 – INCOMPLETE EXAMPLES ............................................................. 212

# CONCLUSION – THE PROPHETIC ROLE OF CHRISTIAN ANARCHISM ............................................................................................. 214

  "CHRISTIAN ANARCHISTS" AND "CHRISTIAN ANARCHISM" ..................... 215
  THE KINGDOM OF GOD IN HISTORY ....................................................... 217
    *"Hastening" God's kingdom* ........................................................... 217
    *History's mysterious unfolding* ....................................................... 219
    *The temptation of normal political action* ........................................ 221
  RELENTLESS PROPHECY AT THE MARGINS ............................................ 225
    *Love, justice, and social ontology* .................................................. 225
    *Christian anarchists as prophets* ..................................................... 229
    *Distinguishing church and state* ...................................................... 232
  CHRISTIAN ANARCHISM'S ORIGINAL CONTRIBUTION .............................. 235

# EPILOGUE ............................................................................................. 240

# BIBLIOGRAPHY ................................................................................... 242

# INDEX ................................................................................................... 265

# Acknowledgements

This book is the product of six years of doctoral research undertaken at the University of Kent, in Canterbury, England. Since the defence of that thesis in September 2008, the taking on of various academic duties and responsibilities have prevented me from making major revisions to the text, and therefore from integrating into it the related material which I have come across or read since. Apart from adding a few references to such material and other minor modifications, the book is not significantly different from the original thesis.

The aim of the thesis was to produce a clear and accessible synthesis of all the Christian anarchist publications I managed to come across and study during my research, as well as a comprehensive set of references to these. The aim of the original, hardback version of this book was to present both that synthesis and its references to a wider audience. This abridged, paperback version presents almost exactly the same text, but without the original version's detailed comments and references in the footnotes – the main aim being to thereby make the book more affordable. The footnotes of the current version therefore only contain the most important comments and reference details (such as for *verbatim* quotations). Those who wish to study the Christian anarchist literature and its context in more depth will find the full comments and references in the hardback version. As to the main text, the only changes to it are the current paragraph, the rectification of a few typos, and the addition of two bracketed comments where the text refers to extensive footnotes only present in the original. By implication, just as with the hardback version, given that the Introduction's function is to set the context, locate the book in the wider literature, and introduce the Christian anarchist thinkers relied on for the rest of the book, readers less interested in such preliminaries can skip these and jump straight to Chapter 1.

I would not have been able to complete my PhD without the financial support of my parents. Their love, care and patience, along with that of my (then) partner Tânia Gonçalves, provided the ideal climate for my research to take root, grow and bear fruits. My gratitude to all three of them is immense.

My doctoral work was supervised mainly by Dr Stefan Rossbach. His comments on my work were always sympathetic and helpful, and even when he took issue with Christian anarchists, his feedback was always informed by a concern for me to improve my case and hence theirs. Those he supervises are envied by those he does not, and the Department of Politics and International Relations at Kent owes a lot to him for his dedication to research students as Director of Research. I am also grateful to Dr Peter Moore and Dr Joseph Milne, whose invitation to return to Kent and to sit in numerous modules in theology and religious studies was instrumental in setting the context for me to start my PhD. They also both acted as supervisors from time to time, and especially in Joseph's case, as friend and collaborator too. My thanks also go to my examiners, Professor David McLellan and Dr Ruth Kinna.

My work benefited from the stimulating feedback and friendship of numerous research students in politics and in religious studies. They cannot all be listed here, but deserving special mention for their impact on my doctoral work are, in the religious studies crowd, Duane Williams, David Lewin, Todd Mei, Brian Edwards and Geoffrey Cornelius, and in the politics crowd, James Schillabeer (whose careful proofreading of my thesis was of tremendous help), George Sotiropoulos, and Charles Devellennes. Fanny Forest has also been of great support in helping me convert my thesis into this book.

I have also found help and inspiration among the academic networks I have joined and the conferences they organised. These include the Anarchist Studies Network and the broader Political Science Association it belongs to, the Society for the Study of Theology, the Religion and Politics standing group of the European Consortium of Political Research, and the Research on Anarchism and Anarchist Academics mailing lists. To those networks (among others), and more to the point to their members who have helped me articulate and improve my work, I owe another big "thank you."

Finally, I wish to thank all those activists of love and justice whose passion and commitment are an inspiration to those who are ambassadors of the same objectives within academia. This includes many anarchists, many Christians, but also many others who dedicate time and effort to the improvement of the lives of others. To them, to all of the above and to all those reading these pages, I hope that this book can convey enthusiasm and stimulate thought in the way the Christian anarchist literature did to me over the years.

# Introduction – Christian "Anarchism"?

Christianity and anarchism are rarely thought to belong together. Surely, the argument goes, Christianity has produced about as hierarchic a structure as can be, and anarchism not only rejects any hierarchy but is also often fervently secular and anti-clerical. Ciaron O'Reilly warns, however, that Christian anarchism "is not an attempt to synthesise two systems of thought" that are hopelessly incompatible, but rather "a realisation that the premise of anarchism is inherent in Christianity and the message of the Gospels."[1] For Christian anarchists, Jesus' teaching implies a critique of the state, and an honest and consistent application of Christianity would lead to a stateless society. From this perspective, it is actually the notion of a "Christian state" that, just like "hot ice," is a contradiction in terms, an oxymoron.[2] Christian anarchism, therefore, is not about forcing together two very different systems of thought – it is about pursuing the radical political implications of Christianity to the fullest extent.

A generic "theory" of Christian anarchism, however, has yet to be enunciated. Several writers have adopted a Christian anarchist position, and some of these writers are aware of some of the others who have come to the same position, but a detailed and comprehensive synthesis of the main themes of Christian anarchist thought has yet to be produced.[3] That is, an overall theory of Christian anarchism has yet to be outlined. The central aim of this book is to do just that – metaphorically-speaking, to weave together the different threads presented by individual Christian anarchist thinkers, to arrange into a symphony the similar melodies played by each of these theorists. In other words, this book delineates Christian anarchism by bringing together the main insights of individual Christian anarchist thinkers.

But first, such a perspective must be located in the broader literature, both in political theology and in political thought – the first task of this Introduction. This makes it possible to then spell out in more detail the main aims of this book, its originality, and its chapter structure. The more substantial part of this opening chapter then introduces each of the thinkers who contribute to this generic outline of Christian anarchism.

## Locating Christian anarchism

In order to clarify what is original about Christian anarchism, it is necessary to first contextualise it in the wider literature in both politics and theology.

---

[1] Ciaron O'Reilly, "The Anarchist Implications of Christian Discipleship," *Social Alternatives* 2/3 (1982), 9 (in which "Christianity" is spelt "christianity").
[2] Leo Tolstoy, "Church and State," in *On Life and Essays on Religion*, trans. Aylmer Maude (London: Oxford University Press, 1934), 338.
[3] The words "synthesise," "synthesis" and their derivates are used here not in the Hegelian sense of reaching a new idea by resolving the conflict between an initial proposition and its negation, but in the original and etymological sense of generating a new unified whole by combining different elements.

## *In political theology*

The modern, Western assumption that religion and politics are best kept separate has been coming under increasing strain lately, from a variety of angles. Recent scholarship, for example, has questioned the motives and the historical origins of the claim that religion should be kept out of politics in the first place. William T. Cavanaugh in particular argues that the very "creation of religion" as a set of private and therefore apolitical beliefs "is correlative to the rise" of the modern state, in other words that the modern liberal myth of their necessary separation was a far from innocent product of the state's successful outmanoeuvring of the church for power and legitimacy in sixteenth and seventeenth century Europe.[4] Even the typical Christian rationalisation for this separation – the "distinction of planes" interpretation of the "render unto Caesar" passage – was absent "until at least the late medieval period," contends Cavanaugh.[5] Hence whether secular or Christian, the rationale for the separation of religion and politics has been questioned.

Moreover, a growing body of scholars has made the case for the direct and indirect political implications of Jesus' teaching to be fully recognised. John Howard Yoder's *Politics of Jesus*, for instance, is an eminent example of such scholarship.[6] His book also helpfully provides a very comprehensive set of references to the many other studies that have similarly emphasised the political nature and context of Jesus' teaching. Partly thanks to such work, "political theology" is an increasingly popular field of study in academic circles (despite the uneasiness caused by this term's association with Carl Schmitt).[7] Nowadays, therefore, while it is possible to disagree on whether the political side of Jesus' teaching was the most important, it is increasingly difficult to argue that there is no such political dimension to it.

Away from the theory, in practice, scholars have also noted that there has been something of a resurgence of religion in politics in the past decades, even – if not especially – in the hitherto allegedly secularised West, which has witnessed the increasing "collective mobilisation of Christians in large numbers

---

[4] William T. Cavanaugh, "A Fire Strong Enough to Consume the House: The Wars of Religion and the Rise of the State," *Modern Theology* 11/4 (1995), 403. This topic is addressed in more detail in Chapter 3 and in the Conclusion.
[5] Cavanaugh is not saying that the distinction of planes was absent until the late Middle Ages (some Christian anarchists accuse Augustine, for instance, of making precisely such a distinction, as noted in Chapter 3) – but that the *interpretation of the "render unto Caesar" passage* as implying such a distinction was absent until then. William T. Cavanaugh, *Torture and Eucharist: Theology, Politics, and the Body of Christ* (Oxford: Blackwell, 1998), 191. The Christian anarchist interpretation of this passage is explained in Chapter 4.
[6] John Howard Yoder, *The Politics of Jesus: Vicit Agnus Noster*, Second ed. (Grand Rapids: William B. Eerdmans, 1994), especially chap. 1.
[7] Carl Schmitt (who never regretted his enthusiasm for Nazism) coined the term "political theology" to describe the secularisation of theological concepts, the theological ancestry of secular concepts. Following Johann Baptist Metz, however, the term has also been used to describe "theology doing politics," so to speak – that is, theology that concerns itself with the political. It is obviously in that latter sense that the term is being used is this book.

## Introduction – "Christian Anarchism"?

across a wide range of issues."[8] Yet perhaps the most famous example of recent political engagement by Christians has come not from the West but from the "theologies of liberation" of Latin America (and beyond), where churches have mobilised to resist oppressive regimes and more recently the perceived oppression inherent in global capitalism. These and other examples demonstrate that religion continues to inform politics, despite the confident predictions of certain Enlightenment thinkers.

For Christian anarchists, however, although encouraging and in the right direction, none of these trends go far enough. For them, the conventional Christian legitimisation of the state ought to be seriously reconsidered. Jacques Ellul, for example, argues that while one of the two "tendencies" in the New Testament does seem "favorable" to the state (based "mainly" on Romans 13), the other, "more extensive" tendency which is "hostile" to it (based on the Gospels and Revelation) should also be given due attention.[9] He finds it "strange" that "the official Church since Constantine has consistently based almost its entire 'theology of the State' on Romans 13 and the parallel texts in Peter's epistles."[10] Christian anarchists are also deeply sceptical of the view that the head of state somehow acts as God's ambassador for its population, or that the state is otherwise divinely appointed – although of course, as one of them puts it, "Those who live off the loot would be very pleased for you to believe that."[11] They note, for instance, that "it is the state and the powers behind it that" crucified Jesus,[12] and that perhaps the poor and those who are being persecuted by the state are better candidates to the title of God's "ambassadors" on earth.[13]

A central aim of this book is to explore the detail of such Christian anarchist criticisms of the received Christian wisdom on the state, and to thereby contribute to the wider literature in political theology. More specifically, the Christian anarchist understanding of the political implications of Jesus' teaching and example is explained in Chapters 1 and 2; their bitter criticism of both church and state for their collusion since Constantine in Chapter 3; and their interpretation of the "render unto Caesar" passage and of Romans 13 in Chapter 4. Both Chapters 4 and 5 also describe the sort of mobilisation which Christian anarchists expect from Christians today. Each of these Chapters, therefore, has a bearing on the contemporary theological debates on the theoretical and practical political implications of Christianity.

---

[8] The quotation is from Jonathan Bartley, *Faith and Politics after Christendom: The Church as a Movement for Anarchy* (Milton Keynes: Paternoster, 2006), 56, whose book is very much addressed to Christians on this very topic.
[9] Jacques Ellul, "Anarchism and Christianity," in *Jesus and Marx: From Gospel to Ideology*, trans. Joyce Main Hanks (Grand Rapids: William B. Eerdmans, 1998), 166.
[10] Ellul, "Anarchism and Christianity," 166-167.
[11] Llewellyn H. Rockwell, Jr., *The Ten Commandments Question*, available from http://www.lewrockwell.com/rockwell/commandments.html (accessed 21 November 2007), para. 3.
[12] Bartley, *Faith and Politics after Christendom*, 191.
[13] Peter Maurin, *Easy Essays* (Washington: Rose Hill, 2003), 8.

## *In political thought*

Aside from political theology, Christian anarchist thought also contributes to wider political thought, and in particular, obviously, to anarchist thought. Here is not the place to discuss the often misjudged association of the term "anarchism" with violent chaos and disorder. It should suffice to note that anarchism is a recognised school of political thought with a very broad range of (sometimes contradictory) voices reflecting on important political themes, such as those of freedom, power, economic justice, and the best methods to approach these. Violence, far from being universally supported among anarchists, is justified by some but also roundly rejected by many, and is thus a topic of passionate debate among anarchists to this day – a debate on which Christian anarchists have a particularly pointed contribution to make (as Chapter 1 to 3, in particular, make clear).

Christian anarchism has long been acknowledged as a peculiar variant of anarchism. For some anarchists, it is to be welcomed as another strand of the very diverse tradition that is the anarchist school of thought. For others, however, the association of Christianity and anarchism is not without potentially serious problems, for several reasons.

For a start, many classic anarchist thinkers were atheistic or at the very least agnostic, and there is certainly what Nicolas Walter describes as "a strong correlation between anarchism and atheism."[14] Colin Ward furthermore explains that "The main varieties of anarchism are resolutely hostile to organised religion."[15] Yet the same commentators also grant that anarchism *need* not necessarily be atheistic, that there even seems to be anarchist elements in Buddhism and Taoism, and of course that thinkers like Leo Tolstoy have famously made the case for a peculiarly Christian type of anarchism as well. Anarchist conclusions, therefore, do not necessarily depend on atheistic premises.

Ellul argues that anarchism's "complaints against Christianity" usually "fall into two categories: the essentially historical and the metaphysical."[16] The prime example of the former is the anarchist blaming of the church for colluding with the state to persecute and oppress the masses. Almost all anarchists are extremely critical of organised churches for this reason. As Chapter 3 shows, however, so are most Christian anarchists. A strong anticlericalism is therefore present in *both* secular and Christian anarchism, although both also note that a minority of revolutionary churches and rebellious sects also form part of the Christian legacy.

Related to this historical complaint is the one that "religions of all kind generate wars."[17] True though this may be, the twentieth century demonstrates

---

[14] Nicolas Walter, "Anarchism and Religion," *The Raven: anarchist quarterly 25* 7/1 (1994), 8.
[15] Colin Ward, "Anarchist Entry for a Theological Dictionary," *The Raven: anarchist quarterly 25* 7/1 (1994), 22.
[16] Jacques Ellul, *Anarchy and Christianity*, trans. George W. Bromiley (Grand Rapids: William B. Eerdmans, 1991), 23. Some of these "metaphysical" complaints cannot be taken up here, because they are broad criticisms raised by atheists or agnostics against religion more generally. Ellul sketches a response to the classic objection about God allowing evil ("if God is both good and omnipotent, how come there is evil on earth?") on pages 41-43, and to the objection that God's providence rules out freedom on pages 35-37. He also criticises the notion of God as "first cause" on pages 37-41.
[17] Ellul, *Anarchy and Christianity*, 24.

that secular ideologies are no less culpable of similar bloodshed. Nonetheless, Ellul accepts the accusation and comments that he has "never understood how the religion whose heart is that God is love and that we are to love our neighbours as ourselves can give rise to wars."[18] (As Chapter 3 shows, Christian anarchists do actually have an explanation for this: they blame the deceptive manipulation of the Christian message by ruling elites.) Ellul also admits that Christianity "claims exclusive truth," but he refuses to blame this for these wars, insisting instead that "faith cannot be forced" by war or coercion because it "has to come to birth as a free act," otherwise "it has no meaning."[19] Either way, the point here is that Christian anarchists like Ellul are just as critical as secular ones of the sort of Christianity that has waged wars, especially when under the pretence of converting non-Christians to the faith (see Chapters 3 and 5).

Another – this time "metaphysical" – complaint raised by anarchists against Christianity is often encapsulated by the Bakuninist motto: "no gods, no masters."[20] Anarchism, it is claimed, necessarily implies the rejection of all masters, including therefore that greatest master of all: God. Here, Christian anarchists respond by questioning "simplistic representations of God" as an autocratic ruler.[21] Nekeisha Alexis-Baker recalls that in the Bible, "God is also identified as Creator, Liberator, Teacher, Healer, Guide, Provider, Protector and Love," so that anarchists and Christians alike who are "making monarchical language the primary descriptor of God" in fact "misrepresent" his "full character."[22] Ellul similarly argues that even in the Old Testament, "the first aspect of God is never that of the absolute Master," and that human beings are always free to act or not according to his commandments (this is clarified further in Chapter 2).[23] Therefore, in response to this anarchist complaint, Christian anarchists contend that much is misunderstood about the nature of God if he is just seen as an autocratic ruler or as some sort of "Super Santa-Claus" or "Benevolent Despot," as Hennacy puts it.[24]

Nonetheless, Christian anarchists' anarchism does – perhaps somewhat paradoxically – derive from the authority they ascribe to God and to Jesus' teaching in particular (this point is revisited several times in this book). It is precisely this acceptance of God's authority that leads to their negation of all human authority. Yet most anarchists can also be said to derive their anarchism from the authority they ascribe to their understanding of freedom, for instance, or

---

[18] Ellul, *Anarchy and Christianity*, 26.
[19] Ellul, *Anarchy and Christianity*, 26-27.
[20] On this issue, McLellan (following Durkheim and Bellah) makes the interesting point that "Images of God *do* often mirror existing dispositions of political authority," which suggests that the misperception of God as an absolute ruler is not unconnected to the rise of absolute rulers on earth. David McLellan, *Unto Caesar: The Political Relevance of Christianity* (London: University of Notre Dame Press, 1993), 7 (McLellan's emphasis).
[21] Nekeisha Alexis-Baker, "Embracing God, Rejecting Masters," *Christianarchy* 1/1 (2005), 2.
[22] Alexis-Baker, "Embracing God, Rejecting Masters," 2. Note, however, that a slightly different Christian anarchist view (as summarised in its title) is expressed in [Anonymous], *Why I Worship a Violent, Vengeful God Who Orders Me to Be Loving and Non-Violent* (Vine and Fig Tree), available from http://members.aol.com/Patriarchy/predestination/Jesus.htm (accessed 4 November 2005).
[23] Ellul, *Anarchy and Christianity*, 34.
[24] Ammon Hennacy, *The Book of Ammon*, ed. Jim Missey and Joan Thomas, Second ed. (Baltimore: Fortkamp, 1994), 43.

equality.[25] Whether secular or religious, therefore, the anarchist rejection of the state often follows from the priority attributed to something which is then interpreted as logically incompatible with the state. That Christian anarchists ascribe authority to God may be unusual for secular anarchists, but not that authority is ascribed (and anarchism derived therefrom) *per se*. Besides, as Dorothy Day reiterates in response to this anarchist complaint, the authority of God, unlike that of the state, is one which can be accepted or rejected of one's own free will.[26] Nothing therefore precludes one from at the same time accepting the authority of God and rejecting human authority, from being both a Christian and an anarchist.

In any case, the fact remains that regardless of these various anarchist complaints about Christianity, an outline of Christian anarchism that encompasses all its main thinkers has never yet been articulated. By addressing this lacuna, this book not only clarifies the Christian anarchist contribution to political thought, but also thereby makes possible a better informed discussion on the place of religion in anarchist thought and thus in politics more generally.

While on this subject, it is worth noting in passing that there is something of a debate among Christian anarchists as to how to characterise their blending of Christianity and anarchism. Some prefer to speak of "parallels," "overlap," similar "general orientation" or "shared history" between Christianity and anarchism, thus seeing the two as in the end quite distinct yet also as potentially fruitful dialogue partners.[27] Others prefer to speak of Christian anarchism as the only logical political conclusion that can be derived from Christianity – one of them pointing out, for example, that he has "a problem with the term Christian anarchism […] if it implies that there can be *authentic* forms of Christianity that aren't anarchic."[28] Hence while some prefer to speak of "Christianity and anarchism"[29] or of a "Christian+anarchist position,"[30] thus

---

[25] On anarchism not necessarily implying an absolute rejection of all authority, see, for instance R. B. Fowler, "The Anarchist Tradition of Political Thought," *The Western Political Quarterly* 25/4 (1972), 741-742; Ruth Kinna, *Anarchism: A Beginner's Guide* (Oxford: Oneworld, 2005), 67-76.
[26] Hennacy, *The Book of Ammon*, 151.
[27] [Anonymous], "From an Old Christian Anarchist Manuscript," *The Digger and Christian Anarchist*, issue 36, April 1990, 7 (where it is argued that Christianity and anarchism can each bring something to the other); Nekeisha Alexis-Baker, "Embracing God and Rejecting Masters: On Christianity, Anarchism and the State," unpublished article sent by email by its author to me on 17 November 2005, 1-2 (for the notion of a shared history, though not in those exact words), 11 (for "overlap"); Michael C. Elliott, *Freedom, Justice and Christian Counter-Culture* (London: SCM, 1990), chap. 5 (where Elliott draws the similarities between anarchist thought and Christianity); Ellul, *Anarchy and Christianity*, 105 (for "general orientation"); Justin Meggitt [?], "Anarchism and the New Testament: Some Reflections," *A Pinch of Salt*, issue 10, Summer 1988, 10-12 (where the two are described in parallel – though the use of the word "parallel" itself to describe this exercise is mine).
[28] The quote is from Chris Goodchild, "Christian Anarchism," unpublished pamphlet distributed by London Catholic Workers at the London Anarchist Bookfair in October 2003, 1 (Goodchild's emphasis). From this perspective, to rephrase the observation, which Kinna attributes to an "anti-globalizer," that anarchism can be seen as "liberalism on steroids," Christian anarchism would be seen as "Christianity on steroids." Kinna, *Anarchism*, 37.
[29] For instance: Ellul, "Anarchism and Christianity."; Ellul, *Anarchy and Christianity*; Roger Young, *Christianity and Anarchism: A Match Made in Heaven* (Strike the Root), available from http://www.strike-the-root.com/52/young/young1.html (accessed 8 November 2007).
[30] Alexis-Baker, "Embracing God, Rejecting Masters," 2.

underlining their distinction, others are happy to speak of "Christianarchy"[31] or perhaps of a "Christian (anarchist)"[32] position, thus stressing the logical continuity from a Christian premise to anarchist conclusions.

No one is claiming, however, that anarchism and Christianity are the same or that they are interchangeable. They obviously each have their own heritage and tradition, and it is not unreasonable to want to make this clear while also promoting dialogue between the two. Anarchism is certainly not all there is to Christianity. The point which some describe as the overlap of the two separate traditions, however, seems to be precisely where others argue that Christianity logically leads to some form of anarchism. In other words, it is precisely where Christianity is taken to necessarily imply an anarchist critique of the state and the vision of a stateless society that these otherwise separate traditions, despite their separate beliefs and values, do share a common orientation. They are not the same, but it is where Christianity is understood to imply a form of anarchism that they share something that very much belongs to both. The aim of this book is to focus on this overlap, and therefore solely on the anarchist political implications of Christianity. That is, this book focuses on the view that Christianity implies a (peculiarly Christian) type of anarchism.

## Outlining Christian anarchism

By outlining Christian anarchism, therefore, this book presents a unique contribution to both political theology and political thought. It is important, however, to be clear as to what this book covers and what it must ignore.

### *Aims, limits, and originality*

The boundaries of this book are defined by its focus on Christian anarchist thought: because it focuses on Christian anarchist *thought*, this book does not examine the countless millenarian sects and movements which could be classed as Christian anarchist, but concentrates on the theoretical case for the Christian rejection of the state; because it focuses on *Christian* anarchism, it does not discuss other forms of religious or secular anarchism; and because it focuses on Christian *anarchism*, this book is not concerned with Christian pacifism, with theologies of liberation that are favourable to the state, or with any of the many more examples of Christian radicalism or alternative movements that are not explicitly anarchist.

Nonetheless, because in its politicisation of Christianity and denunciation of oppression, Christian anarchism appears so similar to other theologies of liberation, key differences between the two are noted when doing so

---

[31] For instance: Dave Andrews, *Christi-Anarchy: Discovering a Radical Spirituality of Compassion* (Oxford: Lion, 1999); Elliott, *Freedom, Justice and Christian Counter-Culture*, xiv; Roger, "Christianarchy," *A Pinch of Salt*, issue 2, March 1986; Michael Tennant, *Christianarchy?* (Strike the Root), available from http://www.strike-the-root.com/51/tennant/tennant5.html (accessed 21 November 2007).

[32] This particular rendering is mine. The issue of how to best describe this thinking is revisited briefly in the Conclusion.

clarifies the originality of Christian anarchism (especially in Chapters 2 and 4, and in the Conclusion).[33] Christian pacifism also shares a lot with Christian anarchism (just like secular pacifism with anarchism), but their differences become obvious especially in Chapters 1 and 2. Crucial differences with secular anarchism are also noted where relevant, particularly in Chapter 4. Also, despite the explicit focus on thought, individual and communal examples of Christian anarchist practice are also listed in this book (in Chapter 6), but only because Christian anarchist thinkers themselves frequently refer to these movements as illustrations of their thought.

Many more overlaps and similarities can be found between Christian anarchist thought and many other themes, writers and traditions which sit just outside its boundaries. There are even many instances where Christian anarchist thought is not dissimilar in its exegesis to orthodox Christian theology. Very few such similarities are noted in this book, however, because without such tight focus on Christian anarchist thought, the path would be open for seemingly endless noting of, and referencing to, analogous lines of thinking outside Christian anarchist thought. Hence while the reader will most probably find parallels here or there between what is being said and this or that famous or less famous theory or perspective, these parallels are not drawn out in this book. The fleshing out of many such parallels and the potential dialogue between Christian anarchism and thinkers in other traditions must therefore remain subjects for future study.

The main aim of this book is to articulate a generic outline of Christian anarchism. To do so, it relies almost completely on the existing writings of individual Christian anarchist thinkers, quoting them extensively in the process. In a sense, therefore, the thought that this book conveys outline is not novel or original. Yet these different Christian anarchist voices have never been synthesised or combined before into a comprehensive and overarching outline of Christian anarchism. They are similar and complementary, but they have never yet been made to speak together as one. In a way, Christian anarchism as a school of thought is both assumed and proposed by this book. It is presented as if it already exists as a tradition, but doing so also thereby constitutes it as a tradition at the same time. The originality of this book lies in this presentation of Christian anarchism as a coherent perspective, in this weaving together of separate Christian anarchists into what thereby begins to resemble a school of thought.

In any school of thought, of course, there are also disagreements. Different thinkers come from different angles, and sometimes these differences can lead to major controversies. Such open rows have been largely absent in the Christian anarchist literature, presumably in large part because its thinkers have yet to consider themselves as part of such a varied school of thought, in dialogue with others within it. Still, there are certainly important variations and potentially serious tensions between Christian anarchists on some issues. To list but three

---

[33] It would seem that the relation between Christian anarchism and liberation theology (which often openly acknowledges a strong Marxist inspiration) is not dissimilar to the relation between secular anarchism and Marxism: in both cases, one finds important similarities between the two, but also important (and similar) differences. This parallel relationship between secular and Christian anarchism and their Marxist counterpart could indeed be an interesting topic for further research.

examples: Tolstoy's rationalistic approach to Christianity sits uncomfortably with Day's faith in the Sacraments; Christian anarcho-capitalists' take on private property is diametrically opposed to that of most other Christian anarchists (thus mirroring the comparable contrast in secular anarchism); and there also seem to be potentially serious disagreements between Vernard Eller's emphasis on Romans 13 and the stance taken by many Christian anarchist activists. This book, however, concentrates on the similarities, on the general coherence of the main line of thought presented by all those thinkers when taken together. Their differences are noted in passing where appropriate, and in some cases (especially that of the last example), they are discussed in some detail. The emphasis, however, is on the general coherence. Exploring the tensions remains another task for further research.

While every effort has been made to include all the relevant literature into this generic outline of Christian anarchism, there is always room for more. This book intends to be as comprehensive as possible in its coverage of Christian anarchist thinkers and certainly in its thematic breakdown of Christian anarchism as a generic theoretical perspective, but it does not claim to be the final word on the topic. It is hoped that future scholarship can add more voices to this book, especially thinkers prior to the nineteenth century – and perhaps the best candidate for possible future inclusion is Gerrard Winstanley.[34] With the exception of Peter Chelčický (explained below), such pre-nineteenth century thinkers have been excluded here in part because the modern state had not risen to its full industrial power yet (and anarchism as an explicit position had not yet been articulated in response to it), but also mainly and simply because including these thinkers would have required several more years of research.[35] Nevertheless, although some of these thinkers would no doubt enrich the outline

---

[34] Winstanley is not included here for two main reasons: time restrictions, and the fact that the debateable nature of his credentials as Christian *anarchist* would seem to imply that he is not a thinker central to any generic outline of Christian anarchism. His specifically *anarchist* credentials are somewhat debatable because his writings seem to focus mostly on criticism of the private ownership of land rather than of the "state" as such (though to expect him to refer to the "state" would of course be somewhat anachronistic, and many anarchists touch on this land issue as well), and he seems to have later favoured a form of (albeit elected and hence, for his time, revolutionary) government with some degree of coercion. It is interesting that the editor of a Christian anarchist paper changed its title from *The Digger* (in direct reference to Winstanley's movement) to *The Digger and Christian Anarchist*, justifying his decision as a deliberate distancing from Winstanley because of his discomfort with elements of Winstanley's thinking, as explained in Kenny Hone [?], "Editorial," *The Digger and Christian Anarchist*, issue 12, October 1986, 1. Having said this, Winstanley is excluded from this book more out of lack of time to consider him properly than out of a deliberate desire to exclude him, and his voice may indeed deserve to be added to the Christian anarchist chorus as a result of future research. A good case for his inclusion is provided by Valerio Pignatta, *Dio L'anarchico: Movimenti Rivoluzionari Religiosi Nell'inghilterra Del Seicento* (Milano: Arcipelago Edizioni, 1997). Finally, note that another thinker from that period who might be seen as Christian anarchist is Abiezer Coppe. See Peter Pick, "A Theology of Revolutions: Abiezer Coppe and the Uses of Tradition," in *Religious Anarchism: New Perspectives*, ed. Alexandre J. M. E. Christoyannopoulos (Newcastle upon Tyne: Cambridge Scholars Publishing, 2009).

[35] Also, the further back one goes into the past, the more one tends to have to rely on secondary sources and accounts of radical Christian thinkers, and the more difficult it becomes to get a comprehensive and authentic picture of their ideas. The original writings of many such radicals may also often not have been translated into English. All this in turn implies that even more time needs to be set aside to properly consider such pre-nineteenth century Christian radicals.

of Christian anarchism presented here, they would probably not radically upset the thematic breakdown of this book. To refer to a previous analogy, their distinct melodies would most probably fit the symphony rather than force a major rewrite of it.

Also ignored in this book are any criticisms which could be mounted against Christian anarchism in general or Christian anarchist exegesis in particular. Since a generic and comprehensive outline of Christian anarchism has never been produced before, this book focuses on doing just that – a task which on its own makes this a long enough manuscript. It is therefore necessarily one-sided: it takes the Christian anarchist perspective and makes a detailed case for it by collating the contributions of individual Christian anarchist thinkers. Some reflections on Christian anarchism are offered in the Conclusion, but most of the critical and reflective input has gone into drawing out the overall coherence of the many Christian anarchist voices, methodically weaving them together, and presenting Christian anarchism as a coherent perspective rather than critiquing it. To paraphrase Darrell J. Fasching, with this book, "I do not so much attempt to stand outside of [Christian anarchism] and judge it as to get inside it and clarify it."[36] The aim has been to give a fair hearing to the numerous sets of arguments presented by Christian anarchism, to let Christian anarchists speak rather than to mount criticisms at every turn. Such criticisms must therefore remain yet another topic of further research, but such research will now be able to build upon the synthesising work of this book.

Therefore, this book can act as a first important step towards a better understanding of Christian anarchism in political theology and political thought. Moreover, it also opens up areas of potential dialogue for instance with other trends in anarchism, with pacifist thinking, with liberation theology, and in general with the growing literature on religion and politics. It provides a unique perspective to Christians pondering how their faith is to inform their politics. It might also be of interest to non-Christians who are curious about the political dimension of what continues to be one of the world's most widespread religions. Obviously, it also makes available to Christian anarchist activists and similar Christian radicals a fairly comprehensive summary that weaves together many of the thinkers they might have read so far on the topic. Indeed, it will also be relevant to those who have studied other aspects of some of these thinkers, by clarifying that side of their thinking. This is especially the case for Tolstoy, whose Christian anarchism is rarely given serious academic attention. In synthesising Christian anarchism and presenting it as a tradition, therefore, this book is – I hope – potentially relevant to a wide range of (academic and lay) thinkers, Christians, and activists.

## *Technical issues*

At this stage, a few technical points on the referencing, language and Biblical approach of this book are in order.

---

[36] Darrell J. Fasching, quoted (by Goddard in his thesis on Ellul) in Andrew Goddard, *Living the Word, Resisting the World: The Life and Thought of Jacques Ellul*, ed. David F. Wright, et al. (Milton Keynes: Paternoster, 2002), xvii.

On referencing, given that one of the intentions behind this book is to present a source for references on Christian anarchism, extensive use of footnotes is made, either to point to the original Christian anarchist source where an assertion that is made in the text can be found or explained, or to provide more detail on a point when providing this detail in the text would be tangential to the main line of argument (however, as explained in the Acknowledgements, these very extensive footnotes have here been trimmed down to the bare minimum, so readers interested in such references and tangential discussion points will find these in the original, hardback version of this book).[37] Footnotes for quotations always point to original page numbers, except for internet pages for which the precise paragraph where the quote can be found is numbered.[38]

On language, no definitions of the words "state," "government," "power" or "authority" are presented in this book. This is mainly because Christian anarchists do not all refer to them in exactly the same way, and since extensive use of quotations is made throughout the book, any strict definition would regularly need to be qualified to reflect the slightly different meaning attributed by different Christian anarchists. A fairly clear sense of what is being criticised by Christian anarchists does nevertheless emerge in the first three Chapters anyway, and Chapter 3 does briefly revisit this question of the terminology employed by Christian anarchists.

The words "non-violence," "non-resistance" and "pacifism" are also not defined in this book, again because individual Christian anarchists can sometimes have slightly different meanings in mind when using them. Nonetheless, a tension between the first two words, and specifically between the different understandings of Jesus' teaching which their choice betrays, becomes evident by Chapter 4, where it is discussed in more detail.

Another key word for which a definition is avoided is the word "church," because usually, what is being said in the text about the existing church refers not to one particular church or denomination but to almost all churches in Christianity, to the Christian church generically-speaking.[39] A clearer picture of what it is about the existing church that Christian anarchists dislike is drawn in Chapter 3, and Chapter 5 portrays the "true," ideal church or community which they understand Jesus' teaching to have implied.

While on language, it is worth confessing that the language of several of the quotations in this book is clearly male-centric, especially from authors who wrote prior to the feminist revolution. Although it is impossible to assert with certainty whether these authors meant their words to apply to both genders, it goes without saying that in quoting their words in this book, my intentions are for these to be interpreted as applying to all, in a gender-neutral way.

---

[37] Note that when a referencing detail is not specified in the original source but I am able to make an informed guess about it, the uncertain detail is included but accompanied by a quotation mark inside square brackets.
[38] This applies to pages in ".html" format (since these are basically just one – potentially very long – "page"). Quotations from internet pages in ".pdf" format are listed by page number.
[39] Note also, in passing, that the words "church" and "state" are written in lower case, except in quotations, where the case used by the author of the quote is always maintained. The same logic applies to "non-violence" and "non-resistance." That is, the words include a hyphen except in some quotations, where the particular preference of the author being quoted is always respected.

Another somewhat outdated form of vocabulary present in the book appears through the choice of the King James Version for all Bible quotations.[40] This is because the English translations of Tolstoy and Chelčický all opt for this version, as does Adin Ballou in his own writings, and the book contains many quotations from these authors which deliberately hint at Bible passages using the wording of the King James Version.

With regards to the Bible, this book pays no attention to the important debates in Biblical scholarship on the relative authenticity of different sections of it. The four Gospels are taken at face value, assumed to be valid accounts of the life and teaching of Jesus.[41] The aim here (in line with that of Christian anarchists) is to make the case for an anarchist understanding of the political implications of these Gospels as they stand, not to engage in debate over their reliability.

Not all Christian anarchists agree on the value of other parts of the New Testament, but this is noted where relevant. The Old Testament is mostly ignored, partly because the New Testament is traditionally understood to fulfil it, but mainly simply because Christian anarchists generally have very little to say about it.[42]

Some Christian anarchists take very different views on theological dogma derived from the Bible. Those differences that are relevant to Christian anarchism are noted, but those that are not are ignored.[43] Likewise, where the different hermeneutical methods adopted by Christian anarchists have a bearing on their political commentary of a passage, this is noted, but otherwise these differences are ignored.

It will become clear that most Christian anarchists approach the Bible with a modern mindset, interpreting its commandments as fairly literal propositions and frequently paying little attention – in their political exegesis at least – to any layers of meaning beyond the merely literal and political.[44] For reasons made clear in Chapter 3, in typically protestant ("*sola scriptura*") fashion, they bypass traditional exegesis and rely only on scripture for their understanding of Jesus' teaching.[45] This hermeneutic approach is of course questionable, but such questioning would take this book beyond its immediate remit. The limited

---

[40] The italics and the phonetic syntax used by the King James Version have been removed, however, as they are unnecessary for this exegesis.

[41] As noted below, Tolstoy was the Christian anarchist who most seriously doubted the account of the four Gospels, going as far as writing his own, harmonised and rationalised version of Jesus' life and teaching.

[42] Apocryphal texts are also ignored because Christian anarchists themselves generally ignore them.

[43] Tolstoy's rationalistic understanding of what it means for Jesus to be the "Son of man," for instance, is probably very different to that of Catholic Christian anarchists. But since none of them explicitly argues for direct political implications to be derived from it, differences such as these are ignored here.

[44] Of course, some Christian anarchists are more interested than others in such other layers of meaning.

[45] Indeed, Tolstoy's approach to the Gospels is described as "radically protestant" in Antony Flew, "Tolstoi and the Meaning of Life," *Ethics: An International Journal of Social, Political, and Legal Philosophy* 73/2 (1963), 116. Interestingly, Voltairine de Cleyre, a (secular) anarchist, is also reported to have described anarchism itself as "a sort of Protestantism," in Kinna, *Anarchism*, 17. The parallels between the protestant method, anarchism and Christian anarchism certainly make an interesting subject for future research – but once again, too big a digression for this particular book.

aim of this book is to weave together the different interpretative threads of Christian anarchist thinkers, not to evaluate the soundness of their hermeneutic methods.[46]

## The structure of this book

The main body of the book consists of six Chapters, split into two main Parts. Part I describes the Christian anarchist critique of the state, and Part II, the Christian anarchist response.

Chapters 1 and 2 focus on the Christian anarchist exegesis of key Bible passages, on the interpretation of these passages as implying a rejection of the state. Chapter 1 singles out the Sermon on the Mount because of the central importance accorded to it by Christian anarchists, and Chapter 2 turns to other Bible passages, mostly from the four Gospels but also from other books in both the Old and New Testaments. By contrast to these two exegetical Chapters, Chapter 3 focuses on the state and church in practice, outlining the Christian anarchist critique of both institutions for their perceived collusion in deceiving and oppressing the masses.

Part II then considers the Christian anarchist response to the state's contemporary prominence. Chapter 4 discusses the direct Christian anarchist response to the state and the potential for some degree of civil disobedience, examining Romans 13 and the "render unto Caesar" passage in the process. Chapter 5 describes the other side of the response: the example to be set by the "true" church, by this alternative community witnessing to the truth of the Christian teaching. In a sense, whereas Chapter 4 outlines the negative response to the state, Chapter 5 outlines the positive response as the "true" church. Chapter 6 then lists the examples of individual and collective witness which are either praised or inspired directly by Christian anarchist thinkers – examples, therefore, of the Christian anarchist response.

In the Conclusion, some reflections are offered on the name and defining characteristic of Christian anarchism, on the Christian anarchist understanding of history, and on the original and perhaps "prophetic" role played by Christian anarchism in its unfolding.

## Christian anarchist "thinkers"

There remains to introduce the main protagonists of Christian anarchist thought, the separate threads that this book weaves together into a generic outline of Christian anarchism. What qualifies this diverse range of thinkers as "Christian anarchists" is specified in each case below, but on a general note, each of these "Christian anarchists" (as they are often hereafter referred to) have something to contribute to the perspective that Christianity logically implies a form of anarchism, that anarchism logically follows from Christianity – the defining characteristic of Christian anarchism. These thinkers have either written openly

---

[46] Besides, such an evaluation would necessarily concern much modern exegesis – a major task on its own.

about something they describe as Christian anarchism, are widely described by others as Christian anarchists, or have something to say which helps strengthen the case for Christian anarchism. What is of interest here is not their particular life or social context, or even how solid a commitment they might have made to Christian anarchism, but that at the level of ideas, they contribute to a generic outline of Christian anarchism. That their writings on this particular issue combine to produce a fairly coherent body of thought is both assumed and demonstrated by the remainder of this book.[47]

## Leo Tolstoy

Russian aristocrat Leo Tolstoy (1828-1910) is of course one of the world's most acclaimed authors of literature, but he is also by far the most frequently cited example of this peculiarly Christian form of anarchism that is the subject of this book. His Christian anarchism was an outcome of an intensive existential quest for the meaning of life, a quest which ended only once he converted to his idiosyncratic understanding of Christianity around 1879. There is much debate as to whether this conversion should be seen as a clear rupture in his thinking (as he himself certainly liked to portray it) or a natural continuation of his lifelong intellectual pursuits. As Stepun remarks, however, whether or not Tolstoy's life and thought should be divided into two parts, his *fame* is certainly twofold: as an artist and as a "social prophet."[48] It is only as a social prophet that his legacy is of direct relevance to this book.[49] Besides, it is clear that by the turn of the century, Tolstoy himself considered his views as a thinker to matter more than his artistic prowess: "Like a clown at a country fair grimacing in front of the ticket-booth in order to lure the public inside the tent where the real play is being performed," Tolstoy comments, "so my imaginative work must serve to attract the attention of the public to my philosophic teaching."[50]

Tolstoy's understanding of Christianity was peculiar indeed, although it very much reflected the nineteenth century context in which he lived. For him, Jesus was simply the most rational human being ever to walk the planet, not some supernatural figure that actually flew back into the sky. As Chapter 3 explains in more detail, Tolstoy distrusted all such miraculous elements in both the Bible and

---

[47] Note that strong candidates for inclusion in this survey of Christian anarchist literature, but which crossed my path too late to weave into this book, are: Shane Clairborne and Chris Haw, *Jesus for President: Politics for Ordinary Radicals* (Grand Rapids: Zondervan, 2008); Tripp York, *Living on Hope While Living in Babylon: The Christian Anarchists of the Twentieth Century* (Cambridge: Lutterworth, 2009). Clairborne and Haw's indicative bibliography acknowledges the likes of Day, Yoder, Wink, Cavanaugh and Ellul (to mention only those listed in the remainder of this Introduction) – enough to expect a text in strong sympathy with the Christian anarchism articulated in this book. As to York, his study of the Berrigan brothers, Dorothy Day, Eberhard Arnold and other Christian anarchists of the twentieth century obviously belongs to the Christian anarchist literature.
[48] Fedor Stepun, "The Religious Tragedy of Tolstoy," *Russian Review* 19/2 (1960), 157.
[49] In this book, only Tolstoy's non-fictional and explicitly political and religious writings are taken into consideration. This does not mean that a Christian anarchist element cannot be discerned in his fictional works – whether those preceding his conversion to Christianity or (especially) those that followed it – but that the discernment of such Christian anarchist tendencies remains a task for future research.
[50] Leo Tolstoy, quoted in Rosemary Edmonds, "Introduction," in *Resurrection*, by Leo Tolstoy, trans. Rosemary Edmonds (London: Penguin, 1966), 8.

the wider Christian tradition – he called them the "rotten apples" of Christianity.[51] What mattered in the Christian message, for him, was only the revolutionary but (for Tolstoy) eminently rational teaching and example of Jesus, which he saw as best summarised in the Sermon on the Mount. He brushed aside the tradition, and studied the Bible very closely – indeed even rewriting a harmonised version of the Gospel purged from supernatural distractions. For him, the essence of Christianity was to be found in the moral principles articulated by Jesus.

His rationalistic take on Christianity is rarely shared by other Christian anarchists, but it is not necessary to agree with his dislike of the supernatural to be able to follow his powerful arguments on Jesus' teaching and example. It was the development of these arguments that led him to become such a bitter critic of church and state. That is, as Chapter 1 makes clear, Tolstoy's Christian anarchism follows from his rationalistic interpretation of Jesus' teaching, especially as summarised in the Sermon on the Mount. He wrote countless essays and books on the topic, but the most often cited one among anarchists is *The Kingdom of God Is within You* (although *What I Believe* is just as good and comprehensive).[52]

In the academic literature on anarchism, Tolstoy is usually credited with having made the most detailed case for Christian anarchism, if he is not even described as the *only* known example of Christian anarchism. He is also often recognised as one of the classic thinkers of the broad anarchist pantheon. Like several of these classic thinkers, however, Tolstoy himself avoided the word "anarchism" to describe his thought, because he associated the word with the violent revolutionaries which he strongly disagreed with. His understanding of anarchism as an intellectual position improved over time, however, and he eventually accepted this term to describe his position as long as it was understood that his anarchism was strictly non-violent and based on the Sermon on the Mount.

Among Christian anarchists, Tolstoy is also generally acknowledged as the best known Christian anarchist thinker. Several Christian anarchists refer to him or quote him, and many more seem to suggest that they are familiar with his writings even though they might choose not to engage with these in any detail. It may be that Tolstoy's extreme rationalism had deterred several Christian anarchists from such a more thorough engagement with him. Again, however, one need not agree with Tolstoy on this to be able to follow his Christian anarchist line of reasoning. In any case, further investigation into Christian anarchism quickly reveals that there are actually quite a few other thinkers who have developed a similar position, and most of them approach Christianity in much less rigidly rationalistic a way than Tolstoy.

---

[51] Leo Tolstoy, "What Is Religion, and Wherein Lies Its Essence?," in *On Life and Essays on Religion*, trans. Aylmer Maude (London: Oxford University Press, 1934), 272.
[52] Leo Tolstoy, "The Kingdom of God Is within You," in *The Kingdom of God and Peace Essays*, trans. Aylmer Maude (New Delhi: Rupa, 2001); Leo Tolstoy, *What I Believe <My Religion>*, trans. Fyvie Mayo? (London: C. W. Daniel, [1902?]). *The Kingdom of God Is within You* is rather long and can be quite repetitive at times. *What I Believe* is more clearly structured, and focuses more on Tolstoy's exegesis of key Bible passages. Moreover, he opens the former by answering the many letters and comments he received in response to the latter.

## Jacques Ellul

Perhaps the most important of these other Christian anarchist thinkers is French scholar Jacques Ellul (1912-1994). Ellul is known today mostly for his critical work on technology and the technological society, of which the modern state is just another symptom. He wrote extensively, usually covering each given topic from both a theological and a sociological perspective, clearly distinguishing the two approaches.[53] Comparatively few of his writings, however, are targeted specifically at the state itself. The most directly relevant for this book is his *Anarchy and Christianity*, but several other books of his are also relied upon where appropriate.

Unlike Tolstoy, Ellul happily employed the word "anarchism" as a thoughtful political position to hold, and certainly demonstrated his familiarity with thinkers like Bakunin, Proudhon and Kropotkin. At times, he even suggests an awareness of Christian anarchist thinkers. He himself maintained that he did not believe a true anarchist society could ever come about, but he just as adamantly insisted that "the anarchist position [is] the only acceptable stance in the modern world."[54] For him, even though "the realizing" of "an anarchist society" is "impossible," the "anarchist fight," the "struggle" for such a society is nonetheless "essential."[55] This ambivalence is explained further below in the book.

What Ellul adds to Tolstoy is his anarchist exegesis of many more passages from the Bible, including the Old Testament. His work therefore complements Tolstoy's narrower focus on the Sermon on the Mount. Besides, Ellul's approach to Christianity was not as unusual as Tolstoy's, being grounded instead in traditional Protestant (especially Calvinist) theology. His approach may therefore be more comfortable than Tolstoy's for Christians who belong to that tradition. Ellul's contribution to Christian anarchist thought is therefore an important one. His work is certainly praised by several other Christian anarchists.

## Vernard Eller

One author who makes clear his appreciation of Ellul is American academic Vernard Eller (1927-2007), author of a book published around the same time as Ellul's and titled *Christian Anarchy*. In that book, he repeatedly associates himself with the Christian anarchist position which he elaborates. His own Christian background is that of the Anabaptist/Brethren tradition – again therefore a position which some Christians might find more sensible than Tolstoy's.

His contribution to Christian anarchism, however, is somewhat contentious. Because of the submissive response which he advocates to the state, those Christian anarchists who are inclined to more confrontational activism have been very critical of Eller's views. Yet Eller's input is valuable precisely for his exegesis of Romans 13 and the "render unto Caesar" passage, on which his advocacy of such submission (which he sees as subversive in a peculiar way, as

---

[53] The distinction between these two strands to his work is explained in Goddard, *Living the Word, Resisting the World*, part 1.
[54] Ellul, "Anarchism and Christianity," 156.
[55] Ellul, *Anarchy and Christianity*, 19 (he explains this statement in the pages that follow).

explained in Chapter 4) is based. The disagreement between him and such activists on how to respond to the state touches on a topic important enough to constitute the main theme of Chapter 4, so it will not be resolved here. What should be noted here is only that Eller certainly considers himself as a Christian anarchist, and that his book has evidently been noticed by other Christian anarchists. His contribution is therefore very relevant to this book, and he cannot be excluded from the Christian anarchist school of thought even if some in that school find his presence disconcerting. If anything, such disagreements only make for potentially interesting debates within such schools.

## Michael C. Elliott

Another important contribution to Christian anarchist thought comes from Michael C. Elliott's *Freedom, Justice and Christian Counter-Culture* – a book for which "Christianarchy" was at some point contemplated as an alternative title.[56] In that book, Elliott provides an anarchist interpretation of a number of Biblical passages, reinforcing therefore the input of the Christian anarchist thinkers mentioned above. Indeed, that book acts as an excellent introduction to Christian anarchism.

By contrast to *this* book, however, Elliott's book does not attempt to weave together the different lines of thinking articulated by Christian anarchist thinkers. It reads more as a call for Christians to embody this Christian "counter-culture," introducing them to communist and anarchist thinking and drawing parallels with Jesus' teaching and example as narrated in the Bible. Elliott himself seems to have studied a number of other Christian anarchist thinkers, but aside from the odd reference, they do not figure much in that book. Also, perhaps as a result of the absence of the word "anarchism" in the title, it seems not to have been noticed by many Christian anarchists to this day. Nevertheless, Elliott's contribution to Christian anarchist thought is important, both as an introduction to the topic and through his reflections on several key passages in the Bible.

## Dave Andrews

Australian thinker Dave Andrews (born 1951) did name one his books by the title which Elliott briefly considered: *Christi-Anarchy*. Like Elliott, he seems to be aware of many of the key Christian anarchist thinkers, though also like Elliott, he does not discuss them in any detail.

Andrews' writings are more pragmatic than those penned by most Christian anarchist thinkers. He repeatedly encourages Christians to reflect on some of the most challenging political passages in the Gospels and, crucially, to act upon them in their own community, to put Jesus' teaching to practice. His books and essays therefore blend reflections on Gospel passages with a considerable number of moving examples of community life and personal sacrifice which illustrate the politically revolutionary potential of Jesus' teaching

---

[56] Elliott, *Freedom, Justice and Christian Counter-Culture*, xiv (for his remark about the alternative title).

when taken literally. He also often refers to work which he has been involved with in his own community in Brisbane.

His input into Christian anarchist thought thus comes both from his reflections on various Bible passages and from the many moving examples which he uses to illustrate these. Given that his writings are very recent, he is not cited by the many Christian anarchists who lived and published on the topic long before him. His work does however clearly belong to the Christian anarchist school of thought.

## Key writers in the Catholic Worker movement

The Catholic Worker movement, which is still mostly based in the United States, is by definition a movement rather than just a group of thinkers. As with most movements, however, it was founded by visionaries who committed their vision into writing, not least, of course, in the newspaper after which it is named and which is at the heart of the Catholic Worker community. First published in 1933 (and sold ever since at the price of one cent), this newspaper has multiplied into many local versions of the *Catholic Worker*, each published by local communities brought together by the ideas of its founders. Although the majority of the columns of these newspapers do not amount to systematic and scholarly publications on Christian anarchism, they do nonetheless sometimes touch on more theoretical issues and thus contribute to a generic outline of Christian anarchism. Moreover, as Chapter 6 explains, Catholic Worker communities provide moving illustrations of Christian anarchism put to practice.

That the paper is explicitly Catholic does not mean that its members are not sometimes very critical of the Catholic Church, or that they have all vowed to abide by the will of the Pope. Instead, it reflects the respect and awe of many Catholic Workers for many of the traditional Catholic mysteries, dogmas and rituals, and for the work of several of the Catholic Church's famous theologians. Catholic Workers also point to the many examples of loving witness and community life which are also part of the Catholic legacy as a counter-side to its darker side, which they nevertheless openly acknowledge.

From the beginning, Catholic Workers happily described themselves as anarchists – although sometimes preferring the terms "personalist" or "libertarian" so as not to arouse misunderstanding and confusion. The Catholic Worker movement is certainly recognised as Christian anarchist by both secular and Christian anarchists.[57] Both its key writers and its many contributors to newspaper columns therefore contribute, each in their own way, to the generic outline of Christian anarchism presented by this book.

---

[57] Note that the United States government also considers the Catholic Worker movement to be subversive: *The New York Times* reported on 20 December 2005 that the government had been spying on domestic groups, including the Catholic Worker, referring to it as "semi-communistic ideology," according to Jim Reagan, "The Sweet Fruit of the Spirit," *The Catholic Worker*, issue 73, May 2006, 8.

## Dorothy Day

One of the two main founders of the movement is Dorothy Day (1897-1980), who by the time of her death had, according to Ellsberg, "achieved iconic status as the 'radical conscience' of the Catholic church in America."[58] In her autobiography, she explains how she was always concerned about social injustice and quickly found herself frequenting socialist and anarchist circles, including the Industrial Workers of the World.[59] She studied anarchist thinkers such as Kropotkin, Ferrer, Godwin, Proudhon and Tolstoy – though her praise for the latter was usually confined to his fictional work, with its emphasis on peasant life and hard manual labour. Prayer was always important in Day's life, and she eventually joined the Catholic Church, drawn not only by its liturgy but also by its late nineteenth century social teaching and by the exemplary life of some of its more radical saints (see Chapter 6).

Day saw no problem in combining her Catholicism with her anarchism. She was a keen activist and ended up behind bars several times. She wrote countless columns in the *Catholic Worker*, as well as an inspiring autobiography. Her direct contribution to Christian anarchist *thought* is perhaps not the most significant, but some of her reflections on social issues and Bible passages are certainly pertinent enough to Christian anarchism for some of her views to be weaved into this book. Along with the Catholic Worker movement, she is often cited by several other Christian anarchists.[60] She is also loved and venerated as a mother by most Catholic Workers, and indeed even being considered for possible canonisation by the Catholic Church.

## Peter Maurin

The other main founder of the Catholic Worker movement is Frenchman Peter Maurin (1877-1949), who quickly became Day's partner, lover and "master."[61] Maurin saw himself as a thinker, expressing his thought in scores of short "easy essays" which he saw the *Catholic Worker* as an essential vehicle for. His intellectual influences ranged from Aquinas to Kropotkin, including Bloy, Berdyaev, Mounier and a number of papal encyclicals. Obituaries reporting his death appeared both in papers from the Industrial Workers of the World and in *Osservatore Romano* (the official Vatican paper) – a reflection of his status as both an important Catholic and a notable voice of the revolutionary Left.

Maurin advocated a revolution based on roundtable discussions, houses of hospitality and farming communes (as explained in more detail in Chapter 6). Like Day, he happily described himself as an anarchist, but preferred the term "personalist" because it tied him to a particular trend in Catholic thinking which he saw as the Catholic variant of anarchism. He is therefore

---

[58] Robert Ellsberg, "Preface to the Anniversary Edition," in *Selected Writings: By Little and by Little*, by Dorothy Day (Maryknoll: Orbis, 2005), xi.
[59] Dorothy Day, *The Long Loneliness: The Autobiography of the Legendary Catholic Social Activist* (New York: HarperSanFrancisco, 1952), 36-67.
[60] Besides, the director of the Federal Bureau of Investigation indirectly confirmed her subversive status by considering her "a threat to national security" according to Jim Creskey, *A Most Unusual Saint* (The Tablet), available from http://www.thetablet.co.uk/articles/6828 (accessed 14 February 2007), para. 5.
[61] That word is hers, from Day, *The Long Loneliness*, 11.

recognised by other Christian anarchists as one of them, and as the other founder of perhaps the most famous modern Christian anarchist movement. As with many Catholic Workers, however, his input into the present outline of Christian anarchist *thought* is relatively minor, although some of his passing reflections are indeed quite pertinent at times.

## Ammon Hennacy

The third main figure of the Catholic Worker movement is American campaigner Ammon Hennacy (1893-1970). Unlike Day and Maurin, however, his allegiance to the Catholic Church wavered, as demonstrated by the change of title of his book from *The Autobiography of a Catholic Anarchist* to *The Book of Ammon*. His Christian anarchism was always Tolstoyan at heart: he concurred with Tolstoy, in particular his focus on the Sermon on the Mount, his suspicious hermeneutics and his distrust of institutional churches. Hennacy later explained his temporary conversion to Catholicism as motivated mostly by his love and admiration for Day, and once he recanted from it, he resumed his fierce criticism of all churches. Despite this, he is widely regarded as an influential figure in the Catholic Worker movement, and certainly as an important Christian anarchist.

Hennacy was very much an activist, and (as Chapter 4 shows) has been credited with steering the Catholic Worker movement towards more confrontational forms of Christian anarchist activism. His main contribution to Christian anarchist thought comes from numerous passing comments and reflections which he spelt out in his lengthy autobiography. Like Andrews, he also offered a short definition of Christian anarchism – definition which he repeatedly and wholeheartedly identified with.[62] His book also demonstrates his knowledge of anarchist thinkers such as Berkman (whom he met in prison), Goldman, Malatesta, Kropotkin, Proudhon, Godwin, Bakunin, and – above all – Tolstoy. There is no doubt, therefore, that Hennacy belongs firmly to the Christian anarchist tradition.

## Ciaron O'Reilly

An equally active but present-day Catholic Worker activist is Ciaron O'Reilly (born 1960), who has been engaged in various recent protests, acts of civil disobedience and trials in England, Ireland, and his native Australia. He often refers to fellow Catholic Workers in his writings, but also to some of the thinkers whose writings help support Christian anarchist thought and who are introduced further below (namely: Yoder, Wink and Myers). His work has been noticed and cited by other secular and Christian anarchists, and some of it is indeed also relevant to the present book.[63] Like other Catholic Workers, therefore, he figures in this book partly thanks to some of his reflections on Christian anarchism, and partly for his example in putting these reflection to practice, as described in Chapter 6.

---

[62] Hennacy, *The Book of Ammon*, xix.
[63] Like Day and the Catholic Worker as a whole, he has also been watched and indeed interviewed by government forces – specifically by a counter-terrorism squad in Australia, and Special Branch officers in the United Kingdom, according to Ciaron O'Reilly, *Remembering Forgetting: A Journey of Non-Violent Resistance to the War in East Timor* (Sydney: Otford, 2001), 24-27, 58.

## Writers behind other Christian anarchist publications

Apart from the *Catholic Worker* and its contributors, several other regular Christian anarchist publications have provided useful input into this book.

### Stephen Hancock (A Pinch of Salt)

One such publication was *A Pinch of Salt*, fourteen issues of which were published in England in the late 1980s. 800 to 1000 copies of the paper were usually printed and then mailed out and distributed across the island and beyond. Admired by British Christian anarchists, it has very recently been revived under new editorship (see Chapter 6).[64]

The original paper was started by a group of people, but Stephen Hancock quickly became its main editor. Aside from humorous and thoughtful reflections from Hancock, the paper reprinted a variety of articles, letters from readers and other contributions sent to it on a number of topics dear to Christian anarchism (again, see Chapter 6 for more detail).

The paper proudly portrayed itself as an anarchist journal and included references to a range of secular anarchists such as Malatesta, Proudhon, Bakunin, Kropotkin, Guérin and Ward. It also often reported on liberation theology and (especially) on the Ploughshares movement, and it frequently referred to the writings of other Christian anarchists, including Chelčický, Tolstoy, Ellul, Eller and all the Catholic Workers introduced above, several of the supportive thinkers introduced below (namely: Ballou, Yoder, Wink), and many of the pre-modern examples of forerunners of Christian anarchism listed in Chapter 6.

In other words, the paper clearly embedded itself in the Christian anarchist tradition. Its columns varied widely in style, but several of these have certainly provided useful contributions or corroborations to the present outline of Christian anarchism.

### Kenneth C. Hone (The Digger and Christian Anarchist)

Around the same time in Canada, Kenneth C. Hone was publishing a Christian anarchist paper eventually called *The Digger and Christian Anarchist*. It ran to a total of 36 issues, but the paper's style was less rigorous, less colourful and less humorous than *Pinch* – which is perhaps why it usually printed only around 150 copies. The editors of the two papers corresponded, met and sometimes reprinted one another's articles, but compared to *Pinch*, *The Digger*'s articles tend to read as somewhat undigested and casual at times. Whereas *Pinch* brought together and reprinted contributions from a substantial number of people, *The Digger* was more of a personal journal for Hone's reflections. Nevertheless, just like *Pinch*, it frequently referred to anarchist thinkers. From the Christian anarchist literature, *The Digger* included references to Chelčický, Tolstoy, Berdyaev, Catholic Workers, as well as to some of the pre-modern examples described in Chapter 6 – Winstanley in particular. Like *Pinch*, therefore, it clearly rooted itself in the Christian anarchist tradition, and like *Pinch*, some of its columns have provided sometimes helpful input into this book.

---

[64] Today's *Pinch* also has a blog: http://apos-archive.blogspot.com/.

### Contributors to The Mormon Worker

Very recently, a newspaper which openly purports to provide a Mormon version of the *Catholic Worker* has been launched. Although *The Mormon Worker* is too young to be cited by other Christian anarchists, its columns praise several of the thinkers introduced here and thereby explicitly locate the paper in the Christian anarchist tradition. Some of the articles which appear in the issues published to date are very well written, and are therefore cited where relevant in this book.

### Andy and Nekeisha Alexis-Baker (Jesus Radicals)

A vibrant, mostly American Christian anarchist online community has gathered under the auspices of the Jesus Radicals website, the prime movers behind which seem to be Andy and Nekeisha Alexis-Baker. A section of the website contains short essays by its members, some of which have been useful for this book. The website also hosts a discussion forum and includes videos and links to other texts and websites. Jesus Radicals cells have already organised several annual conferences in the United States, the United Kingdom and in the South Pacific. Christian anarchist thinkers cited at these conferences (recordings for which are usually made available through the website) or in the Jesus Radicals essays, or otherwise recommended as further reading on their website, include the main Catholic Workers introduced above, Ellul (who the Jesus Radicals seem to hold in particularly high regard), Tolstoy, Eller, Andrews, Cavanaugh and Yoder (the last two are introduced below). Hence the Jesus Radicals provide a series of online and offline fora for the discussion of Christian anarchist ideas, and some of their online publications are certainly meticulous and original enough to have been weaved into this book.

### Bas Moreel (Religious Anarchism newsletters)

A final regular publication worth mentioning here is the *Religious Anarchism* newsletter published online by Dutchman Bas Moreel, three issues of which so far have discussed Christian anarchism. Moreel started these newsletters in reaction to what he saw as the poor treatment of religion in anarchist and atheist papers. The newsletters themselves are usually quite basic, concerned mostly with giving a taster to the uninformed reader of the religious anarchism chosen for the given newsletter. Still, some of them have been helpful in the present outline of Christian anarchism.

## William Lloyd Garrison

All the thinkers and publications mentioned so far are undeniably rooted in the Christian anarchist tradition. Several other thinkers, however, have also published material that has been described as Christian anarchist, even if for some reason or other their identification with the Christian anarchist tradition is not always straightforward or unproblematic.

One such writer is William Lloyd Garrison (1805-1879), one of the most famous champions of the abolition of slavery in the United States. What makes him slightly problematic is that his full commitment to Christian anarchism only lasted for a few years, when he drifted away from his otherwise fairly tight focus on slavery and towards a more general critique of all government. He later recanted from such anarchism, indeed whipping up support for the Civil War and campaigning for specific Presidential candidates. Garrison was always an agitator, concerned more often with agitating as such rather than with intellectual consistency. Nonetheless, he drafted, during his Christian anarchist phase, one of the most passionate summaries of Christian anarchism, a declaration which Tolstoy later reprinted in *The Kingdom of God Is within You*.[65] For that declaration and for his brief Christian anarchist phase, he is included in this book – but outside from that period, he was certainly no Christian anarchist.

## Hugh O. Pentecost

American pastor Hugh O. Pentecost (1848-1907) is similar to Garrison in promoting Christian anarchism only for a few years. Unlike Garrison, however, he explicitly used the word "anarchism," and was at pains to separate the term and its advocates from popular misconceptions about it. Where Garrison preached through his newspaper columns, Pentecost preached through sermons to his congregation (he had studied to become a Baptist priest but went on to set up his own congregation). Like Garrison, however, he later renounced and even dismissed his Christian anarchist phase, and found work as a District Attorney. He does not seem to have been noticed by any other Christian anarchist, but some of the sermons which he preached during his anarchist phase are cited in this book when relevant to Christian anarchism.

## Nicolas Berdyaev

Russian philosopher Nicolas Berdyaev (1874-1948) is sometimes quoted as a Christian anarchist. He rejected this association, however, and deliberately distanced himself from Tolstoy's thought, which he was familiar with. Yet his critique of (especially Marxist) socialism and his references to Christian theology do resonate with Christian anarchism. His writings are much more abstract than other Christian anarchists', relying more on Christian dogma than Biblical passages and criticising what he saw as dangerous monist and collectivist philosophies. His *The Realm of the Spirit and the Realm of Caesar* condemns socialism for such monism and advocates a Proudhonian type of world federalism. He may have had reservations about his association with anarchism, but his Christian philosophy does openly criticise statist tendencies. Besides, he did accept that the kingdom of God which he longed for could "only be envisaged in terms of anarchism."[66] Therefore, although he was uneasy with the term and quite abstract in his thinking, some of his writings do resonate strongly with and indeed enhance the Christian anarchist position, and where this is so, this is noted and incorporated into this book.

---

[65] William Lloyd Garrison, "Declaration of Sentiments Adopted by the Peace Convention," in *The Kingdom of God and Peace Essays*, by Leo Tolstoy, trans. Aylmer Maude (New Delhi: Rupa, 2001).
[66] Nicolas Berdyaev, "The Voice of Conscience from Another World: An Introduction," in *Essays from Tula*, by Leo Tolstoy, trans. Free Age Press (London: Sheppard, 1948), 14.

## William T. Cavanaugh

William T. Cavanaugh is a contemporary Catholic American theologian belonging to the school of thought known as Radical Orthodoxy. He is critical of the state's violent and jealous expropriation of power and authority from the church and speaks of the eucharistic church as an alternative to the state. He argues that the Eucharist is "a key practice for Christian anarchism" in the necessary challenging, by Christians, of the "false order of the state."[67] He rarely refers to other Christian anarchists in his writings, but his work is recommended by the Jesus Radicals. Cross-referencing between Cavanaugh and other Christian anarchists is therefore minimal, but his ongoing work on the questionable origins of the secular state and on how Christians ought to respond to the state's assumed omnipotence is relevant to a generic outline of Christian anarchism, hence his inclusion here.

## Jonathan Bartley

In Britain, Christian campaigner Jonathan Bartley (born 1971) recently published a book whose subtitle is *The Church as a Movement for Anarchy*.[68] The book, however, is less concerned with Christian anarchist thought than with encouraging Christian churches to dissociate themselves from the state and embrace more bottom-up methods and structures of campaigning and organisation. Bartley does mention Tolstoy, Ellul, Eller, Wink, Yoder and Myers, and he looks forward to a stateless society, but he offers little detailed theoretical thinking (in the sense of making the case that Christianity logically implies anarchism) of his own. His book thus acts more as a popular and pragmatic introduction to Christian anarchism than a systematic discussion of Christian anarchist thought.

Aside from that book, Bartley is Co-Director of *Ekklesia*, a Christian think-thank that carries forward some of what he advocates in his book and brings together several commentators who share that perspective. Bartley also does a lot of work with the media, appearing regularly on television and on the radio.

One can therefore argue over the extent to which the work that Bartley has been involved in should be considered theoretical, but his book and some of the articles produced by *Ekklesia* are nonetheless weaved into this book when doing so proves helpful in outlining Christian anarchism.

## Christian anarcho-capitalists

On the internet, one also finds several usually fairly short pages and essays making the case for a free-market type of Christian anarchism. As with its secular equivalent, Christian anarcho-capitalism seems to be largely an American phenomenon, intellectual credit is often given to Murray Rothbard, and the crucial difference with other anarchists is the issue of private property. This book

---

[67] William T. Cavanaugh, "The City: Beyond Secular Parodies," in *Radical Orthodoxy: A New Theology*, ed. John Milbank, Catherine Pickstock, and Graham Ward (London: Routledge, 1999), 182, 194.
[68] Bartley, *Faith and Politics after Christendom*.

does not seek to resolve this disagreement over property. Instead, it incorporates the persuasive arguments made by Christian anarcho-capitalists on a variety of issues, and notes, where relevant, the points at which Christian anarcho-capitalists take views which conflict with those of other Christian anarchists.

### James Redford

Perhaps the most systematic defence of Christian anarcho-capitalism is James Redford's "Jesus Is an Anarchist." Parts of that essay, however, could be improved by more balanced and more meticulous argumentation. Some passages are well argued and useful, but other passages are unconvincing and poorly justified. Tellingly perhaps, the case for private property is rather weak and evasive. Nevertheless, Redford's essay is cited and debated among (Christian and secular) anarcho-capitalists on the internet. Moreover, since some of its sections are thorough and convincing enough and certainly resonate with the thinking of other Christian anarchists, Redford's essay has been included in this book.

### Kevin Craig (Vine and Fig Tree)

The case for Christian anarcho-capitalism is also made by Kevin Craig in a number of interlinked internet pages, which are usually anonymous and officially published by "Vine and Fig Tree." Craig describes himself as belonging to both the radical Left (illustrated, he argues, by his stay in a Catholic Worker community for ten years) and the radical Right (for his anarcho-capitalism, that is). His web pages vary in style and rigour, but several of them make interesting arguments and cite plenty of Bible passages that strengthen the case for Christian anarchism. Very often, however, their focus is specific to the United States and its public. Moreover, some of the assertions expressed in these pages are simplistic and deliberately inflammatory. Classed under "socialism," for instance, which Craig clearly abhors, are "Stalinist Industrialism" and "Washington bureaucrats" alike.[69] In other words, Craig's pages are a mixed bag of thoughtful reflections and rather crude rants. Therefore, only what they contain which is of relevance to a generic outline of Christian anarchism has been included here.

### Strike the Root, Lew Rockwell and Libertarian Nation essayists

The *Strike the Root*, *Lew Rockwell* and *Libertarian Nation Foundation* websites all describe themselves as against the state and for the free market. All three supply banks of short essays by a number of authors (who sometimes refer to one another's essays) on anarcho-capitalism, some of which take the Christian perspective. Several of these essays are very well written and discuss key Bible passages or theoretical arguments for Christian anarchism, and have therefore provided valuable contributions to this book.

### George Tarleton

The last author for whom the title "Christian anarchist" seems applicable is Great Briton George Tarleton, because he published a book titled *Birth of a Christian*

---

[69] [Anonymous], *The Christmas Conspiracy* (Vine and Fig Tree), available from http://thechristmasconspiracy.com (accessed 10 April 2007).

*Anarchist*. That title, however, can be deceptive: although the book briefly mentions Proudhon and Bakunin and claims, in passing, that Jesus was an anarchist, it is not an exposition of Christian anarchism. No scholarly argument is presented for why Christianity would imply anarchism, no mention is made of any Christian anarchist, and in the end, one is left with the feeling that the word "anarchism" was chosen mainly to describe Tarleton's eccentric and perhaps indeed somewhat anarchic practice of Christianity.[70] It certainly contains very little of direct value to Christian anarchist thought. The aim of this book being to weave together a generic outline of Christian anarchism, references to Tarleton are minimal.

## *Supportive thinkers*

On top of the Christian anarchist thinkers introduced thus far, the case for Christian anarchism sometimes finds support in arguments put forward by a number of thinkers who do not themselves reach the anarchist conclusions that these arguments could lead them to.

### *Peter Chelčický*

Starting with the oldest, the one thinker prior to the nineteenth century whose thought has been weaved into this book is Czech reformer Peter Chelčický (c.1390-c.1460). As he preceded by several centuries both the rise to power of the state (as explained in Chapter 3) and the very adoption of the term "anarchism" as a thoughtful political position, he could not really fully develop his argument towards the explicitly anarchist conclusions reached by later Christian anarchists. Nonetheless, he is included here for a number of reasons.

Firstly, his input is very pertinent to Christian anarchist thought, especially on several key Bible passages and on criticisms of the church (see especially Chapters 3 and 4). He might not have reached the more fully-fledged anarchist conclusions that others reached several centuries later, but his lines of argument go a long way towards such conclusions. Secondly, because of his writings, he has been noted and praised by other Christian anarchists, especially Tolstoy. Indeed, Chelčický's style is very similar to Tolstoy's and his argument sometimes frequently echoes Tolstoy's. Thirdly, he is described by many of the scholars who have written about him as one of the clearest example of an anarchist *avant la lettre*. These commentators accept that to call Chelčický an anarchist is somewhat anachronistic since anarchism did not yet exist as a school of thought, but they identify him as a truly unique forerunner of Christian anarchism nonetheless. Finally, including him has not been excessively time-consuming since the only English translation of his main Christian anarchist publication, *The Net of Faith*, has recently been made available on the internet. In short, Chelčický has been recognised as a Christian anarchist by many, and as the numerous references to him in this book demonstrate, his contribution is indeed very pertinent to the present outline of Christian anarchism.

---

[70] Tarleton was involved in the "house church movement," which he describes as anarchic.

### Adin Ballou

Another supportive writer is American Adin Ballou (1803-1890), a staunch pacifist – his preferred term was "non-resistant" – who preached and wrote some of the most moving and compelling arguments for Jesus' Sermon on the Mount to be taken literally. The similarities with Tolstoy led the two to correspond with one another, though they disagreed on a number of issues. Ballou however always rejected anarchism both as a label *and* as a theory or as a possibility. Nonetheless, he was extremely critical of "human government."[71] Besides, that he found himself obliged to rebut accusations of "anarchism" suggests that his arguments were indeed sometimes heard to logically imply such anarchism. Several (secular and Christian) anarchists certainly do describe him as a Christian anarchist. Whether or not they are correct is not an issue which this book pretends to settle, but where his writings do support Christian anarchist thought – especially on non-resistance but also on numerous other Biblical passages – they have been included in this book.

### Ched Myers

Another American author whose writings bring him close to Christian anarchism is Ched Myers, who wrote an impressive political exegesis of the whole of Mark's Gospel.[72] His work is esteemed by several Christian anarchists – especially those with an activist inclination. His study of Mark certainly resonates strongly with Christian anarchist thought, yet he stays clear from reaching explicitly anarchist conclusions, locating himself instead in Marxist liberation theology. Apart perhaps from his criticism of "leaderless groups," however, there is little in his book that separates him from Christian anarchism.[73] Indeed, his exegesis very much implies the sort of Christian anarchism outlined by this book. It is for this reason that his work has been taken into account here.

### Walter Wink

The logic with acclaimed American theologian Walter Wink (born 1935) is fairly similar: like Myers, his work is admired by a few Christian anarchists, he locates himself in liberation theology rather than Christian anarchism, and he advocates a sort of activism that is at odds with Eller's understanding of Christian anarchism. His work on a political interpretation of Jesus' teaching and of Paul's "powers," however, does sometimes lend support to Christian anarchist thought – hence his inclusion in some of the arguments developed in this book.

### John Howard Yoder

Another American scholar whose work is pertinent to this book is John Howard Yoder (1927-1997), a famous Mennonite and pacifist whose pivotal contribution in the study of the political implications of Jesus' teaching has already been noted. Unlike the previous two authors, there is substantial evidence that Yoder

---

[71] Adin Ballou, *Christian Non-Resistance in All Its Important Bearings*, Second ed. (Oberlin: www.nonresistance.org, 2006), available from http://www.nonresistance.org/literature.html (accessed 28 March 2007), 37, 88-89.
[72] Ched Myers, *Binding the Strong Man: A Political Reading of Mark's Story of Jesus* (Maryknoll: Orbis, 1988).
[73] Myers, *Binding the Strong Man*, 280, 434.

studied many Christian anarchist thinkers. There are also plenty of references to him in that Christian anarchist literature, and his lines of reasoning often do lead to anarchist conclusions. Yet he made it clear that he did not advocate Christian anarchism, mainly by defending the police function of the state. Nevertheless, where his work does support the case for Christian anarchism, it has been included in this book.

### Archie Penner

The same applies to (considerably less famous) Canadian Mennonite Archie Penner. That is, his Christian study of the state repeatedly makes arguments that run parallel to Christian anarchist thought, though ultimately he stops short of any clearly anarchist conclusions.[74] His exegesis of numerous Bible passages, however, has proven useful to making the case for Christian anarchism.

All these writers and thinkers have made it into the pages of this book. A few others also appear here and there because their writings support the Christian anarchist perspective, but have not been introduced here either because they belong to one of the networks listed above or because their contribution is only quite modest. Now that the context, the originality, and the thinkers who inform this book have been introduced, the generic outline of Christian anarchism can begin. The next Chapter embarks on this task by pulling together the Christian anarchist exegesis of Jesus' Sermon on the Mount.

---

[74] Archie Penner, *The New Testament, the Christian, and the State* (Hagerstown: James Lowry/Deutsche Buchhandlung, 2000), 86, 118-122.

# Part I – The Christian Anarchist Critique of the State

# Chapter 1 – The Sermon on the Mount: A Manifesto for Christian Anarchism

Jesus' Sermon on the Mount is seen by many Christians – anarchist or not – as a moving summary of his message to the community of Christian disciples. Augustine describes it as "a perfect standard of Christian life," Hans Küng as "the core of Christian ethics."[1] Christian anarchists concur. Andrews, for instance, sees the Sermon as a "summary of Christ's rules" in which the "teaching of Christ [is] epitomized."[2] For Tolstoy as well, the Sermon on the Mount stands out as the most pertinent summary of this teaching: "In no other place does Jesus speak with such solemnity; nowhere else does he enunciate so many moral, clear, and comprehensible rules, appealing so straight to the heart of every man; nowhere else does he speak to a greater or more various mass of simple folk."[3]

At the same time, as Penner puts it, the Sermon on the Mount is also "one of the most acute exegetical battlegrounds of the New Testament," in particular over the section in which Jesus speaks of love and non-resistance.[4] It is therefore not surprising to find many Christian anarchists commenting, sometimes at length, on the pronouncements of Jesus in the Sermon. The purpose of this Chapter is to combine these scattered comments into one aggregate commentary, one generic Christian anarchist exegesis of the Sermon on the Mount.

Scholars often emphasise the parallels between Jesus' long Sermon on the Mount in Matthew's Gospel and the much shorter Sermon in the Plain in Luke's.[5] A discussion of whether these two Sermons are narratives of the same event, however, falls outside the scope of this book. Their content is very similar. Matthew's longer version covers the content of Luke's, and since it is this content that matters for Christian anarchism, this Chapter follows Christian anarchist thinkers in focusing almost exclusively on the Sermon on the *Mount*.

It will become obvious to the reader coming from a traditional Christian background that the Christian anarchist interpretation can frequently be quite different to more conventional exegeses of these passages. As Chapter 3 makes clear, however, Christian anarchists attribute this discrepancy to, at best, innocent misreading, and at worst, deliberate deceit on the part of established commentators. Christian anarchists therefore consciously bypass these traditional interpretations and try to base their exegeses solely on scripture. Tolstoy, for

---

[1] Aurelius Augustine, *The Sermon on the Mount Expounded, and the Harmony of the Evangelist*, ed. Marcus Dods, trans. William Findlay and S. D. F. Salmond (Edinburgh: T. and T. Clark, 1873), 1; Hans Küng, *Christianity: Its Essence and History*, trans. John Bowden (London: SCM, 1995), 52.
[2] Dave Andrews, *Not Religion, but Love: Practicing a Radical Spirituality of Compassion* (Cleveland: Pilgrim, 2001), 65.
[3] Tolstoy, *What I Believe*, 13.
[4] Penner, *The New Testament, the Christian, and the State*, 38.
[5] Matthew 5:1-7:29; Luke 6:20-49.

example, openly admits that he found himself "in the strange position of having to search for the meaning of [Jesus'] teaching as for something new."[6] This Chapter follows Christian anarchists in ignoring the tradition in order to present the pure Christian anarchist reading of the text. Traditional commentaries, as well as the Christian anarchist reasons for bypassing them, are mentioned only in Chapter 3.

For Tolstoy – the most cited exemplar of a Christian anarchist thinker – the Sermon on the Mount held a very special place. Tolstoy had struggled with a deep existential crisis for years when, while pondering a specific verse of this Sermon, suddenly came "a clear comprehension of all the teaching of Jesus," and "all that before had seemed obscure became intelligible."[7] This understanding brought his existential torment to a close, it unlocked for him the essence of Jesus' teaching, and it was based on this understanding of Christianity that he began launching his bitter attacks on the state and on the church. That crucial verse which Tolstoy saw as the key to Christianity is the famous verse where Jesus invites his disciples not to resist evil, but to turn the other cheek instead.

Not all Christian anarchists follow Tolstoy in elevating that single verse as high as he does, but all see in it and in the Sermon on the Mount a moving articulation of Jesus' central teaching of love and forgiveness. Most would agree that the Sermon on the Mount forms an ideal blueprint, a manifesto, as it were, for any truly authentic Christian community. And even if they do not all see the passage on not resisting evil as the absolute essence of Christianity, most Christian anarchists share the analysis of human society which Tolstoy develops from his exegesis of that passage. Moreover, just as with Tolstoy, the starting point for most Christian anarchists is not so much a critique of the state as an understanding of Jesus' radical teaching on love and forgiveness which, when *then* contrasted to the state, leads them to their anarchist conclusion.

The most important passage to examine from the Sermon on the Mount is therefore the one where Jesus calls for his disciples not to resist evil. The first and biggest section of this Chapter reviews, in detail, the various clusters of interpretation made by Christian anarchists (and selected pacifists) on this passage in order to draw out its anarchist implications. The second section considers the instruction not to judge; the third, that to love our enemies; and the fourth, that not to swear oaths. The fifth section briefly mentions the Golden Rule. The sixth relays the few and rather less relevant reflections of Christian anarchists on the remaining passages of the Sermon, except the passage where Jesus claims not to be destroying but fulfilling the Old Law, which is examined in more detail in the seventh section. The Chapter is then brought to a close by the eighth and final section, which returns to the idea that the Sermon on the Mount should guide the practice of the Christian community.

---

[6] Tolstoy, *What I Believe*, 66.
[7] Tolstoy, *What I Believe*, 18.

## 1.1 – Resist not evil

The instruction not to resist evil, a defining passage in the Christian Bible, comes in verses thirty-eight to forty-two of the fifth chapter of Matthew's Gospel, where Jesus tells his disciples:

38. Ye have heard that it hath been said, An eye for an eye, and a tooth for a tooth:
39. But I say unto you, That ye resist not evil[8]: but whosoever shall smite thee on thy right cheek, turn to him the other also.
40. And if any man will sue thee at the law, and take away thy coat, let him have thy cloak also.
41. And whosoever shall compel thee to go a mile, go with him twain.
42. Give to him that asketh thee, and from him that would borrow of thee turn not thou away.[9]

The subsections which follow elaborate the main sets of comments Christian anarchists make about these verses, beginning with a closer look at Jesus' three illustrations of non-resistance to show why these are politically significant. The second subsection introduces the view that what Jesus demands is not unresponsive passivity but a very purposeful reaction. The third shows that Jesus is calling for his disciples to rise above the law of retaliation, and thus prepares the ground for the fourth subsection, which discusses Christian anarchist reflections on the cycle of violence, and the fifth, which explains why Christian anarchists believe Jesus to be proposing a method to overcome it. The sixth and final subsection then clarifies why the preceding exegesis drives Christian anarchists to their anarchism, to their criticism of the state.

### 1.1.1 – Jesus' three illustrations

Elliott and Wink interpret Jesus' three brief illustrations one by one in order to show that in Jesus' historical context, these had immediate political connotations which can often be missed by exegetes who are foreign to that context.

On the first illustration, Wink begins by asking: "Why the right cheek?" He then explains that, in those times, "the left hand was used only for unclean hands," which means the attacker must have used the right hand – but, in that case, "the only way one could strike the right cheek with the right hand would be with the back of the hand."[10] In that context, he suggests this would be "unmistakably an insult," a humiliation.[11] Elliott reaches the same conclusion albeit from a slightly different angle: he notes that "Hitting someone in the face, particularly in front of witnesses, was in those times, just as it is today, a

---

[8] The Greek word in the original text is πονηρώ, which can be *grammatically* translated both as "evil" *and* as "him that is evil" or "the evildoer." The *meaning* of the expression, however, points to "evil" in general rather than to some specific entity "that is evil." The majority of the versions of the Bible, therefore, have opted for a translation into "evil" in the broad sense. In their own translation, Christian anarchists (and Christian pacifists) sometimes fluctuate between one variant and the other. Either way, these alterations have little consequence on the formulation of Christian anarchist thought since Christian anarchists nevertheless always *interpret* it as meaning "evil" in the broad sense.
[9] Matthew 5:38-42 (King James Version's italics removed).
[10] Walter Wink, *Jesus' Third Way* (Philadelphia: New Society, 1987), 15.
[11] Wink, *Jesus' Third Way*, 15.

humiliation and a loss of dignity for the victim in Middle-East society."[12] Jesus, both Wink and Elliott suggest, is depicting a situation which his followers would immediately recognise as humiliating, and which, in that society, would consequently call for an appropriate, equally forceful and humiliating response to uphold one's dignity and honour.

The response Jesus recommends, however, goes against these local expectations. For Elliott, what Jesus is saying is: "Don't retaliate. Don't behave in the way your enemy expects you to behave. Do what your attacker least expects: behave in the opposite way."[13] In effect, by turning the other cheek, "the cycle of violence is unexpectedly interrupted."[14] This, Elliott contends, confuses the attacker, who now "is no longer in control of the process he initiated. He is, in a very real sense, disarmed!"[15] Similarly, Wink claims that turning the other cheek "robs the oppressor of the power to humiliate," which forces the attacker to regard the victim "as an equal human being."[16] Both Elliott and Wink therefore agree that Jesus' surprising response in this first illustration disempowers the attacker and forces him to regard the victim in a different light.

Elliott and Wink bring a similar perspective to the other two responses illustrated by Jesus. In the second one, they note that by pointedly handing over his cloak in response to being sued for his coat, the victim would end up naked. Yet Elliott argues that nakedness in that context would be offensive, and that the community would blame the person who brought this about more than the actual victim. Along the same lines, Wink contends that this nakedness would register "a stunning protest" against the social and legal system that brought this about; that the "entire system" would thus be "publicly unmasked;" but that this unmasking "offers the creditor a chance to see, perhaps for the first time in his life, what his practice causes, and to repent."[17] So, again, Jesus' recommendation in this illustration would be "a practical, strategic measure for empowering the oppressed" against, in this case, such unfair use of the legal system.[18]

Regarding the third illustration, both Elliott and Wink agree that Jesus is here making a reference to a then established military practice, whereby a soldier could force a civilian to carry his pack, but for one mile only. Once again, here, Jesus' proposed response throws the soldier "off-balance," by depriving him "of the predictability of your response."[19] Doing twice as much as what is usually allowed, Elliott argues, is "a way of subverting authority" in that "the victim is claiming the power to determine for himself the lengths to which he is prepared to go."[20] So yet again, Jesus' illustration of non-resistance implies a critique of the expectations of his contemporary society and seeks to empower the victim through a counter-intuitive response.

---

[12] Elliott, *Freedom, Justice and Christian Counter-Culture*, 176.
[13] Elliott, *Freedom, Justice and Christian Counter-Culture*, 176.
[14] Elliott, *Freedom, Justice and Christian Counter-Culture*, 176.
[15] Elliott, *Freedom, Justice and Christian Counter-Culture*, 176.
[16] Wink, *Jesus' Third Way*, 16.
[17] Wink, *Jesus' Third Way*, 18-19.
[18] Wink, *Jesus' Third Way*, 19.
[19] Wink, *Jesus' Third Way*, 21.
[20] Elliott, *Freedom, Justice and Christian Counter-Culture*, 177.

Elliott further argues that the three illustrations cover the three "strategies which the enemy is most likely to employ" against followers of Jesus: "physical intimidation, manipulation of the legal system, and military co-option," each of which "involves a form of violence."[21] According to Elliott, therefore, Jesus' examples have immediate political significance: they illustrate three typical kinds of violence within that political context and three unexpected, subversive yet non-violent responses to it.

### 1.1.2 – A purposeful reaction

Moreover, a point which Christian anarchists (and pacifists) are keen to emphasise is that Jesus' non-resistance is not just some completely inactive, uncaring acceptance of evil, but a very specific, strategic response – a response which Jesus illustrates clearly with his three examples. Here, however, views diverge among Christian anarchists as to exactly what kind of action is allowed and what kind of resistance is forbidden: resistance to certain *types* of evil, resistance *by evil*, or *any* resistance at all. These very important disagreements are discussed in detail in Chapter 4. Here, what should be noted is that non-resistance as it is illustrated by Jesus is a purposeful and determined type of response.

Wink, for instance, who (as explained in the Introduction) is not a Christian anarchist but more of a militant pacifist, maintains that an accurate translation of the Greek does not suggest "the passive, doormat quality" which many Christians "cowardly" adopt, but that Jesus' statement "is arguably one of the most revolutionary political statements ever uttered."[22] He thinks that "court translators" turned "nonviolent resistance into docility," and that a "proper translation" of the Greek word for "resist" would be: "violent rebellion, armed revolt, sharp dissention." Thus according to Wink, Jesus was saying: "Do not strike back at evil (or, one who has done you evil) in kind. Do not give blow for blow. Do not retaliate against violence with violence." Jesus, Wink continues, "was no less committed to opposing evil than the anti-Roman resistance fighters. The only difference was over the means to be used: *how* one should fight evil." There are three possible responses to evil: passive "flight," violent "fight," or "militant nonviolence."[23] For Wink, a correct translation of the Greek verb shows that Jesus was rejecting the first two options and recommending the third. He was not preaching inaction, but a very radical type of reaction.

Ballou, whose position is perhaps best described as on the cusp between Christian anarchism and pacifism, is of a similar opinion to Wink's. Based on Jesus' examples, he argues that the precise type of resistance Jesus forbids is: "resistance of personal injury by means of injury inflicted."[24] He therefore believes the word resistance should not "be taken in its widest meaning" but "in the strict sense of the Saviour's injunction," which would consequently

---

[21] Elliott, *Freedom, Justice and Christian Counter-Culture*, 177.
[22] Wink, *Jesus' Third Way*, 12.
[23] All the quotations since the previous footnote are taken from Wink, *Jesus' Third Way*, 13.
[24] Adin Ballou, *Christian Non-Resistance* (Friends of Adin Ballou), available from http://www.adinballou.org/cnr.shtml (accessed 12 February 2007), chap. 1, para. 48.

mean that "Evil is to be resisted by all just means, but never with evil."[25] Both Wink and Ballou therefore seem to interpret Jesus' instruction as forbidding violent or evil responses to evil, but not necessarily political resistance as such.

However, Tolstoy, who after all is the conventional exemplar of classic Christian anarchism, sometimes appears to disagree. In his version of the Gospel, Jesus says: "Do not fight evil by evil, and not only do not exact at law an ox for an ox, a slave for a slave, a life for a life, but do not resist evil *at all*."[26] He seems to be interpreting the word resistance in the widest possible sense. When read this way, Jesus' recommended reply does not admit any form of resistance at all. And yet somewhere else, Tolstoy writes that "Jesus says, 'You wish to destroy evil *by evil*, but that is unreasonable. That there may be no evil, do none yourselves.'"[27] This time, Tolstoy seems to imply that there is a form of response, perhaps even of resistance, which might not be tainted by evil. Tolstoy thus does not appear fully consistent in his interpretation of Jesus' teaching. Sometimes he interprets Jesus' command to forbid all forms of resistance; sometimes he interprets it to forbid only violent resistance. These important issues are returned to in Chapter 4.

The point to note here is that although there may be disagreement among Christian anarchists and pacifists about exactly what form of reaction is allowed by these verses, they all (Tolstoy included) insist that the Christian response is a very real and very radical *reaction*. In Bartley's words, "nonviolence does not mean inaction, but rather means not being violent in the actions we *do* take."[28] Thus, as Elliott appreciates, what Jesus offers is a genuine strategy, which consist in both not resisting and doing more than is demanded.[29] This is a form of action, a genuine, purposeful, tactical reaction.

### *1.1.3 – Beyond lex talionis*

In these verses, therefore, Jesus is prescribing and describing a radical type of reaction. This radical response, coupled with Jesus' introductory words ("Ye have heard that hath been said […] But I say unto you"), implies a disapproval of something about his political context. That something, for Christian anarchists, relates to the cycle of violence inherent in a non-Christian society's administration of justice, and more specifically in *lex* (or *jus*) *talionis*, the law of retaliation which is respected in the Old Testament.

First, however, it is necessary to note that *lex talionis* is not a licence for unlimited violence. Penner explains that in the Old Testament settings which Jesus is referring to, "the expression […] amounts to a statement of principle based on literal exactions in some areas of civil and criminal justice," and it was

---

[25] Adin Ballou, "A Catechism of Non-Resistance," in *The Kingdom of God and Peace Essays*, by Leo Tolstoy, trans. Aylmer Maude (New Delhi: Rupa, 2001), 14.
[26] Leo Tolstoy, "The Gospel in Brief," in *A Confession and the Gospel in Brief*, trans. Aylmer Maude (London: Oxford University Press, 1933), 165 (emphasis added).
[27] Tolstoy, *What I Believe*, 87 (emphasis added).
[28] Bartley, *Faith and Politics after Christendom*, 174-175 (Bartley's emphasis).
[29] Elliott, *Freedom, Justice and Christian Counter-Culture*, 175, 178.

therefore aiming at "the administration of justice" on the basis of reciprocity.[30] Penner makes clear that "redress for wrong was meant as much as the idea of retaliation," that the purpose of it "was to curb crime and sin and to maintain civil order among the Hebrews," and that therefore "the injunction was not a permission to exercise private and hateful revenge in the sense in which the word is often used currently."[31] The idea behind *lex talionis* is that of justified retaliation, "to mete out punishment on the basis and with the intent of justice."[32] Equally important, however, is how this "fair" and "just" level of retaliation can be used by the two parties as a basis for reaching an alternative solution: a "fair" and "just" level of compensation. *Lex talionis* therefore provides the basis for either retributive (punishment of the offender) or restorative (compensation by the offender) justice. These principles, Penner remarks, were not used only in the times of Jesus, but are also "basic in civil and criminal law today."[33]

In the above verses, however, Jesus calls for his disciples, when wronged, not to "seek revenge or redress through legal or coercive means."[34] In order to "limit the level of retaliation taken in a world caught up in relentless cycles of revenge," argues Andrews, God once ordered human beings not to be excessive, to take only one eye for one eye, not more; but here Jesus is pushing the same intention further: "We were called to move from unlimited violence to limited violence by the command to only take an 'eye for an eye.' And we were called to move on from violence to nonviolence by the command to 'turn the other cheek.'"[35]

Hennacy, Bartley and Yoder all agree. For Hennacy, "in the earlier Bible times, if a man knocked out an eye of another man, according to tradition, he'd be lucky to get off with being lynched at once. The Jews were trying to lessen the severity of this," and what Jesus is here proposing is "to go a bit farther."[36] For Bartley, Jesus "made it clear that [*lex talionis*] was not enough" and instead urged "forgiveness and what many would see as the creation of an upward spiral of peace."[37] Hence, for Yoder, "What in the old covenant was a limit on vengeance [...] has now become a special measure of love demanded by concern for the redemption of the offender."[38]

Both commands are informed by the same intention, but non-resistance to evil goes further that the more rigid law of reciprocity. Indeed, this is one of the senses in which Jesus "fulfils" rather than "destroys" the law, by rearticulating it based on its original purpose (this theme is addressed in more detail later in this Chapter, as well as in the Conclusion). Jesus is instructing his disciples to move beyond the *lex talionis* of the Old Testament, to push its

---

[30] Penner, *The New Testament, the Christian, and the State*, 40.
[31] Penner, *The New Testament, the Christian, and the State*, 41.
[32] Penner, *The New Testament, the Christian, and the State*, 42.
[33] Penner, *The New Testament, the Christian, and the State*, 38.
[34] Penner, *The New Testament, the Christian, and the State*, 42.
[35] Both quotations from Andrews in this paragraph are from Dave Andrews, *Subversive Spirituality, Ecclesial and Civil Disobedience: A Survey of Biblical Politics as Incarnated in Jesus and Interpreted by Paul*, available from http://anz.jesusradicals.com/subspirit.pdf (accessed 17 July 2006), 1.
[36] Hennacy, *The Book of Ammon*, 491.
[37] Bartley, *Faith and Politics after Christendom*, 191.
[38] John Howard Yoder, "The Political Axioms of the Sermon on the Mount," in *The Original Revolution: Essays on Christian Pacifism* (Scottdale: Herald, 1998), 49.

original intentions even further. For Christian anarchists, the reason for which Jesus does this has to do with the way the law of retaliation can – and usually tends to – spiral out of control and degenerate into an unrelenting cycle of violence and revenge.

## 1.1.4 – The cycle of violence

Christian anarchists interpret Jesus' instruction as a comment not just on the Old Law, but also on human practice past and present. This subsection and the next therefore convey, in considerable detail, Christian anarchist reflections on the potential cycle of violence inherent in *lex talionis*, and their understanding of Jesus' non-resistance in light of that.

It will become obvious that Christian anarchists are quick to generalise Jesus' comments on *lex talionis* to the broader political question of how to deal with evil and achieve justice in society as a whole. They reflect on the use of violence as a method to achieve any kind of justice – from personal or collective retribution all the way to the much broader visions of social justice articulated by competing schools of political thought. They also thus broaden the notion of evil in a similar way to include not just personal evil but also social, political and economic evil and injustice. This broadening of the apparently more immediate meaning of these verses may not appear fully justified at first, but as Chapter 2 shows, it accords with Jesus' broader teaching and example. Besides, it resonates with the long established debate in more conventional Christian theology on the theological and ontological relation between love and justice – a theme examined in the Conclusion. Jesus' three examples admittedly illustrate a narrower set of instances of evil, but they are merely illustrations of his reinterpretation of the much broader principle of *lex talionis*, itself a principle aiming at the achievement of justice in society.

Christian anarchists begin by noting that forceful resistance is almost universally accepted as the justified method for humanity to confront injustice. Ballou observes that "The almost universal opinion and practice of mankind is on the side of resistance of injury with injury."[39] Hennacy remarks the same, adding that "It [is] plain that this system [does] not work."[40] "The earth," Ballou regrets, "has been rendered a vast slaughter-field – a theatre of reciprocal cruelty and vengeance."[41] Why? Because "The wisdom of this world has relied on the efficacy of injury, terror, EVIL, to resist evil," says Ballou.[42] Tolstoy is of the same opinion: the whole history of humankind for him betrays incessant and yet ultimately failed attempts to resist evil with evil, to deal violently with problems of violence, to wage wars in order to preclude other wars.

This method, however, only multiplies evil. Because human beings often fail to see that another's violence was to him only fair retaliation for an original offence, they get caught in an unending cycle of vendettas. If the justice of the retaliation is not recognised by its victim, what to one party is only fair

---

[39] Ballou, *Christian Non-Resistance*, chap. 1, para. 17.
[40] Hennacy, *The Book of Ammon*, 30.
[41] Ballou, *Christian Non-Resistance*, chap. 1, para. 17.
[42] Ballou, *Christian Non-Resistance*, chap. 1, para. 68.

retaliation becomes unjustified aggression to the other. Reciprocating evil with evil may *sometimes* appear just, but more often than not, it is thereby multiplying evil. Intrinsic to *lex talionis*, therefore, is the risk of it sparking a cycle of violence. Tolstoy quotes Ballou's explanation:

> He who attacks another and insults him, engenders in him the sentiment of hatred, the root of all evil. To offend another because he has offended us, on the specious pretext of removing an evil, is really to repeat an evil deed, both against him and against ourselves – to beget, or at least to free and to encourage, the very demon we wish to expel. Satan cannot be driven out by Satan, untruth cannot be cleansed by untruth, and evil cannot be vanquished by evil.[43]

Or as Tolstoy puts it, "One wrong added to another wrong does not make a right; it merely extends the area of wrong."[44] An eye for eye eventually makes the whole world go blind.[45] It is hard to overestimate how important this realisation is for all Christian anarchists, especially Tolstoy, Hennacy and Ballou. They believe Jesus exposed this cycle of violence and showed humankind a way out of it. It is therefore worth looking in more detail at some of the reflections made by Christian anarchists on this vicious circle of violence.

Ellul, in his book devoted to the subject, asserts that there are five laws of violence. One of these is that "Violence begets violence – *nothing else*."[46] We think that laudable ends sometimes justify slightly unfortunate means. Most Christian anarchists passionately disagree. Violent means only produce further violence, and they fatally corrupt and destroy even the worthiest of aims. To revise the popular dictum, the end simply does not, ever, justify the means. "When evil means are employed," Berdyaev insists, "these ends are never attained: the means take central place, and the ends are either forgotten, or become purely rhetorical."[47] Countless human goals have been fatally compromised by the violent means which were adopted in an attempt to reach them but which ended up taking centre stage while the original goal became more and more distant and elusive.

Nonetheless, moral aims are necessary preconditions for violent means to be adopted in the first place. As another of Ellul's laws of violence highlights, proponents of violence always try to justify it both to others and to themselves by evoking venerable goals: "Violence is so unappealing that every user of it has produced lengthy apologies to demonstrate to the people that it is just and morally warranted."[48] This is understandable, and proponents of violence can rarely be accused of evil intentions: they usually genuinely and

---

[43] Ballou, "A Catechism of Non-Resistance," 17.
[44] Leo Tolstoy, quoted in George Kennan, "A Visit to Count Tolstoi," *The Century Magazine* 34/2 (1887), 257.
[45] These words are usually attributed to Mohandas K. Gandhi, but the exact reference for them is nonetheless never specified. Whether or not he did say these words, they do eloquently sum up his critique of violence as a means to any end. In any case, as Chapter 6 demonstrates, Gandhi's doctrine of non-violence was in fact strongly influenced by his reading of Tolstoy.
[46] Jacques Ellul, *Violence: Reflections from a Christian Perspective*, trans. Cecilia Gaul Kings (London: SCM, 1970), 100 (Ellul's emphasis).
[47] Nicolas Berdyaev, *The Realm of Spirit and the Realm of Caesar*, trans. Donald A. Lowrie (London: Victor Gollancz, 1952), 88.
[48] Ellul, *Violence*, 103.

wholeheartedly believe that the superior ends they long for can be achieved by the violent means they succumb to. Berdyaev remarks that "no one ever proposes evil ends: evil is always disguised as good, and detracts from the good."[49] Yet the resort to violence is precisely where evil seeps in.

Besides, using violence or coercion to impose a social vision upon rebellious minorities is bound to fail. Tolstoy argues that since "there is in human society an endless variety of opinions as to what constitutes wrong and oppression," authorising violence for any one cause inevitably guarantees a vicious cycle of evil tit-for-tat, "a universal reign of violence."[50] Those who are coerced will only obey while they are weaker than the tyrants, under fear of threats. However "As soon as they grow stronger they naturally not only cease to do what they do not want to do, but, embittered by the struggle against their oppressors and everything they have had to suffer from them, they [...], in their turn, force their opponents to do what *they* regard as good and necessary."[51] Revolutionary violence promises counter-revolutionary violence.

One of the fundamental problems with violent methods, Christian anarchists argue, is that "once we consent to use violence ourselves, we have to consent to our adversary's using it, too."[52] This is because, Ellul continues, "We cannot demand to receive treatment different from that we mete out. We must understand that our own violence necessarily justifies the enemy's, and we cannot object to his violence."[53] Adopting violence as a method to attain one's goals implies the recognition of violence as an acceptable method in the first place. Thus in responding to violence with violence, says Yoder, "We agree with the other party that his weapons are right and thereby really loose our right to tell him that what he is doing is wrong."[54] According to Tolstoy, that is precisely "where the danger of employing violence lies: all the arguments put forward by those who employ it can with equal or even greater justification be used against them."[55] By smiting back when smitten on the right cheek, one is conceding that smiting is an acceptable type of action. One side's violence will always be seen by the other side as legitimising its own choice of violent methods.

Worse, the use of violence creates justifications for further violence. On top of implicitly conceding that violence is an acceptable method, the use of violence actually becomes a justification, almost an invitation, as it were, for a violent reply. This is another of Ellul's laws of violence, that "violence creates violence."[56] That is, "every act of violence can explain and seek to justify itself as a response to an earlier act of violence" – hence the danger inherent in *lex*

---

[49] Berdyaev, *The Realm of the Spirit and the Realm of Caesar*, 87.
[50] Leo Tolstoy, quoted in Kennan, "A Visit to Count Tolstoi," 259.
[51] Leo Tolstoy, "The Law of Love and the Law of Violence," in *A Confession and Other Religious Writings*, trans. Jane Kentish (London: Penguin, 1987), 163 (Tolstoy's emphasis).
[52] Ellul, *Violence*, 99.
[53] Ellul, *Violence*, 99.
[54] John Howard Yoder, "Peacemaking Amid Political Revolution," (Elkhart: Associate Mennonite Biblical Seminary, [1970?]), available from http://www.jesusradicals.com/library/yoder/peacemakingamidrevolution.pdf (accessed 16 May 2006), 60.
[55] Tolstoy, "The Kingdom of God Is within You," 269.
[56] Ellul, *Violence*, 95.

*talionis*.[57] Violent acts aggrieve those who are targeted, as well as their families and friends. These people will typically seek justice in violent retaliation. Hence using violence gives the opponent good reasons for more violence in return. Conversely, this violent retaliation "makes the attacker feel he is right, that all humans are just the same, they must always use weapons to defend themselves," says pacifist Richard Gregg.[58] In short, violence obscures its initial aim, validates itself as a method, and justifies more violence in return.

Moreover, Ellul's first law declares that "Violence becomes a habit of simplification of situations, political, social, or human. And a habit cannot quickly be broken."[59] Evil overcomes us, and we are "led to play evil's game – to respond by using evil's means, to do evil."[60] The world is accustomed to this game, caught in the delusional habit of the efficacy of violence (this is further discussed in the Conclusion). Yoder puts it succinctly: "Violence is always, apparently, the shortest and surest way;" but he immediately adds: "And in the long run that appearance always deceives."[61] We have a habit of thinking that violence can help us achieve our aims, but in the long run, all it does is add momentum to the destructive cycle of violence.

"As fire will not put out fire," Tolstoy therefore believes, "so evil will not destroy evil."[62] Even if we think we are right, we must resist the temptation to force others to obey our will. As Garrison explains, "physical coercion is not adapted to moral regeneration;" evil means do not teach moral virtues.[63] Besides, according to Tolstoy's Jesus, "every man is full of faults and incapable of guiding others. By taking revenge, we only teach others to do the same."[64] The very fact that violence sometimes appears to works in the short run only teaches exactly that – that violence appears to work, not that the user of violence was correct.

Christian anarchists urge every human being to decide where they stand on this. The question of how to respond to evil cannot be avoided. *Lex talionis* appears to offer a solution, but inherent in it is a tendency for reciprocal violence to spiral out of control. Jesus indirectly exposed this logic by advising to go beyond it. On the face of it, however, humanity has so far declined to heed this advice. Yet by opting for violent means either to respond to violence or to try to reach at times admittedly very worthy goals, the world has ensnared itself in a self-reinforcing cycle of violence and resistance. For Christian anarchists, Jesus makes clear that it is in the choice of means that the fatal mistake is committed. For the vicious cycle of violence to be broken, humanity needs an alternative method for responding to injustice and reaching moral aims.

---

[57] Goddard, *Living the Word, Resisting the World*, 168.
[58] Richard B. Gregg, *The Power of Nonviolence*, Abridged ed. (Lusaka: M. M. Temple, 1960), 46.
[59] Ellul, *Violence*, 94.
[60] Ellul, *Violence*, 173.
[61] John Howard Yoder, "The Theological Basis of the Christian Witness to the State," (Elkhart: Associate Mennonite Biblical Seminary, 1955), available from http://www.jesusradicals.com/library/yoder/witnesstostate.pdf (accessed 16 May 2006), 24.
[62] Tolstoy, *What I Believe*, 49.
[63] Garrison, "Declaration of Sentiments Adopted by the Peace Convention," 7.
[64] Tolstoy, "The Gospel in Brief," 269.

## 1.1.5 – *Overcoming of the cycle of violence*

Christian anarchists firmly believe Jesus both taught and lived out such an alternative, and that he best expressed it in those verses counselling non-resistance: "the sub-principle of Christian Non-Resistance," Ballou maintains, is that "Evil can be overcome only with good."[65] It is not an easy method, and at first, it can appear counterintuitive: Ellul indeed stresses that non-resistance implies "seeking another kind of victory, renouncing the marks of victory" (more on this in Chapter 4 and in the Conclusion).[66] Christian anarchists however believe it is the only real alternative for humankind, "the only possible way of breaking the chain of violence, of rupturing the circle of fear and hate."[67]

At the same time, no Christian anarchist pretends it is painless. Overcoming evil with love requires a willingness to endure violence or evil without doing violence or evil in return, even – in fact, especially – when treated unjustly. Hence it requires forgiveness since "by definition," explains Andrews, it "means making the sacrifice that is necessary to accept an injustice without demanding satisfaction in return."[68] That sacrifice is precisely the "relinquishing [of a person's] right to restitution or retaliation in order to restore a relationship."[69]

Returning good for evil, Andrews says, "may not transform every bad relationship into a good friendship; but [...] is the *only* thing that ever has or ever will."[70] Only such an attitude of love, non-violence and forgiveness makes healing possible. It forces "the oppressor to see you in a new light" and to reconsider the situation.[71] This opens "the possibility of the enemy's becoming just as well," which is important because as Wink continues, "Both sides must win."[72] Non-resistance, and its concomitant willingness to suffer unjustly, clears the ground for reconciliation because it exposes the destructive violence of the situation and makes a moving plea to overcome it. It lays bare the cycle of violence and it refuses to prolong it.

Some might object that non-resistance is contrary to human nature in that it goes against the natural instinct of self-preservation. Ballou replies that actually, non-resistance is "the true method of self-preservation."[73] He recalls that resistance always tend to be justified by self-defence:

> It professes to eschew all aggression, but invariably runs into it. It promises personal security, but exposes its subjects not only to aggravated assaults, but to every species of danger, sacrifice and calamity. It shakes the fist, brandishes the sword, and holds up the rod in terrorem to keep the peace, but constantly excites, provokes, and perpetuates war. It has been a liar from the beginning. It has been a Satan professing to cast out Satan, yet confirming

---

[65] Ballou, *Christian Non-Resistance*, chap. 1, para. 73.
[66] Ellul, *Violence*, 173.
[67] Ellul, *Violence*, 173.
[68] Dave Andrews, *The Crux of the Struggle*, available from http://www.daveandrews.com.au/publications.html (accessed 3 December 2006), 29.
[69] Andrews, *The Crux of the Struggle*, 29.
[70] Andrews, *Not Religion, but Love*, 106 (Andrews' emphasis).
[71] Wink, *Jesus' Third Way*, 23.
[72] Wink, *Jesus' Third Way*, 32.
[73] Ballou, *Christian Non-Resistance*, chap. 4, para. 10.

the power and multiplying the number of demons which possess our unfortunate race. It does not conduce to self-preservation, but to self-destruction, and ought therefore to be discarded.[74]

The usual method of self-preservation "constantly [runs] into the very wrongs it aimed to prevent."[75] Like begets like, therefore "the disposition to injure begets a disposition to injure."[76] In other words, resistance divides and actually destroys humanity – whereas non-resistance actually preserves it. Accordingly, Ballou concludes that non-resistance is not contrary but "in perfect accordance with" the "laws of nature."[77] It is the only method which can preserve humanity in the long run.[78]

Christian anarchists thus firmly believe in a strict continuity between ends and means. They believe these cannot be separated because the means eventually become the ends. Violence leads to violence, resistance to resistance. By the same token, peace, love and forgiveness can only begin with peaceful, loving and forgiving pioneers. The cycle of violence cannot be broken by cathartic or exemplary acts of violence; it can only be overcome by love and non-resistance. "[That] there may not be violence," Tolstoy insists, "it is necessary that *no-one under any pretext whatever should use violence, especially under the most usual pretext of retribution*."[79] The only means to reduce violence in the world, Tolstoy deduces, "is the submissive peaceful endurance of all violence whatever."[80]

Of course, such non-resistance is not easy. In the words of an Indian poet, "True love is not for the faint-hearted."[81] Non-resistance requires an absolute commitment, and this means a willingness to suffer, even to die, rather than to resist. Thus non-resistance is not cowardly; it requires courage. Gandhi observed that "bravery consists in dying, not in killing."[82] (This readiness to pay the ultimate price is discussed in more detail later, notably in Chapters 2 and 5.)

---

[74] Ballou, *Christian Non-Resistance*, chap. 4, para. 12.
[75] Ballou, *Christian Non-Resistance*, chap. 4, para. 17.
[76] Ballou, *Christian Non-Resistance*, chap. 4, para. 37.
[77] Ballou, *Christian Non-Resistance*, chap. 4, para. 33.
[78] There is an inconsistency in Ballou's argument: *humanity* might preserve itself by not resisting, but an *individual* might perish. Non-resistance preserves humanity as a whole, but not necessarily individuals facing injury. Ballou, however, still believes that an individual has better chances of survival by not resisting, as he suggests in Adin Ballou, *Non-Resistance in Relation to Human Governments* (www.nonresistance.org), available from http://www.nonresistance.org/literature.html (accessed 28 March 2007), 15-16. In any case, this also touches on the important theme of personal sacrifice, which is discussed again in Chapters 2 and 5. The point here is that while there may be a case for humanity's *collective* natural instinct to be one of non-resistance, that case would have to be formulated slightly differently to apply to human beings' *individual* natural instinct – and Ballou does that, but elsewhere.
[79] Leo Tolstoy, "The End of the Age: An Essay on the Approaching Revolution," in *Government Is Violence: Essays on Anarchism and Pacifism*, ed. David Stephens, trans. Vladimir Tchertkoff (London: Phoenix, 1990), 25 (Tolstoy's emphasis).
[80] Tolstoy, "The End of the Age," 26.
[81] Kabir, quoted in Anna Davie, "Setting Prisoners Free: A Workshop on an Anarchist Christian Response to Imprisonment," paper presented at *God Save the Queen: Anarchism and Christianity Today*, All Hallows Church, Leeds, 2-4 June 2006, available from http://uk.jesusradicals.com/Setting_the_Prisoners_Fre.pdf (accessed 4 June 2006), 4.
[82] Gandhi, quoted in Myers, *Binding the Strong Man*, 286.

Non-resistance involves courage because it demands a willingness to suffer, perhaps even to die (but not kill).

Besides, non-resistance is what Jesus commands, and Tolstoy is adamant that "Jesus really means what he says."[83] Indeed, Tolstoy only made sense of these verses when "he admitted to himself that perhaps Jesus meant that saying literally."[84] He explains that he had been distracted by trying to explain the passage allegorically, even though, deep down, he knew that it expressed "the vital principle of Christianity."[85] The teaching, however, could not be clearer:

> It may be affirmed that the constant fulfilment of this rule is difficult, and that not every man will find his happiness in obeying it. It may be said that it is foolish; that, as unbelievers pretend, Jesus was a visionary, an idealist, whose impracticable rules were only followed because of the stupidity of his disciples. But it is impossible not to admit that Jesus did say very clearly and definitely that which he intended to say: namely, that men should not resist evil; and that therefore he who accepts his teaching cannot resist.[86]

When he asked his disciples not to resist evil, Jesus meant it. Moreover, as Chapter 2 illustrates, Jesus practiced what he preached both throughout his life and in his very death.

So, to repeat and sum up, Jesus says (according to Tolstoy): "The teaching of the world is that men should do evil to one another, but my teaching is that they should love one another."[87] Jesus rejects the violence of the world by preaching non-resistance. His teaching overcomes the cycle of violence by refusing to resist. A faithful follower of Jesus – a Christian – therefore cannot resist, cannot participate in violence, and only by thus following Jesus' instruction might help overcome the world's vicious cycle of violence.

## 1.1.6 – Anarchist implications

State theory and practice, however, reveal an attitude at odds with this fundamental teaching of Jesus. Put simply, the state is founded on violence. In order for it to enforce law and order, the state demands from its citizens a monopoly over the legitimate use of force. Hence coercion is essential to government. The famous "social contract" postulated by Hobbes, Locke and (to a lesser extent) Rousseau rests precisely on the (hypothetical) consent, by a group of individuals, to grant the state a monopoly over the legitimate use of violence – allegedly to preserve order and security in an otherwise chaotic and sinful world.[88] For Hennacy, this means that "all governments – even the best – were founded upon the policemen's club: upon a return of evil for evil, the very

---

[83] Tolstoy, *What I Believe*, 15.
[84] Aylmer Maude, *The Life of Tolstóy: Later Years* (London: Oxford University Press, 1930), 33.
[85] Tolstoy, *What I Believe*, 19.
[86] Tolstoy, *What I Believe*, 18-19.
[87] Tolstoy, "The Gospel in Brief," 297.
[88] Incidentally, Ellul does not even agree with "social contract" theory that the state's mandate comes from the people's consent for it to rule over them. Instead he thinks that "the state is legitimized when the other states recognise it" – the consent of the governed is less important than the consent of other power holders that this or that state shall govern over this or that territory. Ellul, *Violence*, 84.

opposite of the teachings of Christ."[89] The state is founded on the very thing Jesus prohibits.

Christian anarchists reject the differentiation between "violence," with its negative connotations, and the state's use of "force." Ellul writes:

> I refuse to make the classic distinction between violence and force. The lawyers have invented the idea that when the state applies constraint, even brutal constraint, it is exercising "force;" that only individuals or nongovernmental groups (syndicates, parties) use violence. This is a totally unjustified distinction. The state is established by violence – the French, American, Communist, Francoist revolutions. Invariably there is violence at the start.[90]

Violence is employed at the start, and it permeates the day-to-day administration of government whenever "force" is involved. Ellul thus speaks of "administrative violence" and the "violence of the judicial system."[91] The state, he therefore insists, "cannot maintain itself save by and through violence."[92]

The resulting tragedy is that although the state promises to protect from evil, it itself "produces evil and extends it," says Berdyaev.[93] Civil law, according to Chelčický, "encourages a continuing fall of man," because it "perpetuates lawsuits, punishments, and revenge: it returns evil for evil."[94] For Christian anarchists, law is thus an inadequate and unchristian response to violence since it is itself another form of violence.

The state is also more visibly violent and therefore unchristian in another way: it wages war. In doing so, it breaks not only Jesus' instruction not to resist evil, but also one of the much older Ten Commandments, namely: "Thou shalt not kill."[95] Chelčický believes this was an "absolute" command which "God never revoked."[96] Yet as Berdyaev remarks, "murder is committed in an organized way and upon a colossal scale by the state."[97] A letter to *A Pinch of Salt* notes that "states institutionalise killing by maintaining armed forces."[98] The army's institution attests to the state's disregard for the commandment not to kill. It is the state's killing machine, its ultimate tool with which to murder and resist evil.

Some might retort that a distinction should be made between murder and war. To those, Ballou asks rhetorically:

---

[89] Hennacy, *The Book of Ammon*, 62.
[90] Ellul, *Violence*, 84.
[91] Jacques Ellul, quoted in Goddard, *Living the Word, Resisting the World*, 50.
[92] Ellul, *Violence*, 84.
[93] Berdyaev, *The Realm of the Spirit and the Realm of Caesar*, 83.
[94] Enrico C. S. Molnár, *A Study of Peter Chelčický's Life and a Translation from Czech of Part One of His Net of Faith*, ed. Tom Lock (Oberlin: www.nonresistance.org, 2006), available from http://www.nonresistance.org/literature.html (accessed 28 March 2007), 99 (quoting Chelčický).
[95] Exodus 20:13.
[96] Respectively: Peter Brock, *The Political and Social Doctrines of the Unity of Czech Brethren in the Fifteenth and Early Sixteenth Centuries* (The Hague: Mouton and Co., 1957), 60; Molnár, *A Study of Peter Chelčický's Life*, 14 (quoting Chelčický).
[97] Nicolas Berdyaev, "Personality, Religion, and Existential Anarchism," in *Patterns of Anarchy: A Collection of Writings on the Anarchist Tradition*, ed. Leonard I. Krimerman and Lewis Perry (Garden City: Anchor, 1966), 159.
[98] Frits ter Kuile, "Anarcho Theologie," *A Pinch of Salt*, issue 12, March 1989, 16.

> How many does it take to metamorphose wickedness into righteousness? One man must not kill. If he does it is murder. Two, ten, one hundred men acting on their own responsibility must not kill. If they do it is still murder. But a state or nation may kill as many as it pleases and it is no murder. It is just, necessary, commendable, and right. Only get people enough to agree to it, and the butchery of myriads of human beings is perfectly innocent. But how many men does it take?[99]

Christian anarchists see no valid reason to distinguish between people acting on their own and people doing the same thing through the state. Christian commands apply in both cases. Hennacy even finds support on this in Pope Benedict XV, who he quotes as having said that "The Gospel command of love applies between states just as it does between individual men."[100]

Both at home and abroad, then, the state directly contravenes the related commandments not to kill and not to resist evil. Hennacy affirms that "all government denies the Sermon on the Mount by a return of evil for evil in legislatures, courts, prisons, and war."[101] Of his own (American) government, he says that it "represents the largest single example of the organised return of evil for evil, both in foreign relations and in domestic affairs."[102] Through war and capital punishment, the state responds to evil with murder. A Christian should neither kill nor resist evil, yet the state does both.

Moreover, as Ballou explains, "what [a man] does through others he really does himself."[103] Therefore human beings might find themselves resisting injury with injury "as constituent supporters of human government."[104] That is,

> if a political compact [...] requires, authorizes, provides for, or tolerates war, bloodshed, capital punishment, slavery, or any kind of absolute injury, offensive or defensive, the man who swears, affirms or otherwise pledges himself, to support such a compact [...] is just as responsible for every act of injury done in strict conformity thereto, as if he himself personally committed it.[105]

When the state resists evil, its citizens who have consented to it holding power to resist evil are just as responsible for its behaviour as they would be if they had resisted evil themselves. What the state commits with my implicit or explicit consent, I am doing myself through it.

To put it as mildly as a contributor to *A Pinch of Salt*, the renunciation of violence taught by Jesus therefore "places a massive question [mark] against any use of violence by christians or any approval of social structures which themselves embody the legitimation of the use of violence and coercion within territorial bounds – like states."[106] Christians should neither coerce fellow human beings nor empower others to do so through legislation. It is because of this

---

[99] Ballou, quoted in Tolstoy, "The Kingdom of God Is within You," 13.
[100] Benedict XV, quoted in Hennacy, *The Book of Ammon*, 373.
[101] Hennacy, *The Book of Ammon*, 124.
[102] Hennacy, *The Book of Ammon*, 259.
[103] Ballou, "A Catechism of Non-Resistance," 16.
[104] Ballou, *Christian Non-Resistance*, chap. 1, para. 51.
[105] Ballou, *Christian Non-Resistance*, chap. 1, para. 53.
[106] David Mumford, "The Bible and Anarchy," *A Pinch of Salt*, issue 14, March 1990, 8.

absolute commitment to non-violence that Christian anarchists refuse to endorse the institution and conduct of the state.

Moreover and for the same reasons, Christian anarchists reckon that a true Christian cannot use courts of law to seek redress. Ballou explains that Jesus' instruction "forbids not merely all personal, individual, self-assumed right of retaliation, but all revenge at law."[107] According to Tolstoy, if any use of force is forbidden, then so are "all legal proceedings in which force is actually or implicitly employed to oblige any of those concerned [...] to be present and take part."[108] Aylmer Maude (Tolstoy's friend, biographer and translator) thus concludes that "This teaching involves nothing less than the entire abolition of all compulsory legislation, Law Courts, police, and prisons, as well as all forcible restraint of man by man."[109] Christianity, that is, involves anarchism.

Hennacy therefore concludes that "Anarchism is the negative side" of "Pacifism and the Sermon on the Mount."[110] According to Christian anarchists, anarchism is closer to the "social order" envisaged by Jesus than any alternative "of which force is a component."[111] They believe Christian anarchism to be "an inevitable corollary of Christian pacifism."[112] It is because it returns evil for evil that Hennacy would abolish the state. It is because he thought that "the very existence of governments and state apparatuses [make] domestic violence and international war inevitable" that Tolstoy was an anarchist.[113] It is because they take Jesus' words in the Sermon on the Mount literally, and because they consider the state to be, both in theory and practice, in flagrant contravention of these, that Christian anarchists believe anarchism to be an inevitable corollary of Christianity.

Brock explains that, "like other anarchists," Christian anarchists such as Tolstoy "wished to base the organization of society on consent, on cooperation, and not on force."[114] Christian anarchists do not envision a chaotic society, but an organised one based on real consent, love and mutual help rather than the fictional granting of the legitimacy of violence to some monstrous Leviathan. Quite what such a society would look like is discussed in Chapter 5.

Guseinov observes about Tolstoy's anarchism that "one cannot deny his consistency."[115] Christian anarchists move in consistent logical steps from Jesus' command not to resist evil, through their assessment of state violence in both theory and practice, to their ultimate rejection of the state. Tolstoy encapsulates the apparent simplicity of this logic in an often quoted syllogism of

---

[107] Ballou, *Non-Resistance in Relation to Human Governments*, 12.
[108] Maude, *The Life of Tolstóy*, 36.
[109] Maude, *The Life of Tolstóy*, 36.
[110] Hennacy, *The Book of Ammon*, 99.
[111] Evacustes A. Phipson, "A Happier Social Order," *A Pinch of Salt*, issue 14, March 1990, 10.
[112] Note that Peter Brock was using this turn of phrase to express a slightly different point. The full sentence reads: "We may agree that anarchism is not an inevitable corollary of Christian pacifism; yet it appears, at least to me, as an essential element of Tolstoyism." Peter Brock, *Pacifism in Europe to 1914* (Princeton: Princeton University Press, 1972), 459.
[113] Brock, *Pacifism in Europe to 1914*, 460.
[114] Peter Brock, *The Roots of War Resistance: Pacifism from the Early Church to Tolstoy* (New York: Fellowship of Reconciliation, 1981), 73.
[115] A. A. Guseinov, "Faith, God, and Nonviolence in the Teachings of Lev Tolstoy," *Russian Studies in Philosophy* 38/2 (1999), 100.

his: "Government is violence, Christianity is meekness, non-resistance, love. And, therefore, government cannot be Christian, and a man who wishes to be a Christian must not serve government."[116]

So, according to Tolstoy, every would-be Christian faces a choice: God or the state, Jesus' teaching and example or state theory and practice. It is "impossible," he says, "at one and the same time to confess the God-Christ, the foundation of whose teaching is non-resistance to evil, and yet consciously and calmly labour for the establishment of property, tribunals, kingdoms, and armies."[117] He further believes that this choice is inevitable, that every single person must decide where they stand on this issue. He writes:

> Perhaps Christianity may be obsolete, and when choosing between the two – Christianity and love or the State and murder – the people of our time will conclude that the existence of the State and murder is so much more important than Christianity, that we must forego Christianity and retain only what is more important: the State and murder.
>
> That may be so – at least people may think and feel so. But in that case they should say so![118]

People should openly admit to have chosen what they have chosen and not pretend they have been able to combine the two, because each of these alternatives directly repudiates the other. It is either Christianity, or the state.

Further Christian anarchist criticisms of the state (including state violence) are outlined in Chapter 3. What matters here is that for Christian anarchists, in both theory and practice, the state is founded on violence and maintains itself through violence, a behaviour directly opposed to Jesus' instruction not to resist evil. Moreover, if the state cannot but be violent, it follows that a perfectly Christian society would have done away with it. If the state cannot but be violent, then in preaching non-resistance to evil, Jesus prescribes a form of anarchism.

## 1.2 – Judge not

Anarchism follows not just from non-resistance to evil, but also from other key passages in the Sermon on the Mount. One such passage, which Tolstoy frequently analyses alongside the commandment not to resist evil, is where Jesus says the following:
1. Judge not, that ye be not judged.
2. For with what judgement ye judge, ye shall be judged: and with what measure ye mete, it shall be measured unto you again.
3. And why beholdest thou the mote that is in thy brother's eye, but considerest not the beam that is in thine own eye?
4. Or how wilt thou say to thy brother, Let me pull out the mote out of thine eye; and, behold, a beam is in thine own eye?

---

[116] Leo Tolstoy, "Letter to Dr. Eugen Heinrich Schmitt," in *Tolstoy's Writings on Civil Disobedience and Non-Violence*, trans. Aylmer Maude (New York: Bergman, 1967), 129.
[117] Tolstoy, *What I Believe*, 22.
[118] Leo Tolstoy, "Address to the Swedish Peace Congress in 1909," in *The Kingdom of God and Peace Essays*, trans. Aylmer Maude (New Delhi: Rupa, 2001), 540.

> 5. Thou hypocrite, first cast out the beam out of thine own eye; and then shalt thou see clearly to cast out the mote out of thy brother's eye.[119]

Tolstoy explains Jesus to here be saying to his disciples: "You cannot judge, for all men are blind and do not see the truth. [...] And those who judge and punish are like blind men leading the blind."[120] Moreover, "[men] cannot judge one another's faults because they are themselves full of wickedness."[121] Since no human being is faultless, castigating other persons for their faults is both ill-advised and hypocritical.

This, in turn, further explains why men should not resist evil. The two injunctions are connected in that since "every man is full of faults and incapable of guiding others," men should not condemn, take revenge or resist evil.[122] Because one cannot judge evil properly in the first place, to act upon that judgement by resisting the alleged evil is unwise. Instead of judging, Christian should patiently forgive even what to them looks evil. Ballou writes that true followers of Christ "deem it their duty to forgive, not punish – to yield unto wrath and suffer wrong, without recompensing evil for evil, referring their cause always unto Him who has said, 'Vengeance is mine; I will repay.'"[123]

These words which Ballou quotes come from Paul's Epistle to the Romans.[124] They refer back to the Old Testament, but Christian anarchists sometimes mention Old Testament passages in their interpretation of Jesus' instruction not to judge. While interpreting a passage from Isaiah, for instance, Eller argues that "There is only One who is qualified to serve as Judge of all the earth, who not only can say what justice is but also is capable of bringing it to be the actual state of affairs."[125] True justice, Eller argues, can only be brought about by "Judge Jehovah," so "we would better let God do it his way from the outset."[126] The Christian who has faith in God must also have faith in God's judgement and in his execution of justice, which is also why he should abstain from impersonating God and judging his fellow human beings.

Men are ill-equipped to make laws and judge other men as good or wicked, let alone punish them for it. Hence, while an omniscient God can punish evil-doers, "it is not to be done by men to men, and the Son of God has bid men not to do it."[127] Judgement is God's prerogative. Hence Jesus clearly forbade human judgment. However startling this may seem, Tolstoy therefore insists that Jesus' instruction not to judge further condemns all earthly tribunals: if we are not supposed to judge and condemn our fellows, then neither can that be done through courts of justice. Our judicial system is unchristian not only because it resists evil, but also because it involves judging – both forbidden by Jesus. As a

---

[119] Matthew 7:1-5 (King James Version's italics removed).
[120] Tolstoy, "The Gospel in Brief," 165-166. See also: Tolstoy, "The Gospel in Brief," 288.
[121] Tolstoy, "The Gospel in Brief," 288.
[122] Tolstoy, "The Gospel in Brief," 269.
[123] Ballou, *Non-Resistance in Relation to Human Governments*, 10-11.
[124] Romans 12:19.
[125] Vernard Eller, *Christian Anarchy: Jesus' Primacy over the Powers* (Eugene: Wipf and Stock, 1987), 257 (emphasis removed).
[126] Eller, *Christian Anarchy*, 254, 256.
[127] Tolstoy, *What I Believe*, 64.

result, a Christian can neither be a judge, nor take part in any trial, nor take a fellow human being to court. Christians must stay clear of human courts.

Tolstoy usually discusses the instructions not to resist evil and not to judge together, because even though they have a slightly different focus, they both condemn the state's resistance to what it has judged to be evil. To judge and to resist are different acts, but they are related, especially in the state. The former places more emphasis on legislation and the judicial system, the latter on the police force and the army. Either way, they both criticise functions of the state which are fundamental to its existence. They both inform the Christian anarchist position.

## 1.3 – Love your enemies

Another instruction from the Sermon on the Mount which Christian anarchists interpret as implying a critique of the state comes right after the verses on non-resistance. Here, Jesus says:

43. Ye have heard that it hath been said, Thou shalt love thy neighbour, and hate thine enemy.
44. But I say unto you, Love your enemies, bless them that curse you, do good to them that hate you, and pray for them which despitefully use you, and persecute you;
45. That ye may be the children of your Father which is in heaven: for he maketh his sun to rise on the evil and on the good, and sendeth rain on the just and on the unjust.
46. For if ye love them which love you, what reward have ye? do not even the publicans the same?
47. And if ye salute your brethren only, what do ye more than others? do not even the publicans so?
48. Be ye therefore perfect, even as your Father which is in heaven is perfect.[128]

Christian anarchists and pacifists develop two overlapping lines of interpretation on these verses: one of these focuses on the implied condemnation of patriotism and war; the other argues that loving one's enemy is the litmus test of Christianity.

Tolstoy concentrates on the condemnation of patriotism and war. He admits to have been initially puzzled by the commandment, because it appears to be "an unattainable moral ideal," and because unusually, Jesus is not quoting the Old Testament "with verbal exactness" but using words "which were never spoken."[129] Tolstoy then realised, however, that "'neighbour' in the Jewish tongue simply meant a Jew," as parallel passages in the Bible indeed confirmed.[130] Likewise, Tolstoy explains, "The word 'enemy' is seldom used in the Gospels in a private or personal sense, but almost always in a public and national one."[131] Both Penner and Ballou agree, and add that Jesus is here

---

[128] Matthew 5:43-48 (King James Version's italics removed).
[129] Tolstoy, *What I Believe*, 88-89.
[130] Tolstoy, *What I Believe*, 90.
[131] Tolstoy, *What I Believe*, 90-91.

deliberately reinterpreting the Old Testament notions of "neighbour" and "enemy."[132] Indeed for Ballou, these notions had been misapprehended, and Jesus in fact draws out their "true" and intended meaning.[133] Tolstoy thus concludes that in these verses,

> All the passages, spread over the different books of the Scriptures, in which it is prescribed to the Jews to oppress, slay, and destroy other nations, are brought together by Jesus into one saying, "Thou shalt hate or do evil to thine enemy." He says, "You have been told to love your own people, and to hate the enemy of your race, but I tell you to love all without distinction of nationality."[134]

According to Tolstoy, Jesus simply tells us to love people of other nations as well as our own countrymen. He says: "If you are attached only to your own countrymen, remember that all men are attached to their own countrymen, and wars result from that."[135] The "snare," Tolstoy explains, arises from the "false belief" that one's good is bound up with the good of one's countrymen, "and not, as it is really, with the good of all men on earth."[136]

Yet if the new rule is "to make no difference between our own and other nations," then this rule also requires "never to act in conformity with such a difference, that is, never to provoke or take part in war, and to treat all men of what nationality soever as though they belonged to our own."[137] Any manifestation of lower feelings towards foreigners compared to one's own nationals being outlawed, anything that incites such differentiation must also be forbidden. Hence, to the extent that the state takes part in war, provokes it or otherwise differentiates between "us" and "them," it is behaving in an unchristian manner.

For Tolstoy, therefore, Jesus is also ultimately outlawing patriotism. As Chapter 3 discusses in more detail, Tolstoy refuses to accept that there might be a good kind of patriotism, because Jesus' teaching unequivocally condemns all favouritism towards one's countrymen. For Tolstoy, Jesus says: "Treat foreigners as I have told you to treat one another. To the Father of all men there are no separate nations or separate kingdoms: all are brothers, all sons of one Father. Make no distinctions among people as to nations and kingdoms."[138] Tolstoy interprets the Parable of the Good Samaritan as being precisely about treating foreigners as neighbours.[139] A Christian should "do good to all men without distinction."[140] Whenever the state stirs up patriotism and national preferences, it is thereby disobeying yet another of Jesus' instructions.

Moreover, Chelčický argues, "Wars and other kinds of murder have their beginning in the hatred of the enemy and in the unwillingness to be patient

---

[132] Ballou, *Christian Non-Resistance*, chap. 1-2; Penner, *The New Testament, the Christian, and the State*, 45-46.
[133] Ballou, *Christian Non-Resistance*, chap. 1, para. 66.
[134] Tolstoy, *What I Believe*, 91 (emphasis removed).
[135] Tolstoy, "The Gospel in Brief," 166.
[136] Tolstoy, *What I Believe*, 215.
[137] Tolstoy, *What I Believe*, 92.
[138] Tolstoy, "The Gospel in Brief," 166-167.
[139] Tolstoy, "The Gospel in Brief," 229-230. (Luke 10:25-37)
[140] Tolstoy, "The Gospel in Brief," 288.

with evil."[141] Therefore "if Christians really believed in this commandment of love, [...] the sword would immediately fall from their hands, all conflicts and wars would cease among them [...]; and should they be hurt and oppressed by others, they would not strike back with their sword but patiently suffer all evil."[142] Many Christian theologians have tried to argue that love of enemy does not prevent killing, as long as one's inner disposition is one of love and charity; but as Chapter 3 shows, Christian anarchists have no time for these arguments, which they consider to be both pure hypocrisy and a betrayal of Jesus. For them, conflicts continue to plague the world "because men do not trust the Son of God enough to abide by his commandments."[143]

Christian anarchists believe that true Christians have the faith and the courage to do what Jesus demands. Love of enemies might be very difficult, but that only makes it an even more revealing criterion to identify genuine followers of Jesus. According to Chelčický, "The whole test of a Christian comes to this: is he willing to love his enemies?"[144] Wink says that this is "the litmus test of authentic Christian faith."[145] Of course, it is not easy: it calls to love "even the ones who have caused the greatest pain by taking precious life," because such love "does not depend upon the nature or 'lovableness' of the object of love."[146] It is not easy. But it is what Jesus asked his followers to do.

Besides, "love of enemies is based on imitation of God."[147] As Jesus himself makes clear, it imitates God's love for all – good or evil – in his Creation. That, Yoder argues, is the sense in which Jesus' instruction to be "perfect" as God is "perfect" should be understood. He explains:

> we are asked to "resemble God" just at this one point: not in His omnipotence or His eternity or His impeccability, but simply in the undiscriminating or unconditional character of His love. This is not a fruit of long growth and maturation; it is not inconceivable or impossible. We can do it tomorrow if we believe. We can stop loving only the lovable, lending only to the reliable, giving only to the grateful, as soon as we grasp and are grasped by the unconditionality of the benevolence of God. "There must be no limit to your goodness, as your heavenly Father's goodness knows no bounds."[148]

Hence according to Yoder, "the perfection to which Jesus calls his hearers [...] is not flawlessness or impeccability, but precisely the refusal to discriminate between friend and enemy, the in and the out, the good and the evil."[149] It is easy to love our friends. What Jesus taught and lived, however, was to love and forgive both the good and the evil, just as God does.

---

[141] Molnár, *A Study of Peter Chelčický's Life*, 135 (quoting Chelčický).
[142] Molnár, *A Study of Peter Chelčický's Life*, 134 (quoting Chelčický).
[143] Molnár, *A Study of Peter Chelčický's Life*, 135 (quoting Chelčický).
[144] Molnár, *A Study of Peter Chelčický's Life*, 134 (paraphrasing Chelčický).
[145] Wink, *Jesus' Third Way*, 49.
[146] Scott Langley, "End the Death Penalty Now!," *The Catholic Worker*, issue 73, May 2006, 3; Penner, *The New Testament, the Christian, and the State*, 46.
[147] Laurie Johnston, "Love Your Enemies – Even in the Age of Terrorism?," *Political Theology* 6/1 (2005), 88.
[148] Yoder, "The Political Axioms of the Sermon on the Mount," 48.
[149] Yoder, *The Politics of Jesus*, 225 (footnote 216).

Furthermore, just as non-resistance helps overcome the cycle of violence, love of enemies helps overcome the associated cycle of hatred. Wink explains:

> Love of enemies is the recognition that the enemy, too, is a child of God. The enemy too believes he or she is in the right, and fears us because we represent a threat against his or her values, lifestyle, and affluence. When we demonize our enemies, calling them names and identifying them with absolute evil, we deny that they have that of God within them which still makes transformation possible.[150]

The challenge, he therefore suggests, is to "find God in my enemy."[151] That is the only way to convert someone else to one's cause, because "no one can show others the error that is within them, as Thomas Merton wisely remarked, unless the others are convinced that their critic first sees and loves the good that is within them."[152] Love of enemies opens the possibility of reconciliation.

This obviously relates to the above discussion of ends and means. Enmity stirs up more enmity and hence perpetuates itself in a vicious circle. Laurie Johnston suggests that "the real enemy is not any human person or group, but rather *enmity itself*."[153] To overcome the vicious circle, enmity must be dried up in the heart, by cultivating love. In the long run, by such love, enmity will be overcome: "Love your enemies and you will have none."[154]

The state, however, does none of that. It treats its nationals differently to foreigners. It stirs up patriotism, prepares for war and goes to war. It discriminates between good and evil domestically. It institutionalises love of friends and hatred of enemies. It does not even try to pretend to mirror God's unconditional love for all. For Christian anarchists, therefore, on this account as well, the state is an unchristian institution.

## 1.4 – Swear not at all

There is another, much simpler way in which the state contravenes one of Jesus' instructions from the Sermon on the Mount. It concerns swearing and oath taking, a topic on which Jesus says the following:

33. Again, ye have heard that it hath been said of them of old time, Thou shalt not foreswear thyself, but shalt perform unto the Lord thine oaths:
34. But I say unto you, Swear not at all; neither by heaven; for it is God's throne:
35. Nor by the earth; for it is his footstool: neither by Jerusalem; for it is the city of the great King.

---

[150] Wink, *Jesus' Third Way*, 49.
[151] Wink, *Jesus' Third Way*, 49.
[152] Wink, *Jesus' Third Way*, 51.
[153] Johnston, "Love Your Enemies – Even in the Age of Terrorism?," 104.
[154] Tolstoy reports that this is said in *Teaching of the Twelve Apostles*, but he gives no reference details for these words to be traced to back to their original source. Leo Tolstoy, "Bethink Yourselves!," in *Recollections and Essays*, trans. Aylmer Maude (London: Oxford University Press, 1937), 250.

36. Neither shalt thou swear by thy head, because thou canst not make one hair white or black.
37. But let your communication be, Yea, yea; Nay, nay: for whatsoever is more than these cometh of evil.[155]

Tolstoy is the only Christian anarchist to discuss in detail this instruction's implication for the state. So even though other Christian anarchists, such as Ballou and Chelčický, come to the same conclusion, it is Tolstoy's exegesis that will be followed here.

Tolstoy begins by stating that unlike some of the other instructions of Jesus, this one only troubled him "by its clearness, by its simplicity and easiness."[156] Jesus simply enjoins his followers never to swear, in other words never to bind themselves to any oaths. Why would Jesus command this? Tolstoy explains: "If it be the teaching of Jesus that one should always fulfil the will of God, how can a man swear to fulfil the will of a fellow-man? The will of God may not accord with the will of a man."[157] It is impossible to know in advance what will be required by the Christian demands to love and forgive, hence one should not bind oneself with an oath that may compel to act against the will of God. For this reason, Tolstoy writes, "every oath is an evil."[158] He insists that "For a Christian to promise obedience to men or to laws made by men is as though a workman, having hired out to one master, should at the same time promise to carry out any order given him by someone else. Man cannot serve two masters."[159] It is impossible to swear allegiance to the state at the same time commit oneself to follow Jesus. Swearing was therefore condemned by Jesus.

Tolstoy believes that his reading is further confirmed by several other passages in the New Testament. For instance, he draws attention to the Epistle of James. There, James plainly reiterates Jesus' position: "But above all things, my brethren, swear not, neither by heaven, neither by the earth, neither by any other oath: but let your yea be yea; and your nay, nay; lest ye fall into condemnation."[160] This injunction seems as clear as Jesus' – do not swear, ever.

Tolstoy also reads the episode of Peter's three denials as a confirmation of this logic.[161] Peter initially assures Jesus that he will defend him, and Jesus, according to Tolstoy, replies that "A man cannot pledge himself to do anything."[162] Sure enough, eventually, Peter repeatedly swears not to have known Jesus, and the cock crows. Peter should never have sworn, just as Jesus had warned him.

Tolstoy also links to this commandment the two passages on the payment of taxes which are discussed in detail in Chapter 4. In the temple tax episode, Jesus is asked whether everyone is bound to pay the taxes, to which in the Gospel according to Tolstoy, Jesus replies: "If we are sons of God we are bound to no one but God, and are free from obligations. But if they demand the

---

[155] Matthew 5:33-37.
[156] Tolstoy, *What I Believe*, 81.
[157] Tolstoy, *What I Believe*, 83.
[158] Tolstoy, "The Gospel in Brief," 164.
[159] Tolstoy, "The Kingdom of God Is within You," 233.
[160] James 5:12 (King James Version's italics removed).
[161] Matthew 26:31-35, 69-75; Mark 14:27-30, 66-72; Luke 22:31-34, 55-62; John 13:36-38, 18:25-27.
[162] Tolstoy, "The Gospel in Brief," 295.

tax from you, then pay: not that you are under obligation to do so but because you must not resist evil."[163] Followers of Jesus must have no forsworn obligation to do what other men demand. Their sole allegiance is to God through Jesus.

Tolstoy lists the "render unto Caesar" passage immediately after this one, and portrays it as making the same point. He then has Jesus say: "Your Orthodox teachers go about everywhere making people swear and vow that they will fulfil the law. But by this they only pervert people."[164] Those in authority seek to bind people into future allegiance, but this should be refused, "for every oath is extorted from men for evil purposes."[165]

One such "evil purpose" is the establishment of state power. "Oath taking," R. V. Sampson explains for Tolstoy, "is fundamental to military and therefore political power. The oath of allegiance creates the legal basis for the maintenance of the disciplined unity of large numbers of men, on which all State power ultimately rests." Jesus' saying, he therefore concludes, "indirectly [strikes] at the roots of Caesar's military power."[166] To refuse to swear oaths is to deny the state the basis of its power.

In *The Kingdom of God Is within You,* Tolstoy illustrates this process with a telling example, by quoting the words that Kaiser Wilhelm pronounced when addressing German soldiers:

> "Recruits!" said he. "You have sworn fidelity to me before the altar and a minister of God. You are still too young to understand the full importance of what has been said here; but take care above all to obey the orders and instructions given you. You have sworn fidelity to me, lads of my Guard: that means that you are now my soldiers, that you have given yourselves to me, body and soul. For there is now but one enemy – my enemy. In these days of socialistic sedition it may come to pass that I command you to fire on your own kindred your brothers, even your fathers and mothers – which God forbid – and even then it will be your duty to obey my orders without hesitation."[167]

By swearing an oath of allegiance to the state, one becomes a tool of the state; and as the state's tool, one will be forced to betray Christ.

It should be noted that the connivance of the clergy in swearing such deadly oaths of allegiance to the state was not missed by Tolstoy. Indeed, he laments that "In very truth the chief obstacle to understanding the law against the swearing of oaths, has been that so-called Christian teachers have boldly forced men to take oaths on the Gospel itself; in other words, have forced them to do by the Gospel what is contrary to the Gospel."[168] For Tolstoy, "the snare arises from the name of God being used to *sanction* deceit."[169] Terry Hopton explains that Tolstoy condemns the church's involvement here because "such oaths appear to bind the individual to commit violence in God's name, in absolute disobedience

---

[163] Tolstoy, "The Gospel in Brief," 227. (Matthew 17:24-27.)
[164] Tolstoy, "The Gospel in Brief," 228. (Matthew 22:15-22.)
[165] Tolstoy, *What I Believe*, 85.
[166] Both quotations in this paragraph are from R. V. Sampson, *Tolstoy: The Discovery of Peace* (London: Heinemann, 1973), 172.
[167] Tolstoy, "The Kingdom of God Is within You," 225 (Tolstoy's emphasis).
[168] Tolstoy, *What I Believe*, 84-85.
[169] Tolstoy, *What I Believe*, 213 (Tolstoy's emphasis).

to His will."[170] Swearing on the Bible is clearly inconsistent, therefore either candidly ill-advised or wilfully hypocritical. Chapter 3 returns to Tolstoy's distrust of the church.

In any case, whenever the state requires oaths of allegiance from its citizens or soldiers, it breaches Jesus' instruction. Jesus made clear that his followers should "say Yes when it is yes" and "No when it is no," but that "every oath is evil."[171] For Christian anarchists, whenever the state requires oaths of allegiance, it is unchristian – it is "evil."

## 1.5 – The Golden Rule

Later in the Sermon, Jesus pronounces what is often described as (the Christian version of) the Golden Rule: "Therefore all things whatsoever ye would that men should do to you, do ye even so to them: for this is the law and the prophets."[172] According to Tolstoy, this summarises all the other instructions articulated by Jesus in the Sermon: "All these commandments are contained in one: All that you wish men to do to you, do you to them."[173]

The Golden Rule indeed encapsulates the logic behind the commandments explained so far. For Andrews, the Sermon on the Mount is an "unpacking [of] the specific implications of the Golden Rule."[174] Do not do to others what you would not want them to do to you, because whatever you do to them, you can reasonably expect them to do to you in return. Hence do not resist, use violence, judge or bind others by oaths of allegiance if you do not want others to resist you, use violence against you, judge you or bind you by oaths of allegiance. Likewise, love your enemies if you want them to do the same. Love one another and love will eventually be returned to you.

A member of the Catholic Worker movement explains that this Golden Rule is "[at] the root of anarchist morality […]. If you would not be exploited, then you must not exploit others. If you would not be ruled, then you must refuse to rule others."[175] Yet because of its monopoly over the allegedly legitimate use of force, it is impossible for the state to abide by the Golden Rule, Redford argues, as by definition, this monopoly implies that "governments do to their subjects what they outlaw their subjects to do to them."[176] Hennacy agrees that the Golden Rule accords with Christian anarchism, and contrasts it with "other systems of society" which "depend upon manmade laws and the violence of the State."[177] To use violence, Tolstoy says, is "to do what he to whom

---

[170] Terry Hopton, "Tolstoy, God and Anarchism," *Anarchist Studies* 8 (2000), 37.
[171] Tolstoy, "The Gospel in Brief," 164-165.
[172] Matthew 7:12.
[173] Tolstoy, "The Gospel in Brief," 167.
[174] Dave Andrews, *Plan Be: Be the Change You Want to See in the World* (Milton Keynes: Authentic, 2008), 4.
[175] Robert Ellsberg, quoted in Mary C. Segers, "Equality and Christian Anarchism: The Political and Social Ideas of the Catholic Worker Movement," *Review of Politics* 40/2 (1978), 225.
[176] James Redford, *Jesus Is an Anarchist: A Free-Market, Libertarian Anarchist, That Is – Otherwise What Is Called an Anarcho-Capitalist*, available from http://praxeology.net/anarchist-jesus.pdf (accessed 14 August 2006), 6.
[177] Hennacy, *The Book of Ammon*, 200.

violence is done does not wish," and is therefore unchristian.[178] The Golden Rule thus implies a rejection of the state's self-assumed right to coerce its citizens into submission.

## 1.6 – Reflections on other passages in the Sermon

The most important passages of the Sermon on the Mount for Christian anarchism have now been considered. Before discussing the extent to which Jesus breaks or fulfils the Old Law, it is worth noting in passing some of the comments which Christian anarchists make about other passages of the Sermon. These comments do not really bear directly upon their anarchist conclusions on the state as such, but they do hint at further criticisms of state and church officials.

### *1.6.1 – Be not angry*

Two of Jesus' five new commandments at the end of the fifth chapter of Matthew have been left out so far. The first of these is where Jesus instructs his followers not to be angry:

21. Ye have heard that it was said by them of old time, Thou shalt not kill; and whosoever shall kill shall be in danger of the judgement:
22. But I say unto you, That whosoever is angry with his brother without a cause[179] shall be in danger of the judgement: and whosoever shall say to his brother, Raca, shall be in danger of the council: but whosoever shall say, Thou fool, shall be in danger of hell fire.
23. Therefore if thou bring thy gift to the altar, and there rememberest that thy brother hath ought against thee;
24. Leave there thy gift before the altar, and go thy way; first be reconciled to thy brother, and then come and offer thy gift.
25. Agree with thine adversary quickly, whiles thou art in the way with him; lest at any time the adversary deliver thee to the judge, and the judge deliver thee to the officer, and thou be cast into prison.
26. Verily I say unto thee, Thou shalt by no means come out thence, till thou hast paid the uttermost farthing.[180]

Christian anarchists (and pacifists) offer different reflections on this passage.

Yoder points out that the three punishments in verse twenty-two are "of mounting severity," and that "[the] most serious hatred is seen not in the act but in the inner attitude towards the brother."[181] Jesus is shifting the sin from the actual act of killing to the judgemental attitude that precedes it. Ernest Crosby

---

[178] Leo Tolstoy, quoted in Guseinov, "Faith, God, and Nonviolence in the Teachings of Lev Tolstoy," 100.
[179] "Without a cause" does not appear in the original Greek and has been withdrawn in most subsequent translations of the Bible. As discussed in Chapter 3, Christian anarchists believe that its insertion in the King James Version is an example of the way in which court translators and theologians have manipulated Jesus' teaching to suit their own (unchristian) purposes.
[180] Matthew 5:21-26.
[181] Yoder, "The Political Axioms of the Sermon on the Mount," 50-51.

agrees: "the great evil is not killing but the anger against a brother."[182] The implication for the state would be that it breaches Christian demands even before the act of killing (in war or capital punishment), when it passes judgement on the intended victim and thus starts rationalising its eventual murder.

Ellul argues that these verses confirm his view that "all kinds of violence are the same" – physical, economic or psychological.[183] According to Ellul, Jesus "declared that there is no difference between murdering a fellow man and being angry with him or insulting him."[184] The state, for Ellul, is violent not just by military coercion, but also by economic injustice and by brainwashing and other forms of propaganda.

Tolstoy draws parallels between these verses and some of the Gospel passages on forgiveness: when injured, we should cultivate forgiveness instead of letting anger overcome us, not least since we are so ill equipped to judge one another in the first place. This subject is examined in Chapter 2.

Tolstoy also explores why Jesus is so disapproving of the words "Raca" and "fool." He explains that "Raca" means "a man not worthy to be called a man," a "lost man."[185] According to Tolstoy, Jesus' point is therefore to identify typical justifications for anger, such as calling the other a fool or a lost man. The temptation of counting only a few other men as equal "and despising the rest as insignificant men of no account (raca), or as stupid and uneducated (fools)," is the chief cause of the separation of men, Tolstoy argues.[186] Jesus wants peace and equality among human beings and that is why he is frowning upon anger and discrimination, because, as Crosby argues, "brotherly love is [...] imperilled" by "standing aloof from others, by refusing to recognize them as equals."[187] To the extent that the state creates and perpetuates discrimination, however, it is maintaining hierarchies which become easy justifications for anger and eventually murder.

It should be noted that not all Christian anarchists condemn anger outright. In Christian anarchist newspapers, for instance, while some see anger as "a tool of domination," others believe that there is "a kind of anger that is healthy" which consists of a healthy concentration of energies, compared to "another kind of anger" which is dangerous because it is violent and murderous.[188] The intricacies of this distinction, however, are not fully articulated. Besides, this argument is not rooted in an exegesis of the above verses.

Andrews, however, quotes Stassen and Gushee to relay their point that Jesus does not actually command not to be angry (which indeed he does not, at least not as clearly as he spells out the ensuing commandments), that the statement is in fact "descriptive, not prescriptive, of 'a vicious cycle that we often

---

[182] Ernest Howard Crosby, *Tolstoy and His Message* (BoondocksNet Edition), available from http:www.broondocksnet.com/editions/tolstoy/index.html (accessed 18 August 2003), chap. 4, para. 8.
[183] Ellul, *Violence*, 97.
[184] Ellul, *Violence*, 99.
[185] Tolstoy, *What I Believe*, 72.
[186] Tolstoy, *What I Believe*, 209.
[187] Crosby, *Tolstoy and His Message*, chap. 4, para. 8.
[188] Barbara Deming, "On Anger," *A Pinch of Salt*, issue 1, September 1985, 10-11; Richard Hamilton, "Anger: An Anarchist Perspective," *The Digger and Christian Anarchist*, issue 36, April 1990, 9.

get stuck in.'"[189] This would of course resonate with the above discussion on the cycle of violence. Andrews also emphasises that Jesus was angry twice, and once called his opponents fools.[190] One of the two cited instances of that "anger" is the temple cleansing episode which is discussed in Chapter 2 – but it is worth noting that the Greek word for "anger" does not appear in that text. Nevertheless, the words for "anger" and "fool" do appear in the other two instances reported by Andrews: once, Jesus does "look with anger" at those who query his healing of a man on the Sabbath; and once, he does call scribes and Pharisees "fools."[191] Twice, it seems, Jesus does not live up to what he seems to be preaching in this commandment.

Andrews argues that it is both "unrealistic" and "unbiblical" to understand Jesus as asking us never to be angry.[192] He believes that what Jesus is calling for is "self-restraint," for an anger that is not "aggressive."[193] He admits that "There is great danger in getting angry" because "we want to hit back at people" or "call them names."[194] But, based on his translation of the Greek for "meekness" in the Beatitude concerning the meek, he believes that Jesus blesses those with "neither too much anger, nor too little anger, but just the right amount of righteous indignation to address any grievous wrong."[195] The important thing, for him, is to channel this anger "constructively," by practicing "proactive self-control by learning to 'turn the other cheek.'"[196] For Andrews, therefore, the commandment not to be angry is not as clear as might first seem: Jesus is not outlawing anger but commending reconciliation, and he appears to consider some amount of anger legitimate as long as it is channelled constructively, with self-restraint and without ever returning evil for evil.

This apparent contradiction must here be left unresolved. Christian anarchists offer no solution other than Andrews' contention that Jesus actually did not prescribe his followers not to be angry at all. That contention, however, is not unproblematic. On the face of it, and certainly according to other Christian anarchists, the phrasing of Jesus' saying does suggest he is prescribing behaviour and not just describing vicious cycles – indeed, why describe the cycle if not also to at least implicitly point out a way to overcome it? Besides, in this section of the Sermon, Jesus is deliberately referring to ancient prescriptions, which he reviews and "fulfils" with what looks like another, modified, prescription. Here, then, Jesus apparently diagnoses anger as the source of this particular vicious cycle, and preaches reconciliation as a cure. If anger is not altogether condemned, it certainly seems to be frowned upon. Still, it may be that the emphasis is best placed more on promoting reconciliation than on reproving anger (Chapter 4

---

[189] Dave Andrews, *A Spiritual Framework for Ethical Reflection*, available from http://www.daveandrews.com.au/publications.html (accessed 3 December 2006), 4.
[190] Andrews, *Plan Be*, 23-24 (where he also argues that Jesus was quite angry at the death of Lazarus); Andrews, *A Spiritual Framework for Ethical Reflection*, 4. (Matthew 21:12-17, 23:17; Mark 3:5; John 11.)
[191] Mark 3:5 and Matthew 23:17 respectively.
[192] Andrews, *Plan Be*, 46.
[193] Andrews, *Plan Be*, 7.
[194] Andrews, *Plan Be*, 23.
[195] Andrews, *Plan Be*, 22. (Matthew 5:5.)
[196] Andrews, *Plan Be*, 24-25.

revisits this theme of reconciliation). Be that as it may, this difficulty does not impact much upon the Christian critique of the state as a violent and thus unchristian institution. It may be that Jesus twice failed to follow his own instructions, but that is of little consequence to his implied criticisms of the state – except that it allows the toleration of some righteous indignation in these criticisms.

### 1.6.2 – Commit no adultery

This applies even more to the only other of the five commandments so far left out of the discussion, where Jesus says that adultery, which is forbidden, in fact begins in the heart.[197] Tolstoy is the only Christian anarchist to spend any time on this commandment. He reads it as implying both that one should only have one partner for life and that sensuality destroys the soul.[198] None of this has much relevance for Christian anarchism, except perhaps to the extent that he considered the church to have deliberately mistranslated the meaning of the original Greek to "pervert and conceal" Jesus' teaching.[199] Tolstoy's many criticisms of the church are addressed in Chapter 3. The verses on adultery, however, are of no significance for the Christian anarchist critique of the state.

### 1.6.3 – Seek no praise

Towards the middle of the Sermon on the Mount, Jesus makes some recommendations about almsgiving, praying and fasting, namely that these things should not be done so as to seek praise and recognition from the community.[200] Tolstoy simply repeats these remarks, but in a language that makes them refer even more obviously to church leaders, past *and present*. Again, therefore, this is relevant for this book only as further criticism of the church. That is all Christian anarchists have to say about those verses.

### 1.6.4 – The Beatitudes

The Beatitudes, with which the Sermon begins, also appear to amount to an (at the very least) indirect snipe at rich and comfortable church or state officials.[201] Christian anarchists, however, tend to cite these verses without spending any time articulating an interpretation of them – though still clearly implying this very criticism of public and ecclesiastical officials. The only exception to this is Andrews, who spends a whole (but short) book on the Beatitudes – which he playfully calls "Be-Attitudes." He interprets these as a synopsis of the Sermon and of the attitudes which it calls Christians to adopt. He summarises "the virtues that are blessed" in these Beatitudes as follows:

---

[197] Matthew 5:27-32.
[198] Tolstoy, "The Gospel in Brief," 163-164, 226-227, 287; Tolstoy, *What I Believe*, 73-81, 210-212.
[199] Tolstoy, *What I Believe*, 80.
[200] Matthew 6:1-16.
[201] Matthew 5:3-12. (See also Luke 6:20-26.)

Focusing on the poor (not status or riches). *Humility.*
Grieving over the injustice in the world. *Empathy.*
Getting angry but not getting aggressive. *Self-restraint.*
Seeking for justice (not vengeance). *Righteousness.*
Extending compassion to all in need. *Mercy.*
Being wholehearted in a desire to do right. *Integrity.*
Working for peace in a world at war. *Non-violence.*
Suffering for just causes (patiently). *Perseverance.*[202]

Of course, in his interpretation of the first blessing, Andrews articulates in some detail the criticism of the rich and comfortable which other Christian anarchists usually leave implicit – indeed he lists many of the other Gospel passages which he reads as similarly "uncompromising" on the subject.[203] For him, too many commentators omit the numerous passages in which Jesus confronts the political, economic and social injustice of his society.[204] Besides, Andrews regrets that the Beatitudes are rarely taken seriously or taught in churches. For him, "To *quote* these Be-Attitudes is religious – but to *act* on them is revolutionary."[205] In any case, the relevance of the Beatitudes for Christian anarchism mainly consists in providing more reasons to criticise rich and comfortable church and state elites.

## 1.6.5 – Worry not about security

Another passage of the Sermon which Christian anarchists often just cite without much elaboration is where Jesus points to the birds and the lilies and says that, like these, his disciples should not worry about what they will eat or wear, but should seek first the kingdom of God and that "these things shall be added unto [them]."[206] Here, Christian anarchists do sometimes include a few comments with their quotations from these verses. Andrews, for example, says that "The issue is that we need to stop eating and drinking to excess, and to start hungering and thirsting for justice."[207] Day interprets it to mean that people should not worry about security all the time – the very worry which leads them to further empower the state in the hope that it will guarantee this sought-after security.[208] Pentecost denounces a similar worry about the economy.[209] Others, like Tolstoy, simply repeat that we should not be afraid or anxious about the future when trying to live according to the Sermon on the Mount, because God will provide for us if we do live according to it. For Christian anarchists, therefore, these verses imply that

---

[202] Andrews, *Plan Be*, 7 (he then spends the rest of the book teasing out those statements).
[203] Andrews, *Plan Be*, 9-14.
[204] This sentence is heavily paraphrased from Andrews, who writes: "Many people say that Jesus said a lot about love, but very little about political, economic and social justice. But Jesus constantly confronted the injustice in his society. The Synoptic Gospels record 40 instances – not counting parallel passages – of Jesus specifically and repeatedly confronting both Roman and Jewish authorities with the injustices they perpetrated in Israel." Andrews, *Plan Be*, 33.
[205] Andrews, *Plan Be*, 66 (Andrews' emphasis).
[206] Matthew 6:19-34.
[207] Andrews, *Not Religion, but Love*, 93.
[208] Tom Cornell, *My Dorothy Day* (Casa Juan Diego), available from http://www.cjd.org/paper/dday.html (accessed 14 February 2007), para. 10.
[209] Hugh O. Pentecost, *A Gigantic Poorhouse*, available from http://www.deadanarchists.org/Pentecost/poorhouse.html (accessed 22 November 2007), para. 21.

people should not worry about how to live in a stateless world. They should stop worrying about the future and focus first and foremost on doing God's will.

### 1.6.6 – Be the salt and the light

Finally, Christian anarchists also mention Jesus' comparison of his disciples with the "salt of the earth" and the "light of the world."[210] Yoder explains that "it is assumed that there should be something about the behaviour of His disciples which will communicate to the world around."[211] For Ballou, being the salt and the light means not waiting "till the bad cease from aggression" to be good, but "to suffer wrong rather than do wrong, 'to overcome evil with good.'"[212] The idea is that the disciples should be the medium by which the salt and the light, that is, the message of Jesus, should be brought to the world. The disciples are the seeds of Christianity. The very title of *A Pinch of Salt* is indeed a direct reference to this. Christians should therefore speak out and not shy away from denouncing the state when it behaves in an unchristian way.

## 1.7 – Fulfilling the Old Law

Before this Chapter can be brought to a close, a more detailed discussion is required of one last passage from the Sermon on the Mount. That passage has been studied heavily by Christian theologians throughout the centuries, because it throws light upon the relation of the New Testament with the Old, upon the extent to which Jesus is transforming the Old Law with his instructions in the Sermon on the Mount. Just before Jesus enumerates his five reinterpretations, he says:

17. Think not that I am come to destroy the law, or the prophets: I am not come to destroy, but to fulfil.
18. For verily I say unto you, Till heaven and earth pass, one jot or one tittle shall in no wise pass from the law, till all be fulfilled.
19. Whosoever therefore shall break one of these least commandments, and shall teach men so, he shall be called the least in the kingdom of heaven: but whosoever shall do and teach them, the same shall be called great in the kingdom of heaven.
20. For I say unto you, That except your righteousness shall exceed the righteousness of the scribes and Pharisees, ye shall in no case enter into the kingdom of heaven.[213]

Christian anarchists do not all understand these verses in exactly the same way. Taken together, and in light of the five instructions which follow, they make two broad sets of at first seemingly contradictory comments on those verses: they often insist that Jesus is still marking a break with the Old Testament, but they explain the way in which this nevertheless amounts to a fulfilment of it.

---

[210] Matthew 5:13-16.
[211] Yoder, "The Political Axioms of the Sermon on the Mount," 41.
[212] Ballou, *Christian Non-Resistance*, chap. 4, para. 16.
[213] Matthew 5:17-20 (King James Version's italics removed).

For a start, Elliott notes that in his ministry, Jesus "does not hesitate to break the Law and to encourage others to do so as well," especially as regards what is permitted on the Sabbath.[214] Jesus might claim to be somehow fulfilling the Law, but he also makes a point of refusing to abide by what he sees as inauthentic strictures claimed to derive from it. Elliott goes even further: he argues that Jesus had to "[take] steps to avoid both the official condemnation and the public alienation which would occur if he were seen to be espousing radical ideas," and that "Jesus' strategy in this respect was publicly to declare that he was not concerned to change anything, but was, on the contrary, a staunch defender of orthodoxy."[215] Yet at the same time, "in the verses which immediately follow these, Jesus takes some of the particular requirements of orthodoxy [...] and begins to radically reinterpret them."[216] What Jesus means by "fulfilling" is therefore clearly not just some unquestioning obedience to what is presented as the Law. Jesus explicitly reviews five commands from the Old Law and reinterprets them in a new way.

"However salutary [the Mosaic] statute," Ballou therefore claims, "the great Master of Christians has abrogated it."[217] For example, "so far as Moses and his expounders enjoined the infliction of penal personal injuries in resistance of injuries, and for the suppression of evil doing, Jesus Christ prohibits the same."[218] The prohibition of resistance to evil "is made precisely coextensive in all its bearings with the allowances and injunctions of the Olden Code."[219] Jesus' prohibition of oaths, resistance or hatred of enemies now applies to the very same extent that the older Law permitted them.

If this is not accepted, Ballou writes, and therefore if Jesus' instructions are not seen as abrogating the commandments he relates them to, then Christians are faced with a clear contradiction over what Jesus forbids but the Old Law allows. Yet if so, Ballou continues, "is it not worth as much *for* non-resistance as *against* it?"[220] If there is a contradiction, then one reading is just as potentially valid as the other: the view that the Old Law takes primacy is no more justified than the view that Jesus abrogates it. Furthermore, those arguing that Jesus does not abrogate but confirm the Old Law would have to accept that

> It would carry us back, and bind us hand and foot to Judaism, with its every *jot* and *tittle*. It would re-enact the whole ceremonial, as well as moral and penal code of the Mosaic dispensation! Circumcisions, sacrifices, and all the commandments, *least* as well and *greatest*, would be made binding on us.[221]

If Jesus does not abrogate the Old Law, then Christians should abide by every single instruction of the Old Law.

Tolstoy insists that the Old Law is incompatible with Jesus' instructions and that is impossible to abide by both. He has Jesus say: "The old teaching of external service to God cannot be combined with my teaching of

---

[214] Elliott, *Freedom, Justice and Christian Counter-Culture*, 76.
[215] Elliott, *Freedom, Justice and Christian Counter-Culture*, 161.
[216] Elliott, *Freedom, Justice and Christian Counter-Culture*, 162.
[217] Ballou, *Non-Resistance in Relation to Human Governments*, 13.
[218] Ballou, *Christian Non-Resistance*, chap. 2, para. 12.
[219] Ballou, *Christian Non-Resistance*, chap. 2, para. 13.
[220] Ballou, *Christian Non-Resistance*, chap. 2, para. 27 (Ballou's emphasis).
[221] Ballou, *Christian Non-Resistance*, chap. 2, para. 28 (Ballou's emphasis).

active love of one's neighbour. To unite my teaching with the old is like tearing a piece from a new garment and sewing it onto an old one."[222] He even hears Jesus as saying that his contemporaries' understanding of Mosaic Law was "false" and "full of contradictions."[223] Tolstoy therefore accuses the church of deliberately misleading Christians by pretending that "fulfilment" should mean that the Law of Moses remains binding. Whenever "a teacher preaches [...] a new law of life", Tolstoy argues, "he must necessarily annul the old."[224] Jesus makes a point of reinterpreting the Mosaic Law – indeed, Tolstoy notes, "for this he is reproached with destroying the law of God; and for this he is put to death."[225] It is precisely because he challenges the old order that Jesus is seen as a threat and eventually crucified. For Tolstoy, in the Sermon, Jesus clearly establishes "five new, clear, and definite commandments," and these should therefore supersede the Mosaic commandments in terms of practical advice.[226] Therefore, as far as a Christian in concerned, the primary source for Christian principles should be the teaching of Jesus.

Craig appears to disagree with Tolstoy. For him, the above verses show that "Jesus makes plain the continuity between his ministry and that of [...] the Old Testament."[227] He believes that Jesus did not reject but defend the Old Law against the "pseudo-righteousness of the Pharisees," and that this is visible for instance when Jesus says: "it is *lawful* to do well on the sabbath days."[228] Jesus actually defends the law against the interpretation of his contemporary religious leaders.

Nonetheless, just after he declares that he fulfils the law and the prophets, Jesus does radically reinterpret five of its commandments. So the question remains: in what sense is Jesus "fulfilling" the law? Besides, if it is so obvious that Jesus upholds the Old Law, why does he also make a point of asserting that he has not come to "destroy" it? Eller cites Bornkamm to explain that Jesus is deliberately dissociating himself from two positions: one which regards Jesus as a revolutionary and wants to completely discard the "burdensome" torah, and another which sees the torah as the strict recipe for social order. Instead of either of these positions, Eller claims that "[Jesus'] move is to punch *through* the torah to get the Giver who stands behind it."[229] How so?

Yoder argues that in each of the five instances in which Jesus comments on the Old Law, he reinterprets it "in the same direction" as the original command.[230] Yoder explains: "What Jesus meant by 'fulfillment' was thus a quite literal filling full, a carrying on to full accomplishment of the intent of the earlier moral guides. It is therefore a most striking contrast, not to the Old Testament, but to its interpretation by current tradition; 'righteousness of the

---

[222] Tolstoy, "The Gospel in Brief," 152. (Luke 5:33-39.)
[223] Tolstoy, "The Gospel in Brief," 200, 209, 279. (John 7:10-24, 10:1-10.)
[224] Tolstoy, *What I Believe*, 57.
[225] Tolstoy, *What I Believe*, 65.
[226] Tolstoy, *What I Believe*, 67.
[227] [Anonymous], *Why I Worship a Violent, Vengeful God*, para. 14.
[228] Matthew 12:12 (emphasis added).
[229] Eller, *Christian Anarchy*, 81-82 (Eller's emphasis).
[230] Yoder, "The Political Axioms of the Sermon on the Mount," 44 (emphasis removed).

scribes and Pharisees.'"[231] Jesus is fulfilling the law and the prophets by carrying the intent of their pronouncements further in the same direction. What he is critiquing is the rigid interpretation of the Old Law, not the Old Law's intention.

Even if he contrasts Jesus' and Moses' commandments much more markedly, Tolstoy actually reaches a similar conclusion. He studies occurrences in the Gospels of the word "law" and eventually concludes that "Jesus by no means rejects what is eternal in the old law; but when the Jews speak to him of the law as a whole, or of its peculiar forms, he says that it is impossible to put new wine into old skins."[232] Jesus does not destroy the Old Law, but he reinterprets it beyond the strictures which contemporary interpreters had confined it to.

For example, Ballou notes, when Jesus abolished the oath, he did not abolish the truth but exalted it.[233] Yoder agrees: "the same concern for veracity and for limiting the quasi-superstitious use of the name of God, which had *begun* by calling for truthfulness in swearing, takes a further step *in the same direction* by rejecting the oath itself as a concession to dishonesty and as an abuse of the name of God."[234] Similarly, Yoder explains that (as mentioned earlier in the Chapter) *lex talionis* was intended as a "limitation upon vengeance," a limitation which Jesus pushes "a powerful step further [...] in the direction set by the ancient rules."[235] Ballou agrees: non-resistance did not absolve his disciples "from one iota of the law of love – the obligation to love their neighbors as themselves."[236] Jesus, he says, "drew" that obligation "from the ark of the Mosaic Testament, all mildewed and dusky with human misapprehension, and [...] showed that the 'neighbor' intended was any human being." Thus "[the] true principle was in" the Old Law, "but men could not clearly perceive it."[237]

That is the sense in which Jesus "fulfils" the law: he radically reinterprets it according to its original intentions. On this, all things considered, all Christian anarchists appear to agree. Craig emphasises the continuity, Tolstoy and Elliott emphasise the difference, but all would appear to agree that there is continuity in the intention, albeit difference in the instruction. The discussion of Jesus' fulfilment of the Old Law, and in particular the related debate on love's fulfilment of justice, is picked up again in the Conclusion. For now, the point to note is that overall, the Christian anarchist reading of these verses stresses that

---

[231] Yoder, "The Political Axioms of the Sermon on the Mount," 45.
[232] Tolstoy, *What I Believe*, 60.
[233] Ballou, *Christian Non-Resistance*, chap. 2, para. 29.
[234] Yoder, "The Political Axioms of the Sermon on the Mount," 44-45 (Yoder's emphasis).
[235] Yoder, "The Political Axioms of the Sermon on the Mount," 44.
[236] Ballou, *Christian Non-Resistance*, chap. 2, para. 30.
[237] Ballou, *Christian Non-Resistance*, chap. 1, para. 66 (for the previous sentence as well). Even so, Ballou does accept that the Old Testament is "unequivocally against" non-resistance if "taken independently of the Christian revelation." However, he says: "I do not admit the Old Testament to be as clearly, fully, and perfectly the word of God as the New Testament [...]. It is to be held in reverence as the prophecy and preparative of the New Testament – the foreshadow of better things to come." Moreover, he says, "the New Testament claims to supersede the Old, and the Old, by prophecy, type, and shadow, announced beforehand the coming in of a more glorious dispensation [...] In affirming this, I only affirm what both Testaments unequivocally declare respecting themselves and each other. To question it is virtually to question the credibility of both." Ballou, *Christian Non-Resistance in All Its Important Bearings*, 25, 28.

Jesus criticises not so much the Old Law as rigid and legalistic interpretations of it by the elites, and that he "fulfils" the Old Law in the sense that he radically reinterprets it based on its original intentions. Whereas the strict interpretation of the law tends to authorise coercive legislation to ensure that all abide by its every jot and tittle, Jesus' reinterpretation of it recovers its original intention and subverts any reliance on such official strictures – but this is explored in more detail in the Conclusion.

## 1.8 – A manifesto for Christian anarchism

Jesus' reinterpretation of the Old Law, for Christian anarchists, therefore amounts both to a set of indirect, implied criticisms of state theory and practice, and to a blueprint for the life of the Christian community – a theme which is elaborated in Chapter 5. The Sermon is thus a political document, a manifesto for a Christian anarchist society. It touches on all the main points of the Christian (anarchist) political vision and how to reach it. Day thus writes that the Sermon "answered all the questions as to how to love God and one's brother."[238] It amounts to a complete "philosophical, moral, and social doctrine," says Tolstoy.[239] For him, Jesus gives mankind "practical rules for life" which would lift it from the vicious cycle of violence it is caught in, and move it towards "the kingdom of peace on earth."[240]

Tolstoy moreover rejects the view that the Sermon, this "vital Christian teaching," is "impracticable."[241] He accepts that it might be difficult, but believes that what matters is constant progress in its direction. For him, "These commandments are, as it were, signposts on the infinite road to perfection towards which mankind is moving."[242] That this road may be difficult does not make the commandments any less binding. Jesus' words may be "hard words," quips Maurin (quoting Stevenson), "but the hard words of a book were the only reason why the book was written."[243]

Of course, to show that this Christian (anarchist) manifesto is not impossibly utopian, those who claim to follow Christ need to live by it. Maurin writes, in his typical playful style, that "The Sermon on the Mount will be called practical when Christians make up their mind to practice it."[244] Yet as Andrews (quoting Kurt Vonnegut) bemoans, the "most vocal" Christians "demand that the Ten Commandments be posted in public buildings" but none of them "demand that the Sermon on the Mount, the Beatitudes, be posted anywhere."[245] Christians

---

[238] Day, *The Long Loneliness*, 141.
[239] Tolstoy, "The Kingdom of God Is within You," 49.
[240] Respectively: Tolstoy, *What I Believe*, 98, 203.
[241] Tolstoy, "The Kingdom of God Is within You," 106.
[242] Tolstoy, "The Kingdom of God Is within You," 111.
[243] Robert Louis Stevenson, quoted in Maurin, *Easy Essays (2003)*, 137.
[244] Maurin, *Easy Essays (2003)*, 180.
[245] Kurt Vonnegut, quoted in Dave Andrews, "Heaven on Earth: Trinity, Community and Society," unpublished draft book sent by email by its author to me on 8 November 2006, later edited and eventually published as *A Divine Society: The Trinity, Community, and Society* (West End: Frank Communications, 2008), 145 (emphasis removed).

seem to elevate the Old Law as the ideal to live up to, but not the teaching of the teacher they profess to follow.[246] Christian anarchists wish the same energy and commitment were given to the Sermon: "What a fine place this world would be," writes Maurin, "if Fundamentalist Protestants tried to exemplify the Sermon on the Mount."[247]

Christian anarchists, for their part, do try to exemplify it. Day says of both Maurin and Hennacy that they were constantly guided by the instructions of the Sermon. One writer to *A Pinch of Salt* professes to be trying to take the Sermon literally, and adds that there is "no real justification" for doing otherwise.[248] Andrews describes how the Sermon became his community's "manifesto" when he lived in India.[249] These and other attempts by Christian anarchists to live out the Christianity they profess are reviewed in more detail in Chapter 6. The point to note here is that Christian anarchists do try to follow the instructions of the Sermon.

In short, Christian anarchists take seriously the political implications of Jesus' instructions, especially non-resistance of evil. Tolstoy claims that it "should be the binding principle of our social life."[250] For him, Jesus tells mankind: "You think that your laws correct evil; they only increase it. There is only one way of extirpating evil – to return good to all men without distinction. You have tried your principle for thousands of years; try now mine, which is the reverse."[251] Jesus is thus calling for his disciples to transcend *lex talionis*, to love and forgive evildoers in order for the cycle of violence which has blighted humanity to be overcome. For Christian anarchists, this cannot but require a rejection of state theory and practice. Moreover, they argue that the state also contravenes – or through it obliges its citizens to contravene – the rest of the Sermon on the Mount. For Christian anarchists, therefore, the Sermon contains "the most revolutionary teaching in the world."[252] It calls for revolution by its implied criticism of the state, but it also instructs Christians on how to behave in order for them to lead that revolution – a revolution which, as the next Chapter shows, Jesus further taught and practiced throughout the rest of his life.

---

[246] In a special report on religion and public life, the *Economist* mentions the following striking statistic when discussing, in passing, the sometimes worrying ignorance by militant religious converts of their founding texts: "although 83% of Americans regard the Bible as the word of God, half of them do not know who preached the Sermon on the Mount." Of course, Americans are only mentioned as one of several examples, there is no suggestion that all Christian Americans are militant, and ignorance of who preached the Sermon on the Mount does not imply ignorance of some of its content. Nonetheless, the statistic does come as something of a surprise, and certainly seems to confirm that the Christian anarchist interpretation of Christianity is bound to sound quite radical today. [Anonymous], "O Come All Ye Faithful," *The Economist*, issue 385, 3 November 2007, 9.
[247] Maurin, *Easy Essays (2003)*, 193 (see also: 146).
[248] Kenny Hone [?], "The Gift," *A Pinch of Salt*, issue 3, Pentecost 1986, 12.
[249] Andrews, "Heaven on Earth," 103.
[250] Tolstoy, *What I Believe*, 41.
[251] Tolstoy, *What I Believe*, 41.
[252] Hennacy, *The Book of Ammon*, 62.

# Chapter 2 – The Anarchism Implied in Jesus' Other Teachings and Example

Christian anarchists develop their critique of the state primarily from their interpretation of the Sermon on the Mount, in particular the verses counselling non-resistance, but they see the rest of the New Testament as further confirming this anarchist position. Not only in the Sermon did Jesus preach non-resistance, writes Tolstoy, "but throughout his life and in his death he practised as he preached."[1] Christian anarchists point to several New Testament passages to prove this. Some even read segments of the Old Testament as validating their perspective: for a contributor to *A Pinch of Salt*, the whole Bible thus "puts continually in question all coercive exercise of human authority."[2]

The aim of this Chapter is to summarise Christian anarchists' interpretations of Bible passages other than the Sermon on the Mount. However, only those passages which enough Christian anarchists make substantial comments on can be included here – this will anyway cover the overwhelming majority of Christian anarchist commentaries on Bible passages. Limited space again also makes it impossible to contrast their exegeses to more conventional ones. By and large, they ignore traditional commentaries anyway – the next Chapter explains why. Note also that two Gospel passages are deliberately left aside until Chapter 4: the "render unto Caesar" saying and the related temple tax episode.

The first section below reviews some Christian anarchist comments on the Old Testament, especially the Book of Samuel. The Chapter then unfolds chronologically through Jesus' life, first highlighting the very political nature of the expectations surrounding Jesus' ministry, then discussing Jesus' third temptation in the wilderness, then the Christian anarchist view on exorcisms and other miracles performed by Jesus. This is followed by an outline of Jesus' repeated teaching on forgiving, not judging, and being a servant to one another. His allegedly violent cleansing of the temple comes next, followed by his arrest, trial, crucifixion and resurrection. Due to the interesting comments offered on it by Christian anarchists, a short section also reports their take on the Book of Revelation, and explains why other part of the New Testament are left aside for now. The Chapter then concludes by summarising Christian anarchists' thoughts on the Gospel passages where Jesus is sometimes alleged to have legitimised violence.

---

[1] Tolstoy, *What I Believe*, 43.
[2] Mumford, "The Bible and Anarchy," 8.

## 2.1 – The Old Testament

Few Christian anarchists comment a great deal on the Old Testament, perhaps because they are often not sure what to make of much of it. Yoder remarks that "the picture of the God of the ancient Israelites as a God of war has been an occasion for caricature and embarrassment for Christians."[3] This God of war is particularly awkward for Christian anarchists given their insistence on non-resistance to evil.

Tolstoy is predictably the least ambiguous about his dislike for the Old Testament. Aylmer Maude explains that "he regarded it as religious literature of varying quality, containing much that is excellent and some of the best literary art the world has produced, but much also that is crude, primitive, and immoral."[4] Yoder therefore classes Tolstoy in the category of Christians who deal with the Old Testament by setting it aside "on the grounds of a 'new dispensation' after the model of Jesus' repeated 'but I say to you' in Matthew 5" (as Chapter 1 explains).[5]

That categorisation applies to most Christian anarchists: their typical stance with respect to the Old Testament is to emphasise that it was imperfect, that God's revelation is anyway fulfilled in the teachings of Jesus, and that therefore a Christian ought to derive practical guidance for life first and foremost (if not solely) from the New Testament. Nevertheless, Christian anarchists do offer a few scattered comments on the Old Testament. By far the most elaborate commentaries focus on the first book of Samuel.

### 2.1.1 – 1 Samuel 8

Christian anarchists claim that up until Samuel, the Israelites had no king, no central government, but what Andrews calls a "decentralized federation of tribes."[6] Ellul explains that "When an important decision had to be made, with ritual sacrifices and prayers for divine inspiration, a popular assembly was held and this had the last word."[7] Ultimately, however, God alone was Israel's king and lawmaker, "Israel's head."[8] This ultimately theocratic form of government was precisely "one of the most significant differences from [the Israelites'] pagan neighbours," comments Michael Tennant.[9] According to Chelčický, the Israelites thus "lived safely under the protection of God and His laws."[10] The Law dictated by God to Moses was seen as "good and trustworthy," remarks Stephen Carson, and since it left out prisons, taxes, and – crucially – executive and legislative

---

[3] Yoder, *The Politics of Jesus*, 86.
[4] Maude, *The Life of Tolstóy*, 39.
[5] Yoder, *The Politics of Jesus*, 87.
[6] Andrews, *Subversive Spirituality, Ecclesial and Civil Disobedience*, 2.
[7] Ellul, *Anarchy and Christianity*, 46.
[8] Ellul, *Anarchy and Christianity*, 46.
[9] Michael Tennant, *Government as Idolatry* (Strike the Root), available from http://www.strike-the-root.com/3/tennant/tennant1.html (accessed 21 November 2007), para. 4.
[10] Molnár, *A Study of Peter Chelčický's Life*, 93 (quoting Chelčický).

bodies, this Mosaic political system was basically a form of anarchy.[11] Tennant for his part concedes that the Mosaic structure can be seen as "a form of government, but," he insists, "it was not an independent institution which claims a monopoly on violence,"[12] and it was "highly decentralized."[13]

If Israel was struck by disasters like successive military defeats, famine or idolatry, and especially plunder by foreign raiders, then a judge would exceptionally be appointed to restore order. "A judge," Heppenstall however maintains, "was someone who offered advice, who took on a priestly role during ritual sacrifices, who had a charismatic leaning, and was moved by the Spirit to act or speak in a certain way, felt to be the will of God, but who never accepted the title of king, because all power is God's."[14] Judges were considered to have a special relationship with God and were therefore expected to interpret God's will for the community. Moreover, Ellul notes that "Apparently, when the 'judges' had played their part they effaced themselves and rejoined the people."[15] Judges therefore possessed only a limited form of authority.[16]

The Israelites, however, flirted with the idolatrous idea of appointing a human king. The first but ultimately unsuccessful attempt to be ruled by a king took place after Gideon was judge, but only Tennant articulates a nonetheless convincing anarchist commentary on it.[17] The more important attempt, in that it successfully established Israel's dynasty of kings, took place under Samuel's spell as judge. The Bible says that Samuel was old and had been a judge for many years when the elders of Israel approached him and asked him for a king in order "to be like other nations"[18] – which as Tennant remarks, "was, of course, precisely what God did *not* want them to be."[19] Ellul writes that in the context of their continuing war with the Philistines, the Israelites "also thought that a king would be a better military leader."[20] Scripture however tells of Samuel being displeased at this demand and praying to the Lord, who then says to Samuel:

---

[11] Stephen W. Carson, *Biblical Anarchism*, available from http://www.lewrockwell.com/orig/carson2.html (accessed 8 November 2007), para. 3-6.

[12] Tennant, *Christianarchy?* , para. 6. Elsewhere, he writes that in Israel, "there was to be no human king – and, in fact, no central government of any kind. God chose specific leaders – Moses, and later, Joshua – to communicate his decrees to the people and to guide them into the promised land. God established the laws – laws which applied equally to the leaders and to the population at large (see Lev. 4, for example) – and the punishments to be meted out to those who failed to obey. Moses, acting on advice from his godly father-in-law, selected 'capable men from all the people – men who fear God, trustworthy men who hate dishonest gain' and appointed them 'as officials over thousands, hundreds, fifties, and tens' (Ex. 18:21). Thus, government was highly decentralized, with only the 'difficult cases ... brought to Moses' (Ex. 18:26). [...] Of course, in cases of extreme disobedience, the Lord reserved the right to inflict punishment himself." Tennant, *Government as Idolatry*, para. 5.

[13] Tennant, *Government as Idolatry*, para. 5.

[14] Annie Heppenstall, "Anarchy and the Old Testament," paper presented at *God Save the Queen: Anarchism and Christianity Today*, All Hallows Church, Leeds, 2-4 June 2006, available from http://uk.jesusradicals.com/otanarchy.pdf (accessed 4 June 2006), 5.

[15] Ellul, *Anarchy and Christianity*, 47.

[16] Tennant writes that "They had little to no power over the people; and again, they were held to the same standards." Tennant, *Government as Idolatry*, para. 6.

[17] Tennant, *Government as Idolatry*, para. 6-9.

[18] 1 Samuel 8:5, 20.

[19] Tennant, *Christianarchy?* , para. 7 (Tennant's emphasis).

[20] Ellul, *Anarchy and Christianity*, 48.

"they have not rejected thee, but they have rejected me, that I should not reign over them."[21]

That passage is very revealing to Christian anarchists. For a start, Carson remarks that "Given our contemporary faith in the State, you would think that G-d [...] would praise the Israelites for realizing they needed a ruler."[22] Instead, however, his answer through Samuel "is a sobering reminder of how deeply heretical our modern faith in the State is."[23] As Eller explains, God's answer makes it clear that "the people's demand for worldly government amounts to a *rejection* of God and his government."[24] Chelčický agrees: "In asking for a temporal ruler, the Jews scorned God and His law."[25] They thus "committed a grievous sin," says Carson, through this "tremendous lack of faith in G-d."[26]

Thus Israel's monarchy, for Craig, was established as a result of "a desire to be like the demonic States around Israel, a rejection of the Lord's priestly calling to be a holy nation, and a rejection of God's Law as given to the Patriarchs."[27] The more general conclusion from this passage, according to Craig, is that "The movement towards centralization of power under political mediators is a rejection of God."[28] Hence for Chelčický and indeed all Christian anarchists, "The state has its origin in man's pride and rebellion against God."[29]

Andrews reckons that Israel had been a society based on trust in God's guidance, "But when it came to the crunch, they abandoned the 'politics of trust' in God and embraced the 'politics of security' in a king, an army, and a military-industrial complex."[30] Ellul agrees that "political power rests on distrust [...] of God."[31] The Israelites' demand for a king exposes their loss of trust in God. God's reply to Samuel indeed indicates that the Israelites' request is a form of idolatry, of serving other gods (more on this below).[32]

God then asks Samuel to warn them of the consequences: the king will take their sons as soldiers, their daughters as cooks, their servants as slaves, their land and sheep as treasures, and they will regret their decision to have a king – but it will be too late. For Christian anarchists, God is clearly warning the Israelites of the likely abuses of power which would result from their decision to opt for human government. Ellul even reads God's warning to imply that "political power is always dictatorial, excessive, and unjust."[33] Carson does not make exactly the same generalisation, but still notes that "the Bible makes it

---

[21] 1 Samuel 8:7.
[22] Carson, *Biblical Anarchism*, para. 7.
[23] Carson, *Biblical Anarchism*, para. 8.
[24] Eller, *Christian Anarchy*, 199 (Eller's emphasis).
[25] Molnár, *A Study of Peter Chelčický's Life*, 93 (paraphrasing Chelčický).
[26] Carson, *Biblical Anarchism*, para. 11.
[27] [Anonymous], *Ninety-Five Theses in Defense of Patriarchy* (Vine and Fig Tree), available from http://members.aol.com/VF95Theses/thesis.htm (accessed 20 April 2007), thesis 38.
[28] [Anonymous], *Ninety-Five Theses in Defense of Patriarchy*, thesis 37.
[29] Molnár, *A Study of Peter Chelčický's Life*, 30.
[30] Andrews, "Heaven on Earth," 44 (emphasis removed).
[31] Ellul, "Anarchism and Christianity," 165.
[32] Nekeisha Alexis-Manners, *Deconstructing Romans 13: Verse 1-2*, available from http://www.jesusradicals.com/essays/theology/Romans13.htm (accessed 28 October 2005), 2; Tennant, *Government as Idolatry*, para. 12-17. (1 Samuel 8:8.)
[33] Ellul, "Anarchism and Christianity," 165.

absolutely clear that the change from Mosaic anarchy to what by today's standards would be 'limited government' will have terrible consequences."[34]

Nonetheless, God is also willing to grant the Israelites their wish. According to Alexis-Manners, this "provides a clue to the character of God and God's leadership."[35] God always allows the Israelites to "act on their desire" even though he disagrees.[36] God even selects Israel's first two kings to show that "He will try to work with us through the system we choose," says Carson.[37] Still, Carson adds, "that does not constitute a ringing endorsement of the State as the best system of government."[38] For Eller, even though God does not approve of human government, he accepts or tolerates it.[39] This confirms what is said in the Introduction about God not being an absolute Master. For Andrews, God is thus "committed to democracy – as opposed to autocracy."[40]

Despite Samuel's warning, however, the Israelites insist they want a king, and Saul becomes king. "Thus did Israel destroy its unique character," comments Tennant, "by preferring an idol, in the form of a king, to the one true God who had heretofore ruled over them."[41] Elliott observes that "From this point on, the quest for political aggrandisement becomes an integral part of the new national consciousness."[42] Moreover, for Christian anarchists, God's warning about the consequences of this decision is exemplified by the kings who follow, including David and Solomon: to quote Myers, "The Davidic tradition of kingship [...] resulted only in the realization of Samuel's worst fears: militarism, economic control, and slavery."[43]

Heppenstall furthermore notes that "as the story goes, it is not the fault of [the king] that kingship [is] a disaster," but "the fault of the people, in their gross lack of faith in God in the first place."[44] The establishment of political power and all its resulting abuses is a result of the people's forsaking of God and desire to conform to and imitate what is done among pagan nations. The story of 1 Samuel 8 therefore shows that monarchy "was founded in Israel [...] in direct opposition to the will of God," and out of idolatry.[45] For Christian anarchists, the obvious conclusion is that "rejection of the state [...] is a necessary part of declaring allegiance to God," a theme that is returned to throughout this book.[46]

---

[34] Carson, *Biblical Anarchism*, para. 11.
[35] Alexis-Baker, "Embracing God and Rejecting Masters," 4.
[36] Alexis-Baker, "Embracing God and Rejecting Masters," 5.
[37] Carson, *Biblical Anarchism*, para. 15.
[38] Carson, *Biblical Anarchism*, para. 15.
[39] Eller, *Christian Anarchy*, 199-200.
[40] Andrews, *Subversive Spirituality, Ecclesial and Civil Disobedience*, 4. "Democracy" here is clearly meant as the opposite of "autocracy." This seems to imply a type of fully consensual and participatory democracy – a form of anarchism – rather than the liberal, representative democracy that comes to mind when referring to "democracy" today.
[41] Tennant, *Government as Idolatry*, para. 14.
[42] Elliott, *Freedom, Justice and Christian Counter-Culture*, 74.
[43] Myers, *Binding the Strong Man*, 446.
[44] Heppenstall, "Anarchy and the Old Testament," 6.
[45] Linda H. Damico, *The Anarchist Dimension of Liberation Theology* (New York: Peter Lang, 1987), 2.
[46] Alexis-Baker, "Embracing God, Rejecting Masters."

## 2.1.2 – Other Old Testament passages

Apart from a few brief and passing comments, Christian anarchists have comparatively very little to say about the political implications of other passages from the Old Testament – with two notable exceptions. One such exception is Ellul. He claims that the passages from the Old Testament that "tell how God opposed his people's use of 'normal' means of settling conflicts [...] and bade them put their trust in" him are "innumerable."[47] Moreover, Ellul devoted entire books to demonstrate the implications of specific sections of the Old Testament for political questions. However, these studies are not directly relevant to this book in that they do not contribute much to Ellul's Christian *anarchism*, which he develops fully almost only in *Anarchy and Christianity*.

The other – less significant – exception is Craig, whose "Ninety-Five Theses" do make plenty of references to Old Testament texts to validate his anarchist stance; but the "theses" themselves are very short and seem to assume that their obviousness is automatically confirmed by the cited passages. For example, Craig simply asserts that there were no states in the Garden of Eden.[48] Likewise, he notes that Nimrod, who "left the Godly Family to form a 'State,'" has a name that means "let us rebel" – which confirms the Christian anarchist take on Samuel.[49] Craig cites plenty of passages in that manner, but he does not really engage with them in any real depth.

Other Christian anarchists have even less to say on the Old Testament before Samuel and the kings. One example of a cursory remark is Chelčický's observation that civil authority "began with Cain's lust for power when he built the first city," an episode which Ellul elaborates in some detail.[50] Jason Barr offers a few interesting reflections on Genesis and Ecclesiastes.[51] On the Exodus, a theme so important to liberation theology, Christian anarchists note only very briefly that, in the story, God sets his people free by throwing off the king and calling them towards a new and much more anarchist type of community – they do not echo liberation theologians in elaborating the metaphor as a paradigm of humanity's current condition.[52] Heppenstall also make a couple of passing comments on Leviticus, as Mumford does on Deuteronomy – but again, they do not develop any comprehensive exegesis.[53] Similarly, Carson's helpful contribution is limited to his comments on Mosaic Law, Samuel and Israel's kings.[54]

---

[47] Ellul, *Violence*, 168.
[48] [Anonymous], *Ninety-Five Theses in Defense of Patriarchy*, thesis 2.
[49] [Anonymous], *Ninety-Five Theses in Defense of Patriarchy*, thesis 15.
[50] Molnár, *A Study of Peter Chelčický's Life*, 112 (quoting Chelčický). For Ellul's interpretation of Cain's founding of the first city, see Jacques Ellul, *The Meaning of the City*, trans. Dennis Pardee ([Grand Rapids?]: William B. Eerdmans, 1993).
[51] Jason Barr, *Radical Hope: Anarchy, Christianity, and the Prophetic Imagination*, available from http://propheticheretic.files.wordpress.com/2008/03/radical-hope-anarchy-christianity-and-the-prophetic-imagination.pdf (accessed 11 March 2008), 4-5 (on Ecclesiastes), 10-11 (on Genesis).
[52] Andrews, "Heaven on Earth," 37-42; Charley Earp, "Christianity and Anarchism" (audio file on compact disc, rec. 5-6 August 2005).
[53] Heppenstall, "Anarchy and the Old Testament," 3-4; Mumford, "The Bible and Anarchy," 8.
[54] Carson, *Biblical Anarchism*.

The only Old Testament theme which several Christian anarchists consider in a little more depth and from an anarchist perspective ties into the preceding interpretation of Samuel, and concerns the prophets: they argue that "the prophetic tradition was born from the oppression resulting from monarchical rule."[55] In Ellul's words, "for every king there was a prophet [who] was most often a severe critic of royal acts."[56] For Christian anarchists, the many famous prophets of the Old Testament – as well as some of the psalms – were voicing God's rebuke to the kings for their abuses of political power and for their failure to care for Israel's needy, thus reminding the people not to trust these human leaders. The prophets each express God's disapproval of a society which has rejected him.

David Mumford also notes that through "the last of the major prophets," Ezekiel, God's response to the behaviour of Israel's ruling class was "not to try to replace one ruling class with another but to announce that a time will come when His divine kingship will be resumed."[57] For Christians, of course, this divine kingship is resumed through Jesus Christ – a point which is further discussed later in this Chapter, as well as in the Conclusion.

Ellul makes a few more observations on Israel's "good" and "bad" kings,[58] on the Bible's depiction of government of a foreign people,[59] and on the end of the Jewish monarchy.[60] Heppenstall also offers passing observations on monarchy after the exile,[61] and Yoder reads Chronicles in a way that resonates with the Christian anarchist perspective.[62]

All in all, therefore, Christian anarchists' interpretation of the Old Testament is dominated by their understanding of 1 Samuel 8 and its implications for the rest of Jewish history up to Jesus. In the end, Ellul concludes that according to the Old Testament, "Political power never has any value in itself. On the contrary, Scripture radically repudiates, challenges, and condemns it whenever it claims to exist as political power rather than as a sign. [...] We can therefore conclude that the Old Testament never in any way validates any political power."[63] In any case and having said that, it is almost only on the New Testament that Christian anarchists ground their understanding of the anarchist consequences of Jesus' message.

## 2.2 – Expectations of a political messiah

When it comes to the New Testament, Christian anarchists point out that even before he began to preach, Jesus was expected to be a very political kind of

---

[55] The original sentence is here inverted. Damico, *The Anarchist Dimension of Liberation Theology*, 3.
[56] Ellul, *Anarchy and Christianity*, 51.
[57] Mumford, "The Bible and Anarchy," 8.
[58] Ellul, "Anarchism and Christianity," 165-166 (for the quote); Ellul, *Anarchy and Christianity*, 50-51.
[59] Ellul, "Anarchism and Christianity," 163-164.
[60] Ellul, *Anarchy and Christianity*, 53-55.
[61] Heppenstall, "Anarchy and the Old Testament," 8-9.
[62] Yoder, *The Politics of Jesus*, 79-82.
[63] Ellul, "Anarchism and Christianity," 166.

messiah. For a start, according to Yoder, John the Baptist's ministry – which prepares the way for Jesus' – "had a pronounced political character."[64] John was imprisoned by Herod Antipas because of the fear that he might trigger a political insurrection. That is to say, it was precisely the politically revolutionary character of John's proclamations that led to him being silenced.

Christian anarchists also cite Mary's Magnificat as further evidence of political expectations.[65] In it, Yoder argues, "we are being told that the one whose birth is now being announced is to be an agent of radical social change."[66] Jesus, he continues, is expected to "break the bondage of his people."[67] Charley Earp reads it as the expectation of a new Exodus, this time from Rome.[68] José Porfirio Miranda adds that the liberation is not just from historical Rome, but from "every class of rulers."[69] Heppenstall also notes that "Mary's words do not talk about a restoration of the monarchy," which some factions expected the coming messiah to be about, but "they talk about the bringing down of the mighty and the proud wherever they are."[70] There is already a hint that the kingdom which Jesus will proclaim will not take the familiar hierarchic form of a state.

Further evidence of the politically revolutionary character of Jesus' expected ministry comes from the events around his birth. Both Alexis-Baker and Redford point out that for Herod Antipas to slaughter all the children aged two and younger in the hope of killing Jesus, he must have considered him a threat to the political structure.[71]

Jesus himself further confirms these messianic expectations when he proclaims the beginning of his ministry in the Nazareth synagogue.[72] For Andrews, the passage which Jesus quotes from Isaiah, about releasing the captives and setting the oppressed free, is a "heartfelt, anarchistic manifesto" which Jesus thereby adopts as "his mission in life."[73] Yoder agrees that Isaiah's language is political, that the messianic expectations are deliberately expressed in social and political terms, and that Jesus' proclamation that this is "fulfilled" announces the immediate implementation of a new social and political restructuring of relations.[74]

Hence for Christian anarchists, the messianic expectations surrounding the coming of Jesus have strong political overtones. The messiah is expected to take on Roman and Jewish state authorities and present a new model of social and

---

[64] Yoder, *The Politics of Jesus*, 23. (See Matthew 3, 11:1-19, 14:1-12; Mark 1:1-15, 6:14-29; Luke 1:57-66, 3:1-22, 7:18-35; John 1:19-34.)
[65] Luke 1:46-55. One example of Christian anarchists just quoting the Magnificat without any explanation, as if self-evident, can be found in [Anonymous], "He Has Scattered the Proud..." *A Pinch of Salt*, issue 5, December 1986, 2. Walter, a non-Christian anarchist, agrees that the Magnificat resonates with anarchism: Walter, "Anarchism and Religion," 4.
[66] Yoder, *The Politics of Jesus*, 22.
[67] Yoder, *The Politics of Jesus*, 22.
[68] Earp, "Christianity and Anarchism".
[69] José Porfirio Miranda, quoted in Damico, *The Anarchist Dimension of Liberation Theology*, 90.
[70] Heppenstall, "Anarchy and the Old Testament," 9.
[71] Alexis-Baker, "Embracing God and Rejecting Masters," 6; Redford, *Jesus Is an Anarchist*, 3-5. (Matthew 2.)
[72] Luke 4:14-30.
[73] Andrews, *Christi-Anarchy*, 109.
[74] Yoder, *The Politics of Jesus*, 28-33.

political relations to replace them. Political subversion is expected, as is a radically different form of political constitution.

## 2.3 – Jesus' third temptation in the wilderness

Just before he announces the beginning of his ministry, Jesus spends forty days in the wilderness, where he is tempted three times by Satan.[75] Although Elliott and Yoder stress the political significance of all three of these temptations,[76] most Christian anarchists focus on the third (in Matthew, that is, which corresponds to the second temptation in Luke). This third temptation consist in this: Satan shows Jesus "all the kingdoms of the world, and the glory of them," and offers to give them to him, provided he will "fall down and worship" him.[77]

Christian anarchists begin by noting that Satan's offer of the "kingdoms of the world" must be valid for the episode to qualify as a *bona fide* temptation – which is what the text describes it to be. Some commentators have suggested that Satan must be lying about his authority over the world's kingdoms (authority which Satan implies in Matthew but claims explicitly in Luke), but Christian anarchists disagree. Jesus, they note, does not dispute Satan's claim: he does not call him a liar or call his bluff, so he seems to accept that Satan does indeed control the kingdoms of the world. Satan is not lying; his offer is genuine.

Hence for Christian anarchists, in Ellul's words, "according to these texts all powers, all the power and glory of the kingdoms, all that has to do with politics and political authority, belongs to the devil."[78] As Redford remarks, if all the kingdoms of the world have indeed been "delivered unto" Satan for him to give "to whomever he wishes," then "All Earthly, mortal potentates have quite literally made a pact with Satan!"[79] The state derives its power and authority from Satan.

The devil offers all the power of the state to Jesus, but for this, Jesus must "fall down and worship" him. Jesus of course refuses Satan's offer, because, he says, "it is written, Thou shalt worship the Lord thy God, and him only shalt thou serve."[80] Ellul therefore deduces that "a person can exercise political power only if he worships the power of evil."[81] Ultimately, Alexis-Baker explains, the temptation is "a question of allegiance."[82] One can follow either Christianity and its implied anarchism, or the state and its implied betrayal of God. "If one chooses the path of God," she continues, "then the choice must be a complete one. There is no room for allegiance to the state and its claim to legitimacy,

---

[75] Matthew 4:1-11; Luke 4:1-13.
[76] Elliott, *Freedom, Justice and Christian Counter-Culture*, 157-158; Yoder, *The Politics of Jesus*, 24-27.
[77] Matthew 4:8-9.
[78] Ellul, *Anarchy and Christianity*, 58.
[79] Redford, *Jesus Is an Anarchist*, 23. (Luke 4:6.)
[80] Matthew 4:10.
[81] Ellul, "Anarchism and Christianity," 168.
[82] Alexis-Baker, "Embracing God, Rejecting Masters," 2.

demand for obedience, rights to violence and desire for loyalty from its citizens."[83]

Moreover, what the story also implies is that Jesus was tempted (by Satan) to transform society from above. Damico comments that he "could have chosen the way of domination to lead the people out of their oppressive situation but instead he chose the way of service."[84] Jesus, she says, "recognizes the evil of an option to command and rule."[85] Thus Jesus is implicitly distancing himself from the Zealots and their method, a contemporary group of Jewish rebels who wanted to overthrow Roman rule in Palestine by taking power. Jesus rejects this temptation, and is thereby indicating that "Political power is incompatible with God's earthly promise and it must be rejected."[86]

This absolutely fundamental question of how to change society is discussed in Chapters 4 and 5. The point to note here is that Christian anarchists read the third temptation of Jesus as a renunciation by Jesus of what Crosby calls "all the ordinary means of improvement."[87] For Elliott, all three temptations are "the account of a person analysing methodologies for mission and action;"[88] and in the third, Jesus rejects the "strategy" and "role" of "world leader."[89] Jesus thus refuses "the authoritarian role of king," says a contributor to *A Pinch of Salt*.[90] Kingship and human government, Ballou writes, are animated by "the old serpent of violence" which "he who would rule must first worship;" but instead of this, Jesus "[chooses] the pain and shame of the cross, in preference to the fame and glory of universal empire on such a condition."[91] Moreover, later in the Gospel, "when he perceived the determination of the people to proclaim him a king, he promptly placed himself beyond their reach."[92] Jesus consistently refuses the role of king or political leader as it is commonly understood.

Jesus is also thereby clarifying what his status of messiah is all about. His contemporaries expected the messiah to overthrow political oppressors and restore the Jewish monarchy. In this story, Jesus faces this temptation and rejects it, "perhaps in order to warn [his disciples] about a similar temptation," says Joachim Jeremias.[93] Andrew Lawrence remarks that "this rejection is echoed later in Jesus' ministry" when the "real meaning of messianic 'kingship'" is revealed.[94] That is, shortly before his arrest,

> Jesus turns his gaze towards Jerusalem in the expectation, not of triumph as the world understands it, but of rejection and ignominious execution at the hand of the powers. That his lord – that THE Lord – should fail to "lord it over" those who fall under his dominion is more than Peter can bear to hear. It does not compute. Yet his suggestion that "no such thing should ever

---

[83] Alexis-Baker, "Embracing God, Rejecting Masters," 2.
[84] Damico, *The Anarchist Dimension of Liberation Theology*, 78-79.
[85] Damico, *The Anarchist Dimension of Liberation Theology*, 79.
[86] Damico, *The Anarchist Dimension of Liberation Theology*, 89.
[87] Crosby, *Tolstoy and His Message*, para. 32.
[88] Elliott, *Freedom, Justice and Christian Counter-Culture*, 157.
[89] Elliott, *Freedom, Justice and Christian Counter-Culture*, 158.
[90] Meggitt [?], "Anarchism and the New Testament," 11.
[91] Ballou, *Christian Non-Resistance*, para. 81.
[92] Ballou, *Christian Non-Resistance*, para. 82.
[93] Joachim Jeremias, quoted in Eller, *Christian Anarchy*, 10.
[94] Andrew Lawrence, "Power Politics and Love," *A Pinch of Salt*, issue 12, March 1989, 8.

happen" meets with a rebuke until then reserved for the very Prince of the devils: "Get behind me, Satan! You are an obstacle to me. You are thinking not as God does, but as human beings do." (Matt. 16:23)

Having slammed the door shut on Peter's (that is, our) way of thinking, Jesus immediately throws open a window on a new world, a non-violent order of things in which the logic of earthly triumph does not hold: "Whoever wishes to come after me must deny him or herself, take up their cross, and follow me. For whoever wishes to save their life will lose it, but whoever loses their life for my sake shall find it." (Matt. 16:24-25).[95]

These latter passages are further explained later in this Chapter. What is significant to note here is the important implication of the third temptation: that Jesus rejects the type of political leadership which people were expecting from the messiah. Later, he reinterprets his messianic role in a very different light; but here, Jesus rejects the top-down method of political leadership, and as Eller notes, the identification of political power "as a *temptation* places him distinctly in 'anarchy'" over against those who believe some form of human government to be "elected and sponsored by God."[96]

For Christian anarchists, therefore, Jesus' third temptation in the wilderness is another example of his rejection of the state, which derives its power and authority from Satan.

## 2.4 – Exorcisms and miracle healings

Moving on to Jesus' ministry itself, it is worth noting, in passing, that Christian anarchists (as defined in the Introduction) make almost no comment at all on the various exorcisms and miracle healings which Jesus performs throughout his ministry. The only exceptions are Tolstoy, Pentecost and Myers – and the latter is not even strictly speaking a Christian anarchist, although a radical exegete whose views resonate very strongly with the Christian anarchist position. The only apparent explanation for the general omission of the miracles from Christian anarchist interpretations is that their political significance seems minimal. Yet as Tolstoy but especially Myers show, when interpreted allegorically, they do carry political – albeit not necessarily strictly *anarchist* – connotations.

Pentecost and especially Tolstoy, however, thoroughly dislike the irrational element of these miracle stories. No reader educated in physics, chemistry and other such sciences, Tolstoy argues, can possibly believe any of the many supernatural miracles of either the Old or New Testament.[97] He thinks that Christ's miracles were only added later "to confirm men's faith," but that today they undermine true faith because they are unnecessary and divert attention from the important moral guidelines of Jesus' teaching.[98]

Nonetheless, Tolstoy does include some of Jesus' miracles in his version of the Gospel, but he writes them in a way that makes the Tolstoyan

---

[95] Lawrence, "Power Politics and Love," 8 (Lawrence's emphasis).
[96] Eller, *Christian Anarchy*, 10.
[97] Tolstoy, "The Gospel in Brief," 120; Tolstoy, "The Kingdom of God Is within You," 88-89.
[98] Leo Tolstoy, "Introduction to an Examination of the Gospels," in *A Confession and the Gospel in Brief*, trans. Aylmer Maude (London: Oxford University Press, 1933), 106.

moral interpretation more transparent – blindness, for instance, now only means a lack of understanding – and he still deliberately excludes those miracles for which no such rational interpretation can be formulated. As Maude explains, therefore, "In treating of the Gospel miracles, Tolstóy was interested only in what moral they convey;" he was more interested in the truth they told rather than their physical event.[99] In any case, even if he includes the miracles in his Gospel, he does not really spend any time discussing them or elaborating their anarchist implications.

By contrast, Myers meticulously and convincingly explains the allegorical and political meaning of all the exorcisms and miracle healings of Mark's Gospel by hearing them in the social and textual context in which they were written. Gospel miracles, he argues, function to subvert the dominant social, political and religious order.[100] For instance, in Capernaum, Jesus exorcises a demon who is pleading on behalf of scribal authorities.[101] He then begins his healing ministry "to restore the *social* wholeness denied to the sick/impure by this symbolic order."[102] His healings of a leper and a paralytic are attacks on the purity code and the debt system respectively.[103] The exorcism of the Gerasene demoniac, with all its military imagery alluding to foreign occupation, allegorically amounts to a very political repudiation, a challenge to the powers.[104] In that manner and in considerable detail, Myers emphasises the political significance of these and other Gospel miracles.

Therefore, although this side of Jesus' ministry is hardly commented upon by Christian anarchists, its subversive political implications can be demonstrated. Jesus' exorcisms and miracle healings may not contribute directly to Christian anarchist thought, but they do indirectly shore it up when read following Myers' exegetical approach.

## 2.5 – Forgive seventy-seven times

Having discussed the messianic expectations around Jesus' ministry, his temptations in the wilderness and some of the miracles he performs, the time has come to explore some of the famous sayings uttered by Jesus in the course of his ministry. The next three sections consider, in turn, Jesus' pronouncements on forgiveness, non-judgement, and service.

Jesus repeatedly preaches forgiveness.[105] When his disciples ask him whether forgiving "seven" times is enough, he pointedly answers that it is not, that they should forgive "seventy-seven" times – as if to say they should never give up forgiving.[106] Why strive so much to forgive again and again? Because for

---

[99] Maude, *The Life of Tolstóy*, 41.
[100] Myers, *Binding the Strong Man*, especially chap. 2 and 4.
[101] Myers, *Binding the Strong Man*, 141-143. (Mark 1:21-28.)
[102] Myers, *Binding the Strong Man*, 146 (Myers' emphasis). (Mark 1:30-39.)
[103] Myers, *Binding the Strong Man*, 152-155. (Mark 1:40-2:15.)
[104] Myers, *Binding the Strong Man*, 190-194. (Mark 5:1-21.)
[105] For instance, Matthew 6:9, 14-15, 18:21-22; Mark 11:25-26; Luke 6:37.
[106] Andrews, *The Crux of the Struggle*, 39. (Matthew 18:21-22.)

Christian anarchists, only thus can humanity break out of the cycle of violence which was examined in Chapter 1.

Moreover, Andrews writes, "What Jesus says is so important about forgiveness is not that we *preach* is, but that we *practice* it."[107] But that is not what we do, bemoans Hennacy, since "We make retroactive laws and hang our defeated enemies," since we use the state to avenge and punish.[108] Yet to forgive seventy-seven times, says Hennacy, "means no Caesar at all with his courts, prisons, and war."[109] Forgiveness means not punishing wrongdoers, but striving to love them, bless them, and, to quote Ballou again, "referring [one's] cause always unto Him who hath said, 'Vengeance is mine, I will repay.'"[110] Hence the forgiveness preached by Jesus undermines the state's instruments of coercion. Ballou thus considers the Gospel's repeated passages on forgiveness to be further proof of his radical and strict interpretation of turning the other cheek.

Moreover, he remarks that "Jesus is not speaking of mere envious grudges" when he asks us to forgive, but he "presupposes a real injury done, which, according to the common law, [...] might rightfully be punished."[111] What are to be forgiven are not trivial faults or torts, but very real and painful injuries. Paul Gonya, one of the Christian preachers whose speeches in the days that followed the horrific terrorist attacks of 11 September 2001 are reported by Laurie Johnston, seems to confirm this view. He says: "Let's face it: Either these spiritual truths we claim to believe work all the time, or they don't work at all. When Jesus said, 'Forgive your enemies,' *these* are the kind of people he was talking about, not just some guy who cut you off in traffic."[112] Later on, he writes that it "isn't about who we blame; it's about how we heal" – even if the blame is justifiable.[113] Jesus is calling for his followers to forgive precisely those whose offence would justify legitimate retaliation.

Jesus also explains that his disciples should forgive if they want to be forgiven themselves. For Ballou, he "reminds us that we have all sinned against our Father, and are justly punishable at his hands," and that if we are hoping for God's grace and mercy, we should exercise it ourselves.[114] "Yet," he notes, "millions of professing Christians authorize, aid, and abet war, capital punishment, and the whole catalogue of penal injuries. Still they daily pray God to forgive their trespasses *as they forgive*!"[115] In the Lord's Prayer, Christians ask to be forgiven *as they themselves forgive*, yet foolishly they continue to perpetrate punishments and retaliation through the state. If they really sought God's forgiveness, they would strive to forgive even the worst offences, and they would disentangle themselves from the state's instruments of retaliation. Pushed to its

---

[107] Andrews, "Heaven on Earth," 146 (Andrews' emphasis).
[108] Hennacy, *The Book of Ammon*, 125.
[109] Hennacy, *The Book of Ammon*, 432.
[110] Adin Ballou, "Non-Resistance: A Basis for Christian Anarchism," in *Patterns of Anarchy: A Collection of Writings on the Anarchist Tradition*, ed. Leonard I. Krimerman and Lewis Perry (Garden City: Anchor, 1966), 145.
[111] Ballou, *Christian Non-Resistance*, chap. 2, para. 49.
[112] Paul Gonya, quoted in Johnston, "Love Your Enemies – Even in the Age of Terrorism?," 102 (Gonya's emphasis).
[113] Gonya, quoted in Johnston, "Love Your Enemies – Even in the Age of Terrorism?," 103.
[114] Ballou, *Christian Non-Resistance*, chap. 2, para. 50.
[115] Ballou, *Christian Non-Resistance*, chap. 2, para. 51 (Ballou's emphasis).

80    Christian Anarchism

ultimate logical implications, Jesus' counsel to forgive further confirms that what follows from Christianity is anarchism.

## 2.6 – Not judging one another

Further evidence of Jesus' implied critique of the state comes from his pronouncements on not judging one another, especially the famous passage where he refuses to condemn the adulteress.[116] That story evolves thus: scribes and Pharisees bring to Jesus a woman caught in adultery, claim that according to the Law of Moses she should be stoned, and ask for Jesus' opinion. Initially, Jesus stoops down and writes on the ground, but when he is again asked for an answer, he says "He that is without sin among you, let him first cast a stone at her," and he stoops down and writes on the ground again.[117] Embarrassed by their own sin, the people all walk away, and Jesus addresses the woman and says that as no-one has condemned her, neither does he.

In Hennacy's definition, Christian anarchism is based precisely upon that answer of Jesus to the Pharisees – as well as upon the Sermon on the Mount.[118] Indeed, the two are connected: "Jesus gave us the method of overcoming evil when he said to the woman caught in sin, 'He without sin among you first cast a stone at her.'"[119] Yet, he notes, "if you vote for anyone who makes a law [...], or if you vote for the governor or president who appoints the hangman or the jailer – then these men are your servants; they are your arm to throw the stone and you deny Christ."[120] Christians who are not sinless condemn and stone one another through the long arm of the state. They do the opposite of what Jesus teaches in this passage.

It should be noted that Andrews interprets Jesus' teaching on judgement, including this passage, in a different way than other Christian anarchists. Unlike them, he claims that "Christ doesn't actually prohibit making judgements."[121] For Andrews, Jesus says: "Judge for yourself what is right."[122] But he warns (in the Sermon passage discussed in Chapter 1): "Do not judge unless you are prepared to be judged. If you judge you'll be judged by the very same standards that you apply to others."[123] According to Andrews, Jesus thus "wanted people to accept responsibility for their own problems and accept the responsibility of making their own judgements," and he therefore explained that "they shouldn't project the responsibility onto anyone else either – particularly the *experts*."[124] Hence for Andrews, in the episode with the adulteress, Jesus

---

[116] John 8: 1-11.
[117] John 8:7.
[118] Hennacy, *The Book of Ammon*, xix.
[119] Hennacy, *The Book of Ammon*, 339.
[120] Hennacy, *The Book of Ammon*, 365.
[121] Andrews, *A Spiritual Framework for Ethical Reflection*, 2.
[122] Andrews, *A Spiritual Framework for Ethical Reflection*, 2. (Luke 12:57.)
[123] Andrews, *A Spiritual Framework for Ethical Reflection*, 2. (Matthew 7:1-2.)
[124] Andrews, *A Spiritual Framework for Ethical Reflection*, 2 (Andrews' emphasis). See also Andrews, *Plan Be*, 40-41.

"refused to assume the role of *judge for them*."[125] He wanted people to "judge for themselves."[126]

Andrews, however, is rather unique among Christian anarchists in holding this position. As Chapter 1 explains, most Christian anarchists believe Jesus to have instructed Christians not to judge at all. Either way, although they reach this same conclusion from a different exegetical route, both Andrews and these other Christian anarchists interpret Jesus' instructions to mean that the state's courts of justice are unchristian institutions – be it simply because they judge, or, for Andrews, because they judge on others' behalf.

For Christian anarchists, this implied rejection of human courts of justice is clear from the Sermon on the Mount, but it is also further confirmed in other Gospel passages. Tolstoy's following quote illustrates this:

> Jesus says, "Resist not evil": the object of the courts is to resist evil. Jesus says, "Return good for evil": the courts render evil for evil. Jesus says, "Do not classify men as good or bad": the courts are occupied only in making this distinction. Jesus says, "Forgive all men; forgive not once, not seven times, but without end; love your enemies, do good to those that hate you": the courts do not forgive, but punish; they render not good but evil to those whom they call the enemies of society.[127]

A few lines down, Tolstoy also notes that Jesus "directly denies the justice of the sentence against the adulteress, on the ground that man has no right to judge because he is himself guilty."[128] He also repeats that he whose eye has a beam in it should not behold the mote in the eye of another, that the blind should not lead the blind lest both fall into the ditch.[129] And again, in the commandment not to resist, Jesus says that if someone wants to sue you in the courts for your coat, you should give him your cloak also. For Tolstoy, therefore, Jesus "forbids every one to go to law," and since he repeatedly enjoins forgiveness, "a Christian cannot be a punishing judge."[130]

Furthermore, Tolstoy continues, Jesus' disciples clearly understood this. The Epistle of James and the Epistle of Paul to the Romans both warn Christians against judging one another.[131] According to Tolstoy, both authors recognise that the only way to oppose the tribunals that persecuted Christians was by denying the principle on which they rested, just as Jesus told them to do. In fact, Tolstoy observes that the earliest teachers of the Church "invariably distinguished their teaching from all others" precisely by "never admitting in it either compulsion or judgement."[132] Not judging one another and not resisting evil, according to Tolstoy, were the defining principles of the early Christian community.

For Christian anarchists, therefore, Jesus' explicit and implicit teaching on judgement clearly condemns the state's juridical system. Christians

---

[125] Andrews, *A Spiritual Framework for Ethical Reflection*, 3 (Andrews' emphasis).
[126] Andrews, *A Spiritual Framework for Ethical Reflection*, 2 (emphasis removed).
[127] Tolstoy, *What I Believe*, 30.
[128] Tolstoy, *What I Believe*, 30.
[129] Tolstoy, *What I Believe*, 30. (Luke 6:37-42.)
[130] Tolstoy, *What I Believe*, 31.
[131] Tolstoy, *What I Believe*, 32-35. (James 4:11-12; Romans 2:1-4.)
[132] Tolstoy, *What I Believe*, 36.

should not judge one another (or for Andrews they should at least not call upon third parties to do so), and therefore when the state's institutions judge and condemn, they behave in direct contradiction to Jesus' instructions.

## 2.7 – Being servants

Another passage which Christian anarchists refer to in order to consolidate their position is where Jesus teaches about service, in reply to James and John's demand to sit on his right and left hand in his kingdom.[133] Jesus tells them that they do not know what they are asking, and he then says that even though the Gentiles have rulers who exercise lordship and authority over them, it shall not be so among his disciples, that to be the greatest among his disciples, they need to be like servants.

Craig points out that the original Greek word for the "authority" which is exercised by Gentiles and which Jesus rejects is $\alpha\rho\chi\varepsilon\iota\nu$, the same word which *an*-archism defines itself as a negation of.[134] Jesus is counselling against "archism" – that is, he is counselling "anarchism." As to the word used for how Gentile rulers "exercise lordship," Lawrence explains that it means "'to compact,' and by implication 'to hoard.'"[135] Hence Jesus is telling his disciples that "a favored position in the new order of things is one of suffering servanthood" in contrast to the Gentiles' "'hoarding' of power and privilege."[136] Ellul also notes that Jesus makes no distinction between different Gentile rulers: they all "lord it over their subjects," which to Ellul suggests that "There can be no political power without tyranny."[137] All pagan government is equally authoritarian.

Jesus, however, "does not advocate revolt" against such tyrannical power, but instead tells his disciples: "do not be so concerned about fighting kings. Let them be. Set up a marginal society which will not be interested in such things, in which there will be no power, authority, or hierarchy."[138] Jesus is telling his disciples not to emulate social hierarchies. At the end of the passage, Jesus further clarifies the nature of his own leadership: he has come not to be served, but to serve.[139] And elsewhere in the Gospel, he confirms that the same is expected from his disciples: "he that is greatest among you shall be your servant."[140] Jesus is therefore consistently appealing for an anarchist community of mutual service instead of one of lordship and authority.

Christian anarchists understand that Jesus is thus clearly denouncing the more common notions and expectations of leadership. For Redford, Jesus "rebukes the supposed 'authority' of the Earthly 'rulers;'"[141] for Andrews, "All

---

[133] Matthew 20:20-28; Mark 10:35-45.
[134] [Anonymous], *The Christmas Conspiracy*.
[135] Lawrence, "Power Politics and Love," 8.
[136] Lawrence, "Power Politics and Love," 8.
[137] Ellul, *Anarchy and Christianity*, 61.
[138] Ellul, *Anarchy and Christianity*, 62.
[139] Andrews, *Not Religion, but Love*, 93; Andrews, *Subversive Spirituality, Ecclesial and Civil Disobedience*, 4. (Matthew 20:28; Mark 10:45.)
[140] Matthew 23:11.
[141] Redford, *Jesus Is an Anarchist*, 26.

oppressive forms of politics [are] denounced;"[142] and for Mumford, "Jesus sets his face firmly against any leader/led division."[143] Among Christians, says Ballou, "There must be no political strife for the highest place; no patronizing lordship; no Gentile love of dominion; but they that really occupy the highest place, must prove themselves worthy of it, by an entire willingness to take the lowest."[144]

Crucially, Jesus does not challenge James' and John's regarding of him as an authority or as a leader, but he challenges them on their apparent understanding of the way in which such authority or leadership is to be exercised. As Myers puts it, "Jesus here does not repudiate the vocation of leadership, but rather insists that it is not transferred executively. Leadership belongs only to those who learn and follow the way of nonviolence – who are 'prepared' not to dominate but to serve and to suffer at Jesus' side."[145] Jesus is calling for Christians to be leaders only by virtue of them being great exemplars of non-resistance, vying, as Ballou says, "not for the prerogative of inflicting physical suffering for righteousness' sake, but for the privilege of enduring it."[146] As explained later in this Chapter, the consequence of this vocation of "servant leadership" is the suffering of the cross, which true followers of Jesus are expected to embrace willingly and wholeheartedly.[147]

Finally, Yoder remarks that Jesus does not reprimand James and John "for expecting him to establish some new social order," but, again, he "reprimands them for having misunderstood the character of that new social order which he does intend to set up."[148] Jesus does intend to challenge political and religious authorities and to propose an alternative form of community, but this is to be achieved through leadership by suffering servanthood, not through the lordship and authority practiced by Gentiles. Jesus rejects leadership by coercion and favours leadership by example. It is precisely this alternative form of leadership which makes Jesus' teaching an anarchist alternative to the established order of things.

## 2.8 – The temple cleansing

The next passage for which the Christian anarchist perspective needs to be explained is Jesus' famous cleansing of the Jerusalem temple, where he overturns tables, brandishes a whip, casts out the moneychangers, and proclaims: "It is written, My house is the house of prayer: but ye have made it a den of thieves."[149]

Christian anarchists emphasise that the temple was an important religious, political and economic symbol. For Elliott, therefore, what Jesus attacks

---

[142] Andrews, "Heaven on Earth," 53
[143] Mumford, "The Bible and Anarchy," 8.
[144] Ballou, *Christian Non-Resistance*, chap. 2, para. 62.
[145] Myers, *Binding the Strong Man*, 278.
[146] Ballou, *Non-Resistance in Relation to Human Governments*, 9-10.
[147] The expression "servant leadership" is borrowed from Myers, *Binding the Strong Man*, 260 and passim.
[148] Yoder, *The Politics of Jesus*, 38.
[149] Matthew 21:12-16; Mark 11:15-18; Luke 19:45-48; John 2:13-17.

in nothing less than "the most powerful ideological symbol of all."[150] Elliott furthermore rejects the "conservative reading" which explains Jesus' actions "in terms of his 'righteous anger' over the sullying of a religious shrine with commercial activities." For him, the temple was not just a religious institution, but it also "functioned as the political and economic apparatus of the state." It was "the final arbiter in all criminal, political and religious matters;" it exercised a policing role; and, "to all intents and purposes," it also acted as "the state treasury." It therefore "represented an immense concentration of power" – not unlike our modern state. Hence Elliott considers Jesus' actions as going much deeper than "an argument for the separation of commercial and religious activities," but as actually embodying "the frustrations and the aspirations of all the world's oppressed." Jesus' actions are a clear protest against the temple state's immense power, and it is precisely for this reason that the authorities redouble their efforts to "destroy him."[151]

Myers argues along similar lines, but more closely highlights the economic interests behind the temple's sacrificial system. He says that for the author of the Gospel of Mark, "the temple state and its political economy represented the heart of what was *wrong* with the dominant system."[152] Moreover, Myers contends that "commercial activity was an entirely *normal* aspect of any cult in antiquity;" that the temple "was *fundamentally an economic institution*;" and that it is "the *ruling-class interests* in control of the commercial enterprises in the temple market" that Jesus is therefore attacking.[153] Hence, by citing the "den of thieves" passage from scripture, Jesus is criticising "the sacrificial system *as robbery*."[154] According to Myers, this episode is the key to understanding Jesus' whole apocalyptic struggle against the political, economic and religious order.[155] For him, it epitomises Jesus' stance against his contemporary authorities, and it illustrates how the "practice of forgiveness becomes the replacement of the redemptive/symbolic system of debt represented in the temple."[156] Jesus' teaching of forgiveness subverts the temple state's economic power.

Other Christian anarchists make similar points but in a less elaborate way. Redford shares Myers' view that Jesus' protest is directed at the fraudulent idea, on which the commercial activities he attacks is based, that sins can be atoned through animal sacrifices.[157] Andrews contends that the moneychangers

---

[150] Elliott, *Freedom, Justice and Christian Counter-Culture*, 166.
[151] All the quotes between the previous and this footnote are from Elliott, *Freedom, Justice and Christian Counter-Culture*, 180-181. See Mark 11:17 and Luke 19:47 for the words quoted by Elliott in this last sentence.
[152] Myers, *Binding the Strong Man*, 80 (Myers' emphasis).
[153] Myers, *Binding the Strong Man*, 300 (Myers' emphases).
[154] Myers, *Binding the Strong Man*, 302 (Myers' emphasis).
[155] Myers, *Binding the Strong Man*, 299-306.
[156] Myers, *Binding the Strong Man*, 306.
[157] Redford, the Christian anarcho-capitalist, believes that it is a mistake to interpret this episode "as being some sort of revolt by Jesus on the bad aesthetics of commerce being conducted inside God's temple." For him, commercial activities are perfectly acceptable as long as they are conducted in good faith. But here, "what [Jesus] was saying was that the people who bought these animals to be sacrificed to atone for their sins were being *ripped-off* – i.e., that the animal sacrifices weren't doing anything for their sins." Therefore, says Redford, "having determined that the priests were defrauding their patrons He took appropriate libertarian action (per Rothbardian theory in particular) by using retaliatory force against these thieves" (Rothbard is one of the main thinkers of anarcho-capitalism).

were exploiting the vulnerability of worshippers, and that Jesus became angry at such "exploitation of the worst kind."[158] For Hennacy, what aroused Jesus' anger was "hypocrisy in the Synagogue."[159] Note, however, that as mentioned in Chapter 1, the word "anger" does not actually appear in the text. Jesus must have been upset to act as he did, and for Christian anarchists, he was upset at more than just the commercial activities in the temple, but the view that Jesus was angry is informed more from popular representations of Jesus' actions than from scripture itself.

Nonetheless, Christian anarchists see Jesus' overturning of the tables and driving out of traders and their animals as dramatic and symbolic "direct action," a form of "propaganda by the deed" against what the temple symbolises. Myers even talks of "some kind of barricade or 'guerilla ban' on all further activities for that day."[160] For some Christian anarchists, true Christians should follow Jesus' example and engage in similar direct action against the state. For them, "Love is confrontational."[161]

Other Christian anarchists are uneasy with the aggressiveness of such confrontations. Day, for instance, after confirming that the "justification for a Christ who urges militant action" is indeed this story of the temple cleansing, writes: "I can only answer in these other words of His: 'Let him who is without sin among you, cast the first stone.'"[162] Thus not all Christian anarchists are comfortable with the idea put forward by some that Christians should engage in militant direct action. Those that think so, however, usually cite the temple cleansing to make their point. Either way, this whole debate is examined in more detail in Chapter 4.

Another important debate around this passage centres on the extent to which Jesus uses violence in cleansing the temple. Wink for instance believes that it was "a fairly violent act, even if it caused no casualties."[163] For Elliott as well, Jesus' expulsion of the traders is carried out "with a certain degree of violence."[164] Most Christian anarchists, however, argue that any violence is extremely limited, and that it is never directed at people.

Crosby, for example, points out that only John mentions a whip, that "he alone mentions also the sheep and oxen," and that it is therefore obvious that "the whip was merely used as the ordinary method of driving the cattle."[165] In a letter to Crosby, Tolstoy writes that "It is an old but unfounded libel upon Christ to suppose that the expulsion of the cattle from the temple indicates that Jesus beat people with a whip."[166] Yet as Yoder regrets, the whip is often used as a

---

Hence, for Redford, Jesus is not really protesting about the concentration of power, but about the commercial sham involved in that situation. Redford, *Jesus Is an Anarchist*, 34-35.

[158] Andrews, *Not Religion, but Love*, 65-66.
[159] Hennacy, *The Book of Ammon*, 433.
[160] Myers, *Binding the Strong Man*, 302.
[161] [Anonymous], "Cleansing of the Temple," *A Pinch of Salt*, issue 1, September 1985, 12.
[162] Dorothy Day, *Selected Writings: By Little and by Little*, ed. Robert Ellsberg (Maryknoll: Orbis, 2005), 344-345.
[163] Wink, *Jesus' Third Way*, 36.
[164] Elliott, *Freedom, Justice and Christian Counter-Culture*, 80.
[165] Crosby, *Tolstoy and His Message*, chap. 5, para. 11.
[166] Leo Tolstoy, "Letter to Ernest Howard Crosby," in *Tolstoy's Writings on Civil Disobedience and Non-Violence*, trans. Aylmer Maude (New York: Bergman, 1967), 181.

precedent for Christians' use of violence.[167] For him, however, the better translation of Jesus' action – which more recent translations of the Bible have adopted – is that he "cast out" or "drove out" the animals from the temple. According to Yoder, "'cast out' (*exebalen*) posits no violence; elsewhere in the New Testament is means simply 'send away.'"[168] Penner remarks that this word is most often used by Jesus for the casting out of demons, and agrees that there is no evidence of any force or violent coercion in this passage.[169] Andy Baker makes the same points: to "drive out" does not imply violence but simply to "send away," hence Jesus "did not hit anyone," and the animals were not beaten but whipped only enough for them "to start moving away."[170]

To those who suppose that Jesus must have been more violent than the text describes, Ballou replies: "as I have an equally good right to imagine how Jesus acted on the occasion, I shall presume that he did nothing unworthy of the principle, the character, and spirit that uniformly distinguished him."[171] Although there can be no definitive proof either way, given Jesus' main teaching, the absence of violence is more probable than its presence. In any case, in Myers' view, "too much attention has been given to the futile pursuit of trying to reconstruct a historical event, which serves as a pretext for debates about whether such an action should be considered violent or not."[172] For Myers, the symbolic and ideological aspect of Jesus' action is what is more important.

Either way, says Baker, "Jesus' action in no way can be seen to legitimate Christian violence."[173] (Besides, according to Hennacy, even if Jesus did use his whip on the moneychangers, "He did not try to exterminate their families or imprison and kill them," and therefore his actions are no Christian justification for war.[174]) Jesus' cleansing of the temple, although symbolically and politically potent, does not legitimise Christian violence. What it does confirm, however, is his opposition to such concentration and abuse of religious, political and economic power.

More to the point, Maurin remarks, "today nobody dares to drive the money lenders out of the Temple."[175] Christians argue about whether Jesus used violence instead of cleansing their own temple. Yet for Hennacy, "if He came back here He sure would upset some of the plush around here."[176] Tolstoy agrees: if Jesus came now and saw "what is done in his name in church," Tolstoy says, he would "surely" be even more upset than he was then.[177] Moreover, if he were to act as he did then, "he'd be charged with criminal damage" and arrested, as

---

[167] Yoder, *The Politics of Jesus*, 42.
[168] Yoder, *The Politics of Jesus*, 43.
[169] Penner, *The New Testament, the Christian, and the State*, 68-69.
[170] Andy Baker, *Nonviolent Action in the Temple*, available from http://www.jesusradicals.com/essays/theology/temple.html (accessed 16 May 2006).
[171] Ballou, *Christian Non-Resistance in All Its Important Bearings*, 30.
[172] Myers, *Binding the Strong Man*, 299.
[173] Baker, *Nonviolent Action in the Temple*.
[174] Hennacy, *The Book of Ammon*, 432.
[175] Maurin, *Easy Essays (2003)*, 3.
[176] Hennacy, *The Book of Ammon*, 381.
[177] Leo Tolstoy, "A Reply to the Synod's Edict of Excommunication, and to Letters Received by Me Concerning It," in *On Life and Essays on Religion*, trans. Aylmer Maude (London: Oxford University Press, 1934), 223.

Newell notes.[178] A true follower of Jesus, then, should not get distracted by attempts to reconstruct the exact historical event of the temple cleansing, but should boldly expose the contrast between true Christianity and the state, especially when the latter claims for itself some religious or Christian aura.

## 2.9 – Jesus' arrest

Having shown how Christian anarchists read some of Jesus' teachings and some of the incidents of his life, the time has come to turn to their commentaries on his arrest, trial and crucifixion.

The story of Jesus' arrest varies slightly from one Evangelist to the other.[179] Their differences are interesting, but they have little impact on the anarchist implications of the New Testament, and only those details of Jesus' arrest which have anarchist implications are discussed here.[180] The most immediately relevant of these is Jesus' reply (in Matthew) to the disciple (identified as Peter in John) who has just drawn a sword and slashed the ear of one of the priests' servants. Jesus rebukes him by saying: "Put up again thy sword into his place: for all they that take the sword shall perish with the sword."[181]

For most Christian anarchists, this text further corroborates Jesus' teaching on non-resistance. In Tolstoy's version of the Gospel, Jesus' rebuke indeed begins with him repeating the words: "You must not resist evil."[182] When Jesus says that they who take the sword shall perish by the sword, for Christian anarchists, he is simply reiterating the point made in the Sermon on the Mount. That is, "Violence can only give rise to further violence,"[183] and therefore those who resort to violence shall face violence themselves.[184] Thus Jesus is again raising the question of means and ends, says Elliott, "particularly questioning whether a peaceful and just society can be established through violent and unjust tactics."[185] Those who want peace should keep away from the sword and adopt peaceful means, because "those who seek peace, who act in a friendly manner,

---

[178] Martin Newell, quoted in Greg Watts, "Following Jesus in Love and Anarchy," *The Times*, 29 February 2008, available from http://www.timesonline.co.uk/tol/comment/faith/article3461731.ece (accessed 29 February 2008), para. 16.

[179] Matthew 26:47-56; Mark 14:43-52; Luke 22:35-53; John 18:1-11. Tolstoy's version suggests a connection between Peter's use of the sword and his later sorrow at having denied Jesus because, for Tolstoy, he "had fallen into temptation [...] when he tried to defend Jesus." Tolstoy, "The Gospel in Brief," 255-256.

[180] All four Evangelists recount a servant of Jesus using a sword to cut a servant of the high priest's ear, but only John names Jesus' servant as Peter. Jesus' rebuke varies: in Matthew, he says "Put up again thy sword into his place: for all they that take the sword shall perish with the sword;" in Luke: "Suffer ye thus far;" and in John: "Put up thy sword into the sheath;" but there is no rebuke in Mark. Only Luke tells of Jesus healing the wounded soldier. Jesus' comment that those who are arresting him have come like thieves in the middle of the night is mentioned by Matthew, Mark and Luke, but not John. Finally, Jesus' proclamation that this arrest and what is to follow must come for him to "drink the cup" and for scripture to be fulfilled appears in Matthew, Mark and John, but not Luke.

[181] Matthew 26:52.

[182] Tolstoy, "The Gospel in Brief," 254.

[183] Ellul, *Anarchy and Christianity*, 65.

[184] Garrison, "Declaration of Sentiments Adopted by the Peace Convention," 8.

[185] Elliott, *Freedom, Justice and Christian Counter-Culture*, 117.

inoffensively, who forget and forgive offences, for the most part enjoy peace," writes Ballou.[186]

The anarchist implications are similar to those of the Sermon on the Mount. According to Chelčický, "Christ in disarming Peter unbelted every soldier" – Jesus disarmed the most potent source of state power.[187] Yet as Hennacy laments, even in peacetime, "we draft our boys and prepare for more terrible wars."[188] States take the sword and use it, and "as centuries of history have shown," Ellul notes, they in turn get destroyed by it.[189] In that sense, according to Ellul, Jesus' words amount to a reflection on the rise and fall of states through history. But Ellul also adds that "we might also view the saying as a command to Christians. Do not fight the state with the sword, for if you do, you will be killed by the sword."[190] How Christians should respond to the state is discussed in detail in Chapter 4; what matters here is to note that for Christian anarchists, in this saying just as in the Sermon on the Mount, Jesus is both reflecting upon the cycle of violence and counselling against it.

Before moving on to Jesus' trial, there is another element in the story of Jesus' arrest which needs to be looked at. It precedes Jesus' arrest in Luke's Gospel, and it is a tricky passage for Christian anarchists as it seems to contradict the above saying: Jesus tells his disciples that even though in the past, he has sent them without purse, scrip and shoes and yet they lacked "nothing," now, they need to buy a sword because, he says, "this that is written must yet be accomplished in me."[191] They then show him two swords, and he answers that "It is enough."[192]

Different Christian anarchists understand this passage differently: for Tolstoy and Hennacy, Jesus was tired and slightly hesitant; for Ellul, Ballou and others, two swords could not have been enough for defence, so the swords must have had a different purpose than violent defence.

In Tolstoy's version of the Gospel, Jesus tells his disciples that now that he is considered "an outlaw," they need to "get knives" in order to "procure supplies" so that they do not "perish uselessly."[193] Moreover, in his later summary of the same episode, Tolstoy puts this saying in the context of Peter claiming that he will not let Jesus be killed but he will protect him, to which Jesus replies: "If that is so, then prepare for defence, get weapons to defend yourselves and collect your provisions."[194] But, Tolstoy continues, "When Jesus heard the mention of the knives, anguish came over him. And going to a lonely spot he began to pray."[195] For Tolstoy, Jesus "strove with temptation" but eventually concluded that he must not resist evil: "I shall not fight, but shall give myself

---

[186] Ballou, "A Catechism of Non-Resistance," 19.
[187] Molnár, *A Study of Peter Chelčický's Life*, 15 (quoting Chelčický).
[188] Hennacy, *The Book of Ammon*, 125.
[189] Ellul, *Anarchy and Christianity*, 65.
[190] Ellul, *Anarchy and Christianity*, 65.
[191] Luke 22:35-37.
[192] Luke 22:38.
[193] Tolstoy, "The Gospel in Brief," 244.
[194] Tolstoy, "The Gospel in Brief," 295.
[195] Tolstoy, "The Gospel in Brief," 295.

up."[196] For Tolstoy, then, it seems that the "two swords" episode reveals a slight but understandable hesitancy on the part of Jesus, followed by an eventual and final decision against any use of swords.

Hennacy makes a similar point: Jesus was tired and full of agony when he told Peter to buy a sword, but his later rebuttal of Peter when the sword was used conclusively overturns this brief hesitation and reasserts the need for pure non-resistance.[197]

Ellul, however, is among the Christian anarchists who understand this in a different way. He notes the surprising statement from Jesus that two swords are "enough," and writes:

> The further comment of Jesus explains in part the surprising statement, for he says: "It is necessary that the prophecy be fulfilled according to which I would be put in the ranks of criminals" (Luke 22:36-37). The idea of fighting with just two swords is ridiculous. The swords are enough, however, to justify the accusation that Jesus is the head of a band of brigands. We have to note here again that Jesus is consciously fulfilling prophecy. If he were not, the saying would make no sense.[198]

Two swords could not possibly have been "enough" to defend Jesus from his pending arrest, trial and execution, so their sole purpose must have been the fulfilment of prophecy. That is how not just Ellul but also Yoder and Penner understand this intriguing passage.[199]

Penner adds a further dimension to this. Peter, he notes, had been in charge of preparing the Passover, and the said swords have a dual use: as weapons, but also as knifes to cut animals and prepare meat. "This," he concludes, "would suggest that the two knives were present because they had been used in preparing the Supper."[200] He admits that this suggestion is only a probability, but it adds credence to the view that "the purpose of Jesus in asking for swords had no connection with violence, self-defense, or bloodshed. His purpose was to fulfil the Scriptures."[201]

Besides, as Penner admits, using the swords for defence would have been contrary to Jesus' teaching and example, and for Penner, that very contradiction suggests that their purpose could not have been defence.[202] His disciples' use of swords "would involve them in the vicious circle of cause and effect of violence and hatred."[203] Jesus' rebuke to Peter, however, demonstrates that for Jesus, the sword should be used neither in offence nor defence, for both would equally feed into the circle of violence which Jesus' teaching seeks to overcome. Thus according to Ballou, the actual "sequel" of the narrative "[proves] that he caused the swords to be provided, for that occasion, (two only being enough) for the sole purpose of emphatically, finally, and everlastingly

---

[196] Tolstoy, "The Gospel in Brief," 295.
[197] Hennacy, *The Book of Ammon*, 194, 432-433.
[198] Ellul, *Anarchy and Christianity*, 64.
[199] Penner, *The New Testament, the Christian, and the State*, 52-54; Yoder, *The Politics of Jesus*, 45, footnote 44.
[200] Penner, *The New Testament, the Christian, and the State*, 54.
[201] Penner, *The New Testament, the Christian, and the State*, 54.
[202] Penner, *The New Testament, the Christian, and the State*, 53.
[203] Penner, *The New Testament, the Christian, and the State*, 55.

prohibiting the use of the instrument, even by the innocent in self-defense. [...] The moment one of these was wielded in defense of betrayed innocence, it was peremptorily stayed" and Jesus proclaimed the famous saying.[204] That later rebuke, for Crosby, annuls the earlier advice to buy a sword.[205]

For Christian anarchists, therefore, despite the intriguing request to buy a sword, Jesus' words upon his arrest further confirm than violence should never be used by his followers, be that either in offence or in even innocent defence. If the state cannot but take the sword, then it cannot but contradict Jesus' teaching. If it is fundamental to the state that it takes the sword, then Jesus' teaching counsels anarchism.

## 2.10 – Jesus' trial

Following his arrest, Jesus is tried before the Sanhedrin, Pilate and Herod.[206] Christian anarchists comment on Jesus' attitude and responses during these trials, but first, they emphasise that the various charges that are brought against him are all either directly or indirectly political charges.

Jesus is arrested because he is "turning the world upside down," says a contributor to *A Pinch of Salt*.[207] Tolstoy writes that he is crucified because he says he will destroy the temple and rebuild it in three days, and because "he is reproached with destroying the law of God."[208] Admittedly, today these charges may sound more religious than political, but these two spheres were not seen as clearly separate in Jesus' times. Moreover, as Penner contends, although "The guilt of Jesus, as conceived by the Jews, was in the realm of the religious [...], their charge is shifted to a political one as they confront Pilate with Jesus. The charge of blasphemy becomes the political charge of treason."[209]

To both the Jews and the Romans, Jesus is a real political threat, a dangerous "social agitator," as Pentecost calls him.[210] His non-violent teachings and tactics clearly make the political and religious authorities feel quite jittery.[211] Caiaphas, the chief rabbi, famously proclaims that it is better for one man rather than the whole nation to perish: Jesus is a threat, and the national interest dictates that he should be silenced.[212] Myers notes that Jesus is imprisoned alongside Barabbas, who represents a different but equally political, revolutionary threat.[213] For Christian anarchists, therefore, Jesus is charged with "sedition"[214] and

---

[204] Ballou, *Christian Non-Resistance in All Its Important Bearings*, 31.
[205] Crosby, *Tolstoy and His Message*, chap. 5, para. 7.
[206] Matthew 26-26; Mark 14-15; Luke 22-23; John 18-19.
[207] [Anonymous], "The World Turned Upside Down," *A Pinch of Salt*, issue 3, Pentecost 1986, 10.
[208] Tolstoy, *What I Believe*, 45, 65 (respectively).
[209] Penner, *The New Testament, the Christian, and the State*, 61.
[210] Hugh O. Pentecost, *Murder by Law*, available from http://www.deadanarchists.org/Pentecost/murder.html (accessed 22 November 2007), para. 22.
[211] Yoder, *The Politics of Jesus*, 49.
[212] John 18:14. George Tarleton, *Birth of a Christian Anarchist* (Pennington: Pendragon, 1993), 63-67; Tolstoy, "The Gospel in Brief," 291; Tolstoy, "The Kingdom of God Is within You," 403.
[213] Myers, *Binding the Strong Man*, 380; Yoder, *The Politics of Jesus*, 48-49.
[214] Myers, *Binding the Strong Man*, 372.

"subversion."[215] Jesus' trials "hinge on the charge that he was setting himself up, or being set up as a king, and the description 'King of the Jews' is nailed to his gallows," says Elliott.[216]

Moreover, as Myers recalls, "The 'cross' had only one connotation in the Roman empire: upon it dissidents were executed."[217] Myers complains about the "longstanding conspiracy" which insists on "spiritualizing the cross."[218] As Myers clarifies, when Jesus was crucified, the cross was "not a religious icon, but the ultimate deterrent to those who would challenge the sovereignty of Rome [...], an intolerably cruel form of capital punishment."[219] Furthermore, that Jesus is crucified between two bandits confirms that "Jesus is *perceived* by the authorities in terms equal to that of social bandits."[220] Religious and political authorities consider Jesus as an important threat, and that is why they move to silence him. Jesus' anarchist subversion is too compelling for the state to put up with.

When it comes to the actual trials, Ellul argues against the theologians who believe that just because Jesus "showed respect for the authorities, and did not revolt against the verdict, this proves that he regarded the jurisdiction as legitimate, and we thus have a basis for the power of the state."[221] To the contrary, he says, despite the fact that Roman law is so developed and intricate so as to represent an ideal model of justice (and Ellul, who studied Roman law, means this seriously, with no irony at all), this law provides no protection to an innocent man. Despite Roman law, Pilate yields to the mob and condemns him to death "for no valid reason (as Pilate himself recognized!). This, then, is what we can expect from an excellent legal system!"[222] Jesus' submission to the trial is no acceptance of its legitimacy, but "it is an unveiling of the basic injustice of what purports to be justice," concludes Ellul (the fundamental imperfection of the state's administration of justice is discussed again in the Conclusion).[223]

For Ellul, Jesus' silent refusal "to debate," to "excuse himself," or "to recognize that these authorities have any real power," an attitude which is consistent throughout the Gospels but particularly perilous when being tried, is an "attitude [...] of total rejection and scorn for all religious or political authority."[224] Ellul even sees some of Jesus' answers to the high priest and to Pilate as amounting to "a kind of underlying mockery, a defiance or provocation of

---

[215] "Other aspects of the argument," writes Justin [Meggitt?], "include the fact that one of his disciples is a zealot (a political revolutionary), that his disciples were armed at the time of his arrest, that he drove the money lenders from the temple, that he declared the people to be exempt from paying the temple tax and so on." Meggitt [?], "Anarchism and the New Testament," 11.
[216] Elliott, *Freedom, Justice and Christian Counter-Culture*, 180. Yoder and Mumford also remark that the title on the Cross testifies to the political threat Jesus is seen to pose. Mumford, "The Bible and Anarchy," 8; Yoder, *The Politics of Jesus*, 50.
[217] Myers, *Binding the Strong Man*, 245.
[218] Myers, *Binding the Strong Man*, 256.
[219] Myers, *Binding the Strong Man*, 383.
[220] Myers, *Binding the Strong Man*, 387 (Myers' emphasis). By "social bandits," Myers means subversives struggling for social justice and inciting revolt. Myers, *Binding the Strong Man*, 58-60.
[221] Ellul, *Anarchy and Christianity*, 65.
[222] Ellul, *Anarchy and Christianity*, 66.
[223] Ellul, *Anarchy and Christianity*, 66.
[224] Ellul, *Anarchy and Christianity*, 67-68.

authority."[225] Moreover, Ellul understands Jesus to be sometimes accusing the authorities of being cunning and evil, for instance when Jesus remarks that they could have arrested him in broad daylight in the temple but instead chose the cover of darkness to do so. Along the same lines, Ellul maintains that Jesus' proclamation that Pilate's power has come "from above" is an accusation that Pilate's power has come "from the spirit of evil," not from God as some theologians have it (because this would make no sense of the second part of Jesus' saying).[226]

Finally, there is another sentence which Jesus pronounces during his trial before Pilate which Christian anarchists comment on, and it is the famous: "My kingdom is not of this world: if my kingdom were of this world, then would my servants fight, that I should not be delivered to the Jews."[227] For Ellul, Jesus hereby "states explicitly that [he] does not choose to exercise political power," which "in no way suggests that Jesus recognizes the validity of such power – on the contrary."[228] Jesus concedes that he is king, but explains that this kingship is very different to earthly ones which are defended by fighting.[229] Moreover, Eller's paraphrase has Jesus say that "the one, real, true kingdom isn't even *of* this world," which for Eller shows that "Jesus will grant not one bit of weight to Pilate and his Empire."[230] Jesus' kingdom, for Ballou, "is not an outward, temporal kingdom, like those of this world."[231] It is an alternative to earthly kingdoms, but it is radically different to them. The coercive kingdoms of this world are empowered by the prince of this world, Satan, whereas Jesus' kingdom is one of love, forgiveness and non-resistance.

Caesar, Jesus therefore tells Pilate, should not consider him to be a violent revolutionary bent on claiming his throne, for his servants, by definition, would not use force or coercion.[232] "His Kingdom is not of this world," writes Ballou, "and therefore excludes all military and warlike defenses. His ministers are sent forth unarmed, like sheep in the midst of wolves."[233] As further explained in Chapter 4, Jesus therefore submits to Caesar's punishment here on earth. He

---

[225] Ellul, *Anarchy and Christianity*, 71 (69-71 for the general argument).

[226] In the King James Version of the Bible, the text reads: "Thou couldest have no power at all against me, except it were given thee from above: therefore he that delivered me unto thee hath the greater sin" (John 19:11). Ellul concedes that some interpret "from above" to indicate that "Pilate has his power from God." But, he continues, "in this case I defy anyone to explain what is meant by the second part of his reply. How can the one who has delivered up Jesus be guilty if he has been delivered up to the authority which is from God?" A better interpretation, for Ellul, is that "Jesus is telling Pilate that his power is from the spirit of evil. This is in keeping with what we said about the temptations, namely, that all powers and kingdoms in this world depend on the devil. It is also in keeping with the reply of Jesus to the chief priest that we quoted above, namely, that the power of darkness is at work in his trial." Ellul therefore explains the second part of the saying thus: "Jesus is telling Pilate that he has his power from the spirit of evil but that the one who has delivered him up to Pilate, and therefore to that spirit, is more guilty than Pilate himself. Obviously so!" Ellul, *Anarchy and Christianity*, 68-69.

[227] John 18:36.

[228] Ellul, "Anarchism and Christianity," 168.

[229] Tolstoy, "The Gospel in Brief," 258.

[230] Eller, *Christian Anarchy*, 10 (Eller's emphasis).

[231] Ballou, *Non-Resistance in Relation to Human Governments*, 9.

[232] Penner, *The New Testament, the Christian, and the State*, 62.

[233] Ballou, *Christian Non-Resistance*, chap. 2, para. 62.

holds his peace when taunted, ruffled and insulted by the guards.[234] As Ballou writes, "never a word of threatening, reviling, cursing or bitterness escaped him. With a meek and sorrowful dignity he bore all; and at the moment when he could have summoned legions of angels to his rescue, and to the destruction of his foes, lo, he uttered that last victorious prayer: 'Father forgive them, for they know not what they do.'"[235]

Jesus is tried on political charges and punished like a political subversive. He forgivingly accepts this mortal outcome and yet explains that his kingship is misconstrued if it is taken to involve the sort of fighting conducted on behalf of earthly kings. He is a threat to religious and political authorities, to the state, but not in the way that this is commonly understood. Paradoxically, by his very crucifixion, Jesus illustrates and exemplifies the way in which his teaching unmasks and overcomes power of the state.

## 2.11 – Jesus' crucifixion

Jesus' crucifixion raises the apocalyptic notions of "powers" and "messiah," themes which need to be explained before the political meaning of the cross can be explored.

### 2.11.1 – Paul's "powers"

In their commentaries on Jesus' crucifixion, Christian anarchists often refer to Paul's notion of "principalities" and "powers" (usually $\alpha\rho\chi\alpha i$ and $\varepsilon\xi o\upsilon\sigma i\alpha\iota$ in the Greek).[236] Yoder defines these "powers" as "some sort of superterrestrial beings" – which he admits might sound rather "out-of-date" today.[237] Hendrik Berkhof, whose study of Paul's powers is praised by Yoder, explains that the term is borrowed (but modified) from Jewish apocalyptic writings, where it refers to "classes of angels [...] holding authority over forces of nature."[238] Their "role is one of domination,"[239] he explains, and they rule over "human history."[240] When Paul borrows the term, the powers are angels who have authority over natural forces.

Berkhof notes that Paul always refers to them in connection with $\sigma\tau o\iota\chi\varepsilon i\alpha$, which he translates as "definite religious and ethical rules" or "solid" social "structures."[241] For Paul, the powers are the "guardians and trustees" which preserve men "from chaos;" they are the "demands" of "state and society," of "tradition and morality."[242] Hence Paul modifies the apocalyptic sense of

---

[234] Tolstoy, "The Gospel in Brief," 257.
[235] Ballou, *Christian Non-Resistance*, chap. 2, para. 82 (emphasis removed).
[236] Romans 8:38; 1 Corinthians 2:8, 15:24; Ephesians 1:21, 2:2, 3:10, 6:12; Colossians 1:16, 2:15.
[237] John Howard Yoder, "Translator's Preface," in *Christ and the Powers*, by Hendrik Berkhof, trans. John Howard Yoder (Scottdale: Herald, 1977), 5.
[238] Hendrik Berkhof, *Christ and the Powers*, trans. John Howard Yoder (Scottdale: Herald, 1977), 16.
[239] Berkhof, *Christ and the Powers*, 18.
[240] Berkhof, *Christ and the Powers*, 19.
[241] Berkhof, *Christ and the Powers*, 21.
[242] Berkhof, *Christ and the Powers*, 22.

heavenly angels of nature and sees the powers more as "structures of earthy existence," as the soul of social structures such as the state.[243] The powers, in Paul, are the spirits that animate social institutions. Thus, every state is moved by one such spirit or power.[244]

Moreover, according to Berkhof's reading of Paul, these powers are instruments of God's dominion in a fallen world, and, in themselves, they are not necessarily tyrannical – yet they can become so, especially when they become gods and act as ultimate values which demand our absolute loyalty.[245] What this notion of the powers "leads us to suppose," says Ellul, is "that earthly political and military authorities really have their basis in an alliance with spiritual powers, which I will not call celestial, since they might equally well be evil and demonic."[246] The state, writes Ellul, "may fall prey to demons, if the power that it represents refuses to recognise the supremacy of God."[247] As mentioned already in the discussion of the Book of Samuel and as further discussed in the Conclusion, the state becomes unchristian when it elevates itself to the status of a god.

Paul writes that Christians "wrestle not against flesh and blood, but against principalities, against powers, against the rulers of the darkness of this world."[248] For Christian anarchists, therefore, Christians should "gird up their loins, not against the world of flesh and blood, but against spiritual wickedness."[249] They should be "engaging with the powers that lie behind all social institutions."[250] Here, Christian anarchists cite the work of Wink, who writes that Christians are contending "against the spirituality of institutions, against the ideologies and metaphors and legitimations that prop them up."[251] Indeed, Andrews interprets "an-archy" to mean precisely "'against the powers,' as in 'the principalities and powers.'"[252] In that sense, and following Paul, any true Christian must be an anarchist.

It is also through this language of the powers that Ellul understands all the passages of the Bible that "speak of strife, contention, violence."[253] For him, they are all part of the battle *against the powers*: "we must be clear that this is not contention against flesh and blood, but against the powers," insists Ellul.[254] This battle involves no physical violence; it is a "spiritual battle against what

---

[243] Berkhof, *Christ and the Powers*, 23.
[244] Wink, *Jesus' Third Way*, 84.
[245] Berkhof, *Christ and the Powers*, 27-35. This theme is revisited in Chapter 4.
[246] Ellul, *Anarchy and Christianity*, 83.
[247] Ellul, quoted in Goddard, *Living the Word, Resisting the World*, 281.
[248] Ephesians 6:12.
[249] Murray L. Wagner, *Petr Chelčický: A Radical Separatist in Hussite Bohemia* (Scottdale: Herald, 1983), 88.
[250] Bartley, *Faith and Politics after Christendom*, 193.
[251] Walter Wink, *Naming the Powers: The Language of Power in the New Testament* (Philadelphia: Fortress, 1984), 140.
[252] Andrews, *Christi-Anarchy*, 215. As mentioned above, the word usually translated as "principalities" is indeed αρχαί in the Greek, the same word "an-archism" defines itself as a negation of.
[253] Ellul, *Violence*, 161.
[254] Ellul, *Violence*, 161.

constitutes the 'soul' of these material phenomena."[255] Ellul admits that this type of battle is "less visible, less exalting" and "brings you no glory."[256] However, quoting Rimbaud, Ellul maintains that "spiritual warfare is just as brutal as human warfare."[257] Indeed, he adds: "We know what price Jesus paid for waging his battle spiritually."[258] That is, for contending against the soul of the Jewish and Roman authorities, Jesus was executed as a political subversive. The fight against the powers therefore demands important sacrifices.[259]

## 2.11.2 – The defeat of the powers

Nevertheless, Paul says that by his crucifixion, Jesus "disarmed" these powers, "made a public example" of them, and "triumphed" over them.[260] Similarly, Craig writes that through Jesus' execution, Satan was judged and bound.[261] "In Christian thinking," explains Ellul, "the crucifixion of Christ is his true victory over all powers."[262] How can such a paradoxical conclusion be reached? Because as Chelčický understands, "the passion of Jesus reveals the true character of political powers: they are demonic, violent, and out of control."[263]

Wink writes that "They stripped him naked and crucified him in humiliation, all unaware that this very act had stripped them of the last covering that disguised the towering wrongness of the whole way of living that their violence defended. [...] The Law by which he was judged is itself judged, set aside, and nailed to the cross."[264] By the very violence with which the powers execute Jesus, their character is exposed for what it truly is. Myers therefore speaks of the crucified Jesus representing "at once both defendant and prosecutor – depending on which court, 'earthly' or 'heavenly,' is being considered [...]; what appears to be his defeat and the triumph of both Rome and the Sanhedrin (narrated in his trial and execution) [is] *really* his vindication and their judgement."[265] What looks like "an apparent political failure," confirms Bartley, is in fact "a political statement" which is "part of a larger strategy of success."[266]

---

[255] Ellul gives the following phenomena as examples: the state, money, sexuality, and law. Ellul, *Violence*, 163.
[256] Ellul, *Violence*, 162. Nonetheless, it is worth noting that because for Ellul "the powers are *incarnated* in very concrete forms, and their power is expressed in institutions or organizations," he argues that the material battle must be fought, and therefore he sees "a kind of division of labour" whereby "People generally join the material struggle out of their own volition, spontaneously," but "the other war can be waged only by Christians" because only they "can contend against the powers that are at the root of the problem." Ellul, *Violence*, 163-164 (Ellul's emphasis). This distinction between Christians and the rest is addressed again in Chapters 4 and 5.
[257] Arthur Rimbaud, quoted in Ellul, *Violence*, 164.
[258] Ellul, *Violence*, 164.
[259] Ellul, *Violence*, 165.
[260] Colossians 2:15 (these words are from the New Revised Standard Version).
[261] [Anonymous], *Ninety-Five Theses in Defense of Patriarchy*, thesis 55.
[262] Ellul, *Anarchy and Christianity*, 84.
[263] Wagner, *Petr Chelčický*, 51.
[264] Walter Wink, *Engaging the Powers: Discernment and Resistance in a World of Domination* (Minneapolis: Fortress, 1992), 139-140.
[265] Myers, *Binding the Strong Man*, 249 (Myers' emphasis).
[266] Bartley, *Faith and Politics after Christendom*, 222.

Hence what the powers conceive of as their victory is in reality their judgement and defeat.

Therefore as Berkhof puts it, the principalities and powers "are unmasked as false gods by their encounter with very God; they are made a public spectacle."[267] In their "encounter with Christ," religious and political institutions "reveal their tyrannical character."[268] Moreover, their "unmasking is actually already their defeat."[269] Jesus "disarms" the powers because their weapon "was the power of illusion, their ability to convince men that they were the divine regents of the world," and this weapon is "struck out of their hands" by Jesus' refusal to assign them this importance.[270] Yoder argues that although Jesus submitted to the powers, "morally he broke their rules by refusing to support them in their self-glorification" – the violent expression of which is exposed in the crucifixion.[271]

So, while to some, Jesus' crucifixion is the meting out of a deserved punishment to a dangerous subversive, and to others, it represents the "end of the road" for the naïve hopes of a utopian community, to Christian anarchists (and to most Christians), however paradoxical and counterintuitive, "the *crucified* [Jesus] is the fulfilment, rather than negation, of the vocation of messianic kingship."[272] On the cross, Jesus' alternative kingdom is not conclusively crushed but triumphantly exemplified and vindicated. His very crucifixion is his victory over the powers and his inauguration of the kingdom of God.[273]

Indeed, this is what Yoder understands the story of the two disheartened followers of Jesus walking back from his crucifixion to be about: "Jesus' rebuke to the unseeing pair on the road to Emmaus was not that they had been looking for a kingdom, and should not have been," but that "they were failing to see that the suffering of the Messiah *is* the inauguration of the kingdom."[274] For Christian anarchists, then, the "way of the cross" is both "the *via negativa* of resistance to political oppression" and "the positive experimentation of a genuinely new way of social organization" – and these themes are further explored in Chapters 4 and 5.[275]

## 2.11.3 – The crucified "messiah"

As an aside, it is worth noting that Jesus himself, and not just Paul, borrows from and refers his own actions to Jewish apocalyptic writings. This apocalyptic literature, as Elliott notes, "tries to restore national confidence" in a "background of profound political disillusionment."[276] It is therefore "resistance literature at its best" because it promises "a new dawn," a "messianic deliverance" through

---

[267] Berkhof, *Christ and the Powers*, 38.
[268] Berkhof, *Christ and the Powers*, 34.
[269] Berkhof, *Christ and the Powers*, 38.
[270] Berkhof, *Christ and the Powers*, 39.
[271] Yoder, *The Politics of Jesus*, 145.
[272] Myers, *Binding the Strong Man*, 405 (Myers' emphasis).
[273] Myers, *Binding the Strong Man*, 383-384.
[274] Yoder, *The Politics of Jesus*, 51 (Yoder's emphasis). (Luke 24:13-34.)
[275] Myers, *Binding the Strong Man*, 257.
[276] Elliott, *Freedom, Justice and Christian Counter-Culture*, 160.

divine intervention.²⁷⁷ That messianic expectations were attributed to Jesus and that Jesus deliberately reinterprets these in a radical way has already been mentioned above. Yet as noted by Elliott and Yoder, Jesus himself deliberately plays into these political hopes and symbols when he rides into Jerusalem on a donkey, in clear reference to an apocalyptic prophecy of the messianic king's glorious entry into Jerusalem.²⁷⁸ Therefore Jesus deliberately sets himself up as the messianic king, as if to consciously reawaken in his entourage the expectation that he is the long-awaited political messiah.

However, just when Jesus seems to approach the climax of this messianic ministry, the ideal moment to stir up the masses, overthrow the corrupt Roman and Jewish authorities and install himself as the new king – when he rides into Jerusalem on a donkey and engages in direct action in the temple – he is arrested, tried and executed. To those who were expecting a messianic revolution, all apocalyptic hopes seem crushed, nailed with their leader to the cross.

Yet for most Christian anarchists, Jesus is the saviour precisely because he accepted the cross – *that* is the revolution. He is the messiah because he consistently responds to injustice with unwavering love, forgiveness and non-resistance. He does not seek to lead yet another revolutionary government, but instead points to the true kingdom beyond the state. Therefore the crucifixion is indeed the glorious climax of Jesus' messianic ministry. As further discussed in the Conclusion, it reveals the true character of the messiah and the true nature of his kingdom. Jesus' messianic teaching is indeed exalted, not crushed, on the cross.

## 2.11.4 – *The crux of Jesus' political teaching*

According to Myers, Jesus knows that his suffering on the cross is a "political *inevitability*,"²⁷⁹ the "concrete consequence" of his teaching and practice.²⁸⁰ Jesus teaches love, non-resistance and forgiveness, and the question of how far love can really go inevitably demands an answer. With his crucifixion, Jesus answers that love must go to the very end. A martyr of Christian love must be prepared for his own execution.²⁸¹

---

²⁷⁷ Elliott, *Freedom, Justice and Christian Counter-Culture*, 160.
²⁷⁸ Elliott, *Freedom, Justice and Christian Counter-Culture*, 179-180; Yoder, *The Politics of Jesus*, 39-40. (Matthew 21:1-11; Mark 11:1-11; Luke 19:28-40; John 12:12-19.)
²⁷⁹ That is what he understands the dialogue between Peter and Jesus on the nature of Jesus' status as Messiah to be about. He writes: "Jesus drops Peter's Messiah title and replaces it with 'Human One' [which is how Myers translates what is usually translated as 'Son of Man']. Mark has already established within his own story that the Human One is someone who challenges the authority of the scribes and Pharisees. [...] According to the understanding of Peter, 'Messiah' *necessarily* means royal triumph and the restoration of Israel's collective honour. Against this, Jesus argues that 'Human One' *necessarily* means suffering." Myers, *Binding the Strong Man*, 243-244 (Myers' emphasis). (Mark 8:27-38.)
²⁸⁰ Myers, *Binding the Strong Man*, 383.
²⁸¹ As noted elsewhere, "A 'martyr', etymologically, is he who makes himself a witness to his faith. And it is the ultimate testimony to one's faith to be ready to put it to practice even when one's very life is threatened. But the life to be sacrificed, it should be noted, is not the enemy's life, but the martyr's own life." Alexandre J. M. E. Christoyannopoulos, "Turning the Other Cheek to Terrorism:

Andrews explains that there cannot be love and forgiveness without sacrifice, indeed that forgiveness can even be measured by the degree of sacrifice involved.[282] Furthermore, he quotes the words of Gale Webbe, who says that "the only way to conquer evil is to let it be smothered within a willing, living, human being. When it is absorbed there, like a spear into one's heart, it loses its power and goes no further."[283] On the cross, Jesus "absorbed our evil," argues Andrews, and "The cycle of violence stopped there and then."[284] Jesus could have saved himself, but he chose not to, because "He was more concerned about saving the people ridiculing him, than he was about saving himself."[285] Jesus, says Wink, "preferred to suffer injustice and violence rather than be their cause."[286] Jesus' crucifixion is therefore his most powerful illustration of the Sermon on the Mount.

Thus the cross, meant by the authorities to be an exemplary punishment of political subversives, actually "signifies the love of Jesus," writes a contributor to *A Pinch of Salt*.[287] Through it, "Jesus conquered the violence and hatred of this world, not by using that very violence, but by a greater power – the power of love."[288] Jesus' martyrdom on the cross is "a supreme exhibition of love,"[289] and as such, for Andrews, it "lights a beacon for compassion."[290] In Wogaman's words, the cross is therefore both "a maximal expression of human evil – the killing of one who embodied the goodness of God – and [...] a maximal expression of that goodness itself."[291] It is a contrast between love and violence, between goodness and evil, an "*appeal* to humanity" for it to reject "the use of political methods that are violent and coercive," by embracing love and forgiveness instead, and to the very end.[292]

## 2.11.5 – Taking up the cross

However, even though Jesus unmasks, disarms and triumphs over the powers, "the battle continues until the triumph will have been made effective on all fronts and visible to all."[293] The powers may be defeated and condemned on the cross, but they live on, "seemingly victorious."[294] For the principalities and powers to be finally and fully defeated, Christians have to follow Jesus in disarming, making a

---

Reflections on the Contemporary Significance of Leo Tolstoy's Exegesis of the Sermon on the Mount," *Politics and Religion* 1/1 (2008), 41.
[282] Andrews, *The Crux of the Struggle*, 29 (Andrews' emphasis).
[283] Gale Webbe, quoted in Andrews, *The Crux of the Struggle*, 30.
[284] Andrews, *The Crux of the Struggle*, 30.
[285] Andrews, *The Crux of the Struggle*, 41.
[286] Wink, *Jesus' Third Way*, 69.
[287] Charlie, "The Love of Jesus," *A Pinch of Salt*, issue 5, December 1986, 5.
[288] Charlie, "The Love of Jesus," 5.
[289] Abelard, quoted in Andrews, *The Crux of the Struggle*, 26.
[290] Andrews, *Christi-Anarchy*, 155; Andrews, *The Crux of the Struggle*, 30.
[291] J. Philip Wogaman, *Christian Perspectives on Politics*, Revised and expanded ed. (Louisville: Westminster John Knox, 2000), 168 (Wogaman's emphasis).
[292] Wogaman, *Christian Perspectives on Politics*, 168.
[293] Berkhof, *Christ and the Powers*, 40.
[294] Goddard, *Living the Word, Resisting the World*, 101.

public spectacle of and thereby triumphing over their contemporary manifestations.

Every person therefore faces a difficult choice between Jesus and the powers. Jesus warns of the difficulty of following him when he repeatedly says: "Whosoever will come after me, let him deny himself, and take up his cross, and follow me."[295] This "turn of phrase," according to Myers, "could have no other meaning except as an invitation to share the consequences" of daring to challenge political authorities.[296] Yoder insists that it is one of the popular misuses of scripture to interpret "bearing one's cross" as facing the private suffering of "illness and accidents, loneliness and defeat," because Jesus' cross "was the political, legally-to-be-expected result of a moral clash with the powers."[297] Hence Jesus' call for his followers to take up their cross is a call for them to follow his example of love, non-resistance and political subversion to the ultimate sacrifice.

As discussed later in Chapters 4 and 5 discuss, for Christian anarchists, this is the vocation of the church, of the community of Christians. Inevitably, Berkhof notes, contending against the powers will lead to "oppression and persecution. But in this very act of desperation […] their unmasking is repeated and confirmed. They can no longer exist without being forced to uncover their true nature and thereby to abandon their role as gods and saviors."[298] It is a mission of the church to expose the true nature of the principalities and powers, and to thus unmask and triumph over the violence, the self-aggrandisement and the deception of the powers.[299] Yet his can only be done by fighting "nakedly and weakly," by "surrendering" oneself "even unto death."[300]

In this way, explains Myers, "the suffering of the just is somehow in itself efficacious in bringing down the old order and creating the new."[301] Myers asserts that "The threat to punish by death is the bottom line of the power of the state; fear of this keeps the dominant order intact. By resisting this fear and pursuing kingdom practice even at the cost of death, the disciple contributes to the shattering of the powers' reign of death in history."[302] In other words, by "redefining the cross as the way to liberation rather than symbol of defeat and shame," the authority of the powers is subverted, because "the power of death, by which the powers rule, is broken."[303] Accepting and surrendering to death out of love and forgiveness disarms the state, and does so without "increasing the sum of evil in the world."[304] Jesus sets the example with his crucifixion, and he expects his followers to be willing to follow him all the way to the cross.

---

[295] These are the exact words of Mark 8:34, but the same saying can also be found in Matthew 16:24 and Luke 9:23.
[296] Myers, *Binding the Strong Man*, 246.
[297] Yoder, *The Politics of Jesus*, 129.
[298] Berkhof, *Christ and the Powers*, 44.
[299] Berkhof, *Christ and the Powers*, 47-64.
[300] Ellul, *Violence*, 165-166.
[301] Myers, *Binding the Strong Man*, 103 (see also 287). (This notion of efficacy is discussed and critiqued in the Conclusion.)
[302] Myers, *Binding the Strong Man*, 247.
[303] Myers, *Binding the Strong Man*, 428.
[304] Ellul, *Violence*, 174.

In short, the cross is the symbol of Christian anarchism's stance against the state. It represents a willing acceptance of the costliest consequence of contending against the state. It epitomises both the violent injustice of the state and the love, the forgiveness and the non-resistance with which Jesus is responding to it. The cross condemns the violence of the state but also embodies the method to overcome it.

## 2.12 – Jesus' resurrection

The traditional Christian view is that the single most important factor in explaining the spread of Christianity, and indeed in instilling hope among Jesus' dejected disciples after his crucifixion, is his resurrection from the dead. That, however, is not the typical Christian anarchist view. At the same time, Christian anarchists have very little to say on the resurrection. As Chapter 3 makes clear, they view the traditional emphasis placed upon it with deep suspicion, but aside from these suspicions, one struggles to find any mention of the resurrection in Christian anarchist writings.[305]

Tolstoy is the only writer who discusses New Testament passages on the resurrection from a Christian anarchist perspective, and he does so only to disprove the traditional understanding of them. He comments that "Strange as it may seem" – especially in light of the importance ascribed to the event by Christian theologians – Jesus himself "never once said a single word in affirmation of personal resurrection or of the immortality of the individual beyond the grave."[306] Indeed, Tolstoy writes that Jesus denied that belief every time he met it, "and replaced it by his own teaching of Eternal Life in God."[307] This teaching, as Tolstoy understands it, is about "the restoration of life by the transference of man's personal life to that of God" – which feeds into Tolstoy's interesting if idiosyncratic, rationalistic and deistic understanding of Christianity.[308]

The details of Tolstoy's peculiar approach to Christianity cannot be discussed here, but what should be noted is that he questions the traditional interpretation of the resurrection. Tolstoy reviews "the only two passages which are quoted by theologians as witnessing to that teaching" to demonstrate both their mistake and his correctness.[309] He also exposes what he sees as the interpretative errors concerning the fourteen passages where Jesus is alleged to prophesise his own resurrection.[310] Tolstoy's alternative translation of these various passages can be deduced from his own version of the Gospel – which of course ends with Jesus' last breath on the cross, not with any resurrection.[311] For Tolstoy, then, it is a naïve mistake to believe in future *personal* life; what Jesus teaches instead is that life *as a whole* is eternal; and in fact belief in personal

---

[305] One significant exception to this, from both Eller and Ellul, is discussed in the Conclusion.
[306] Tolstoy, *What I Believe*, 126-127 (also 137).
[307] Tolstoy, *What I Believe*, 127.
[308] Tolstoy, *What I Believe*, 128.
[309] Tolstoy, *What I Believe*, 128.
[310] Tolstoy, *What I Believe*, 130-131.
[311] Tolstoy, "The Gospel in Brief," 231-233, 239-240, 247-248, 263, 284-286, 289, 293-296, 302.

resurrection distracts from the more important ethical teaching articulated by Jesus.[312] Tolstoy clearly does not believe in Jesus' resurrection from the dead.

Myers is a little bit more guarded in his treatment of the subject. In part, that is because his book is an exegesis of Mark's Gospel only, the ending of which is disputed. The consensus today is that the original text ends with three women fleeing the empty tomb, and thus with no narrative of the risen Christ. According to Myers, this confirms that the advent of the Son of man has already happened on the cross, and Mark's abrupt ending is therefore a final call for Jesus' disciples to follow him to the cross.[313]

Nonetheless, Myers does not reject the resurrection altogether: he says he agrees "with those who contend that nothing else can explain the genesis of the Christian movement."[314] For him, however, "We do not entirely understand what 'resurrection' means," and therefore "we should be 'holding fast' to what we *do* know: that Jesus still goes before us, summoning us to the way of the cross."[315] Mark, he says, "*means* to leave us to wrestle" with the "'dilemma' of the ending," and it is a betrayal of the gospel to rewrite it as the added endings of Mark have attempted to do.[316] For Myers, it is essential not to separate Jesus into "earthly Jesus and risen Christ," because there is "only one Jesus, and he is still on the road calling us to discipleship."[317]

Myers, then, is happy to accept the mystery of the resurrection as long as Jesus' revolutionary teaching is not brushed aside. The only other Christian anarchist to *explicitly* acknowledge his belief in the resurrection of the dead *in his Christian anarchist writings* is Chelčický – though he still only mentions it in passing.[318] Other Christian anarchists seem to avoid the mysterious subject altogether. Then again, indirect comments and reflections at times seem to imply belief in the resurrection, but little is offered in exegesis or discussion of the event. The devout Dorothy Day, for instance, appears to believe in it. Ellul's theology also appears to be informed by it, as does Eller's interpretation of history. Yet on the whole, Christian anarchists – certainly in their dedicated Christian anarchist writings – offer very few direct commentaries on the resurrection, preferring instead to focus on the many passages of the New Testament which justify their political interpretation of Christianity. Even those who do discuss it, either with respect (Chelčický, Myers) or with suspicion (Tolstoy), ascribe it almost no significance compared to that of the narratives of Jesus' teaching and examples which precede it.

---

[312] Tolstoy, "The Gospel in Brief," 120-121; Leo Tolstoy, "On Life," in *On Life and Essays on Religion*, trans. Aylmer Maude (London: Oxford University Press, 1934), 71-72, 129-139; Tolstoy, *What I Believe*, 131-141. Besides, says Tolstoy, even if you believe in the resurrection, in hell, paradise and other miracles, "nothing of all this need hinder you at the same time from doing those things which Jesus has ordained for you to your good." Tolstoy, "The Gospel in Brief," 204-205.
[313] Myers, *Binding the Strong Man*, 398-401.
[314] Myers, *Binding the Strong Man*, 447.
[315] Myers, *Binding the Strong Man*, 401 (Myers' emphasis).
[316] Myers, *Binding the Strong Man*, 401 (Myers' emphasis), and 401-404.
[317] Myers, *Binding the Strong Man*, 406.
[318] Molnár, *A Study of Peter Chelčický's Life*, 54.

## 2.13 – Revelation

Before bringing this Chapter to a close, it is worth noting a few brief points about the Book of Revelation. The other Books of New Testament (all between the four Gospels, discussed above, and Revelation) are left out of this Chapter for three reasons: first, they do not report much about Jesus' life and teaching but instead consist largely of commentaries on these; second, and probably for that same reason, Christian anarchists have very little to say on them, except on Paul's (and Peter's) counsel to submit to authorities; and third, those Christian anarchist commentaries on Paul (and Peter) are discussed in detail in Chapter 4, because they concern the question of how Christians should respond to state authorities.

On Revelation, however, Christian anarchists have several short reflections to offer, because as Ellul says, "Throughout the book there is a radical opposition between the majesty of God and the powers and dominions of earth," which, to him, "shows how mistaken are those who find continuity between the divine power and earthly powers, or who argue, as under a monarchy, that a single earthly power ought to correspond to the one almighty God who reigns in heaven."[319] Christian anarchists like Ellul therefore bring out the political nature of the symbolism which abounds in Revelation.

Ellul, for example, reflects on the symbolism of the two beasts.[320] Many exegetes have identified the first beast, which rises from the sea, with Rome, but Ellul insists that this "must be universalised" to what Rome represents.[321] Hence he identifies it with the state or political power:

> It has a throne that is given to it by the dragon (chs. 12-13). The dragon, anti-God, has given all authority to the beast. People worship it. They ask who can fight against it. It is given 'all authority and power over every tribe, every people, every tongue, and every nation' (13:7). All who dwell on it worship it. Political power could hardly, I think, be more expressly described, for it is this power which has authority, which controls military force, and which compels adoration (i.e., absolute obedience).[322]

To Ellul, this also further confirms the connection between the state and the devil noted when discussing Jesus' third temptation. The beast from the sea thus represents state sovereignty. As to the second beast, which rises from the earth, Ellul identifies it with political propaganda, and cites the verses that describe it as almost self-evident descriptions of "propaganda in association with the police."[323] Taken together, Ellul therefore explains, the two beasts which defy God thus represent two aspects of political power.

---

[319] Ellul, *Anarchy and Christianity*, 71.
[320] Ellul, "Anarchism and Christianity," 169; Ellul, *Anarchy and Christianity*, 71-73. (Revelation 13.)
[321] Goddard, *Living the Word, Resisting the World*, 283.
[322] Ellul, *Anarchy and Christianity*, 72.
[323] He writes: "It is described as follows. 'It makes all the inhabitants of the earth worship the first beast. ... It seduces the inhabitants of the earth. It tells them to make an image of the first beast. ... It animates the image of the beast and speaks in its name. ... It causes all, small and great, rich and poor, free and slave, to receive a mark on their right hand or on their forehead, so that no one can buy or sell without having the mark of the beast' (13:12-17). For my part, I find here an exact description of propaganda in association with the police. The beast makes speeches which induce people to obey the state, to worship it. It gives them the mark that enables them to live in society. Finally, those that will not obey the first beast are put to death." Ellul, *Anarchy and Christianity*, 72-73.

Other symbols of political power which Ellul points to include the red horseman with the sword, "whose only function is making war, exercising power, and causing human beings to perish," and of course Babylon, "the focus of political power."[324] Babylon, he repeats, does not only represent Rome (as is often presumed), because "it is clear in the text that Rome is equated with supreme political power."[325] Hence with the fall of Babylon, writes Ellul, "What is promised is the pure and simple destruction of political government: Rome, to be sure, yet not Rome alone, but power and domination in every form. These things are specifically stated as enemies of God. God judges political power, calling it the great harlot."[326] For Ellul, therefore, Revelation is loaded with political meaning and confirms the incommensurability of the state and true Christianity.

Moreover, several Christian anarchists and pacifists (namely Yoder, Wink, Penner, Ellul and Elliott) note that the Book also reiterates a difficult message to Christians, who are "portrayed as those who disobey the dictates of the state when its commands abrogate the commandments of God even though their lives are endangered by this disobedience."[327] The Book warns these "true believers" that the powers will persecute them as a result;[328] it warns that their loyalty will be tested "by their willingness to perform the ritual of the state religion;"[329] and it warns that the great harlot will be "drunk with the blood of saints and with the blood of witnesses to Jesus."[330] Yet the true believers – the saints – "are pictured as resting their case with God, [...] patiently waiting for the vengeance and righteous wrath of God."[331] That is, the "horrible, yet I am afraid, absolutely accurate vision," as Wink puts it, is that of the persecuted saints, who are pleading with God and asking how much longer they must endure this terrible persecution, being encouraged in response to patiently wait a little longer, to continue to endure and forgive, to patiently put up with the cross a little longer.[332]

According to Elliott, therefore, Revelation "was composed [...] as a resource manual for persecuted Christians" and "calls God's judgement down upon those who co-operate with the civil authority."[333] For Redford, it is also a warning that the Antichrist "will come to strengthen and empower government during the last days," and a reminder that "the coming of God's true Christ [...] is to be the exact opposite," that Jesus Christ will return "to abolish and utterly annihilate all the governments of the world."[334] In the end, according to Revelation, Jesus will destroy the "kings of the earth."[335] To Redford, therefore,

---

[324] Ellul, "Anarchism and Christianity," 169. (Revelation 6:3-4, 17-18.)
[325] Ellul, *Anarchy and Christianity*, 73 (see also 74).
[326] Ellul, *Anarchy and Christianity*, 74.
[327] Penner, *The New Testament, the Christian, and the State*, 116. (Revelation 13:17, 14:9-12.)
[328] Yoder, *The Politics of Jesus*, 196.
[329] W. M. Ramsay, quoted in Penner, *The New Testament, the Christian, and the State*, 115. (Revelation 2:12-17.)
[330] Ellul is here quoting Revelation 17:6 (and 18:24). Ellul, *Anarchy and Christianity*, 74.
[331] Penner, *The New Testament, the Christian, and the State*, 116. (Revelation 6:10-11.)
[332] Wink, *Jesus' Third Way*, 70. (Revelation 6:10-11.)
[333] Elliott, *Freedom, Justice and Christian Counter-Culture*, 78.
[334] Redford, *Jesus Is an Anarchist*, 53. (Revelation 16:14; 17:2, 9-18; 18:3, 9; 19:19; 20:4.)
[335] Redford, *Jesus Is an Anarchist*, 56.

The Book of Revelation only further confirms that "There can be no honest doubt: Jesus is an anarchist!"[336]

## 2.14 – Allegedly violent passages

In this Chapter, are reported only the commentaries on Bible passages other than the Sermon on the Mount which are made by Christian anarchists. The four Gospels – not to speak of the New Testament or even the whole Bible – are rich enough to include many other episodes which arguably have a bearing upon the political implications of Christianity. Those on which Christian anarchists have commented and which have not been discussed yet are addressed further down, as for instance the tax questions in Chapter 4. The rest, however, must be left aside here due to the limited purpose of this book – to weave together the loose threads of Christian anarchist thought.

Having said that, since Jesus' rejection of violence is so central to Christian anarchism, it might worth briefly mentioning the passing comments made by Christian anarchists on those Gospel passages which seem to imply the contrary. The task, however, is made relatively brief by the small number of these Gospel passages alleged to betray a violent Jesus.

The most typical example claimed to provide a justification of violence has already been discussed above: the temple cleansing, for Christian anarchists, is less an example of violence than one of righteous condemnation of an abuse of religious and political power. Besides, any violence used has as sole purpose the casting out of animals, and is anyway never directed at human beings.

The Christian anarchist view of the intriguing instruction to buy a sword, given by Jesus to his disciples just before his arrest, has also been discussed already. The two swords which Jesus says are "enough," to Christian anarchists, could never have been "enough" for violent defence, and must thus have had an altogether different use than violence – perhaps the cutting of meat in preparation for Passover or the deliberate fulfilment of scripture. Moreover, Jesus' famous saying about swords upon his arrest would seem to cancel out any violent implications of the preceding request to buy one.

Jesus also says, in Matthew: "Think not that I am come to send peace on earth: I came not to send peace, but a sword;" and in Luke: "Suppose ye that I am come to give peace on earth? I tell you, Nay; but rather division."[337] In both cases, the speech continues with Jesus warning that households will be divided about him, and in Matthew, he repeats that to be "worthy" of him, his followers must take up their cross. Ellul is the only Christian anarchist to comment on this passage, and just as all the other violent passages in the Bible, he considers it to be once again about "contention" not "against flesh and blood, but against the powers."[338] For Ellul, it does not legitimise physical violence.

---

[336] Redford, *Jesus Is an Anarchist*, 56.
[337] Matthew 10:34-39; Luke 12:49-53.
[338] Ellul, *Violence*, 161.

2 – Jesus' Other Teachings and Example                                          105

Moreover, even though he never comments on it directly, Tolstoy does relay a revealing version of the two passages in his harmonised translation of the Gospel:
> Not everyone will believe in my teaching. And those who do not believe will hate it because it deprives them of what they love. So dissentions will come from my teaching. It will kindle the world like a fire, and from it strife must arise. There will be dissentions in every house, father against son, mother against daughter. Families will hate those members who understand my teaching, and will kill them. For to him who understands my teaching there will be no meaning in "father," or "mother," or "wife," or "children."[339]

What Tolstoy is thereby suggesting is that Jesus is warning about the division which his teaching will cause among men and women, and about the difficulty of following him to the cross because of the rejection by society and by family members which will result. Jesus is not legitimising or advocating violence, but predicting it, warning that his teaching will stir passions. The passage therefore does not contradict the Christian anarchist reading, but simply forewarns that Jesus' teaching is bound to cause contention and disagreements. Christianity's anarchism will agitate society.

Another passage where Jesus' is said to display violence is when he curses the fig tree for not bearing fruit even though it is not the right season.[340] Myers' exegesis of this passage, which borrows heavily from William Telford, is interesting and convincing, and more importantly corroborates the Christian anarchist perspective. He explains that the barren fig tree "would have been recognized as a metaphor for the temple-based nation and its cultus."[341] He shows how established such a metaphor for the fig tree is, and relates the whole episode to the cleansing of the temple which is actually adjoined to the cursing of the tree. Thus the consequent drying up of the tree's roots is, for Myers, God's judgement of the temple state. Jesus' cursing is a condemnation of this state, but not a condemnation which warrants violence against fellow human beings. The same logic applies to Jesus' frequent and strong denunciation of scribes and Pharisees.

The most famous and debated passages claimed to betray a violent Jesus have thus been looked at from a Christian anarchist perspective. Those believing Jesus to advocate violence usually cite further and relatively less famous passages to validate their views, but these cannot be discussed here because of both lack of space and *lack of comment on them by Christian anarchists*.[342] On the whole, though, the arguments are based on the view that

---

[339] Tolstoy, "The Gospel in Brief," 184.
[340] Mark 11:11-26 (where it frames the Temple cleansing); Matthew 21:17-22 (where it follows it).
[341] Myers, *Binding the Strong Man*, 297.
[342] The "parable of the great feast" (Luke 14:15-24), for instance, is said to show that violence can be used to coerce people to join the church; but a Christian anarchist exegesis would probably emphasise that this remains only a parable and thus presumably carries less weight the direct instructions such as in the Sermon on the Mount. Supporters of a violent Jesus also mention Jesus' support for the amputation of limbs that offend God (Matthew 5:29-30); though the violence is only to be used upon oneself, not others. Others point to the harsh punishments at the Last Judgement which Jesus repeatedly warns about (for instance, Matthew 8:10-12, 10:12-15, 11:20-24); but these punishments are meted by God, not humans, and such harsh language is typical in prophetic warnings (see for example the Book of Revelation). Again, though, Christian anarchists never really discuss interpretations of these passages.

Jesus himself was sometimes violent, not that he explicitly instructed his followers to be violent – yet according to Craig, even though God is indeed perhaps violent and vengeful, the same God still orders him to nevertheless be loving and non-violent.[343]

On balance, however, the vast majority of Christian anarchists believe Jesus to be strictly against any use of violence: that is what his most explicit and direct instructions are about, and proponents of a violent Jesus find themselves relying on relatively minor, indirect and allegorical passages to justify their view. The vast majority of Christian anarchists also disagree that Jesus himself was ever violent, and point to his non-violent acceptance of his arrest, trial and crucifixion as the most powerful exemplification of this. For Christian anarchists, Jesus clearly teaches and embodies love, non-violence and non-resistance, and the state is unchristian precisely because it directly contravenes this teaching.

## 2.15 – Jesus' anarchist teaching and example

Christian anarchists therefore understand Jesus' teaching, and his exemplification of it in his life and death, to amount to both a critique of the state and a vision of a stateless society. They ground their perspective not just in the Sermon on the Mount, but also in numerous other passages in the four Gospels. They even believe that the Old Testament further confirms their view – especially the Book of Samuel. They highlight the political expectations which were inseparable from the long-awaited messiah, and they explain the way in which Jesus' actions force a radical and subversive reinterpretation of the mission of this political liberator. They cite all the passages in which Jesus teaches about forgiveness, service and non-judgement, and they contrast these to state theory and practice. They bring out every instance of Jesus' constant struggle against Satan and the powers, and expose the anarchist significance of Jesus' arrest, trial and crucifixion. In short, as demonstrated in detail in Chapters 1 and 2, they derive their anarchist interpretation from countless instructions explicitly formulated by Jesus, as well as from the way in which he himself exemplified his anarchist teaching in his life and (not least) in his death.

Chapters 1 and 2 thus articulate one of the two major strands of the Christian anarchist critique of the state. The other strand is not so much grounded in scripture. It emerges from Christian anarchism's understanding of the evolution of state and church since Jesus, and its consequent criticism of state and church today. As it amounts to another line of criticism of the state, it needs to be discussed in this Part of the book. Yet whereas the criticism of the state which is outlined in Chapter 1 and 2 begins with *scripture* and then contrasts it to the state, this different criticism begins by analysing state and church *practice* in order to then contrast it to the Christian society envisioned by Jesus. This different line of argument is examined in the next Chapter.

---

[343] [Anonymous], *Why I Worship a Violent, Vengeful God*.

# Chapter 3 – The State's Wickedness and the Church's Infidelity

If Jesus' teaching is as politically radical as Christian anarchists understand it to be, one might wonder why it is not clearly affirmed as so by more Christians. For Christian anarchists, the reason that their reading sounds so new can be surmised from the historical evolution of church teaching and practice. They believe that the church compromised Jesus' teaching in order to sanction the state and derive benefits thereby, to the point that contemporary state violence, which should be denounced by the church, is instead approved of and defended as fully compatible with Christian doctrine.

The aim of this Chapter is to tease out this critique of church and state mounted by Christian anarchists, by outlining their understanding of the historical evolution of church and state since the days of Jesus, by fleshing out the details of their description of the state as violent and thus unchristian, and by going over the main reasons for which many of them express sometimes deep antipathy for the official church. Hence this Chapter outlines the Christian anarchist diagnosis of contemporary Christian societies – why they believe it to be unhealthy, unfair and unchristian. Unlike the previous two Chapters which focus on analysing Bible verses in order to then contrast them to the state, this Chapter focuses on describing state and church theory and practice in order to expose the contrast between these and the teaching articulated by Jesus. The first two Chapters examined the Bible; this one examines the history of church and state.

It should be noted that Christian anarchists' criticisms of church and state are numerous and varied, and that therefore many of these can only be noted here fairly briefly, without exploring all the details of their full argumentation. Their reasoning is sometimes summarised in the footnotes, which anyway always point to the passages in Christian anarchist literature where these criticisms and further elaboration of these can be found.

The first section of this Chapter introduces the Christian anarchist account of the early church's compromise with state power around the time of Constantine, and briefly describes the Christian anarchist opinion of Christendom. The second section begins with a few remarks on the historical emergence of the modern state, goes on to describe the Christian anarchist verdict on its violence, its deceitfulness, and its economic exploitation of the poor, and concludes by portraying the modern reverence for the state as a form of idolatry. The third section outlines the church's arguments in support of state authority which Christian anarchists identify and reject: its misleading reinterpretations of the commandments given by Jesus in the Sermon on the Mount, especially non-resistance to evil, and some of its other legitimisations of state authority. The fourth section summarises many Christian anarchists' deep suspicion of church dogmas: their mockery of the church's claim to authority over truth, their dislike of what, to them, are obscure dogmas and rituals which hide the essence of Jesus' teaching, and their general unease with institutional religion. The Chapter then concludes with the Christian anarchist call for humanity to awaken to true Christianity.

## 3.1 – The history of Christendom

When looking at the history of Christianity, Christian anarchists make one set of comments on the early church and what became of it, and another on the excesses of Christendom since the fourth century establishment of Christianity as the state religion. These are now analysed in turn.

### 3.1.1 – Constantine's temptation of the early church

As further explained in Chapter 6, Christian anarchists understand the early church (to the extent that a good picture of it can be drawn today despite our limited knowledge of it) or (perhaps more appropriately, although Christian anarchists themselves rarely use the plural) the early church*es* to have faithfully strived to apply Jesus' subversive political teaching, at least in the beginning. The early church was a "political community," writes Bartley, and the martyrdom of its saints was often a "political act" which "bore witness to their citizenship of another kingdom" and "was a statement of opposition to the state and its idolatry, violence and injustice."[1]

Gradually, however, Jesus' radical teaching was compromised, especially over the question of military service. Penner explains that for a century and a half, there was hardly any debate on the question, which suggests that the "baptized Christian simply did not become a soldier."[2] The debate intensified after around 170 AD, by which time, perhaps in part as a result of persecution, a number of "Christians" had joined the army and participated in other affairs of the state.[3] Many objected to this within the church, but the consequence was only a growing variety of dissenting factions within the church. Either way, by the end of the second century, significant sections of the Christian church had developed a more sympathetic approach to the affairs of the state.[4]

The more abrupt and symbolic change, however, came with Constantine, Roman emperor from 306 to 327 AD, who called a halt to persecutions of Christians, issued the Edict of Milan which mandated toleration of Christianity, and paved the way for Christianity to become the established state religion later that century. For Christian anarchists, if Constantine had to do this, it was because Christianity had become too "powerful" a "popular mass movement,"[5] because the "Christian truth" was therefore politically "dangerous,"[6]

---

[1] Bartley, *Faith and Politics after Christendom*, 18, 25.
[2] Adolf Harnack, quoted in Penner, *The New Testament, the Christian, and the State*, 24.
[3] Penner, *The New Testament, the Christian, and the State*, 26.
[4] Bartley, *Faith and Politics after Christendom*, 30; Penner, *The New Testament, the Christian, and the State*, 26-27.
[5] Elliott, *Freedom, Justice and Christian Counter-Culture*, 86.
[6] Berdyaev, *The Realm of the Spirit and the Realm of Caesar*, 21.

and because adopting and distorting Christianity could help him unite the fragmented Roman Empire.[7]

Andrews contends that Constantine tempted the clergy by exempting it from certain taxes and army duties, and by promising to silence the more defiant voices within the church using the powers of the state to enforce "unanimous acceptance of the Nicene creed."[8] According to the myth of the "Donation of Constantine" which Chelčický vehemently criticises, Constantine allegedly donated land to Pope Sylvester I and bequeathed Rome to the Holy Roman Church.[9] That is, Constantine tempted the church with political power and economic comfort. The higher clergy was seduced: to borrow Alexis-Baker's words, the church said "'Yes' to the very temptation that Jesus denies."[10] Tempted by Constantine, the church opted for the very political power which Jesus rejects in the wilderness temptations.

Of course, for the church to move from being politically subversive to being more favourable to political powers, significant revisions to Christian theology would be required. To some extent, as already mentioned, this had begun before Constantine.[11] But these revisions accelerated: Penner notes that efforts now focused on arguing for the compatibility of war with the gospels, and that "Athanasius, Ambrose, and Augustine were the *first* Christian theologians to try" to do so.[12] For Christian anarchists, Augustine was particularly important: "If Constantine laid the foundations of Christendom," writes Bartley, "its principal architect was Augustine."[13] He played a central role in revising Christian theology to accommodate an alliance of throne and altar. This essential and detrimental contribution by Augustine and other theologians is further explored later in this Chapter.

The point here is that for most Christian anarchists, the reforms ushered by Constantine were pivotal in the transformation of the church from a subversive anarchist threat to a collaborator with the state. Andrews claims that under Constantine, "Christ, who had turned the Roman empire upside down, was turned into a lap-dog for the Roman emperor."[14] As Tolstoy puts it, "they arranged a Christianity for him."[15] Constantine's empire, Eller explains, could now "become 'Christian' without having to make any changes at all; Christianity had done all the changing."[16] For Tolstoy, this betrayal of Jesus which thereby saw the church become a "tangible fraud" was then sealed by the Council of Nicaea – convened by Constantine.[17]

---

[7] Andrews, *Christi-Anarchy*, 26; Berdyaev, *The Realm of the Spirit and the Realm of Caesar*, 21.
[8] Andrews, *Christi-Anarchy*, 26.
[9] Molnár explains that in Chelčický's times, the "papal theocracy based its whole legal justification on" this alleged Donation, the authenticity of which Chelčický does not seem to doubt, but the validity of which he criticises "on ethical and Biblical grounds." Molnár, *A Study of Peter Chelčický's Life*, 27, 29.
[10] Alexis-Baker, "Embracing God, Rejecting Masters," 2.
[11] Tolstoy, "The Kingdom of God Is within You," 62.
[12] Penner, *The New Testament, the Christian, and the State*, 27-28 (Penner's emphasis).
[13] Bartley, *Faith and Politics after Christendom*, 33.
[14] Andrews, *Christi-Anarchy*, 70.
[15] Tolstoy, "Church and State," 339.
[16] Eller, *Christian Anarchy*, 23.
[17] Tolstoy, "Church and State," 337-343 (the actual expression is quoted from page 342).

Thereafter Christianity, which Andrews says had begun "as a voluntary, non-violent movement," quickly "became a fierce reactionary force" which "ferociously suppressed political dissent."[18] Moreover, O'Reilly writes, "The church as an intentional community disappeared as it became a civil obligation to be a christian."[19] Bartley agrees: Christianity became associated with territory rather than "faith and commitment."[20] From now on, as Berdyaev explains, "the Empire became Christian," and "the Church became imperial" – which, he notes, "should have produced a revolutionary uprising."[21] It did not, and as Penner remarks, the only two other alternatives for true Christians were "Monasticism and the sectarian churches."[22] In the meantime, "To become a 'Christian' soon became the only religiously honourable thing to do."[23] Imperial Christianity spread among the Roman middle classes and other similarly "ungodly persons,"[24] resulting in even further compromises with state power.[25] Those who disagreed with these trends were persecuted, judged and condemned as heretics.

Through the Edict of Milan and the Council of Nicaea, therefore, Constantine inaugurated the alliance of throne and altar that has carried the day for nearly two millennia – even though as O'Reilly remarks, "there have always been groups (large and small) who have refused to burn incense for Caesar."[26] Thus for Christian anarchists like Chelčický, "the Constantinian merger of church and state marked the fall of the church."[27] Constantine's reign marks this fall in history – which is why Tolstoy refers to Constantine as "that canonized scoundrel."[28]

Chelčický depicts this important moment in Christian history through a unique interpretation of the Gospel story of the miraculous inclusion of fishes.[29] This interpretation forms the backbone of *The Net of Faith*, the book which according to Molnár summarises Chelčický's "whole philosophy of life and history" by examining the relation of church and state and the expected response of the true Christian to it.[30] It is worth relaying Chelčický's illustration, which Wagner summarises as follows:

> The net of faith is the law of God, bound together in the faithfulness of those believers loyal to the disciplined life of the early church. Out of the sea of the world, the net hauls in God's elect. But the net has taken in more than ordinary fish. Its binding in the law of God has been ripped through by two

---

[18] Andrews, *Christi-Anarchy*, 26.
[19] O'Reilly, "The Anarchist Implications of Christian Discipleship," 10.
[20] Bartley, *Faith and Politics after Christendom*, 34.
[21] Berdyaev, *The Realm of the Spirit and the Realm of Caesar*, 74.
[22] Penner, *The New Testament, the Christian, and the State*, 28.
[23] Penner, *The New Testament, the Christian, and the State*, 27.
[24] Molnár, *A Study of Peter Chelčický's Life*, 57 (quoting Chelčický).
[25] Elliott, *Freedom, Justice and Christian Counter-Culture*, 173.
[26] O'Reilly, "The Anarchist Implications of Christian Discipleship," 10.
[27] Brock, *The Political and Social Doctrines*, 45; Wagner, *Petr Chelčický*, 96.
[28] That expression is reported by Sampson, but without full reference details, in Sampson, *Tolstoy*, 171.
[29] The story can be found in Luke 5:4-11. Molnár, *A Study of Peter Chelčický's Life*, 25, 33, 49-57 (for the actual interpretation of the passage; Wagner, *Petr Chelčický*, 132-137.
[30] Molnár, *A Study of Peter Chelčický's Life*, 25.

huge predators, the pope and the emperor. [...] The two vicious intruders have thrashed around in the net, venting hostility toward God's ordinances. The net of faith is now so mangled that there remain only the barely visible shreds of the apostle's original net, the primitive church.[31]

Chelčický writes that even though the early churches "remained faithful" to Jesus' teaching "for over three hundred years, [...] the net became greatly torn, when the two great whales had entered it."[32] These two "fat and gluttonous Baals,"[33] as Chelčický calls them, compromised the "law of Christ" by adding "two other laws [...], namely the temporal and the papal law," an addition which led to the immediate deterioration of "the Christian society."[34]

Just like other Christian anarchists, Chelčický argues that instead of reforming the empire to conform to Christianity, Christianity was reformed to conform to the empire and its "laws, offices, courts," and other forms of unchristian violence and coercion, not least war.[35] In other words, instead of giving their trust to and seeking help from God alone, Christians began to give their trust to and seek help from the emperor. Chelčický notes the parallels with the episode from the Book of Samuel examined in Chapter 2, and comments that "whenever man gives preference to human institutions and statutes rather than to the law of God, he chooses for himself other and foreign gods."[36] For Chelčický, therefore, the net of true faith in God alone was rent by Constantine and Sylvester, and the church committed the twin sin of idolatry and betrayal of Jesus' teaching in allying herself "with the state and with the secular methods of power, institutionalism, and coercion."[37]

Perhaps the most immediately visible sign of this fall of Christianity was the adoption of the cross, the ultimate symbol of Jesus' loving sacrifice, by the Roman army. As Tolstoy explains, the state's conquest of the true church was soon complete: "Under Constantine the cross had already appeared on the standard of the Roman Legions. In 416 a decree was issued forbidding pagans to join the army. All the soldiers became Christians: that is, all the Christians, with only a few exceptions, renounced Christ."[38] Soon after that, Andrews writes, "a law was promulgated which threatened any 'heretic' that was discovered in the empire with death," so that "from then on, when it came to the matter of religion, the people in the empire had no choice."[39] What Constantine had started was completed hardly a century later. Rome had successfully corrupted and overcome the threat posed by Christianity's anarchist subversion. Faced by Christianity's growing political force, the Roman state had nominally adopted it and perverted it with the complicity of church elites, tempted as they were by a combination of material comforts and perhaps naïve expectations that by acceding to political power, they might be able to hasten the kingdom of God on earth (a theme further

---

[31] Wagner, *Petr Chelčický*, 132.
[32] Molnár, *A Study of Peter Chelčický's Life*, 68, 73 (quoting Chelčický).
[33] Chelčický, quoted in Wagner, *Petr Chelčický*, 137.
[34] Molnár, *A Study of Peter Chelčický's Life*, 67 (quoting Chelčický).
[35] Molnár, *A Study of Peter Chelčický's Life*, 73-90 (84 for Chelčický's quoted words).
[36] Molnár, *A Study of Peter Chelčický's Life*, 86 (quoting Chelčický).
[37] Molnár, *A Study of Peter Chelčický's Life*, 35.
[38] Tolstoy, "The Law of Love and the Law of Violence," 190.
[39] Andrews, *Christi-Anarchy*, 27.

discussed in the Conclusion). Thus began, for Christian anarchists, the Dark Ages of Christendom.

### 3.1.2 – Christendom and beyond

Christian anarchists see in Christian history since Constantine both the repressive reign of a perverted version of Christianity and examples of resistance by radical thinkers and sects.

On the dark side, Andrews argues that Christian elites, under the Holy Roman Empire, "slowly but surely, took control of the state."[40] During the Middle Ages, the church extended its jurisdiction even further by regularly expanding the scope of canon law; and with the brutal European colonisation of the globe, the church extended its geographical sphere of influence to much of the known world.[41] Throughout this period, Penner therefore comments, "the state was an instrument in the hands of the [fallen] church."[42] The church used the coercive tools of the state, for instance to launch the Crusades, to establish the Inquisition, and to hunt and slaughter rebellious heretics and quell political insurrections. For Christian anarchists, therefore, medieval Christianity was false, violent and vindictive.

Still, Christian anarchists take heart that now and again, dissenting voices expressing what they see as a truer Christianity could be heard, especially during the years of the Reformation. Given that Christian anarchists frequently tend to see them as examples of Christian anarchism, these voices are considered later, in Chapter 6. Here, however, suffice it to note that unfortunately, many of these Christian dissenters did tend to increasingly give in to violence, even sometimes to compromise with the state – thereby losing, from the Christian anarchist perspective, the Christian credentials with which they may have begun.

As discussed in the next section, the Reformation, modernity and the Enlightenment brought about a reconfiguration of church-state relations. Yet for Christian anarchists, even though the church lost much of the state power it had appropriated itself during the Middle Ages, it has nonetheless continued to behave in ways incompatible with Jesus' radical political teaching.[43] Andrews cites the role of the church in the anti-Semitism that fed the Jewish Holocaust, but also the more recent church support for repressive regimes in Latin America.[44] For him, the church is often guilty of disregard for human rights and has a far from innocent hand in "the worst cases of genocide in the twentieth century."[45]

Hence for Christian anarchists like Andrews, "the history of Christianity is as much a litany of cruelty as it is a legacy of charity."[46] These acts of cruelty confront Christians, he adds, and they cannot be discounted too

---

[40] Andrews, *Christi-Anarchy*, 29.
[41] Andrews, *Christi-Anarchy*, 32-35.
[42] Penner, *The New Testament, the Christian, and the State*, 29.
[43] One example often denounced by Maurin is Calvin's legalisation of money-lending at interest, against the teachings of the prophets and the Church Fathers. Maurin, *Easy Essays (2003)*, 78-83 (see also 199).
[44] Andrews, *Christi-Anarchy*, 39-46.
[45] Andrews, *Christi-Anarchy*, 10.
[46] Andrews, *Christi-Anarchy*, 25.

easily.[47] "To the victims" of the violence committed in the name of Christianity, Andrews warns, "Christianity is the Antichrist."[48] It is therefore important to distinguish the wheat from the chaff, the true acts of authentic Christian witness from the violence disloyally committed, supported or implicitly tolerated by the church since Constantine. This Chapter has already cited examples of violence committed by the church; the rest of it exposes state violence and the arguments through which the church has justified its support for and participation in it.

## 3.2 – The modern state and economy

After a brief subsection discussing what Christian anarchists mean by the state, this section summarises Christian anarchism's diagnosis of the modern state: the way in which it perpetuates violence, deception and economic exploitation, and the extent to which unquestioned veneration of it amounts to idolatry.

Because he is by far the most prolific Christian anarchist writer on the subject, Tolstoy figures prominently in this section, and much of what is reported here can also be found in my article for *Anarchist Studies* on Tolstoy's criticisms of the state.[49] Apart from reorganising the argument slightly, the main difference between this section and that article is the inclusion of other Christian anarchists' criticisms when appropriate.

### 3.2.1 – The "state"

As the purpose of this section is to explore Christian anarchist criticisms of "the state," it is worth conceding from the outset that Christian anarchists tend to use words like "state" and "government" somewhat interchangeably. Indeed, as Kinna notes in the first pages of her chapter on anarchist rejections of the state, all anarchists have been accused of not differentiating clearly enough between terms like "state," "government," "power" and "authority," thus making it near impossible to settle on final and universal definitions for these.[50] *Christian* anarchists tend to use the first two terms more frequently that the last two, but a closer look at Kinna's proposed definitions shows that they sometimes also have in mind what other anarchists mean by "power" and "authority."

Kinna delineates the difference between the three "abstract concepts" associated with the state as follows: "By government, anarchists tend to think of a particular system of rule, based on violence. In authority they consider the social relationships sustained by this system, and in power they consider the means by which government secures its authority."[51] She then reviews anarchist rejections of each of these "concepts" of the state.

---

[47] Andrews, *Christi-Anarchy*, 46-47.
[48] Andrews, *Christi-Anarchy*, 61 (emphasis removed).
[49] Alexandre J. M. E. Christoyannopoulos, "Leo Tolstoy on the State: A Detailed Picture of Tolstoy's Denunciation of State Violence and Deception," *Anarchist Studies* 16/1 (2008).
[50] Kinna, *Anarchism*, 45-46.
[51] Kinna, *Anarchism*, 46.

Since they categorically reject the use of violence, Christian anarchists are particularly denunciatory of the state as "government:" like other anarchists, they see government as "rule by the use of physical force" through a mix of both deception and tangible coercion;[52] and like other anarchists, they also detect government violence in state-endorsed economic inequalities and in interstate relations.[53] Christian anarchists also denounce the state as "authority," though only really in the sense of it being morally corrupting by encouraging a type of hypnotic hypocrisy through the reproduction of social roles that obscure the violence of the system.[54] And just like other anarchists, Christian anarchists reject state "power" as discernible in its legal institutions, in the army and in the patriotism that legitimises it.[55]

In the subsections that follow, each of these criticisms is explored in more detail, though the emphasis is placed predominantly on what Kinna discusses as "government." Criticisms of state "authority" and "power" are also mentioned, but only as aspects of the state as "government." This reflects both the main focus of Christian anarchist criticism of the state as violent and the general inconsistency in the choice of terms across the Christian anarchist literature. In light of this inconsistency, and despite this short discussion of definitions, no clear and final definition of terms can be offered here. Suffices to note that the main thrust of the Christian anarchist criticism of the state is directed at its use of violence, deception and economic exploitation, and that in that sense, the concept of "government" delineated by Kinna better captures what Christian anarchists mean by "the state" than "authority" or "power." In any case, as already noted, Christian anarchists often use "government" and "state" as seemingly perfectly interchangeable terms.

Another difficulty raised by the word "state" is that it is a modern word; it was hardly used before the Renaissance. Indeed, the administrative colossus today known as "the state" only really took shape since the Reformation. Nevertheless, in the sense of human beings given or ascribing to themselves the power to legislate and to use violence to enforce such legislation, the "state" did exist long before Jesus. In that sense of the word, one can indeed speak of Jesus' teaching as implying a denunciation of the "state." Still, as the rest of this section illustrates, what Christian anarchists have in mind when they criticise the state is very much the modern state or nation-state.

A very interesting account of the rise of this modern state out of the Reformation and the ensuing "Wars of Religion" is provided by Cavanaugh,

---

[52] Kinna, *Anarchism*, 46.
[53] Kinna, *Anarchism*, 49-52.
[54] Kinna reviews three aspects of authority which anarchists reject: authority as commanding, as controlling and as corrupting. Christian anarchists say very little about the first two. Kinna, *Anarchism*, 53-58. Later in her chapter (pages 69-72) Kinna argues that anarchists do not reject all forms of authority, and she explains this by discussing the distinctions between being *in* authority and being *an* authority, and between natural and artificial authority. Like other anarchists, Christian anarchists are adamant that no human being should have artificial powers of coercion, but of course, they do take the word of God as authoritative even though some of them (Tolstoy, for instance) only do so because they think it is purely rational. Hence while Christian anarchists very much share other anarchists' concerns about human authority, some do ascribe some form of divine authority to Jesus' teaching which other anarchists would frown upon.
[55] Kinna, *Anarchism*, 58-62.

whose analysis is openly influenced by Tilly.[56] Cavanaugh contends that to call the wars out of which the modern liberal state emerged "Wars of Religion" is "an anachronism, for what was at issue in these wars was the very creation of religion as a set of privately held beliefs without direct political relevance."[57] He further contends that these wars "were not the events which necessitated the birth of the modern State" as a sort of "scolding schoolteacher on the playground of doctrinal dispute to put fanatical religionists in their proper place," but that these wars "were in fact themselves the birthpangs of the State."[58]

For Cavanaugh, at stake in the "Wars of Religion" that animated the Reformation were both the privatisation of religion and the nascent state's overpowering of the church as the highest political legislator and administrator. European monarchs wanted to reclaim the political power that the church had appropriated itself during the Middle Ages, a move which required the domestication of the church and the separation of religion from the public and political sphere. The pivotal victory for the emerging state over the church came with the 1648 Treaty of Westphalia, after which, fuelled by war and the spread of nationalism, the state's centralisation of its administrative power and extension of its monopoly over the legitimate use of violence accelerated with little opposition.[59]

The evolution of the state towards its modern manifestation was thus precipitated by the outcome of the Reformation.[60] From the days of Constantine onwards, monarchs and bishops had competed for ultimate political supremacy; the monarchs came out of the Middle Ages as winners. Since then, "the state" gradually developed to become the modern phenomenon captured by the contemporary word to describe it.

Yet the Christian anarchist criticism of the state is not limited to this modern construct: accusations of violence, deception, exploitation as well as human idolatry in many cases echo back way before the word "state" was first coined. These accusations must now be examined in turn, starting with that of state violence.

## 3.2.2 – *State violence*

As already mentioned several times and in particular when discussing the anarchist implications of non-resistance in Chapter 1, Christian anarchists accuse the state of being violent in a number of ways. War is one obvious example, but

---

[56] Cavanaugh, "A Fire Strong Enough to Consume the House."; William T. Cavanaugh, "Killing for the Telephone Company: Why the Nation-State Is Not the Keeper of the Common Good," *Modern Theology* 20/2 (2004); Charles Tilly, "War Making and State Making as Organized Crime," in *Bringing the State Back In*, ed. Peter Evans, Dietrich Rueschemeyer, and Theda Skocpol (Cambridge: Cambridge University Press, 1985).
[57] Cavanaugh, "A Fire Strong Enough to Consume the House," 398.
[58] Cavanaugh, "A Fire Strong Enough to Consume the House," 398 (408 for the middle quote).
[59] For Cavanaugh's view of this process, see Cavanaugh, "A Fire Strong Enough to Consume the House."; Cavanaugh, "Killing for the Telephone Company."; Cavanaugh, *Torture and Eucharist*, 5, 9, 191-197, 216-221.
[60] For how this process has already begun during the Middle Ages, see Cavanaugh, "Killing for the Telephone Company," 246-250; Tilly, "War Making and State Making as Organized Crime."

the state also uses violence and the threat of violence against its own population. Tolstoy hints that this is inevitable: any state activity, some see as good, others as less so, and therefore since some will always disagree, some degree of violence or compulsion will always be required to carry out any state activity.[61] Inevitably, therefore, all states exercise violence and intimidation. No state could act otherwise.

Moreover, for Tolstoy, "the essence of legislation is organised violence."[62] He disagrees with the view that "legislation is the expression of the will of the people."[63] For him, legislation merely expresses the will of those in power, obedience to which can only be achieved by the threat of violent punishment. As a result, Tolstoy's "exact and irrefutable definition of legislation, intelligible to all, is that: Laws are rules, made by people who govern by means of organised violence for non-compliance with which the non-complier is subjected to blows, to loss of liberty, or even to being murdered."[64] Tolstoy is therefore adamant that legislation amounts to slavery. Moreover, by definition, no legislative fix can truly eradicate this slavery – only the abolition of human laws can.

Furthermore, scientific progress only makes things worse. In Tolstoy's words, "every victory over Nature will inevitably serve only to increase" the governing minority's "power" over and "oppression" of the majority.[65] Tolstoy twice quotes Herzen's remark that governments have become "Genghis-Khans with telegraphs" – a technological invention that has now of course been far surpassed.[66] Pentecost gives the example of the electric chair as an invention that allows the state to avoid the uncomfortable spectacle of "sickening contortions" and unpleasant mishaps that accompany the more traditional hangings of criminals.[67] Scientific and technical progress has thus served the governing minority by extending the range of options available to violently oppress the masses.

The same progress has also helped transform the state into a more complex machine, as a result of which the violence this machine perpetrates becomes less obvious, more obscure. The next subsection shows how some of the complexities of the state's organisation obscure the violence it is responsible for. The point to note here is that technical progress has allowed the state to be more violent in increasingly elaborate ways, and at the same time to conceal this violence under these same layers of elaboration and complexity. Technical progress has thus enabled the construction of a "terrible machine of power," says Tolstoy – and yet people "are afraid of anarchists' bombs, and are not afraid of this terrible organization which is always threatening them with the greatest

---

[61] Lyof N. Tolstoï, *What to Do?* (London: Walter Scott), 148.
[62] (The words quoted form the title of section 12.) Leo Tolstoy, "The Slavery of Our Times," in *Essays from Tula*, trans. Free Age Press (London: Sheppard, 1948), 109.
[63] Tolstoy, "The Slavery of Our Times," 109-110.
[64] Tolstoy, "The Slavery of Our Times," 112 (Tolstoy's emphasis removed).
[65] Leo Tolstoy, "Modern Science," in *Recollections and Essays*, trans. Aylmer Maude (London: Oxford University Press, 1937), 185.
[66] Tolstoy, "The Kingdom of God Is within You," 211, 312.
[67] Pentecost, *Murder by Law*, para. 11-16.

calamities."[68] As Hennacy also remarks, even though some anarchists are "bomb-throwers and killers," "the biggest bomb-thrower [is] the government."[69] Thanks in no small part to technical progress, state violence is more threatening and more cunning than that carried out by subversives. Those who see otherwise, for Christian anarchists, are deceiving themselves.

## 3.2.3 – *State deception*

Christian anarchists believe that people are deceived about the violence committed by the state in several ways. One such deception comes with the illusion that democratic government somehow limits, or provides safeguards against, the state's abuses of power.

Christian anarchists refuse to share such a comforting view of democracy. For a start, they note that in the process of seeking election, politicians display a behaviour that is far removed from the sort of temperance, restraint and integrity that could moderate any temptation to abuse the power they seek to be entrusted with. In other words, in their thirst for power, democratic candidates frequently resort to underhand tactics and rarely demonstrate the concern for morality or humanity that would justify the assurance that democratic states are less violent than others. Indeed, for Christian anarchists, the dishonest competition that characterises electoral campaigns is only likely to promote not the best but the worst candidates to office. Hence for Tolstoy, democracy provides no tighter guarantee than its alternatives against abuses of power by those in government.[70]

Likewise, Pentecost remarks that people are quick to criticise abuses of power by foreign dictators, but "they do not see how the same principle applies when it is, as with us, a question of supporting executive officers, judicial functionaries, and military people, who are pushed forward by a few cunning politicians and elected by a very decided minority of the people."[71] Moreover, according to Tolstoy, the idea that democratic states are somehow constitutionally more just is absurd. He writes:

> When among one hundred men, one rules over ninety-nine, it is unjust, it is a despotism; when ten rule over ninety, it is equally unjust, it is an oligarchy; but when fifty-one rule over forty-nine (and this is only theoretical, for in reality it is always ten or eleven of these fifty-one), it is entirely just, it is freedom!

---

[68] Leo Tolstoy, "Patriotism and Government," in *The Kingdom of God and Peace Essays*, trans. Aylmer Maude (New Delhi: Rupa, 2001), 517.
[69] Hennacy, *The Book of Ammon*, 218.
[70] Tolstoy, "The Kingdom of God Is within You," 184-185. Barr moreover notes that even though people vote, this "does not necessarily affect the kinds of policies" which their representatives implement, not least because away from those rare moments of democracy, the election cycle "will likely be heavily influenced by powerful economic entities that are not accountable to the general public." Barr, *Radical Hope*, 8.
[71] He adds: "If among the sixty million people in the United States there are twelve million voters, six million and one can elect a President, who has been selected as one of two candidates by, perhaps, a hundred politicians; selected because with him the best bargain for a division of the tax money with them could be made." Hugh O. Pentecost, *The Sins of the Government*, available from http://www.deadanarchists.org/Pentecost/sins.html (accessed 22 November 2007), para. 2.

Could there be anything funnier, in its manifest absurdity, than such reasoning? And yet it is this very reasoning that serves as the basis for all reformers of the political structure.[72]

Because they view the electoral process with deep suspicion, Christian anarchists doubt that democratic elections actually reflect the free will of the majority; but more importantly, they argue that abuses of power are no less abusive when conducted by a few more people.

Yet many believe that democratic government is less oppressive than its alternatives, and are prepared to die to be governed in this way. For Christian anarchists, this very deception whereby democratic states claim their use of force to be more legitimate actually makes the violence much worse. The claim to moral legitimacy makes it more excusable to commit acts that are in reality no less violent or abusive. Moreover and paradoxically, as Tolstoy points out, this deception turns democratic electorates into willing participants in their own slavery: "a member of a constitutional State is always a slave because, imagining that he has participated or can participate in his Government, he recognizes the legality of all violence perpetrated upon him."[73] Democracy, therefore, is a deceptive form of government: the state is no less violent, but the legitimacy it claims makes the violence appear more acceptable – even to those against whom the violence is directed.

Another state deception denounced by Christian anarchists concerns the hypnotic sense of duty thanks to which each individual cog in the state's violent machinery plays its part and yet evades its responsibility (a deception that is of course further concealed by the impression that "the existing conditions of society" are "the best and most sacred of which human life is possible").[74] As the following quotation demonstrates, Tolstoy believes that the violence of the system is cunningly obscured by the complexity of the machinery that perpetrates it:

> At the bottom of the social ladder soldiers with rifles, revolvers, and swords, torture and murder men and by those means compel them to become soldiers. And these soldiers are fully convinced that the responsibility for their deed is taken from them by the officers who order those actions. At the top of the ladder the Tsars, presidents, and ministers, decree these tortures and murders and conscriptions. And they are fully convinced that since they are either placed in authority by God, or the society they rule over demands such decrees from them, they cannot be held responsible.
>
> Between these extremes are the intermediate folk who superintend the acts of violence and the murders and the conscriptions of the soldiers. And these, too, are fully convinced that they are relieved of all responsibility, partly because of orders received by them from their superiors, and partly because such orders are expected from them by those on the lower steps of the ladder.[75]

At each rung on the ladder, people think they are merely fulfilling their "duty," they are just doing the job they were appointed to do. Some are bound by oaths of

---

[72] Tolstoy, "The Law of Love and the Law of Violence," 165.
[73] Tolstoy, "The End of the Age," 28.
[74] Tolstoy, *What I Believe*, 46.
[75] Tolstoy, "The Kingdom of God Is within You," 351 (the same idea is expressed pages 325-326).

allegiance; others are just honouring their professional function; but they are certainly not answerable for the cruel deeds committed by the state as a whole.

As a result, the moral responsibility that human beings are built to feel is diluted in the system. Tolstoy explains:
> Not a single judge will consent to strangle with a rope the man whom he has condemned to death in his court. No one of higher rank will consent to snatch a peasant from his weeping family and shut him up in prison. [...]
> 
> These things are due to that complicated machinery of Society and the State, which makes it its first business to destroy the feeling of responsibility for such deeds, so that no man shall feel them to be as unnatural as they are. Some make laws, others apply them. Others again train men and educate them in the habit of discipline, in the habit, that is to say, of senseless and irresponsible obedience. Again others, and these are the best trained of all, practise every kind of violence, even to the slaying of men, without the slightest knowledge of the why and wherefore. We need only clear our mind for an instant from the network of human institutions in which we are thus entangled, to feel how adverse it is to our true nature.[76]

This subdivision of tasks explains why people collectively commit such barbarous acts. They deceptively lose sight of the fact that their own contribution is at least partly morally responsible, along with the contribution of all the other individual cogs in the complex machinery, for the violence they inflict upon others (and indeed themselves).

Thus all the units of the state system are hypnotised into feeling they have special duties. They forget that they are just humans beings, equal to other human beings, and instead "represent themselves to others as being [...] some special conventional beings: noblemen, merchants, governors, judges, officers, Tsars, ministers, or soldiers, not subject to ordinary human duties but to aristocratic, commercial, governatorial, judicial, military, royal, or ministerial, obligations."[77] They are intoxicated by their social function and overlook their most basic moral responsibilities as human beings.

Even the ruling classes hypnotise themselves to some extent. Consciously or unconsciously, however, they are responsible for the design and perpetuation of the system: Tolstoy believes that the subdivision of tasks that alleviates any feeling of responsibility for a public execution "is carefully arranged and planned by learned and enlightened people of the upper class."[78] To some extent, state authorities are hypnotised just like everybody else; but as the people lucky enough to get an education, as the people formally in charge of the state machinery, they also ensure that the various tasks of any act of state violence remain cleverly subdivided so as to alleviate anybody's potential feeling of responsibility. Besides, many in the upper classes have every incentive to tolerate this since they "can occupy advantageous positions only under such an organization."[79] The better off have every incentive to perpetuate the collective hypnosis as well as to keep themselves hypnotised.

---

[76] Tolstoy, *What I Believe*, 46-47.
[77] Tolstoy, "The Kingdom of God Is within You," 354.
[78] Leo Tolstoy, "I Cannot Be Silent," in *Recollections and Essays*, trans. Aylmer Maude (London: Oxford University Press, 1937), 396.
[79] Tolstoy, "The Kingdom of God Is within You," 346.

Ultimately, however, the state relies on brute force if and when deception fails. This, in turn, highlights the importance of military conscription, a subject on which Tolstoy has written extensively.[80] For Tolstoy, "The basis of state power is physical violence," and "the possibility of inflicting physical violence on people is afforded chiefly by an organization of armed men trained to act in unison."[81] Therefore "Power always lies in the hands of those who control the army."[82] This army can then be used as a last resort to protect the ruling classes from the masses, the oppressors from the oppressed – indeed for Tolstoy, that is its main purpose. Yet the army is mostly composed of the working classes, who thus paradoxically become accomplices in the state violence committed against them. For them to do that therefore requires "special and intensive methods of stupefaction and brutalisation."[83] Tolstoy thus lists the "methods of instruction" as: "deception, stupefaction, blows and vodka," an overwhelming mix of delusions, coercion and intoxication.[84]

One of the most important deceptions in this regard – the final one to be considered here – is patriotism, which to Tolstoy is nothing but an artificial (and, as explained in Chapter 1, unchristian) preference for one's people "at the expense of a higher unity."[85] Tolstoy argues that patriotism is a "psychotic epidemic" which hypnotises whole nations and prepares them to commit the most terrible barbarities against fellow human beings.[86] It is a crucial deception in the further stupefaction of soldiers because it deludes them into thinking that the violence they commit has a higher purpose, that what they are doing is not upholding a deeply unjust system but defending the values and the territory of the "fatherland."[87]

Tolstoy accuses the ruling classes of deliberately enflaming international rivalries and arms races in order to justify the existence of their armies, so that these same armies can be called upon to defend and expand their privileges. He also denounces the hypocrisy of international peace conferences, because he insists that only through the eradication of armies – a move never seriously considered at such conferences – can real peace be achieved. Moreover, international military alliances convened in the name of peace are for him nothing but alliances for war. Governments may strive to delude people into believing that their intentions are pure, but in reality they continue to cultivate and regularly call upon patriotic feelings in order to consolidate their grip over the army.

In sum, for Christian anarchists, the state relies on a set of powerful deceptions in order to nurture the alleged consent of the same people it commits violence against. Tolstoy speaks of people being hypnotised by these deceptions,

---

[80] When Tolstoy was writing, military conscription was becoming universal and compulsory across the West, a development which he opposed and repeatedly denounced (more on this in Chapter 4).
[81] Tolstoy, "The Kingdom of God Is within You," 183.
[82] Tolstoy, "The Kingdom of God Is within You," 184.
[83] Tolstoy, "The Kingdom of God Is within You," 214.
[84] Tolstoy, "The Kingdom of God Is within You," 341.
[85] Gregg, *The Power of Nonviolence*, 61.
[86] Tolstoy, "Bethink Yourselves!," 212; Leo Tolstoy, "Christianity and Patriotism," in *The Kingdom of God and Peace Essays*, trans. Aylmer Maude (New Delhi: Rupa, 2001), 435-438, 448-449, 458; Leo Tolstoy, "Thou Shalt Not Kill," in *Recollections and Essays*, trans. Aylmer Maude (London: Oxford University Press, 1937), 196.
[87] Tolstoy, "Bethink Yourselves!," 219-222, 229.

a hypnosis which he repeatedly calls for humanity to shake off so that it can outgrow the violent state and realise the true society of peace and love envisioned by Jesus. In his political essays, his aim is to help this process by applying his literary talent to expose the state's violence and deception. The following extract is a good example of such prose, and nicely summarises almost every theme discussed so far in this Chapter:

> Take a man of our time – be he who he may – [...] living quietly when suddenly people come to him and say: "First you must promise and swear to us that you will slavishly obey us in everything we prescribe to you, and obey and unquestioningly accept as absolute truth everything we devise, decide on, and call law. Secondly you must hand over to us part of the fruits of your labour (we shall use the money to keep you in slavery and to prevent you forcibly resisting our arrangements). Thirdly you must elect others, or be yourself elected, to take a pretended part in the government, knowing all the while that the administration will proceed quite independently of the foolish speeches you and others like you may utter, and that things will proceed according to our will – the will of those in whose hands is the army. Fourthly you must at the appointed time come to the law-courts and take part in the senseless cruelties we perpetrate on erring people whom we have perverted – in the shape of imprisonments, banishments, solitary confinements, and executions. And fifthly and finally, besides all this, although you may be on the friendliest terms with men of other nations, you must be ready, as soon as we order it, to consider as your enemies those whom we shall point out to you, and co-operate, personally or by hiring others, in the destruction, plunder, and murder of their men, women, children and aged alike – perhaps also of your own fellow countrymen or even your parents, should we require that."[88]

By explaining the situation in this manner, Tolstoy was hoping to arouse the masses out of their hypnotic submission to this violent, deceptive and exploitative machine. It is now time to turn to the only aspect of this exploitation which has not been discussed so far.

## *3.2.4 – Economic exploitation*

Christian anarchists' criticism of the state extends beyond the purely political into economics (although, on this topic, Christian anarcho-capitalists differ substantially from the majority of Christian anarchists).[89] They accuse the state not only of waging war to exploit foreign lands and peoples, and to thereby enrich its well-to-do classes, but also of deploying its full arsenal domestically to protect what the wealthy classes have stolen from the masses.

---

[88] Tolstoy, "The Kingdom of God Is within You," 238-239.
[89] Christian anarcho-capitalists such as Redford are perfectly happy with private property, usury and so on (themes which are addressed further below in this subsection). Hence they do not follow the majority of Christian anarchists in their criticism of economy, although they do strongly criticise any state interference in the operation of the market. After all, their defining argument is that the market (and, by extension, private property) should be truly and completely free from such public interference. Redford, *Jesus Is an Anarchist*.

On the international scene, according to Christian anarchists, states wage war out of covetousness and lust, to (aggressively) exploit foreign resources and workforces as well as to (defensively) protect these unduly acquired riches. Tolstoy expresses this view by quoting the following words from Lichtenberg: "If a traveller were to see a people on some far-off island whose houses were protected by loaded cannon and around those houses sentinels patrolled night and day, he could not help thinking that the island was inhabited by brigands. Is it not thus," he asks rhetorically, "with the European states?"[90] For Christian anarchists, all states – not just European ones – steal from other nations and then protect their loot behind their cannons and sentinels.

Domestically too, the state is an instrument of legalised robbery.[91] It transfers the wealth of the poor to the rich so that the latter can further consolidate the enslavement of the former. The state claims to protect its citizens from the worst of human nature – from robbers, criminals and the like – and demands taxes to provide this service, yet it thereby behaves precisely like the evil it claims to guard against. For Tolstoy (following Schmitt), the similarity with the mafia is striking: "Governments, justifying their existence on the ground that they ensure a certain kind of safety to their subjects, are like the Calabrian robber-thief who collected a regular tax from all who wished to travel in safety along the highways."[92] The state will keep you safe – that is, it will not attack you – provided that you pay your dues and do not interfere with its business.

Similarly, writes Tolstoy, it is said about the right of property that it "is established in order to make the worker sure that no one will take from him the produce of his labour," yet in practice, "the very thing happens which that right is intended to prevent: namely, all articles which have been, and continually are being, produced by working people, are possessed by, and as they are produced are continually taken by, those who have not produced them."[93] Laws allegedly designed to protect the vulnerable in effect become the means by which they are further exploited. Thus, as Pentecost remarks, instead of being institutions for the meting out of justice, prisons and gallows "are instruments for the intimidation of the poor if they dare to get back some of the wealth that is daily juggled out of their hands."[94]

For Pentecost, the most important source of social injustice is the private ownership of land. He strongly denounces wealthy landowners for keeping large swathes of land out of use, and for extorting rent from those who produce wealth on their land even though they have put no effort into its production. For him, "a taker of ground rent is exactly like a person who compels a starving man to deliver up his bag of gold for a crust of bread."[95] Like other

---

[90] Lichtenberg, quoted in Tolstoy, "Bethink Yourselves!," 253.
[91] The expression is taken from Brock, *The Political and Social Doctrines*, 46.
[92] Tolstoy, "The Slavery of Our Times," 124-125.
[93] Tolstoy, "The Slavery of Our Times," 104-105.
[94] Pentecost, *Murder by Law*, para. 22.
[95] Hugh O. Pentecost, *The Crime of Owning Vacant Land*, available from http://www.deadanarchists.org/Pentecost/vacantland.html (accessed 22 November 2007), para. 22. Pentecost further remarks that the resulting poverty which is produced is also "the nest in which thieves and murderers are hatched." Pentecost, *Murder by Law*, para. 21.

Christian anarchists, he is therefore outraged that instead of preventing such widespread injustice, the state arraigns the worker and supports the landowner.

Without being able to cultivate land freely, Christian anarchists contend, the landless masses become economically enslaved by the wage system. In *The Slavery of Our Times,* Tolstoy marvels at how "for a bare subsistence, people, considering themselves free men, [think] it necessary to give themselves up to work such as, in the days of serfdom, not one slave-owner, however cruel, would have sent his slaves to."[96] For Tolstoy, there are three causes to this apparently freely accepted enslavement: these workers have no land to cultivate and live from; they are regularly forced by the state to pay taxes; and they are tempted and ensnared by the more luxurious habits of city life. Taken together, these factors convince the worker to submit to wage slavery. Thus, Tolstoy concludes, "one way or another, the labourer is always in slavery to those who control the taxes, the land, and the articles necessary to satisfy his requirements."[97]

Tolstoy therefore argues that even though slavery was officially abolished long ago, the post-industrial economic system unmistakably amounts to a form of slavery. Even if "it is difficult to draw as sharp a dividing line as that which separated the former slaves from their masters," because some can be both or move from one category to another, "this blending of the two classes at their point of contact does not upset the fact that the people of our time are divided into slaves and slave-owners."[98] He explains:

> If the slave-owner of our time has not slave John, whom he can send to the cess-pool to clear out his excrements, he has five shillings of which hundreds of Johns are in such need that the slave-owner of our times may choose anyone out of hundreds of Johns and be a benefactor to him by giving him the preference, and allowing him, rather than another, to climb down into the cess-pool.[99]

Today's complex globalised economy may have blurred the boundaries between slave and slave-owner even further, and may have succeeded in hiding all these Johns oceans away from those who keep them in slavery,[100] but the system remains essentially the same, and the work that many workers are forced to resort to is no less degrading. As Hopton remarks, such economic exploitation is "more subtle and more pervasive than direct physical violence" – but it is exploitation nonetheless, indeed exploitation on a greater scale than was allowed by the more visible slavery of the past.[101]

Tolstoy moreover refuses to accept that this system is natural or unchangeable. Most of us, he admits, "shrug our shoulders" and say that despite

---

[96] Tolstoy, "The Slavery of Our Times," 71.
[97] Tolstoy, "The Slavery of Our Times," 100.
[98] Tolstoy, "The Slavery of Our Times," 94-95.
[99] Tolstoy, "The Slavery of Our Times," 95.
[100] Tolstoy notes that the social customs of the aristocracy ensure that a gulf is maintained between the poor and the rich. He would no doubt remark today that the globalisation of the world economy allows to enlarge this gulf by increasing the geographical distance between rich consumers and the sweatshops in which the poor produce what they are consuming. Tolstoï, *What to Do?* , 58.
[101] Hopton, "Tolstoy, God and Anarchism," 39; Tolstoy, "The Slavery of Our Times," 96-97.

the injustice, "we can do nothing to alter it."[102] Most of us try our best not to see the connection between their suffering and our luxurious lives. For Tolstoy, "This wonderful blindness which befalls people of our circle can only be explained by the fact that when people behave badly they always invent a philosophy of life which represents their bad actions to be not bad actions at all, but merely results of unalterable laws beyond their control."[103] Among the excuses which have been invented and which are happily accepted as true since formulated by some respectable expert or other, Tolstoy lists the "Christian" doctrine that this social arrangement is the will of God; the Hegelian idea that the current order is a necessary manifestation of the spirit; and the more recent and more "scientific" view that human society is a perfect organism subject to iron laws which regulate the natural division of labour.[104] With each such excuse, Tolstoy comments, "We say, It is not we who have done all this; it has been done of itself; as children say when they break any thing, that it broke itself. [...] But that is not true."[105]

The "Christian" excuse is examined below, and Tolstoy's intrinsic suspicion of the Hegelian idea is explored elsewhere. As to the third excuse, Tolstoy accepts that some division of labour is indeed natural and appropriate, but he notes that as soon as any coercion is introduced, such division becomes an artificial *usurpation* of labour – in other words, slavery. For Tolstoy, as soon as the state protects and enforces private ownership of land, the resulting division of labour is not natural but imposed. Thus the so-called laws which regulate the division of labour do not describe "the general order of things" but "the condition of people in the whole world."[106] The division of labour in our modern societies is not a result of some eternal and universal law, but the reflection of state-sanctioned economic exploitation – that is, wage slavery.

Christian anarchists are therefore suspicious of most conventional theories about the economy. These theories tend to be articulated by the more comfortable social classes, predictably exalt the status quo as sacrosanct if admittedly slightly unfair, and lead to proposed amendments that are not nearly radical enough since they hinge on the preservation of the foundations of this status quo. In the meantime, the economic enslavement of the masses continues undeterred.

While on the subject of economics, it is worth noting in passing that Tolstoy is also suspicious of money more generally, and economic theories about it. He sees money not as a neutral medium of exchange, but as yet another instrument of slavery, because its functions as wage or as tax are not separable from the violence and coercion which enchain modern slaves to their chore. Along the same lines, Maurin similarly condemns usury (the lending of money at interest) not only as against the teaching of the Prophets, but also as "trying to live on the sweat of somebody else's brow."[107] (Note that Christian anarcho-capitalist James Redford, however, believes usury to be perfectly compatible with

---

[102] Tolstoy, "The Slavery of Our Times," 74.
[103] Tolstoy, "The Slavery of Our Times," 74-75.
[104] Tolstoï, *What to Do?*, 143-146, 154-171; Tolstoy, "The Slavery of Our Times," 75-77.
[105] Tolstoï, *What to Do?*, 133.
[106] Tolstoy, "The Slavery of Our Times," 76.
[107] Peter Maurin, *Easy Essays* (London: Sheed and Ward, 1938), 32.

Jesus' teaching.) For these Christian anarchists, money is yet another tool with which the masses are exploited.

Besides, as several Christian anarchists remember, Jesus himself warns that "No one can serve two masters [...]. Ye cannot serve God and mammon [or money]."[108] Yet despite Jesus' warning, "all our education is to try to find out how we can serve [these] two masters,"[109] and people continue to be tempted "to serve Mammon with all their heart."[110] For Christian anarchists like Tolstoy, however, we must all decide which of the two masters we will serve and which we will give up. Indeed, consciously or unconsciously, that decision has usually already been made: if money has been chosen, God has been renounced. Instead of worshipping God, many "Christians" worship money – that is, they fall prey to idolatry.

## 3.2.5 – The state as idolatry

Christian anarchists accuse other "Christians" of idolatry not only in their worship of money, but also in their worship of the state. Simply put, they contend that the state is a human creation which dethrones God and His laws. As illustrated in 1 Samuel 8, this creation testifies to humanity's lack of faith and trust in God.

Indeed, Pentecost notes that to rely on legislatures, judges or policemen implies "that we have a God who made a lot of laws which are so defective that the universe would go to smash if it were not for these honourables and big-wigs and blue-coat-and-brass-buttons, with all their authority and clubs."[111] To rely on human laws and law-enforcement suggests both a lack of faith in God's laws and providence and an arrogant confidence in humanity's capacity for self-management. The state is therefore "an expression of man's original sin, the desire to be as gods," says one Christian anarchist.[112] It expresses the desire to rule (to make rules), which according to one Christian thinker "is the mother of all heresies."[113] Hence the state embodies the sinful human desire to sit in God's throne.

Furthermore, as Goddard explains, for Ellul, "the state has become a new locus of the sacred in our society."[114] Instead of God, "It is the state that is held responsible for all that occurs and to which people now look for security, protection, and the solution of all their problems. The state in turn thrives upon this religious devotion, encourages it, and demands its citizens' full compliance with all its decisions."[115] People have faith in the state, obey it, and impute to it "the attributes and powers of God."[116] Hence "the cult of the State" is today's

---

[108] Matthew 6:24, Luke 16:13.
[109] Stevenson, quoted in Maurin, *Easy Essays (2003)*, 216.
[110] ter Kuile, "Anarcho Theologie," 16.
[111] Pentecost, *Murder by Law*, para. 20.
[112] [Anonymous], *Ninety-Five Theses in Defense of Patriarchy*, overview to section B (see also section E).
[113] St. John Chrysostom, quoted in an epigraph in Carson, *Biblical Anarchism*.
[114] Goddard, *Living the Word, Resisting the World*, 268.
[115] Goddard, *Living the Word, Resisting the World*, 269.
[116] Tennant, *Government as Idolatry*, para. 3 (for the quoted words).

"golden calf."[117] The state thus does indeed belong to "the realm of the demonic,"[118] as Jesus' third wilderness temptation suggests: it demands worship, and it seeks total power to make and enforce laws.[119] It will not admit any competition from other gods.

Yet in Acts, Peter says clearly that "We ought to obey God rather than men."[120] Ballou portrays this choice as between "human government," which is "the will of man – whether of one, a few, many, or all in a state or nation – exercising absolute authority over man, by means of cunning and physical force," and "divine government," which is "the infallible will of God prescribing the duty of moral agents, and claiming their primary allegiance."[121] The two types of government cannot be combined: Tolstoy insists that God's laws "supplant all other laws,"[122] and he then reiterates that we "cannot serve two masters," and that the oath of allegiance to human government "is the direct negation of Christianity."[123] For Christian anarchists, a true Christian would recognise God as the sole King, Lawgiver and Judge, as sovereign over human society, and would thus reject government by other human beings as idolatry.

(Incidentally, Chelčický remarks that "he who obeys God needs no other authority," because as Paul says, "Love does no wrong to a neighbour; therefore love is the fulfilling of the law."[124] As already discussed in Chapter 1, the Sermon on the Mount fulfils the demands of the Mosaic Law; similarly, some Christian anarchists claim that obeying God in itself makes the Christian somehow fulfil the intentions of most human laws. This, however, needs further elaboration, because sometimes there can be conflict between God's laws and human laws – hence this question is revisited in Chapter 4, where the Christian anarchist response to the state is discussed, and again in the Conclusion, where love's fulfilment of justice is explored further.)

The point for Christian anarchists is that true Christians would not elevate the state to the status of god. Ultimately, one can place one's trust and have faith either in God's law of love, or in the coercive and human state, not both.[125] Hence Christian anarchists speak out against the state, "such a center of power and violence," being "given a Christian name and justification."[126] For

---

[117] Simon Birch, *Religion, Politics and Liberty* (Libertarian Alliance), available from http://www.libertarian.co.uk/lapubs/relin003.pdf (accessed 21 November 2007), 1.
[118] Goddard, *Living the Word, Resisting the World*, 273.
[119] Both Berdyaev and Ellul argue that technology has helped the state turn into a totalitarian, omnipotent god – or rather demon – which should be opposed. See for instance Berdyaev, *The Realm of the Spirit and the Realm of Caesar*, 42, 48, 50-51, 69, 72, 100, 156; Goddard, *Living the Word, Resisting the World*, 206-207, 220-221, 260, 262-273; Wogaman, *Christian Perspectives on Politics*, 55.
[120] Acts 5:29 (see also Acts 4:19-20).
[121] Ballou, *Non-Resistance in Relation to Human Governments*, 3.
[122] Tolstoy, "The Kingdom of God Is within You," 231.
[123] Tolstoy, "The Kingdom of God Is within You," 232-233.
[124] Molnár, *A Study of Peter Chelčický's Life*, 92 (paraphrasing Chelčický – see also 32). (Romans 13:10.)
[125] Tennant, *Christianarchy?*, para. 33; Tennant, *Government as Idolatry*, para. 18. Along these lines, a contributor to *A Pinch of Salt* writes: "There are two ways of educating children and of governing society: through fear and its counter-point hate, or through love." Meggitt [?], "Anarchism and the New Testament," 11.
[126] Molnár, *A Study of Peter Chelčický's Life*, 32.

them, there is a fundamental contradiction between the state and the gospel: one is by nature violent and coercive, the other teaches love and forgiveness, and therefore the term "Christian state" is a contradiction in terms, an oxymoron just like the term "hot ice."[127] Tolstoy therefore calls "blasphemy" the "sanctification of political power by Christianity," because "it is the negation of Christianity."[128]

Tolstoy writes at length about this paradox of trying to combine Christianity and the state. For him, this paradox is visible in the life of the aristocracy, in domestic legislation, in international affairs, but especially in military conscription. He ridicules the irony of teaching the Sermon on the Mount at Sunday school only to then send the same pupils to the army – thus trying to make them both Christians and gladiators.[129] He recalls "the amazement of an Indian converted to Christianity, when, having absorbed the essence of the Christian teaching, he came to Europe and saw how Christians live. He could not overcome his astonishment," Tolstoy continues, "at a sight so completely contrary to what he had expected to find."[130] Tolstoy repeatedly insists that the state and Christianity are completely incompatible:

> Christianity in its true sense puts an end to the State. It was so understood from its very beginning, and for that Christ was crucified. It has always been so understood by people who were not under the necessity of justifying a Christian State. Only since rulers adopted a nominal external Christianity have men begun to devise all those impossible, cunningly spun theories which pretend to make Christianity compatible with the State. But to every serious and sincere man of our time the incompatibility of true Christianity (the doctrine of humility, forgiveness, and love) with the State and its pomp, violence, executions, and wars, is quite obvious. The profession of true Christianity not only excludes the possibility of recognizing the State, but even destroys its foundations.[131]

In sum, for Christian anarchists like Tolstoy, the state is a violent, deceptive and exploitative human creation. To follow it is to deify it. One can either place the Christian God above the state, and thus follow Jesus' Sermon on the Mount, or the state above God, and thus follow human laws. The former is truly Christian, the latter, idolatry. One cannot follow both, despite attempts to convince us of the contrary through the "cunningly spun theories" put forth by conformist theologians.[132] It is now time to analyse these theories from the Christian anarchist perspective.

## 3.3 – Church doctrine in support of the state

Christian anarchists accuse the church of deliberately misinterpreting Jesus' instructions in the Sermon on the Mount, especially the passage counselling non-resistance, in order to conjure Christian support for authority. This section

---

[127] Tolstoy, "Church and State," 338.
[128] Tolstoy, "Church and State," 338.
[129] Tolstoy, "The Kingdom of God Is within You," 139, 146.
[130] Tolstoy, "The Kingdom of God Is within You," 220.
[131] Tolstoy, "The Kingdom of God Is within You," 259.
[132] Tolstoy, "The Kingdom of God Is within You," 259.

outlines these accusations one by one, but each briefly (the footnotes indicate where, in the Christian anarchist literature, further detail can be found). It begins with Jesus' instructions aside from the one not to resist evil, which is important enough to be discussed on its own in the subsequent subsection.

### 3.3.1 – Reinterpretations of Jesus' commandments in the Sermon on the Mount

Christian anarchists blame established theologians for disingenuously reinterpreting Jesus' teaching in order to make it appear compatible with the state, but Augustine is frequently singled out given his pivotal role when Christianity was becoming the official religion of the Roman Empire. To be sure, Augustine's interpretation of Jesus' commandments in the Sermon on the Mount varies considerably from that of Christian anarchists.

One example of Augustine's surprising reading concerns the commandment not to swear oaths, which he interprets as neither forbidding appeals to God as a witness nor indeed swearing in principle. He even argues that making "a good use of an oath" is not evil, because it is "necessary in order to persuade."[133] For Tolstoy, however, this and other similar excuses put forward to justify the swearing of oaths are all dishonest and incompatible with Jesus' simple instruction.[134] As explained in Chapter 1, Tolstoy sees Jesus as clearly proscribing the swearing of oaths, and "the chief obstacle to understanding" this commandment is for him precisely that "so-called Christian teachers have boldly forced men to take oaths on the Gospel itself."[135]

Equally disingenuous, for Christian anarchists, is the reinterpretation of the commandment not to be angry, which conformist theologians have often argued applies somehow only to the *motivation* behind the act, not the act itself. This argument, Tolstoy argues, is founded on the words "without a cause" (forbidding anger "without a cause").[136] Tolstoy explains that based on this clause "[church] Fathers were chiefly occupied with deciding the cases in which anger [is] excusable."[137] Following these church Fathers, most conventional interpretations tolerate angry acts and, in many cases, anger itself – as long as it is not "without a cause." Yet as Tolstoy remarks, "angry people" always "think their anger just;" they think they have a just cause for their anger.[138] Tolstoy thus felt

---

[133] Augustine, *The Sermon on the Mount Expounded*, 43.
[134] The four excuses which Tolstoy lists are: that Jesus himself confirmed the use of oaths when he replied "thou hast said" to the high priest; that Paul calls God to witness several times and that this amounts to an oath; that oaths were prescribed by the Mosaic Law and not revoked by Jesus; and that the only oaths forbidden are the vain ones like those of the Pharisees. Tolstoy considers the first excuse as almost childish: Jesus' reply, he says, plainly does not amount to an oath. Neither does Paul's calling of God to witness – and anyway, as mentioned in the Introduction and in Chapter 4, Tolstoy does not consider Paul reliable. Also, that only vain oaths are forbidden is not an exception that Jesus allows. So the only potential point that could be valid for Tolstoy would be that Jesus does not revoke the prescription of oaths, but for Tolstoy, that is exactly what Jesus does with this commandment in the Sermon. Tolstoy, *What I Believe*, 82-84.
[135] Tolstoy, *What I Believe*, 84-85.
[136] Tolstoy, *What I Believe*, 70-71. (Matthew 5:48.)
[137] Tolstoy, *What I Believe*, 68.
[138] Tolstoy, *What I Believe*, 69.

that the clause "destroyed the whole meaning of the verse."[139] Why forbid anger in situations that in reality never arise? He then consulted different versions of the Bible, and realised that the destructive clause was "an interpolation of the fifth century, not to be found in the most authentic copies of the gospel" – as is now recognised in more recent versions of the Bible.[140] For centuries, however, orthodox interpretations downplayed or even revised Jesus' original meaning based on a clause which appears to have been disingenuously inserted into the original text.

Another commandment which Christian anarchists believe has traditionally been misinterpreted is the one to love our enemies. Augustine's impossible difficulty was to interpret it in a way that did not contradict the articulation of his doctrine of just war, so here again he argued, as Johnston explains, that it refers "to an inner disposition, and not outward action."[141] This position has been developed over time by other theologians, so that the absurd conclusion has been reached whereby it is said that it is fine to murder your enemy as long as a proper inner attitude of love is maintained – a position which, to non-Christians, betrays the hypocrisy of many professed "Christians."[142] An alternative interpretation which Tolstoy also criticises is one whereby "the words of Jesus are generally corrected to mean that, though we cannot love our enemies [because it is too difficult], we may refrain from wishing them or doing them any ill."[143] To Christian anarchists, of course, either of these methods are betraying the original commandment by attempting to justify its opposite – and anyway, early Christians would have never contemplated murder as compatible in any way with their ethos. Yet again, the established interpretations go against both the spirit and the letter of Jesus' clear original intention.

Tolstoy is also critical of the church's interpretation of the commandment not to judge, which it limits to verbal slander. This, to Tolstoy, is incoherent, and a close analysis of the original Greek confirms that what is meant in the text is judgement in the conventional sense of "passing a sentence on" or to "condemn to punishment."[144] Based on this analysis, Tolstoy deduces that the translation into "evil-speaking, or slander, is the most fanciful and unauthorised of all."[145]

Tolstoy also questions the traditional understanding of the commandment not to commit adultery. While this commandment is not important for Christian anarchism, its usual interpretation is nonetheless for Tolstoy yet

---

[139] Tolstoy, *What I Believe*, 69.
[140] (That the clause was added to the original text is now acknowledged in most contemporary versions of the Bible, although it does figure in the King James Version.) Tolstoy, *What I Believe*, 72.
[141] Johnston, "Love Your Enemies – Even in the Age of Terrorism?," 93.
[142] Johnston, "Love Your Enemies – Even in the Age of Terrorism?," 95-96. On page 95, Johnston also remarks that "Limiting the scope of love of enemy is like limiting the category 'neighbor' – a limit which Jesus subverted."
[143] Tolstoy, *What I Believe*, 89.
[144] On the incoherence of the interpretation of it as slander, Tolstoy comments (on pages 37-38): "Why should it be supposed that Jesus, while forbidding as an evil thing the condemnation of our neighbour by words involuntarily breaking from the lips, does not regard as evil, and does not forbid the very same condemnation, when accomplished deliberately, and accompanied by the use of force against the one condemned?" Tolstoy, *What I Believe*, 37-39.
[145] Tolstoy, *What I Believe*, 39.

another example of an "intentional corruption of the text" which "destroys the moral, the religious, the grammatical, and the logical meaning of the words of Jesus."[146]

Christian anarchists like Tolstoy are therefore deeply suspicious of the conventional church's interpretation of the Sermon commandments since Augustine. Too often, the obvious meaning of Jesus' instructions is contradicted. Where this contradiction is even more pronounced, however, is with the commandment not to resist evil.

## 3.3.2 – Reinterpretations of non-resistance

Christian anarchists list various strategies and arguments that they accuse mainstream theologians of using to shy away from the radical implications of Jesus' demand not to resist evil but to turn the other cheek.

The simplest strategy has been to ignore it, to deny that Jesus taught it, or to evade the question altogether. This, Tolstoy explains, was one of the main types of responses he received from church theologians to his earlier exegesis of the passage in *What I Believe*.[147] He says that much was made of his "misunderstanding" of various other Bible passages and of his lack of acknowledgement of key church dogmas, but that the questions he asked were often evaded or falsely said to have been settled long ago.[148] Some, he says, went as far as to deny that Jesus taught non-violence. According to Tolstoy, however, "It is useless to refute such assertions, for the men who make them refute themselves, or rather renounce Christ and invent a Christ and a Christianity of their own."[149]

Another "ingenious" strategy employed by orthodox theologians, says Tolstoy, "consists in declaring that they do not deny this commandment but recognize it like all the others, only they do not ascribe any special and exclusive significance to it as the sectarians do."[150] This view appears honest and legitimate, but as Tolstoy points out, it is rarely lived up to by its professors. Tolstoy demonstrates this by comparing the attitude of these church theologians towards non-resistance with their typical attitude towards adultery. He writes:

> They never point out any cases in which the command against adultery ought to be broken, and always teach that allurements leading men to commit adultery should be avoided. But it is not so with the command about non-resistance.
>
> All the Church preachers know cases in which this law should be broken, and they teach men so. [...] The clergy never advocate the violation of any other commandment, but in regard to the law of non-resistance they openly teach that it is not necessary to take it too literally, and that not merely is it unnecessary to fulfil it always, but that there are conditions when

---

[146] Tolstoy, *What I Believe*, 80.
[147] Tolstoy, "The Kingdom of God Is within You," 34-46.
[148] Tolstoy, "The Kingdom of God Is within You," 35, 42-46.
[149] Tolstoy, "The Kingdom of God Is within You," 37.
[150] Tolstoy, "The Kingdom of God Is within You," 40.

> just the contrary should be done – that is, that men should go to law, wage wars, and execute people. [...]
>
> So it is not true that this command is recognized by the preachers of the Church as of equal significance with the other commandments.[151]

Church theologians claim that it is wrong to place non-resistance on a pedestal and that all commandments should be treated equally, but they themselves do not actually treat and obey all of Jesus' commandments with the same degree of diligence and sincerity.

Another allegedly dishonest interpretation of this commandment, which both Tolstoy and Ballou comment on, consists in claiming that the Sermon indicates "the perfection to which man should aspire, though, poor fallen creature, in bondage to sin, he is incapable of reaching that perfection, and can be saved only by faith, prayer, and divine grace."[152] For Tolstoy, it would be "strange" for Jesus to give "such clear and beautiful rules directly applicable to every individual, well knowing the impossibility of this teaching being carried into practice by the unassisted strength of man."[153] Instead, it seems to Tolstoy that "without even attempting it, both believers and unbelievers alike have decided that it is impossible."[154] Yet as Ballou asks, "Who is to be the judge of what is possible – God, or man? Who is to judge what and how much shall be required – Jesus Christ, or his disciples?"[155] Ballou expects a true follower of Jesus to follow Jesus' instructions. Hence instead of a big church of weak and dishonest "followers" claiming that Christianity is "impossible," Ballou would rather have a much smaller church of honest and courageous Christian martyrs striving to live up to Jesus' tough demands, and honest non-Christians openly admitting that since Christianity comes with such a difficult cross to bear, they cannot consistently profess it.[156]

A similar excuse put forward by mainstream theologians consists in saying that non-resistance is "impracticable" in today's world and that we must therefore "wait until the millennium" before it can be practiced.[157] Ballou rejects this view. For a start, he wonders how "such state as the millennium should ever be developed among mankind" if no-one is prepared to usher it in by acting on this commandment.[158] He also accuses proponents of this argument of presupposing both that Jesus "enjoined on his disciples, duties [...] which he knew they could not perform," and that "Jesus enjoined many particular duties for which there will be no possible occasion in the millennium, and which therefore

---

[151] Tolstoy, "The Kingdom of God Is within You," 41-42.
[152] Tolstoy, *What I Believe*, 14.
[153] Tolstoy, *What I Believe*, 14.
[154] Tolstoy, *What I Believe*, 43.
[155] Ballou, *Christian Non-Resistance*, chap. 6, para. 11.
[156] He further asserts that Jesus, the apostles, and the early church were precisely examples of such martyrdom, and that it was precisely the courage of such martyrs that helped convert "robbers" and "wild savages" to Christianity. Ballou, *Christian Non-Resistance*, chap. 6, para. 11-13.
[157] Ballou, *Non-Resistance in Relation to Human Governments*, 11.
[158] He affirms "that the righteous would exterminate the wicked, in the best sense of the word, were they to act on strict non-resistant principles. They would immediately usher in the millennium, with all its blessings, were they to act on these principles in true and persevering fidelity. How else is it imaginable that any such state as the millennium should ever be developed among mankind?" Ballou, *Christian Non-Resistance*, chap. 6, para. 2.

can never be fulfilled."[159] Indeed, in the millennium, there should be no occasion to practice non-resistance since "there will be no evil-doer to forbear with."[160] In any case, Jesus "gives no intimation" of the "impracticability" of non-resistance "till some future period."[161]

Christian anarchists also comment on other variations on this argument that non-resistance is impracticable, each time demonstrating that it is unchristian.[162] In the end, Tolstoy cannot avoid the conclusion that "Theological writers, in no way hindered by the authority of him whom they confess as God, calmly put a limit to the meaning of his words. [...] They admit his sentiments to be very lofty sentiments, but devoid of all possibility of a practical application to life, since they would destroy the whole of that social order which they feel we have so well arranged."[163] In other words, these commentators have the audacity to claim that Jesus could not have meant to teach what they have decided to interpret as unrealistic and utopian because it would threaten the current political system.[164] Either way, it is on grounds foreign to Jesus' teaching that these commentators are assessing the possibility or the practicality of his commandments.

A slightly different evasion of Jesus' instruction, in line with several aforementioned reinterpretations of other commandments, is the claim that Jesus "does not prohibit the *act*, but only a vindictive, revengeful *spirit* in performing it."[165] Again, the implication seems to be that one can actually resist evil as long as this resistance is not informed by a spirit of resistance. For Ballou, however, this "is to make [Jesus] the mere *echo* of Moses and his expounders; whereas he goes absolutely against the *deed* – the *act* of inflicting evil."[166] Besides, "however gently and politely inflicted," resistance is resistance, and only a spirit of resistance will actually enact it.[167]

Yet another evasion discussed by Ballou is the claim that the commandment only applied to Jesus' *early* followers, because "To resist *then* would be of no avail; it was better therefore patiently to endure."[168] Ballou finds

---

[159] Ballou, *Christian Non-Resistance*, chap. 6, para. 4-5.
[160] Ballou, *Christian Non-Resistance*, chap. 6, para. 8.
[161] Ballou, *Christian Non-Resistance*, chap. 6, para. 7.
[162] Tolstoy for instance rejects the view that the commandment not to resist is meant to be heard allegorically, and insists that this commandment, the essence of Christianity, must be understood literally, because a failure to do so abrogates Jesus' whole teaching: Tolstoy, *What I Believe*, 19-23.
[163] Tolstoy, *What I Believe*, 86.
[164] There is an interesting parallel here with anarchism in general, which is also often dismissed as "a nice idea on paper, but impossible in the real world" (although of course the authority behind that idea, in the case of classical anarchism, is neither Jesus nor God but often – though not always – reason, liberty, or some similar enlightenment value). Kinna, *Anarchism*, 170.
[165] Ballou, *Christian Non-Resistance*, chap. 2, para. 16.
[166] Ballou cites several passages from the Old Testament illustrating Moses' commandments, and concludes that "From these and other passages in the writings of Moses, it will be seen that, notwithstanding the severity of his code, he did not authorize individual hatred, revenge and wanton cruelty in punishing the wicked. To make Christ prohibit *only* a personal, spiteful, malicious, cruel spirit in executing the authorized punishments of the law, is to make his the mere *echo* of Moses and his expounders; whereas he goes absolutely against the *deed* – the *act* of inflicting evil on the persons of offending." Ballou, *Christian Non-Resistance*, chap. 2, para. 19 (Ballou's emphasis).
[167] Ballou, *Christian Non-Resistance*, chap. 2, para. 19.
[168] Ballou, *Christian Non-Resistance*, chap. 2, para. 22 (Ballou's emphasis).

this view astonishing: "What a despicable expediency," he exclaims, "does this ascribe to the Savior! What a *skulking prudence*! Resist not evil when unable to do so!"[169] For Ballou, this argument is "utterly derogatory to the character of Jesus, and utterly unsupported by a single hint in the context," hence it needs not be refuted in any more detail.[170]

A different method which has been employed to evade Jesus' instruction is to cite other Bible passages said to justify violence. Christian anarchists thus accuse many theologians of deliberately searching the Bible in the hope that a justification for violence can be constructed. One obvious place to search into is the Old Testament, with its many laws and wars; but for Tolstoy, the teaching that is then followed is not Jesus' but Moses'; and anyway, as already discussed in Chapter 1 and as Ballou puts it, "*That* resistance of evil which Moses sanctioned and enjoined, Jesus obviously repudiates and forbids," and therefore "The prohibition is made precisely coextensive in all its bearings with the allowances and injunctions of the Olden Code."[171] Aside from references to the Old Testament, passages from the New have also been deliberately misinterpreted to justify "Christian" war. For instance, it is said that if war was really meant to be unchristian, John the Baptist had the opportunity to outlaw it in his reply to the Roman soldier; but for Chelčický, "John, who preceded our Lord Jesus in time, was still under the Law of Moses," hence he "could not have changed the laws (concerning) the (established) order of things."[172] For other theologians, the obligation to care for one's neighbour implies a duty to use force to protect him; but for Tolstoy, this interpretation is both arbitrary and anyway absent from the gospels.[173] Also cited are New Testament passages calling for sacrifice, which have been misused to eulogise military glory even though their actual meaning concerns sacrifice or bearing one's cross but *not* violence or killing.[174] In the end, all these passages may distract from Jesus' commandment not to resist evil, but for Christian anarchists, honestly interpreted, they do not abrogate it.

In any case, even when the commandment not to resist evil is acknowledged, some theologians argue that it applies only to private or small matters, not to public or national ones – again an evasion unwarranted by scripture. Others say that although Jesus did preach non-resistance, "there are malefactors in the world, and if these evil men are not curbed by force the whole

---

[169] Ballou, *Christian Non-Resistance*, chap. 2, para. 22 (Ballou's emphasis).
[170] Ballou, *Christian Non-Resistance*, chap. 2, para. 22
[171] Ballou, *Christian Non-Resistance*, chap. 2, para. 13 (Ballou's emphasis).
[172] Molnár, *A Study of Peter Chelčický's Life*, 107 (quoting Chelčický).
[173] Tolstoy says that it arbitrarily reduces the question to "defining what constitutes danger for another person," which involves "personal judgement." As a result, violence can always be justified, since "there is no case of violence that cannot be justified on the ground of danger threatening somebody." Moreover, while the violence one feels threatened by remains hypothetical, one's own pre-emptive violence is real – that is, while the other may not have been violent and may have left the cycle of violence unaffected, one's own violence is certain to affect it. In any case, as Tolstoy insists, "no such limitation is indicated in [Jesus'] whole life or in his teaching." Tolstoy, "The Kingdom of God Is within You," 39-40.
[174] Leo Tolstoy, "Notes for Soldiers," in *Tolstoy's Writings on Civil Disobedience and Non-Violence*, trans. V. Tchertkoff and A. C. Fifield (New York: Bergman, 1967), 35-37.

world will perish"[175] – an argument which, for Tolstoy, is once again not informed by the text, and opens up an impossible debate on how to all agree on distinguishing the evil from the good.

Augustine, for his part, argues that coercion is a natural part of political authority after the Fall, a necessary pedagogical tool in a sinful world. For Christian anarchists, however, Christian love and non-resistance are meant precisely as an alternative pedagogy to that of punishment and violence. Christian anarchists therefore accuse the church, which was supposed to embody Jesus' radical teaching, of abandoning it and instead following conformist theologians like Augustine, who not only justified punishment and coercion but also was the first to develop "just war" theory – all "to the benefit of state and king."[176] For Christian anarchists, this blessing of violence and war by the church, this "just war theory" which it further developed over the centuries, is horrifying, and further obscures the radical truth of Jesus' teaching.

Myers calls it "the profoundest historical betrayal of the Gospel" for the church to have thus "turned the cross into a sword."[177] Instead of bravely teaching and embodying non-resistance and the turning of the other cheek, to Tolstoy the very essence of Jesus' message, the church shows indifference to it and justifies violence and war. It exalts the Sermon on the Mount in words, but in practice has no intention of following it. It honours dead saints and radicals, but alive it finds them too uncomfortable to deal with, let alone praise.[178] To Christian anarchists, the church is therefore guilty of gradually renouncing Jesus' radical commandments and endorsing the very instruments which had once shed the blood of its martyrs.

It is for that reason that according to Christian anarchists, a proper exegesis of these verses must bypass the church's conventional interpretations. The many Christian teachers who justify violence, for them, are false teachers. Jesus teaches love, non-violence and non-resistance to evil. According to Christian anarchists, whatever the church says, this is obvious to anyone reading the Gospels. Gandhi once observed that "The only people on earth who do not see Christ and his teachings as nonviolent are Christians."[179] For Christian anarchists, provided it is approached with a mind purged from the many layers of

---

[175] Tolstoy, "The Kingdom of God Is within You," 37.

[176] Elliott, *Freedom, Justice and Christian Counter-Culture*, 178-179. Note that while he certainly frequently condemns the violent excesses of the church over the centuries, Andrews appears to be fairly comfortable with Augustine's criteria: he says that "Ambrose and Augustine developed a set of criteria to call those in power – who make war – to be accountable to the principles of justice;" he then briefly describes the eight specific conditions articulated by them with that purpose; and he concludes that "According to these criteria, our current wars are not 'just wars.' As Christians committed to peace and justice, we should robustly oppose these hostilities and actively seek reconciliation with our enemies." It is worth noting, however, that he avoids calling these criteria "Christian" – he just says they are about "justice," and that Christians should oppose current wars, which are unjust. Andrews, *Plan Be*, 57-58.

[177] Myers, *Binding the Strong Man*, 403.

[178] This sentence paraphrases a *Commonweal* editorial cited in Hennacy, *The Book of Ammon*, 312. Pentecost makes the same point: "We worship men who said and did certain things long, long ago, but we persecute and slay the men who say and do substantially the same things today." Hugh O. Pentecost, *Anarchism*, available from http://www.deadanarchists.org/Pentecost/anarchism.html (accessed 22 November 2007), para. 13.

[179] Gandhi, quoted in Wink, *Engaging the Powers*, 216.

conventional interpretation, the Sermon of the Mount's true, radical and politically subversive meaning is obvious for all to see.

### 3.3.3 – Support for political authority

According to Christian anarchists, the church's misinterpretation of Jesus' teaching has one particular purpose: to pave the way for its support of political authority – that is, of the state. But to legitimise this support, on top of playing down the anarchist implications of Jesus' teaching, church theologians have had to devise positive arguments in direct support of the state and its instruments of coercion. These arguments can be divided into two broad sets: those that are based on passages from scripture, and those that are not.

Among the New Testament passages said to imply support for political authority, the most frequently cited must be Romans 13. Chapter 4 discusses Christian anarchists' rejection of the standard interpretations of this passage and their alternative interpretation. Another passage often cited by those supporting the state is the "render unto Caesar" episode, likewise discussed in Chapter 4. Sometimes apologists of the state ground their support on Jesus' reply to Pilate during his trial. The Christian anarchist alternative interpretation is mentioned in Chapter 2. Apologists of the state also sometimes interpret Paul's call for Christians to pray for all, including kings, as biblical foundation for political power. Christian anarchists rarely comment on this particular argument, but Chelčický makes it clear that for him, it is a deliberate misunderstanding of a simple hope that these kings might repent. Several other – less weighty – New Testament passages have also been cited as implying support for authority. For Christian anarchists, however, as shown where these passages are discussed in Chapters 2 and 4, they are all dishonest interpretations of the original text.

Christian apologists of the state also rationalise their support using arguments not directly derived from scripture. These tend to focus on justifying the use of political violence. One way this has been done has been to say that because "God can kill since He is the giver of life and death, [...] Therefore the kings whom God has authorized to rule can kill in the exercise of their justice."[180] Another way has been to see it as "not cruelty but kindliness to punish the sins for God."[181] Similarly, the church has at times argued that any political authority to use force must proceed "from God."[182] Either way, a false distinction between violence and political force (which, as Chapter 1 shows, Christian anarchists reject) has to be maintained "to clear the state of the charge of violence."[183]

Another line of reasoning has consisted in claiming that the church would never be able to maintain its strength and thereby fulfil its mission in the world without the support of the state. Christian anarchists reject this, and Chapters 4 and 5 discuss how they think the church should be striving to fulfil its mission in a world in which the state is as dominant as it is today. They certainly

---

[180] Molnár, *A Study of Peter Chelčický's Life*, 125 (quoting Chelčický).
[181] Molnár, *A Study of Peter Chelčický's Life*, 125 (quoting Chelčický).
[182] Tolstoy, "Church and State," 340.
[183] Ellul, *Violence*, 5.

do not believe that the good ends of Christianity can be realised through the wrong means of the state.

For Christian anarchists, all these arguments which the church has deployed to legitimise its support of the state and its instruments are unchristian, and they actually have a hidden motive: the accumulation and the protection of wealth. The church has "converted faith into a lucrative business," says Chelčický, and the state is happy to shelter the church's luxuries in exchange for divine sanctification.[184] Because it has grown so accustomed to these luxuries, the church is usually happy to defend and consecrate the state's prevailing ideology, whatever the ideology – provided of course that it does not threaten the church's wealth. Hence instead of being a force for an anarchist revolution, the church has usually sided with the establishment and, in times of trouble, with right-wing military dictatorships like that of Franco or Peron rather than with the poor and their revolutionary ideologies.

Thus church and state mutually support one another. Although the precise constitutional details of their relationship has varied greatly over time and place, they have become one another's auxiliary, relying on one another to provide either the ideology or the sheer force required to ensure they both continue to enjoy their power and material comforts. Of course, this has required the church to reinterpret the politically radical elements of Jesus' teaching, but ever since Constantine and Augustine, many church theologians have laboured hard to do just that. The other important deception which Christian anarchists accuse the church of developing in order to further obscure Jesus' subversive message is its set of dogmas, creeds, and other such tenets of faith.

## 3.4 – Deceptive dogmas

Tolstoy has produced some scathing criticisms of church dogmas. Other Christian anarchists have been far less prolific on this particular topic, although one can find scattered hints here and there that suggest that their opinion can often be similar to Tolstoy's. As this section outlines these criticisms, it relies predominantly on Tolstoy.

These criticisms are admittedly not crucial to the main theme of this book, since they do not impact directly on Christian anarchists' critique of the state. It is nonetheless valuable to outline them in that they demonstrate that several Christian anarchists – especially Tolstoy, Hennacy and Chelčický – do take their criticism of the church as far as many other anarchists do, and thus that Christian anarchism does include a significant strand that shares such anticlericalism with significant strands of secular anarchism. At the same time, in order not to delve too much on this sub-topic, the detailed elaboration of most of these criticisms is relegated to the footnotes, and to the texts referenced therein (but as explained in the Acknowledgements, the footnotes were trimmed down to the bare minimum for this abridged version, so readers interested in these fuller elaborations will find them in the original, hardback version of this book).

---

[184] Molnár, *A Study of Peter Chelčický's Life*, 109 (paraphrasing Chelčický).

### *3.4.1 – Sanctimonious self-righteousness*

Christian anarchists believe that one of the church's cardinal sins has been to appoint itself as the sole authority for the interpretation of the Bible. Tolstoy is upset that "the very people Christ denounced came to consider themselves the sole preachers and expositors of His doctrines."[185] Jesus had warned his followers that "the self-styled Orthodox [...] were, and are, the enemies of all that is good," and therefore that such "self-appointed teachers" are "to be feared."[186] He also told his followers "to call no man master or father."[187] Moreover, says Tolstoy, "nowhere [in the Gospels] is anything said of the foundation of what churchmen call the Church."[188] The word "church" is only mentioned twice in the Gospels, once meaning "an assembly of men to settle a dispute," the other "in connexion with the obscure utterance about the rock, Peter, and the gates of hell."[189] Nowhere does Jesus announce the coming of what became the church.

Yet from these two mentions by Jesus, the church has derived its authority and its "monopoly of Christian preaching."[190] Besides, according to Tolstoy, "A slight addition to the Gospels was invented, telling how Christ, when about to go up into the sky, handed over to certain men the exclusive right – not merely to teach others divine truth [...] – but also to decide which people should be saved or the reverse, and, above all, to confer this power on others."[191] Thus the "great priest" of the church, Chelčický writes, "has arrogated to himself divine power, no, the power of the Savior himself, the power to forgive sins, which is God's prerogative" – a prerogative which, he notes, also happens to be very "lucrative."[192] On the basis of this authority, the church tells believers what is right and wrong, defines "heresies" and persecutes its proponents. To Christian anarchists, the parallel with the scribes and Pharisees condemned by Jesus is striking.

Hence for Tolstoy, "the whole fraud" in Christianity "is built up on the fantastic conception of a 'Church.'"[193] In "The Restoration of Hell," Tolstoy describes the creation of the church in a conversation Beelzebub has with his subordinate devils. Beelzebub had "understood that all was lost" when Jesus had

---

[185] Tolstoy, "Letter to Ernest Howard Crosby," 189.
[186] Tolstoy, "The Gospel in Brief," 233-234. (Matthew 23:1-34; Luke 20:46-47)
[187] Tolstoy, "The Kingdom of God Is within You," 63, 76. (Matthew 23:8.)
[188] Tolstoy, "The Kingdom of God Is within You," 63.
[189] Tolstoy, "The Kingdom of God Is within You," 63. (Matthew 16:18, 18:17.)
[190] Tolstoy, "Letter to Ernest Howard Crosby," 189.
[191] Tolstoy, "What Is Religion?," 240-241.
[192] Molnár, *A Study of Peter Chelčický's Life*, 79-80 (quoting Chelčický). He adds (page 80): "Now to go further, he not only initiates such lucrative pilgrimages to Rome from all countries, but he even sends to those countries letters containing the forgiveness of sins and sufferings; (he tells them) not to inconvenience themselves with a long journey to him, that he will forgive them everything provided they pay for it in golden ducats; that the sinner is free to specify what sins he wants to have forgiven and that, if he pays for it, he (the Pope) will grant him in a letter a freedom to sin for as many years as are paid for, even until a man's death if so desired." Chelčický thus complained about the selling of indulgences several decades before Luther (Chelčický wrote this around 1440-1443, and Luther published his ninety-five theses in 1517).
[193] Tolstoy, "Church and State," 333.

just died, since his teaching had been "so clear, so easy to follow, and so evidently saved men from evil."[194] A devil then explains that although things were rosy among followers of Jesus for a while, they gradually began disagreeing on things like circumcision. At that point, explains the devil, "I invented 'The Church.' And when once they believed in 'The Church' I was at peace. I understood that we were saved, and that Hell was restored."[195] Beelzebub then asks the devil to explain what this welcome "Church" is, and the devil spells out Tolstoy's definition:

> Well, when people tell lies and feel that they won't be believed, they always call God to witness, and say: "By God, what I say is true!" That, in substance, is "the Church," but with this peculiarity, that those who recognize themselves as being "the Church" become convinced that they cannot err, and so whatever nonsense they may utter they can never recant it. The Church is constituted in this way: Men assure themselves and others that their teacher, God, to ensure that the law he revealed to men should not be misinterpreted, has given power to certain men, who, with those to whom they transfer this power, can alone correctly interpret his teaching. So these men, who call themselves "the Church," regard themselves as holding the truth not because what they preach is true but because they consider themselves the only true successors of the disciples of the disciples of the disciples, and finally of the disciples of the teacher – God – himself.[196]

For Tolstoy, this arrogant self-righteousness about possessing the truth is what has allowed hell to be restored, and this fraud must be exposed.[197] Tolstoy even wrote an open appeal directly to the clergy, calling it to "forego for a while your assurance that you [...] are the true disciples of the God Christ" – predictably, to no avail.[198]

  Other Christian anarchists are also suspicious of the self-righteousness of the church and its members. Andrews repeats the words of a friend of his, who says that "Religious people love to play a game called 'church.' We all dress up, and go through our paces in the service together, and whoever looks the most religious wins."[199] Hennacy likewise accuses each church of "[praying] more and [doing] less than the other."[200] The church, for them, is hypnotised by its self-importance, and thus forgets about Jesus' subversive teaching.

---

[194] Leo Tolstoy, "The Restoration of Hell," in *On Life and Essays on Religion*, trans. Aylmer Maude (London: Oxford University Press, 1934), 309.
[195] Tolstoy, "The Restoration of Hell," 313.
[196] Tolstoy, "The Restoration of Hell," 313-314.
[197] For Tolstoy, it is also the chief cause of division among Christians, since different churches each believe they hold the truth and seeks to preserve their own tradition. Leo Tolstoy, "A Confession," in *A Confession and Other Religious Writings*, trans. Jane Kentish (London: Penguin, 1987), 73-76; Tolstoy, "Introduction to an Examination of the Gospels," 96-99.
[198] Leo Tolstoy, "An Appeal to the Clergy," in *On Life and Essays on Religion*, trans. Aylmer Maude (London: Oxford University Press, 1934), 282.
[199] He continues: "The prize for the winner is approval. No one gives a damn about really being involved in one another's lives." Andrews, *Not Religion, but Love*, 116.
[200] Hennacy, *The Book of Ammon*, 108.

## 3.4.2 – *Obscure rituals and beliefs*

Indeed, Christian anarchists criticise the church for concealing Jesus' political teaching by prioritising obscure and hypnotic external rituals. Tolstoy maintains that Jesus himself denounces such "external forms of religion" and "ceremonial performances" as "harmful" and "injurious" delusion.[201] Tolstoy goes even further: for him, the sacraments amount to "coarse, degrading sorcery," and belief in the Eucharist, to "blasphemy."[202] Christian anarchists like Tolstoy (hence with the exception of at least the Catholic Workers)[203] therefore see church liturgy as an instrument of deception.

Tolstoy accuses the church of inventing not just obscure rituals but also obscure dogmas and beliefs, again to further distract its flock from Jesus' radical teaching. One example Tolstoy highlights is the church's claim that the Bible is infallible and sacred, and its consequent regard for the Old and New Testaments as "equally divinely inspired."[204] According to Tolstoy, this belief forces the church to seek to justify every bizarre assertion in the Bible, again to the neglect of Jesus' revolutionary teaching. It also "makes the importance of the New Testament consist not in its moral teaching, not in the Sermon on the Mount, but in the conformity of the Gospels with the stories of the Old Testament."[205] Tolstoy believes that this endeavour "harms" the "mind," is morally perverting, and deludes people into thinking that just by "professing this teaching, [...] they are living a really Christian life."[206] Even the four Gospels, for Tolstoy, are not "infallible expressions of divine truth," but the attempt of "innumerable minds and hands" to summarise the teaching of a man who wrote nothing himself – hence they are full of "errors" and inaccuracies.[207] Thus, to claim that the Christian scriptures are infallible is for Tolstoy just another trick to distract from the subversive implications of Jesus' teaching.

Related to this, of course, is the church's affirmation that Jesus does not reject Moses' law, the Christian anarchist position on which is discussed in

---

[201] Tolstoy, "The Gospel in Brief," 265-267.
[202] Tolstoy, "A Reply to the Synod's Edict of Excommunication," 219, 220 (respectively).
[203] Many Catholic Workers, Dorothy Day in particular, regularly attend mass and have faith in the mysterious power of the sacraments.
[204] Tolstoy, "Introduction to an Examination of the Gospels," 103.
[205] The full sentence reads as follows: "Besides the history of the Old Testament you also impart the New Testament to children and to ignorant people in a way that makes the importance of the New Testament consist not in its moral teaching, not in the Sermon on the Mount, but in the conformity of the Gospels with the stories of the Old Testament, in the fulfilment of prophecies, and in miracles, the movement of a star, songs from the sky, talks with the devil, the turning of water into wine, walking on the water, healings, calling people back to life, and finally the resurrection of Jesus himself and his flying up to the sky." Tolstoy, "An Appeal to the Clergy," 287.
[206] Tolstoy, "An Appeal to the Clergy," 288-297. (The first two words are from page 288, and the longer sentence from page 294.)
[207] Leo Tolstoy, "How to Read the Gospels and What Is Essential in Them," in *On Life and Essays on Religion*, trans. Aylmer Maude (London: Oxford University Press, 1934), 207 (in the footnote). See also Tolstoy, "The Gospel in Brief," 121-122. Indeed, if Tolstoy wrote this harmonised version of the Gospel, it was precisely to iron out the inconsistencies between the four competing accounts, and to weed out their irrational sections. On page 128 of his Gospel, Tolstoy also remarks that since the church claims that its position has been inspired by the Holy Ghost, it should call its faith "Holy Ghostism after the name of the last revealer."

Chapter 1. For Tolstoy, this claim is clearly contradictory,[208] and results in a deliberately "cloudy interpretation" of the Sermon on the Mount.[209]

According to Christian anarchists, the church has also intentionally obscured Jesus' condemnation of the rich and preference for voluntary poverty (which is discussed in Chapter 5). Myers, for instance, rejects the standard interpretation of the "eye of a needle" saying,[210] and Pentecost refuses to interpret "ye have the poor always with you" as implying that striving to alleviate poverty is to act against God's intentions.[211] These interpretations, for Christian anarchists, deliberately blur Jesus' clear denunciation of the accumulation of riches.

Yet another theme from the Gospels which is intentionally clouded by "standard interpretations," for Myers, is the narrative of Jesus' last days, traditionally celebrated during "Holy Week."[212] He remarks that

> Conditioned by centuries of liturgical and theological reproductions, we think of the "Upper Room" as a lofty eucharistic moment, rather than the conflict-ridden final hours of a fugitive community in hiding, whose solidarity is crumbling in the face of state power. We envision Gethsemane as Jesus' obedient submission to the preordained plan of salvation history, rather than the deep internal struggle of a leader coming to terms with the consequences of his subversive practice.[213]

Again, the established understanding and liturgy linked to these Biblical passages obfuscates an alternative, more politically subversive reading of them.

Aside from these suspicious interpretations of scripture, Christian anarchists also denounce specific church dogmas as superstitious and absurd. One example which Tolstoy singles out is the Nicene Creed. He maintains that it is "impossible to believe" in both "salvation through faith in the redemption or the sacraments," as posited by the Nicene Creed, and in "applying Christ's moral teaching in [one's] life."[214] For him, this Creed is nonsensical – if it were true, then it would suffice "to communicate it with reasonable persuasion plainly and simply."[215] Instead, the church preaches it through violence and hypnotism, claims Tolstoy, especially directed to children and the uneducated – all this to conceal the radical nature of Jesus' teaching.

Thus several Christian anarchists reject the standard doctrine that Jesus died to atone for our sins. Tolstoy also mocks the doctrine of the Trinity. He argues that if these and other dogmas were crucial tenets of his teaching, then Jesus would have surely made a point of saying so.[216] Tolstoy therefore

---

[208] Tolstoy, *What I Believe*, 64.
[209] Tolstoy, *What I Believe*, 61.
[210] Myers, *Binding the Strong Man*, 274-275.
[211] Hugh O. Pentecost, *First Anniversary Address*, available from http://www.deadanarchists.org/Pentecost/anniversary.html (accessed 22 November 2007), para. 14. (Matthew 26:11, Mark 14:7, John 12:8.)
[212] Myers, *Binding the Strong Man*, 354.
[213] Myers, *Binding the Strong Man*, 354.
[214] Tolstoy, "The Kingdom of God Is within You," 84.
[215] Tolstoy, "An Appeal to the Clergy," 284.
[216] Tolstoy, *What I Believe*, 137. On this topic, while describing Tolstoy's views, Maude writes: "It must strike any one who reads the Gospels with an open mind and compares them with the Church Creeds, that if Jesus knew that God would go on punishing mankind for Adam's sin until atonement

denounces the whole of dogmatic theology as a fraud, "not only false but [...] an immoral deception."[217] Initially, he says, he "wilfully closed [his] eyes" to these dogmas as he tried to embrace church Christianity, but he gradually found himself obliged to "throw aside, one after the other, the propositions of the Church," since they were getting in the way of Jesus' teaching.[218]

Tolstoy thereafter spent much time and effort deriding these dogmas in order to expose their irrationality. "I am hopelessly evil," he writes,

> and I must know it. My salvation is not to be found by guiding my life by the gift of reason, and, having recognized good and evil, by making choice of the good. No, Adam once for all has committed evil for me, and Christ once for all has redeemed Adam's sin, and therefore I, as a mere spectator, have but to lament over the fall of Adam and to rejoice over the redemption by Christ.[219]

Moreover, this life "is an evil, fallen, and degenerate life – a parody of the life which we imagine God meant to give us," and "the chief aim of life is not to try to live this mortal life" according to the Sermon on the Mount, but "to convince ourselves that after this life will begin the real life."[220] As to "reason," not only is it "of no importance," but it is "a temptation and an impertinence."[221] It is obvious from excerpts like these that Tolstoy does not hesitate to use irony to ridicule church dogmas.

Tolstoy therefore sees dogmatic theology as containing the "most incomprehensible, blasphemous and shocking propositions, not merely incompatible with reason, but quite incomprehensible and contrary to morality."[222] He also finds it incredible that "In this demand for belief in the impossible and unreasonable, we go so far that the very unreasonableness of what we ask to be believed is taken as a sign of its truth."[223] For Tolstoy, "To assert that the supernatural and irrational form the essential characteristic of religion is like observing only rotten apples, and then asserting that a flabby bitterness and a harmful effect to the stomach are the prime characteristics of the fruit called Apple."[224] Dogmatic theology, for Tolstoy, is not the prime characteristic of Christianity, and to see it as such is to surrender to the church's obfuscation of Jesus' subversive teaching. Moreover, even though, nowadays, only few people still genuinely believe in these dogmas, the tragedy remains that the church's version of Christianity is accepted as the authoritative one. "Christianity" is understood to be this official and dogmatic Christianity preached by the church.

---

was made, and if Jesus approved of this and made it the chief aim of his life and death to appease such a God, and if, moreover, he knew that men's eternal salvation depends on these things and on their believing rightly about them, it is singularly unfortunate that he forgot to mention the matter and left us to pick it up from obscure remarks made years later by St. Paul, whom he never met, and whose mind, character, and work, differed considerably from his own." Maude, *The Life of Tolstóy*, 32.

[217] Tolstoy, "Introduction to an Examination of the Gospels," 96.
[218] Tolstoy, *What I Believe*, 181.
[219] Tolstoy, *What I Believe*, 103-106.
[220] Tolstoy, *What I Believe*, 137.
[221] Tolstoy, *What I Believe*, 106.
[222] Tolstoy, "Introduction to an Examination of the Gospels," 96.
[223] Tolstoy, *What I Believe*, 152.
[224] Tolstoy, "What Is Religion?," 272.

Yet this perspective on Christianity, according to Andrews, "is essentially static," "admits no questions," and "demands complete conformity."[225] It therefore "rips the heart out of Christianity, replacing the warm, kind-hearted compassion of Christ with cold, hard-headed propositions about Christ, and relating to people, often violently, in terms of an ideology of Christianity, rather than the non-violent love of Christ."[226] As a result, "we tend to treat Christ as our *idol*, someone we'd like to be like, but know we never will be like; rather than our *model*, someone we'd like to be like, and do our best to be sure we are like."[227] Yet "Christ doesn't merely *tell* us the way, he *is* the way."[228] Hence Andrews encourages us to "become less concerned about being 'Christian' and a lot more concerned about being 'Christlike.'"[229] Christian anarchists therefore wish Christians were less preoccupied with performing rituals and preaching dogmatic theology, and more with embodying Jesus' teaching and example.

The difficulty, of course, is that the church has "hidden" the "clearness, simplicity, and reasonableness […] of the teaching of Jesus […] under the veil of cunning," says Tolstoy, "under a pretended teaching which is falsely attributed to him."[230] The church has consciously mixed truth with falsehood, and cemented the mix with a plethora of rules about external worship. It has thus succeeded in keeping the radical truth mostly hidden – to such an extent that to quote Chelčický, people "hold Christian faith to be a heresy, while heresies they often parade around as faith."[231] Christians are convinced they have understood Jesus' teaching, and believe that this teaching "can be accepted without changing our life."[232] They are so hypnotised that they "deceive one another and cannot get out of that enchanted circle," says Tolstoy.[233] If one exposes the contradictions, it causes unease and confusion, because people generally assume that they can trust the learned authorities' pronouncements on Jesus' teaching.

For that matter, Tolstoy believes that many theologians are fully aware of the revolutionary potential of Jesus' teaching – but while they sometimes debate it amongst themselves, they keep it hidden from the masses. If one

---

[225] Andrews, *Christi-Anarchy*, 76-77.
[226] Andrews, *Christi-Anarchy*, 77.
[227] Andrews, *Christi-Anarchy*, 114 (Andrews' emphasis).
[228] Andrews, *Christi-Anarchy*, 115 (Andrews' emphasis).
[229] Dave Andrews, *The Urgent Need for a Global Ethic*, available from http://www.daveandrews.com.au/publications.html (accessed 3 December 2006), 7. See also Andrews, *Christi-Anarchy*, 83-84. Elsewhere, Andrews comments that "One of the problems people have with Christians is that we are not only un-Christ-like, but we also use our Christian theology to rationalize our continuing to be un-Christ-like. […] This sticks in the throats of many non-Christians who hoped Christians might be better." Moreover, "Gandhi […] was not afraid to confront Christians with our misuse of the theology of the cross in rationalizing our continued un-Christ-likeness." Andrews, *The Crux of the Struggle*, 37.
[230] Tolstoy, *What I Believe*, 50.
[231] Molnár, *A Study of Peter Chelčický's Life*, 55 (quoting Chelčický). Andrews quotes Ellul, who says that "Christianity is the very opposite of the revelation of God in Jesus Christ," in Andrews, *Christi-Anarchy*, 69. As to Hennacy, he finds it astonishing "To have to argue with Christians that God would take care of those who seek first the Kingdom; to have to try to prove to a priest that Jesus really meant the Sermon on the Mount; to have to tell so-called metaphysical leaders that their Mammon worship was not important and that 'all things work together for good to those that love God.'" Hennacy, *The Book of Ammon*, 118.
[232] Tolstoy, "The Kingdom of God Is within You," 120.
[233] Tolstoy, "The Kingdom of God Is within You," 86.

reminds them of Jesus' teaching, they become angry and publicly contradict it. Tolstoy cannot avoid the conclusion that church theologians are hypocrites preaching hypocrisy. He reminds them that Jesus roundly condemns such hypocrisy, and warns that false interpretations of his teaching will not be forgiven. As to the laity, Tolstoy calls it to use reason – the one gift which he believes God to have granted to all human beings – to deconstruct traditional interpretations, separate truth from falsehood, and uncover the truly radical potential of Jesus' teaching and example.[234]

Jesus founded neither church nor state – indeed he subverted both – yet church and state elites have managed to hide his teaching behind obscure beliefs and rituals, and use their professed authority to bless the violent state with apparent religious endorsement. These dogmas and ceremonies hypnotise and stupefy the masses into submission – particularly soldiers, the state's guardians and cannon-fodder. Thus institutionalised Christianity, with its textual reinterpretations, theological doctrines and liturgical performances, is itself the heart of the deception which has kept a lid on the revolutionary potential of Jesus' anarchist message.

## 3.4.3 – Institutional religion

Christian anarchists maintain that Jesus did not intend to be the founder of an institutionalised religion. One of Jesus' intentions, for them, was indeed to bypass such human intermediaries and do away with priests. In line with this, the early church was more of a popular movement than an institution – Elliott and Andrews call it the "Jesus Movement."[235] Tolstoy argues that this early church "existed in her purity as long as her teachers endured patiently and suffered," but that this ended "as soon as they became fat and sleek."[236] For Christian anarchists, today's institutionalised "church" bears little resemblance to its oldest ancestor, and must be clearly dissociated from the church or assembly which Jesus initially intended.

Given this assessment on the corruption of the church, several Christian anarchists (with significant exceptions)[237] are very critical of institutionalised or organised religion. Hennacy writes that "All religions are a mockery of God no matter if they were once started by inspired prophets."[238] He frequently and pointedly describes himself as a "nonchurch Christian."[239] He insists that when an organisation becomes more important than its alleged ideal, it

---

[234] Tolstoy understands true "faith" to be precisely about using reason to clarify the truth, and he interprets the famous saying about Peter as the rock of the church to be precisely about that. Tolstoy, "The Gospel in Brief," 212, 219; Leo Tolstoy, "The Teaching of Jesus," in *On Life and Essays on Religion*, trans. Aylmer Maude (London: Oxford University Press, 1934), 388; Tolstoy, *What I Believe*, 149-152.
[235] Andrews, *Plan Be*, 56; Elliott, *Freedom, Justice and Christian Counter-Culture*, 174.
[236] Tolstoï, *What to Do?* , 203-204.
[237] As already noted in the Introduction, Catholic Workers (Day in particular) are generally respectful of the Catholic Church. Maurin was also not necessarily critical of the Pope, as evidenced in Maurin, *Easy Essays (2003)*, 89.
[238] Hennacy, *The Book of Ammon*, 472.
[239] For instance: Hennacy, *The Book of Ammon*, 204, 472.

becomes institutionalised and thus corrupt. In turn, institutionalised religion typically seeks support and protection from the state. Over time, the corrupt and powerful organisation becomes tyrannical and dictatorial. For Tolstoy, as Jesus says, a tree must be judged by its fruits, and since organised religion and its priesthood produces evil fruits, it must be rejected.

Christian anarchists therefore sometimes use strong language against the church and its clergy. The priests, for Tolstoy, "are not only not the pillars of Christianity they profess to be, but are its greatest enemies."[240] The church is a "church of Satan," says one contributor to *A Pinch of Salt*.[241] Chelčický calls the pope the Antichrist, and a contemporary Church Council "an assembly of harlots, assassins of righteous men, and transgressors of all commandments of God."[242] Hennacy, however, concedes that he does not think that churchmen "are knowingly wicked people," but simply that "they are in a bad business."[243]

Not all Christian anarchists use strong language to describe the church and clergy (again, Catholic Workers like Day spring to mind as exceptions), but the majority are very critical of the institutional church and its historical achievements. Either way, implicitly or explicitly, all Christian anarchists call for a frank re-examination of Jesus' teaching and life. All see revolutionary potential in it. All see criticism of the state implicit in it. All see an anarchist society envisioned in it. Few believe the institutional church to be founded in it, and most are very critical of what the church made of it. For them, for true Christianity to be embraced by humanity, Jesus' teaching and example must be examined anew.

## 3.5 – Awakening to true Christianity

For many Christian anarchists, therefore, Christianity has never been properly tried yet on a significant enough scale. Catholic Workers often repeat a quote from Chesterton: "The Christian ideal has not been tried and found wanting. It has been found difficult and left untried."[244] Maurin comments that it "has not been tried because people thought it was impractical. And men have tried everything except Christianity."[245] Hence he says of "Catholic scholars" that they "have failed to blow the dynamite of the Church."[246] For Christian anarchists,

---

[240] Leo Tolstoy, "Letter to a Non-Commissioned Officer," in *Tolstoy's Writings on Civil Disobedience and Non-Violence*, trans. Aylmer Maude (New York: Bergman, 1967), 121.
[241] Kenny Hone [?], "The Church of Satan," *A Pinch of Salt*, issue 14, March 1990, 8.
[242] Molnár, *A Study of Peter Chelčický's Life*, vii, 34, 71 (for the Chelčický quote), 74; Wagner, *Petr Chelčický*, 96 (for the Antichrist comment), 140-143.
[243] Hennacy, *The Book of Ammon*, 468.
[244] Maurin, *Easy Essays (2003)*, 87.
[245] Maurin, *Easy Essays (2003)*, 87.
[246] Maurin, *Easy Essays (2003)*, 3. Hennacy says something similar but using a different analogy: "God is a powerline, and a person can pray and do anything he wishes, but unless he connects with this powerline he is not connected up. It is all talk. If the average person tries to 'connect up' without using a transformer he is likely to get shocked or killed [...]. Churches should be these transformers to do the 'connecting,' but they weaken the current until it hardly means a thing." Hennacy, *The Book of Ammon*, 172.

"The Christian truth about society has not yet been revealed," and Jesus' radical teaching is still waiting to be discovered.[247]

In the meantime, and because Jesus' revolutionary teaching has not been articulated by the church, people have turned their attention to secular, socialist ideals. The poor rightly feel "betrayed by Christianity," remarks Day, and they have therefore sought emancipation in alternative ideals.[248] Tolstoy, however, is very critical of these. For him, not only are progressive secular ideals based on a mistaken understanding of human nature, but they will not truly alleviate the plight of the poor. He believes that nineteenth century socialists and similar proponents of secular ethics are mostly hypocrites giving false hopes to the oppressed (partly because their answers to the big questions of life do not go honestly and deep enough to the full truth about life, reason and violence in the way in which Tolstoy felt his own deliberations did) while continuing to benefit from their privileged position. Either that or they are deluded, for reasons discussed in Chapters 4 and 5. Either way, their secular programme will not address the root of social injustice, because the state is left intact. For Tolstoy, Jesus said that "Men's lives, with their different creeds and governments, must all be changed. All human authorities must disappear."[249] The only revolution that can save humanity, therefore, is the Christian anarchist revolution.

Hence Tolstoy repeatedly calls humanity to bethink and awaken itself out of its hypnotic state, its orthodox trap, and fully embrace Jesus' teaching.[250] He is quite hopeful in that he believes in a natural evolution of humanity from darkness into light, and he believes that the desired awakening can happen at any moment. What is needed is for enough people to see through and shake off orthodox deceptions, to see the truth of Jesus' revolutionary teaching.[251] Just as it took a long time for "Christians" to awaken to the injustice of the slave trade, but they eventually did, one day, they will awaken to the violence and injustice of the state. When enough people will have freed themselves from the deceptions of the state and church, a final push by public opinion will usher the age of true Christianity, of Christian anarchy.[252] People will recognise that the state is violent, cunning and exploitative, that the church's dogmas are deceptive, and its interpretation of Jesus' teaching dishonest. At that point, the loving society envisioned by Jesus might finally come about.

In the meantime, however, Christian anarchists have to live in a world in which the state is strong. Hence they need to decide how to respond to this state, as well as on how to embody Jesus' teaching and example in this context. The first is the theme of Chapter 4, the second, of Chapter 5.

---

[247] Berdyaev, *The Realm of the Spirit and the Realm of Caesar*, 61.
[248] Day, *Selected Writings*, 41.
[249] Tolstoy, "The Gospel in Brief," 293.
[250] The expressions of "bethinking" and "awakening," here paraphrased, are Tolstoy's. Tolstoy, "An Appeal to the Clergy," 307-308; Tolstoy, "The Kingdom of God Is within You," 202, 358-368, 398-407, 420-421; Tolstoy, "The Law of Love and the Law of Violence," 217-219.
[251] The notions of "shaking off" the "deception" and "hypnosis," here paraphrased, are Tolstoy's. Tolstoy, "The Kingdom of God Is within You," 202, 384-385, 393, 420-421. Tolstoy, "Letter to a Non-Commissioned Officer," 124-126.
[252] The expressions of a "push" and "public opinion," here paraphrased, are Tolstoy's. Tolstoy, "The Kingdom of God Is within You," 359-368; Tolstoy, "The Law of Love and the Law of Violence," 199-203.

# Part II – The Christian Anarchist Response

# Chapter 4 – Responding to the State

Having outlined the many Christian anarchist criticisms of the state, it is now time to explore the proposed response to the state's contemporary prominence.[1] That response is made of two fairly distinguishable concerns: how to respond to and interact with the state; and how to build an alternative, stateless society. That is, on the one hand, Christian anarchists have to work out a way in which to interact with the prominent state, a *modus vivendi* that honours Jesus' teaching; and on the other, they have to exemplify the Christian alternative to it, to embody and to thereby demonstrate the possibility of the sort of stateless community life which they understand Jesus to be calling them to. The former is the subject of this Chapter; the latter, of the next.

This Chapter's focus on the Christian anarchist response to the state brings to the fore two important New Testament passages which have been deliberately omitted so far: Paul's instructions to the Christians in Rome that they "be subject unto higher powers," and Jesus' saying about rendering to Caesar what belongs to Caesar. Both passages are often seen as problematic for Christian anarchism since they appear to contradict its basic proposition – after all, do they not clearly instruct Christians to concentrate on spiritual matters, to submit to the authority of the state, and to let the state and its politicians deal with political affairs? Also, there are substantial disagreements among Christian anarchists on how to approach these passages – are not these disagreements further confirmation that their interpretation is mistaken? By considering a wide range of Christian anarchist writings, this Chapter suggests a negative answer to both these questions. That is, despite some real differences, a generic and not too incoherent Christian anarchist interpretation (or set of interpretations) can be sketched out according to which these passages do instruct Christians to stay out of state politics, but they imply an indifference to the state that is peculiarly subversive. For Christian anarchists, this Chapter therefore shows, it is the standard interpretation of these passages that turns out to be false and dishonest.

The first section of this Chapter discusses Romans 13, looking at Christian anarchists' opinion of Paul, at their actual exegesis of the passage, and then at what they make of similar passages elsewhere in the New Testament. In the second section, the two instances where Jesus is giving advice on payment of taxes are interpreted from a Christian anarchist perspective: first the "render unto Caesar" passage from Mark 12, then the curious recommendation about collecting the temple tax from the mouth of a fish, from Matthew 17. The third section then outlines the divergent Christian anarchist positions on civil disobedience: the case against it, the case for it, and the paramount importance of obeying God whatever the case may be. The fourth section then lists a few examples of what Christian anarchists argue to be appropriate responses to the

---

[1] The first three sections of this Chapter have also been published as Alexandre J. M. E. Christoyannopoulos, "Responding to the State: Christian Anarchists on Romans 13, Rendering to Caesar, and Civil Disobedience," in *Religious Anarchism: New Perspectives*, ed. Alexandre J. M. E. Christoyannopoulos (Newcastle upon Tyne: Cambridge Scholars Publishing, 2009).

state's demands, such as on elections, on taxes, and on military conscription. The fifth and final section then considers the Christian anarchist rejection of any violent revolutionary methods in response to the state, and the related conviction that real change can only come about by example rather than by force.

## 4.1 – Paul's letter to Roman Christians, chapter 13

In his study of New Testament passages relevant to the state, Penner summarises the conventional view when he asserts that "The most elaborate and specific body of teaching in the New Testament on the Christian's relation to the state is Romans 13," where Paul writes the following:[2]

1. Let every soul be subject unto the higher powers. For there is no power but of God: the powers that be are ordained of God.
2. Whosoever therefore resisteth the power, resisteth the ordinance of God: and they that resist shall receive to themselves damnation.
3. For rulers are not a terror to good works, but to the evil. Wilt thou then not be afraid of the power? do that which is good, and thou shalt have praise of the same:
4. For he is the minister of God to thee for good. But if thou do that which is evil, be afraid; for he beareth not the sword in vain: for he is the minister of God, a revenger to execute wrath upon him that doeth evil.
5. Wherefore ye must needs be subject, not only for wrath, but also for conscience sake.
6. For for this cause pay ye tribute also: for they are God's ministers, attending continually upon this very thing.
7. Render therefore to all their dues: tribute to whom tribute is due; custom to whom custom; fear to whom fear; honour to whom honour.[3]

Of course, this book argues – as Penner does – that many other passages in the New Testament have inherent implications for the state, but Romans 13 is probably the one with the most explicit reference to it. A few other scattered verses which have been omitted so far also refer directly to the state in a similar vein, but as noted in more detail below, what they say is largely encompassed by Romans 13. As a result, as Eller puts it, a thinker's "handling of Romans 13 (along with Mark 12) is the litmus test" of his Christian anarchism.[4]

Mainstream theologians have made the most of this passage to legitimise the church's support of the state. Ellul thus claims that "the official church since Constantine has consistently based almost its entire 'theology of the state' on Romans 13 and parallel texts in Peter's epistles."[5] Based on Romans 13, establishment theologians have argued that Christians ought to submit to state authorities, even to wield the sword when these request it, because God clearly intends the state to be his main tool to preserve social order and stability – in other words, that the state is sanctified by God, and that Christians should welcome that and collaborate with the state. For many Christian anarchists,

---

[2] Penner, *The New Testament, the Christian, and the State*, 76.
[3] Romans 13:1-7.
[4] Eller, *Christian Anarchy*, 114-115.
[5] Ellul, "Anarchism and Christianity," 166-167.

however, such an interpretation betrays the subtle meaning of this passage. It does not take its context into account, and anyway, it leaves the church with the difficulty of dealing with the "embarrassment" of "tyrants."[6] Once again, therefore, Christian anarchists are suspicious of traditional exegeses, and instead, they articulate an alternative interpretation of their own.

## 4.1.1 – Paul's weaknesses

Before this alternative interpretation can be outlined, it is important to note that Paul himself is also viewed with suspicion by some Christian anarchists.

For a start, several Christian anarchists note that Paul himself did not always submit to Roman authorities, and they demonstrate this by listing his many recorded acts of disobedience. Redford even remarks that Paul proudly cites his punishments for such disobedience as proof of his commitment to Jesus.[7] Was Paul guilty of "evil works"? Was he not doing "that which is good" by spreading the good news? Why then did he incur the "wrath" of rulers? It would seem that either Paul did not abide by his own pronouncement, or that what he meant in Romans 13 must be slightly different to what he is traditionally interpreted to have meant.

Either way, some Christian anarchists also make the point that Christians ought in the first instance to follow Jesus, not Paul, since unlike Jesus, "The apostles can err in their acts."[8] Indeed, for Tolstoy, the church's "deviation" from Jesus' teaching begins precisely with Paul.[9] Hence both Tolstoy and Hennacy (who was strongly influenced by Tolstoy) frankly dislike Paul and see him as at best confusing Jesus' message, at worst betraying it. As to Elliott, he contends that Paul's advice to submit to authorities was informed by his "expectation of Christ's imminent return."[10] For him, Paul advised submission because he mistakenly expected "the present order" to be soon "swept away."[11] The "tragedy," he argues, is that for the church, Paul's instruction "takes precedence over the witness of Jesus."[12] For Christian anarchists like Tolstoy, Hennacy and Elliott, therefore, *Jesus* is the important teacher, and Paul is just an erring follower who has been given too much kudos by the tradition. Beyond this, these particular Christian anarchists have little else to say on Romans 13.

Not all Christian anarchists, however, dislike Paul or view him with such suspicion. Some point out that he seems to be edging towards anarchism

---

[6] Many theologians have sought to argue that somehow Romans 13 does not really apply to tyrants and dictators, but only to peaceful and just forms of government – especially democratic ones – but Ellul has little respect for such "strange casuistry" which anyway does not appear founded on the passage. Ellul, *Anarchy and Christianity*, 79.
[7] (He also remembers that Joseph and Mary disobeyed Herod to protect baby Jesus.) Redford, *Jesus Is an Anarchist*, 13-14.
[8] Penner, *The New Testament, the Christian, and the State*, 98.
[9] Tolstoy, "Church and State," 336.
[10] Elliott, *Freedom, Justice and Christian Counter-Culture*, 52.
[11] Elliott, *Freedom, Justice and Christian Counter-Culture*, 77-78.
[12] (He uses the word "tragedy" in the plural.) Elliott, *Freedom, Justice and Christian Counter-Culture*, 78 (see also 89).

when he says that for Christians, "there is no law."[13] Others remember his advice to contend against the principalities and powers (examined in Chapter 2). Others still try to defend him against allegations that he sought protection from the state – obviously anathema to any genuine anarchist. Either way, not all Christian anarchists see Paul as a traitor. Several try to make sense of Romans 13 rather than reject it outright as dishonest and inauthentic. Their resulting exegesis, they argue, actually ends up paradoxically confirming rather than contradicting the Christian anarchist position.

### 4.1.2 – The Christian anarchist exegesis: subversive subjection

One Christian anarchist interpretation of Romans 13, posited by Redford, is to argue that this is an "ingenious case of rhetorical misdirection."[14] For him, Romans 13 must not be interpreted literally because Paul is not speaking his true mind (partly for reasons mentioned in the next paragraph). Similar arguments have been made by others: Timothy Carter, for instance, suggests that Paul is using the "classic ironic technique of blaming by apparent praise."[15] He sees Paul's apparent reverence for authorities as "deeply subversive" because of this "ironic edge."[16] Both Carter and Redford point to examples of Paul disobeying authorities as proof of him not really meaning for Christians to obey. Such interpretations of Romans 13, however, can – rightly or wrongly – sound more like justifications to brush the text aside than patient attempts to grapple with it and give it a real chance.

Yet both Redford and Carter also note something that several other Christian anarchists take note of as well: Paul's letter is addressed to the Christian community in Rome – the very heart of the Roman empire. It is written at a time when Christians are already being persecuted across that empire. For several Christian anarchists, therefore, Paul is deliberately very cautious in his wording, as his letter could easily be used by Roman authorities as a pretext to step up this persecution. Hence for some Christian anarchists, Paul's advice is largely "pragmatic rather than philosophical:"[17] by submitting to the authorities' wishes, Roman Christians might be able to develop good relations with their persecutors and thereby avoid further conflict. Thus, the historical context of Romans 13 is important to pay attention to. It helps explain why Paul would have deliberately addressed – in *this* letter – the question of Christians' relations to the authorities in the first place, and indeed even perhaps why he may have opted for that "rhetorical misdirection" or "irony" alleged by Redford and Carter.

---

[13] Unfortunately, however, the anarchist interpretation of this passage is nowhere elaborated in great detail – it is usually just cited as evidence of Paul's anarchist credentials. Day, *Selected Writings*, 343; Simon Watson, "The Catholic Worker and Anarchism," *The London Catholic Worker*, issue 15, Lent 2006, 8. (Galatians 5.)
[14] Redford, *Jesus Is an Anarchist*, 14.
[15] Timothy Carter, "Commentary: The Irony of Romans 13:1-8," *Third Way*, issue 28, May 2005, 21. (This commentary was sent to me by Keith Hebden, the current editor of the revived *A Pinch of Salt* – which is why it is mentioned briefly here.)
[16] Carter, "Commentary," 21.
[17] Meggitt [?], "Anarchism and the New Testament," 11.

The textual context of Romans 13:1-7 is even more important, as it throws light on what Paul has in mind when writing these particular verses. Along with Yoder, several Christian anarchists insist that "chapters 12 and 13 in their entirety form a single literary unit."[18] In both chapters, Paul is writing about love and sacrifice, about overcoming evil with good, about willingly offering oneself up for persecution. Interpreting Romans 12 and 13 as a coherent whole, Ellul notes that "there is a progression of love from friends to strangers and then to enemies, and this is where the passage then comes. In other words, we must love enemies and therefore we must even respect the authorities."[19] Eller agrees: these authorities "are brought in as Paul's example of those to whom it will be the most difficult to make the obligation apply."[20] They are "a test case of our loving the enemy."[21] In any case, for Yoder, "any interpretation of 13:1-7 which is not also an expression of suffering and serving love must be a misunderstanding of the text in its context."[22] Hence Paul's message in Romans 13 is to call for Christians to subject themselves to political powers *out of love*, forgiveness and sacrifice.

Seen in that light, Romans 13 is not a betrayal of Jesus' revolutionary Sermon on the Mount (as Tolstoy would have it), but actually an exegesis of it: Romans 12-13 is an "eloquent and passionate statement" of the Sermon applied to the case of the state.[23] In the Sermon, Jesus calls for his followers to love their enemies, to give not only the requested coat but the cloak also, and to bless their persecutors. In Romans 12-13, Paul is doing the same, and applying Jesus' commandments to the authorities.

At the same time, Eller emphasises that to "be subject to" does not mean to worship, to "recognise the legitimacy of" or to "own allegiance to."[24] For him, "It is a sheerly neutral and anarchical counsel of 'not-doing' – not doing resistance, anger, assault, power play, or anything contrary to the 'loving the enemy' which is, of course, Paul's main theme."[25] Hence Paul is not counselling "blind obedience."[26] As explained below, if what the authorities demand conflicts with God's demands, then Christians ought to disobey – but also then submit to any punishment. Ultimately, a Christian's allegiance is only to God, not to the state.

Yet Paul goes on to write that "the powers that be are ordained of God."[27] Does this not suggest divine sanctification of state authorities? Does it

---

[18] He notes the unity of the theme both chapters address, but also some specific verbal cross-references that link the two chapters together. Yoder, *The Politics of Jesus*, 196.
[19] He adds that Paul "is reminding Christians that the authorities are also people (there was no abstract concept of the state), people such as themselves, and that they must accept and respect them, too." Ellul, *Anarchy and Christianity*, 81. See also Ellul, "Anarchism and Christianity," 170.
[20] Eller, *Christian Anarchy*, 197.
[21] Eller, *Christian Anarchy*, 197.
[22] Yoder, *The Politics of Jesus*, 198.
[23] [Anonymous], *Why I Worship a Violent, Vengeful God*, para. 5.
[24] Eller, *Christian Anarchy*, 199.
[25] Eller, *Christian Anarchy*, 199.
[26] Wink, *Jesus' Third Way*, 59.
[27] Romans 13:1. Redford reads this to mean that "the only *true* and *real* authorities are *only* those that God appoints, i.e., one cannot become a *real* authority or ruler in the eyes of God simply because through force of arms one has managed to subjugate a population and then proclaim oneself the potentate. Thus, by saying this Paul was actually rebuking the supposed authority of the mortal

not imply that political powers are always endorsed by God? For Christian anarchist writers, it only means that God "allows" it, not that "he agrees with it" or that these authorities are "good, just, or lovable."[28] Here, they recall 1 Samuel 8, where despite his disappointment with the Israelites' request for a king, God grants them their wish. Chelčický furthermore argues that "The earthly rulers and the state authorities are the punishment of God for disobeying His laws."[29] Thus God does indeed "appoint" state authorities, but reluctantly, only because his commandments are being ignored. It does not imply that anything the authorities do is willed by God, or that, as Penner puts it, "God's moral character is in any way imprinted on the state."[30] Again, "appointing" or "ordaining" is not the same thing as "approving" or "agreeing with."[31]

Nonetheless, since people have lost faith in him and instead place their faith in political authorities, since people will not listen to him anymore, God uses the state as one of his "servants" in his mysterious ordering of the cosmos. Several Old Testament passages describe God using state authorities to punish sins and injustices. The state, it seems, is one of God's tools to maintain some order where his commandments are not being heard.[32]

It is probably in that sense that "rulers are not a terror to good works, but to the evil."[33] The authorities should be feared by those who do evil, but not by those who do good works. Perhaps there is a suggestion that *despite* doing good works and nevertheless being persecuted by the state – which they were – Christians should *not fear* the state. This particular phrase, however, is often avoided in the Christian anarchist literature: Christian anarchists never really seem to fully make sense of it. What they do point out, however, is that it cannot mean that these authorities do not persecute good people: they crucified Jesus, Paul himself was beaten by them, and Christians were being persecuted just as Paul was writing these words. Besides, elsewhere, Paul criticises these authorities, and warns Christians of further persecution.[34] Therefore, this verse cannot mean that the state always praises good works and only ever punishes evil

---

governments as they exist on Earth and are operated by men!" Redford, *Jesus Is an Anarchist*, 15 (Redford's emphasis).

[28] For the first two quotes, see Alexis-Manners, *Deconstructing Romans 13*, 3. For the last one, see Ellul, who writes that "We have to remember that the authorities have attained to power through God. Yes, we recall than Saul, a mad and bad king, attained to power through God. This certainly does not mean that he was good, just, or lovable." Ellul, *Anarchy and Christianity*, 81.

[29] Molnár, *A Study of Peter Chelčický's Life*, 95 (paraphrasing Chelčický).

[30] This touches on an important debate regarding God's ultimate responsibility for the actions conducted by political authorities, a debate which Christian anarchists do not venture into in any detail and which is therefore left out of the main body of this Chapter (although a few reflections related to this are offered further below in this section). Suffice it to say here that this debate concerns not just Christian anarchists, but all Christian theologians, and that most would agree that God cannot be fully responsible for every act ever conducted by political authorities, as this would imply the unacceptable conclusion that God killed Jesus. For more on this, see for instance Penner, *The New Testament, the Christian, and the State*, 65-66, 89-90, 119 (for the quote).

[31] Alexis-Manners, *Deconstructing Romans 13*, 3.

[32] Sometimes, therefore, these authorities are indirectly and unconsciously doing God's work, and according to Eller, if, as a Christians, you were to resist them, "You could find yourself resisting the particular use God has in mind for that empire; at the very least, you definitely are trying to take over and do God's work for him." Eller, *Christian Anarchy*, 203.

[33] Romans 13:4.

[34] Redford, *Jesus Is an Anarchist*, 16-17. (1 Corinthians 2:6-8; 2 Timothy 2:8-9, 3:12.)

ones. What it perhaps does imply is that persecuted Christians should not fear these authorities because in the eyes of God, the works that they do are good, and even if they die, at least their "martyrdom" will "magnify their glory" – much like Jesus' death did.[35]

In any case, even state leaders are subject to God's judgement, and are warned of this (for instance) in Acts 28:20.[36] These leaders do not know the precise purpose God has in mind for their actions: "like a plough in the hands of the ploughman," Chelčický writes, the ruler "does not know what the ploughman intends."[37] God uses state authorities as "instruments in the grand economy of his providence," but at the same time, state leaders "[act] entirely out of [their] own perverse and wicked inclinations" and are "punished" by God accordingly, writes Ballou.[38] It is therefore *unknowingly* that state authorities are acting as God's servants. In turn, their actions and intentions are examined by God, and, where their work is evil, they will themselves eventually incur God's providential wrath.

Yoder moreover recalls that according to Paul, the principalities and powers, "which were supposed to be our servants, have become our masters and our guardians."[39] They "were created by God," but they "have rebelled and are fallen" because "they claimed for themselves an absolute value."[40] Yoder then argues that instead of God "ordaining" these powers, a better interpretation of the text would see him as "ordering" them.[41] That is, "God is not said to *create* or *institute* or *ordain* the powers that be, but only to *order* them, to put them in order."[42] Yet while God "orders" them and uses them for good, they remain rebellious and fallen nonetheless.[43] That God puts them in order does not mean that they "do no wrong, commit no sin, and deserve no punishment."[44] They remain living evidence of humanity's rebellion against God.

It is crucial to bear in mind, then, that if God ordains state authorities, it is only to maintain order *among those who have refused to follow his commandments.* In other words, the state may be valid for non-Christians, but if "all truly followed in Christ's footsteps it would wither away."[45] God uses the

---

[35] Chelčický (whose words are borrowed here) actually goes even further, saying that "if they were killed, it was in accordance with His will; He wanted to test His servants and to magnify their glory through their martyrdom" (which again touches on the debate over God's ultimate responsibility for actions perpetrated by political powers). Molnár, *A Study of Peter Chelčický's Life*, 119 (quoting Chelčický).

[36] Molnár, *A Study of Peter Chelčický's Life*, 120. Tennant also draws a parallel with the Book of Samuel. He writes: "Samuel made it plain that '[i]f you fear the Lord and serve and obey him and do not rebel against his commands, and if both you and the king who reigns over you follow the Lord your God – good! But if you do not obey the Lord, and if you rebel against his commands, his hand will be against you, as it was against your fathers' (1 Sam. 12:14, 15). Similarly, Paul in Romans 13:4 asserts that the human ruler 'is God's servant to do you good,' which therefore implies that the ruler is to abide by God's law and to enforce it upon the ruled." Tennant, *Christianarchy?* , para. 9.

[37] Molnár, *A Study of Peter Chelčický's Life*, 120 (quoting Chelčický).

[38] Ballou, *Christian Non-Resistance in All Its Important Bearings*, 35.

[39] Yoder, *The Politics of Jesus*, 141.

[40] Yoder, *The Politics of Jesus*, 142.

[41] Yoder, *The Politics of Jesus*, 201. On page 172 onwards, he also agrees with the view that to "be subject to" would be better translated as to "subordinate oneself to."

[42] Yoder, *The Politics of Jesus*, 201 (Yoder's emphasis).

[43] Yoder, *The Politics of Jesus*, 141-144.

[44] Ballou, *Christian Non-Resistance in All Its Important Bearings*, 34.

[45] Brock, *The Political and Social Doctrines*, 48.

state in his ordering of the cosmos only because his commandments for a peaceful and just society are not being followed. In a community of Christians, however, these authorities and powers would be redundant. Thus for several Christian anarchists, the state remains a regrettable reality among non-Christians, but only because they refuse to follow Jesus' commandments. The state is violent and unchristian, and God wants *all* humans to overcome it; but as long as Jesus' alternative is not embraced, the state remains God's only way to somehow redress sins and injustices. The state is a symptom of human imperfection, tolerated by God only because he accepts that we have rejected him.

Of course – and disappointingly for non-Christian anarchists – this does imply that Christian anarchist theory is only prescribing anarchism for Christians. Among non-Christians, the state is an acceptable, though regrettable and imperfect, servant of God's justice. This does not diminish in any way the many criticisms Christian anarchists mount against the state. After all, Christian anarchists want to see Jesus' teaching taken up by all – they want the whole society to convert to true Christianity. But at the same time, according to Paul, they are to tolerate the presence of the state as an unfortunate symptom of society's rejection of God.[46] Christianity overcomes the state, but it tolerates it among the heathens. That, for several Christian anarchists, is what Paul is implying in Romans 13. He is reminding Christians of the reasons for the state's existence, but he is also calling them to patiently endure and forgive this pagan rejection of God.

The message behind this, therefore, is to make it plain "that Christians were not a sect out to overthrow Caesar and force their religion on everyone else."[47] Paul's concern is for Christians not to engage in any violent insurrection – despite their persecution. He is telling the Christians in Rome to "stay away from any notion of [...] insubordination," and instead to adopt a loving, "nonresistant attitude towards a tyrannical government,"[48] an attitude which would therefore "set an example of humility and peaceful living for others."[49] In other words, Romans 13 "seeks to apply love in a context where Christians detested the authorities."[50] It does not legitimise the state, but it also makes a point of not legitimising any insurrection against it.[51] It is reminding Christians that Jesus refused to engage in that type of revolutionary politics, that the Christian

---

[46] It should be noted that while this view summarises the conclusion reached by those Christian anarchists who give Paul a chance and see his Epistles as genuinely compatible with Jesus' teaching, it is not one that those who reject him outright – Tolstoy in particular – would subscribe to. For someone like Tolstoy, who universalises Jesus' commandments by grounding them in universal reason, the state is evil and should not be tolerated but overcome – period. Then again, in a sense, for all Christian anarchists, non-Christians are those who have not fully understood or seen the truth. Moreover, all Christian anarchists prescribe tolerance, love and forgiveness of those who err on the side of evil. In the end, therefore, the difficulties which those who reject Paul would feel with the conclusions derived by those who do not are probably less serious than might first appear.
[47] Tennant, *Christianarchy?* , para. 19.
[48] Yoder, *The Politics of Jesus*, 202.
[49] Tennant, *Christianarchy?* , para. 19.
[50] Ellul, "Anarchism and Christianity," 170.
[51] Eller argues that Paul here focuses particularly on delegitimising a violent revolution precisely because of the similarity of Jesus' subversive message with the message of violent revolutionaries. Eller, *Christian Anarchy*, 11, 41, 115, 121-125.

revolution is to happen by setting an example of love, forgiveness and sacrifice instead.

Thus the Christian is to remain indifferent, so to speak, to particular forms of political authority (this important topic is discussed in more detail in the Conclusion). However evil or tyrannical any one of them may be – and there is no denying that they can be very brutal – a follower of Jesus should overcome evil by good: by loving enemies, by turning the other cheek, and by submitting to persecution and possible crucifixion. It is not for the Christian to avenge human injustices, however horrible any one of them may be. In Romans 12:19 (as already noted in Chapter 1), Paul recalls that God said "Vengeance is mine; I will repay." That is, vengeance is denied to the Christian because it belongs to God (and the Christian does not know how God will "avenge" injustices). Eller also interprets Paul as telling Christians not to "set their minds on high things" – that is, for Eller, not to get concerned and distracted by specific political ideologies or utopias.[52] Instead, the only priority is to abide by Jesus' commandments.

Hence, according to this Christian anarchist exegesis, Romans 13 cannot be interpreted as divine sanctification for the state. It accepts the state as ordained by God, but only for those who have rejected God. Thus "It carefully declines to legitimize either Rome or resistance against Rome."[53] For Ellul, "we have no right to claim God in validation of this order," and therefore "This takes away all the pathos, justification, illusion, enthusiasm, etc" that can be associated with specific political authorities (again, this theme is revisited in the Conclusion).[54] Moreover, to quote Tennant, "an exhortation to obey authorities does not imply that those authorities are required to exist in the first place. [...] If there is no state, there is no need to obey it."[55] Besides, as Chelčický remarks, while the passage does counsel submission to the state, it does not provide a justification for Christians to become rulers themselves. Indeed, when Paul was writing this, all authorities were pagan – Romans 13 never considers "Christian" authorities. What Paul is saying in Romans 13 is that Christians should love and forgive state authorities – not that they should participate in their sins.

This does not imply uncritical passivity. Where the state infringes upon God's commandments, the Christian should – as always – side with God, not with the state. Indeed, submission to the state is only a consequence, a derivative of submission to God and God alone. When Christians submit to the state, it is because they are submitting to God. If the state demands something that conflicts with God's commandments, then the state should be disobeyed.

Thus, in apparent reference to Mark 12, Paul concludes Romans 13:1-7 by calling for Christians to "Render therefore to all their dues."[56] This is examined in more detail in the next section, but the gist of it for Christian anarchists is that Christians ought to give to the state what it asks, *unless* doing so conflicts with what God demands. What is required, then, is "passive

---

[52] The passage thus paraphrased by Eller is from Romans 12:16, and, in the King James Version, reads as "Mind not high things." Eller, *Christian Anarchy*, 118-121.
[53] Eller, *Christian Anarchy*, 204.
[54] Ellul, *Anarchy and Christianity*, 88.
[55] Tennant, *Christianarchy?* , para. 18.
[56] Romans 13:7.

subordination" but not "pious obedience to the state."[57] The state should be treated with love and due respect, but "Obedience to secular power has definite limits. In matters contrary to the law of God, the Christian is obliged to refuse obedience" and "must willingly suffer whatever penalties the state imposes."[58] As explained further below, this means that Christians must disobey "Directives such as those to wield the sword, to swear an oath, or to enter a public court to settle a dispute."[59] What is less straightforward is the question concerning the payment of taxes – which is addressed in detail below.[60]

The important point is that, as Ballou writes, "The Christian has nothing to care for but be a Christian indeed."[61] The state is a pagan distraction, to be treated with love and respect, but only because doing so is in line with Jesus' teaching of love and forgiveness – and it is *that* teaching only which the Christian is really abiding by even when submitting to the state.[62] It certainly has nothing to do with any duty to protect certain freedoms or maintain some order in a chaotic war of all against all.

### 4.1.3 – Similar passages in the New Testament

Christian anarchists interpret shorter passages elsewhere in the New Testament along the same lines. The most important of these minor passages is probably 1 Peter 2:13-25, since as Alexis-Manner claims, it is "usually used by supporters of obedience to the government as a trump card" if defeated on Romans 13.[63] For Christian anarchists, however, it is actually just repeating the Sermon on the Mount and Romans 13. Peter's plea for Christians to show respect for the king, for instance, is in line with Romans 13. Even Peter's call for slaves to submit to their masters – which Paul also makes elsewhere – mirrors Romans 13: it is not a defence of slavery, but a call to subvert it by accepting one's subjection to it out of love and forgiveness.[64] Moreover, just as for Paul, Christian anarchists point out that Peter seems not to have always fully abided by his pronouncements – at least not if they are taken to imply total and unquestioning obedience to authorities. Like Paul, Peter's allegiance is first and foremost – indeed *only* – to God, and the respect he shows to the state is never absolute.

The other New Testament passage cited by a Christian anarchist in parallel to Romans 13 is Revelation 13 – despite these two being often cited as an example of contradicting passages. For Eller, the Beast does not represent just the Roman empire but the spiritual essence of what he calls "arkydom" – in other

---

[57] Wagner, *Petr Chelčický*, 51.
[58] Wagner, *Petr Chelčický*, 136.
[59] Wagner, *Petr Chelčický*, 136.
[60] Note that Redford considers any insinuation by Paul that Roman Christian should pay taxes to be yet again a case of "rhetorical misdirection." Redford, *Jesus Is an Anarchist*, 17-18.
[61] Ballou, *Christian Non-Resistance in All Its Important Bearings*, 37.
[62] It certainly has nothing to do with any duty to protect certain freedoms or maintain some order in a chaotic war of all against all.
[63] Alexis-Manners, *Deconstructing Romans 13*, 3.
[64] 1 Peter 2:18-25. For Christian anarchists, the same applies to other New Testament passages on slavery and on accepting one's unfortunate position in life (such as Paul's epistle to Philemon, or 1 Corinthians 7:20-24).

words, the state.[65] And as discussed in Chapter 2, Revelation "does not go on to suggest that Christians should therefore resist, withhold their taxes, or do anything else in opposition to this monster;" but instead, "they are asked to bear patiently whatever injustice and suffering comes upon them *by keeping faithful to Jesus*," and at the same time to "come out of the arkys," to "separate [themselves] (spiritually and psychologically) lest [they] get [themselves] entangled and go down with them."[66] For Eller, therefore, there is no opposition between Romans 13 and Revelation 13: neither differentiates between "good" or "bad" states (they refer to "arkydom" in general) and both advise patience and submission rather than violent revolution.

Thus, however surprising or incoherent it might at first seem, several Christian anarchists argue that Romans 13 calls for Christians to accept and forgive the state, but without granting it any absolute authority.[67] For them, this does not in any way compromise Jesus' implicit criticism of the state or his call for humanity to overcome it, but it simply confirms that Jesus calls for Christians to subvert it through love, service and sacrifice.

## 4.2 – Jesus' advice on taxes

The other New Testament passage often quoted by supporters of the state as proof of the error of Christian anarchism is the following:

13. And they send unto him certain of the Pharisees and of the Herodians, to catch him in his words.
14. And when they were come, they say unto him, Master, we know that thou art true, and carest for no man: for thou regardest not the person of men, but teachest the way of God in truth: Is it lawful to give tribute to Caesar, or not?
15. Shall we give, or shall we not give? But he, knowing their hypocrisy, said unto them, Why tempt ye me? bring me a penny, that I may see it.
16. And they brought it. And he saith unto them, Whose is this image and superscription? And they said unto him, Caesar's.
17. And Jesus answering said unto them, Render to Caesar the things that are Caesar's, and to God the things that are God's. And they marvelled at him.[68]

This passage has often been cited by church theologians to suggest that when pushed on the question, Jesus defended the state's tax system. It has also been used to develop the notion of a division of realms between state and church, whereby the state would be concerned with the material and temporal realm (politics), and the church, with the spiritual and eternal one (religion). For Christian anarchists, both interpretations are illegitimate: Jesus is neither "siding

---

[65] Eller, *Christian Anarchy*, 43-44.
[66] Eller, *Christian Anarchy*, 44-45 (Eller's emphasis).
[67] Such an interpretation is indeed one that is bound to result in "angry objection" from both liberal and conservative quarters, as Yoder reports to have faced in response to the first edition of his book. Yoder, *The Politics of Jesus*, 188 (for the quoted expression)-192.
[68] Mark 12:13-17. See also Matthew 22:15-22; Luke 20:19-26.

with the establishment,"[69] nor dividing realms between politics and religion. Again, therefore, Christian anarchists put forward their own, different interpretation.

### 4.2.1 – Caesar's things and God's things

To begin with, Ellul argues that Jesus must have had "a reputation of being hostile to Caesar" for this question to be asked in the first place.[70] He was already seen as a political threat, and the authorities were trying to entrap him: if he had answered "yes, give tribute to Caesar," then this would have dealt a blow to his following; but answering a clear "no" would have made him liable for immediate arrest.[71] For some Christian anarchists, therefore, Jesus' response is a "politically astute" response to a contentious question, an ingenious reply to avoid the trap set by his detractors.[72]

Furthermore, some Christian anarchists claim that the image and superscription on the coin were a clear infringement of the first and second commandments – in other words, a case of idolatry. Hence Jews caught with the coin were arguably violating the Decalogue.

Ellul moreover explains that "in the Roman world an individual mark on an object denoted ownership."[73] Therefore the coin did indeed belong to Caesar – money does belong to the state.[74] If Caesar wanted his coin back, then this coin should be given back to him. The important question, then, is to define what belongs to Caesar and what belongs to God – because Jesus does also emphasise that what belongs to God should be given to God.[75] For Ellul, what belongs to Caesar is simply "Whatever bears his mark! Here is the basis and limit of his power. But where is his mark? On coins, on public monuments, and on certain altars. That is all. [...] On the other hand, whatever does not bear Caesar's mark does not belong to him. It all belongs to God."[76] Thus, for instance, Caesar has no right over life and death. That belongs to God. While the state can

---

[69] Eller, *Christian Anarchy*, 76. Hennacy also remarks that "It would not seem logical that, by saying 'Render unto Caesar,' which meant giving taxes to kill in war, to spread hatred and lies about the enemy, to return evil for evil, that Jesus would nullify all of his Sermon on the Mount." Hennacy, *The Book of Ammon*, 298.
[70] Ellul, *Anarchy and Christianity*, 59.
[71] Some commentators note that the issue of payment of taxes was a sensitive political issue both when Jesus said this and at the time during which Mark is estimated to have written his Gospel (during the Jewish-Roman war of AD 66-70). In both contexts, Jesus' answer would clearly and pointedly distance him and his followers from the Zealots who favoured armed rebellion against Rome. Eller, *Christian Anarchy*, 78-80; Ellul, *Anarchy and Christianity*, 61; Myers, *Binding the Strong Man*, 312-314; Penner, *The New Testament, the Christian, and the State*, 50.
[72] Elliott, *Freedom, Justice and Christian Counter-Culture*, 52.
[73] Ellul, *Anarchy and Christianity*, 59.
[74] (A close look at the small print of most bank notes reveals that the same logic still applies today.) Note that Christian anarcho-capitalists like Redford disagree on this: for him, Caesar's face on the coin does not make the coin his. Redford, *Jesus Is an Anarchist*, 10-11.
[75] Eller reports Hengel's thesis that this crucial second part of the sentence is what "left them 'amazed,'" and that "the Greek of the connective should be translated 'but' in place of the usual 'and': 'Render to Caesar the things that are Caesar's – *but* to God the things that are God's.'" Eller, *Christian Anarchy*, 77.
[76] Ellul, *Anarchy and Christianity*, 60.

therefore expect us to return its coins and monuments when requested, it has no right to kill dissidents or plunge a country into war.[77]

Christian anarchists indeed maintain that what belongs to God is much broader than what belongs to Caesar: to Jesus' Jewish audience, the debt owed to God is incomparably greater. Besides, money is "the domain of Mammon."[78] For a faithful Jew, the higher obligation is always to God, and, against this, Caesar's claim is almost irrelevant. Myers therefore contends that by his careful answer, Jesus

> is inviting them to act according to their allegiances, stated clearly as *opposites*. Again Jesus has turned the challenge back upon his antagonists: What position do *they* take on the issue? *This* is what provokes the strong reaction of incredulity [...] from his opponents – something no neat doctrine of "obedient citizenship" could possibly have done.[79]

In other words, as Ellul insists, "Jesus does not say that taxes are lawful."[80] Instead, according to Penner, he uses to occasion "to point the Jews to the fact that they had, in effect, accepted the supremacy of Rome, when He made them acknowledge whose coinage they were using."[81] His detractors had not been giving to God what belongs to God: they had betrayed God by their de facto allegiance to Caesar.

For Eller, therefore, the apparent choice between Caesar's things and God's things is "fake," because "Whether a person chooses God or not is the only real issue."[82] By uttering those words, Jesus "makes the distinction between the one, ultimate, absolute choice and all lesser, relative choices."[83] Questions like the payment of taxes "are 'adiaphora' [Greek for 'indifference'] in comparison to the one choice that really counts" – the choice of God above Caesar.[84] We are told several times in the New Testament that we "cannot serve two masters," and the message of this passage is "to absolutize God alone and let the state and all other arkys be the human relativities they are."[85] Seen in this light, Jesus' answer is not so much a defence of the tax system or of the division of realms, but a counsel of subversion by indifference (see the Conclusion for more on this).

Thus, for Christian anarchists like Eller, "civic responsibility is a proper obligation only insofar as it does not threaten our prime responsibility of

---

[77] Ellul, *Anarchy and Christianity*, 60-61. To cite a few more examples of separate "belongings," Ellul writes that the only things which belong to Caesar are those things which he himself "creates;" Myers notes that the land of Israel belongs to God; Penner argues that the verse only admits taxes among things to be rendered to Caesar, and that one could perhaps infer that being made in the image of God, the Jews "owed themselves to God;" and Tolstoy suggests that money and property belong to Caesar, but one's soul, to God. On a different note, Hennacy quotes Day, who said (quoting St. Hilary): "The less of Caesar's you have, the less you have to render." Ellul, "Anarchism and Christianity," 167-168; Hennacy, *The Book of Ammon*, 298 (see also 317, 431); Myers, *Binding the Strong Man*, 312; Penner, *The New Testament, the Christian, and the State*, 52; Tolstoy, "The Gospel in Brief," 228; Tolstoy, "The Teaching of Jesus," 371-372.

[78] Ellul, cited in Eller, *Christian Anarchy*, 11 (see also 195).

[79] Myers, *Binding the Strong Man*, 312 (Myers' emphasis).

[80] Ellul, *Anarchy and Christianity*, 60.

[81] Penner, *The New Testament, the Christian, and the State*, 51.

[82] Eller, *Christian Anarchy*, 11 (also: 77).

[83] Eller, *Christian Anarchy*, 82.

[84] Eller, *Christian Anarchy*, 83.

[85] Eller, *Christian Anarchy*, 83.

giving God what belongs to God."[86] In other words, "let Caesar take his cut," says Eller, "so that you can continue to *ignore* him."[87] Hence if Jesus seems to recognise as appropriate the payment of taxes, it is because that concern is insignificant compared to the one concern that really matters.[88] At the same time, however, what must be denounced is Caesar's attempt to compete with God: the state's tendency to seek to dethrone God and be worshipped and served in his place (a tendency noted in Chapters 2 and 3) – precisely because that touches on the much more important issue of rendering to God what belongs to God.

### 4.2.2 – The temple tax and fish episode

Christian anarchists read the other main passage in which Jesus refers to paying taxes in much the same way. The progression of the dialogue in Matthew 17:24-27 is even more interesting than in the "render unto Caesar" case:

24. And when they were come to Capernaum, they that received tribute money came to Peter, and said, Doth not your master pay tribute?
25. He saith, Yes. And when he was come into the house, Jesus prevented him, saying, What thinkest thou, Simon? of whom do the kings of the earth take custom or tribute? of their own children, or of strangers?
26. Peter saith unto him, Of strangers. Jesus saith unto him, Then are the children free.
27. Notwithstanding, lest we should offend them, go thou to the sea, and cast an hook, and take up the fish that first cometh up; and when thou hast opened his mouth, thou shalt find a piece of money: that take, and give unto them for me and thee.[89]

Ellul thinks that too much attention has focused on the curious and miraculous side of this prescription.[90] For Christian anarchists, it is clear from the dialogue that the state has "no legitimate jurisdiction over" Christians, yet that Christians should nonetheless pay taxes "to avoid offense"[91] – that is, "so as not to stir up trouble."[92] If Jesus ends up asking for Peter to pay the tax, Eller therefore writes, it is "for reasons entirely extraneous to the recognition of any arky."[93]

Eller then compares the justifications given in Romans 13, Mark 12 and this passage as follows:

In Mark 12, the stated reason was "Let Caesar have his coin so he will get off your back and leave you alone to be giving to God what belongs to him."
In Romans 13, it was "Let Caesar have his coin so that you won't be drawn

---

[86] Eller, *Christian Anarchy*, 196.
[87] Eller, *Christian Anarchy*, 196 (Eller's emphasis).
[88] Note that Christian anarcho-capitalists refuse to recognise any validation by Jesus of any form of taxation since, as far as they are concerned, taxes are pure theft.
[89] Matthew 17:24-27.
[90] Ellul, *Anarchy and Christianity*, 63-64. Ellul's interpretation of that fantastic story of fishing out a coin is that, in making that prescription, "Jesus held power to ridicule," that "an absurd miracle" is performed "to show how unimportant the power is." Ellul, "Anarchism and Christianity," 167; Ellul, *Anarchy and Christianity*, 64.
[91] [Anonymous], *Ninety-Five Theses in Defense of Patriarchy*, theses 77-78.
[92] Redford, *Jesus Is an Anarchist*, 11, 49.
[93] Eller, *Christian Anarchy*, 206.

into the disobedience of failing to love him." Now, in Matthew 17, it is "Let Caesar have his coin so as not to be guilty of causing 'offence.'"[94]
The priority is always to follow God and his commandments, and any submission to the state is an epiphenomenon to that.

Yet Eller also points out that in some other instances, Jesus does not seem to mind causing offence.[95] The difference, he argues, is between causing offence "deliberately" and "accidentally."[96] The difference is in what constitutes the main motive. To repeat, what matters is always giving priority to God, and abiding by his commandments. In doing so, one should indeed avoid causing offence to others. Sometimes, however, people might be offended at one's actions when giving priority to God – but if so, "that's their business," says Eller, because offence was never intended and because the only purpose was "to obey God."[97] What should be avoided is the causing of deliberate offence. For Eller, therefore, the proper Christian attitude with respect to taxes is to pay them, because withholding them would turn the causing of offence into a political instrument and thus lose sight of what is much more important: obedience to God.[98]

## 4.3 – Pondering the role of civil disobedience

The above exegeses open up the question of the limits of acceptability of any civil disobedience. On this issue, however, Christian anarchists are somewhat divided.

### *4.3.1 – Against civil disobedience*

The main Christian anarchist who argues against any form of civil disobedience is Eller. For him, one should not engage in "deliberately illegal action" in attempting to counter any particular evil in society.[99] Too often, he says, Christians who try and fail to persuade others react by "turning up the volume," at the "high end" of which is civil disobedience.[100] Such disobedience, according to Eller, presumes that effectiveness is enhanced by "offense-causing."[101] Yet for him, civil disobedience helps neither the "content" nor the "persuasiveness" of the "witness and protest" because it "does not call attention to the truth content of the witness and protest but to the offensive behavior of the witness-protester."[102]

---

[94] Eller, *Christian Anarchy*, 208.
[95] Eller, *Christian Anarchy*, 208.
[96] Eller, *Christian Anarchy*, 208-210.
[97] Eller, *Christian Anarchy*, 209.
[98] He sees "tax payment" (or "an allowing of Caesar to take his taxes") as "the model of all the offense-causing actions of Jesus," which only aims to obey God and has "total disregard of the arkys;" and "tax withholding" as an "arky-faith action" which "[uses] offense as a tactic for influencing events." Eller, *Christian Anarchy*, 208-209 (emphasis removed).
[99] Eller, *Christian Anarchy*, 210.
[100] Eller, *Christian Anarchy*, 210-214.
[101] Eller, *Christian Anarchy*, 214.
[102] Eller, *Christian Anarchy*, 213.

For him, "failure of others to accept" the "truth" does not justify "recourse to questionable methods."[103]

One of Eller's problems with such tactics is that typically, they result in "two worldly arkys condemning each other" – that is, a political climate of mutual, zealous and self-righteous condemnation that polarises society into rival political views.[104] What is lost in the process is the higher aim of obedience to God. For him, any civil disobedience should be accidental to that primary goal. Obedience to God, rather than effectiveness in persuasion, should always remain the guiding principle. Hence one should avoid compromising with power politics. According to Eller, direct action is not the only way to bring about change. Another way, and for Eller the only Christian way, is "voluntary self-subordination."[105] Eller admits that the outcome of this method is uncertain, but he argues that is nonetheless precisely the alternative which Jesus and his early followers taught and lived.

### 4.3.2 – For (non-violent) civil disobedience

For other Christian anarchists, Eller's position is a "total cop-out."[106] It is "naïve," and in effect, it "accepts" or "condones" oppression.[107] They say that "we *are* called to resist, […] to actively confront evil and hatred and violence" – though loving and non-violent means should of course be adopted in that struggle.[108] For these Christian anarchists, the "arrogant state" simply must be confronted, unmasked and subverted.[109]

Moreover, doing so is not unchristian: Jesus himself challenged the authorities, spoke out against them, broke a few rules (on the Sabbath) and even sometimes engaged in militant (but non-violent) direct action. He also warned that Christians will be persecuted and that this will be an "opportunity to bear witness."[110] Furthermore, the cross is "a symbol of resistance to evil," so following Jesus and taking up the cross implies at least some form of resistance as well. Besides, when God and the state require contrary things, Christians are clearly called to obey God, not the state, which would then indeed imply some

---

[103] Moreover, for Eller, however evil the state is (and he repeats that he continues to believe it is), at least democratic laws do make it possible to use more honourable ways of being heard. Eller, *Christian Anarchy*, 216.
[104] Eller, *Christian Anarchy*, 217.
[105] Eller, *Christian Anarchy*, 239.
[106] These words are Stephen Hancock's, the editor of the first fourteen issues of *A Pinch of Salt*, in his review of the book, in Stephen Hancock [?], "Christian Anarchy: Jesus' Primacy over the Powers (Book Review)," *A Pinch of Salt*, issue 8, October 1987, 9, 13.
[107] For the accusations of "political naivety" and "condoning" of "oppression," see Hancock [?], "Christian Anarchy," 13. As to Ellul, he writes that "Christian radicalism […] cannot counsel the poor and the oppressed to be submissive and accepting […] without at the same time constraining the rich to *serve* the poor." Ellul, *Violence*, 150-151 (Ellul's emphasis).
[108] The ending of the full sentence of the latter passage is important: "We are called not to be passive, but to actively confront evil and hatred and violence with love of enemies, forgiveness and self-sacrifice," hence also the insistence on non-violence. [Anonymous], "The Power of Non-Violence," *London Catholic Worker*, issue 12, January 2005, 2-3 (writer's emphasis).
[109] Molnár, *A Study of Peter Chelčický's Life*, 39.
[110] [Anonymous], "The Power of Non-Violence," 3. (Luke 22:12-13.)

form of disobedience to the state – but also patient endurance of the consequences.[111] Hence rather than seeing it as civil disobedience, for them, one should see it as obedience to God.[112]

Some Christian anarchists even speak of acts of disobedience or witness against the state in the language of liturgy. Thus civil disobedience becomes "a prayer," and the confronting of state power a sort of "casting out of demons."[113] Chapter 6 mentions several examples of such language and actions.

Then again, Ellul insists that civil disobedience must not become a political strategy to achieve political goals – whether or not it can indeed be effective as a political strategy. As discussed below, Christians can sympathise with and participate in movements of civil disobedience, but their goal must always remain solely to follow God's commandments.

Moreover, the state's punishment for such disobedience should be fully accepted. Day says of Hennacy that "His refusal to pay federal income tax does not mean disobedience since he has always proved himself to be ready to go to jail, to accept the alternative for his convictions."[114] The penalty for disobedience should thus be patiently and forgivingly endured. Besides, for Christian anarchists, prison is a kind of resting place in today's world, a "new monastery" in which Christians can "abide with honour."[115]

In any case, there can be no denying that there is a tension here, between Jesus' call to turn the other cheek and his cleansing of the temple, between what Eller calls "voluntary self-subordination" and civil disobedience. Yet even so, perhaps the tension can be over-exaggerated somewhat: for Christian anarchists, even turning the other cheek is defiantly trying to unmask an evil (the violence that has just been inflicted), and Jesus' cleansing of the temple was an equally non-violent attempt to unmask another evil (the concentration of power in the temple).

As to Tolstoy, as discussed elsewhere, he seems to have quite genuinely read (perhaps indeed misread) Matthew 5:39's "non-resistance to evil" as "non-resistance to evil *by evil*" – not unlike Wink, as explained in Chapter 1.

---

[111] This sentence is heavily paraphrased from Ballou, *Non-Resistance in Relation to Human Governments*, 4; Ballou, "Non-Resistance," 141-142. Note that even Eller admits that in his argument, he has not analysed this very possibility of the state demanding something that is contrary to the will of God – in which case he is clear that the only course of action is obedience to God and "accidental" disobedience to the state. He then even proposes a "litmus test for making the distinction: If an action of lawbreaking is done solely as obedience to God, then, plainly, whatever media exposure occurs is entirely incidental to the purpose. If, however, media exposure is *sought* and valued, the action must have a political, arky motivation that goes far beyond simple obedience to God." Eller, *Christian Anarchy*, 218-219 (Eller's emphasis).

[112] This paraphrases Archbishop Raymond G. Hunthausen, who said "Some would call what I am urging 'civil disobedience.' I prefer to see it as obedience to God." [Anonymous], *Multi-Denominational Statements* (Jesus Radicals), available from http://www.jesusradicals.com/library/taxes/wartaxes.html (accessed 5 November 2006), under "Roman Catholic Archdiocese of Seattle".

[113] [Anonymous], "A Vote for the State Means..." *A Pinch of Salt*, issue 12, March 1989, 9; Jim Douglass, "Civil Disobedience as Prayer," *A Pinch of Salt*, issue 3, Pentecost 1986, 8-9.

[114] Dorothy Day, "Foreword," in *The Book of Ammon*, by Ammon Hennacy, ed. Jim Missey and Joan Thomas (Baltimore: Fortkamp, 1994), ix.

[115] Douglass, "Civil Disobedience as Prayer," 8 (where the expression "new monastery" comes from); Hennacy, *The Book of Ammon*, 132 (from where the expression "abide with honour" is borrowed).

This ambiguity was picked up by his detractors, and many of his admirers cling on to the non-violent resistance which Tolstoy's reading allows for. As explained again below, Tolstoy himself was happy to disobey and "to fight the Government by means of thought, speech, actions" and the like, and called for Christians to desist from participating in the mechanics of the state's power.[116] He was keen to protest and disobey, though always in a strictly non-violent way.

### 4.3.3 – Obedience to God

So who is right? Are Christians called to engage in civil disobedience? It seems that there can be no nicely detailed and predefined answer to these questions. In the end, as discussed in Chapter 1 and 2, the highest principle and ultimate reference on which all Christian (anarchist) guidelines are based is love. Jesus frequently repeats that love of God and of one's neighbour are the two most fundamental commandments on which the rest of the law subsequently hangs.[117] It follows that if to love God and to love one's neighbour sometimes requires disobeying the state (when obedience to the state would imply a violation of any of these two fundamental commandments), then there might be a case for moderating the purest interpretation of the subsequent command not to resist.

Besides, if Wink is right in interpreting the original Greek as criticising violent resistance and rebellion only, and indeed since (according to Christian anarchism) Jesus does call us to react to state violence and injustice, it seems that some degree of civil disobedience is inevitable for his followers in certain specific situations. Nevertheless, what for Christian anarchists remains clearly contradictory to Jesus' commandments is *violent* resistance. It is whether *non-violent* resistance can sometimes be tolerated that is less clear. Evil certainly calls for a response, but for Christian anarchists, this reaction can never be violent. The spectrum of possible responses to evil ranges quite narrowly from non-resistance to non-violent resistance – but also, in the latter case, submission to any consequent penalty for this resistance. Anything outside this narrow range, however, would seem to amount to a disobedience of Jesus' law of love.

At the same time, Eller's warning seems important enough to heed. For example, Tolstoy's own reaction to violence was to spread his gospel in various essays, plays and novels: his protests were largely verbal; Gandhi, who (as Chapter 6 explains) was inspired by Tolstoy, applied the principle of non-violence much more confrontationally; King and later pacifists pushed it even further into tactical political activism. Similarly, the Catholic Worker movement only adopted more confrontational methods of civil disobedience over time, partly under the influence of Hennacy. What these and other examples in Chapter 6 suggest is that there is perhaps a tendency for what begins as fairly strict non-

---

[116] Leo Tolstoy, "On Anarchy," in *Government Is Violence: Essays on Anarchism and Pacifism*, ed. David Stephens, trans. Vladimir Tchertkoff (London: Phoenix, 1990), 79. Maude also explains that one of the reasons Tolstoy dislikes scientific Marxism is precisely because it tends to prescribe patience rather than action, and that Tolstoy liked Thoreau's *Essay on Civil Disobedience* and translated it into Russian. Aylmer Maude, *Tolstoy and His Problems* (London: Grand Richards, 1901), 44-45, 48.
[117] For example, Matthew 22:36-40; Mark 12:30-31; John 13:34-35.

resistance and obedience to *God* to move along the spectrum of possible actions ever closer to *politically*-driven civil disobedience – and beyond. Eller's fear about turning up the volume might be worth remembering: doing so tends to reveal a gradual creeping towards power politics and a concomitant loss of sight of God.

Thus, even if a variety of actions are in line with a Christian anarchist reading of the Bible, one must perhaps always remain on guard to avoid the sort of degeneration spotted by Eller. Every context might result in different actions being most appropriate to continue to serve God and not the state, but it is crucial to always keep service to God as not just the primary but indeed the only concern that informs such non-violent and (in that sense) accidental civil disobedience. Indeed, for Christian anarchists, *whether obeying or disobeying*, a Christian response to the state is always incidental to the Christian obedience to God.

## 4.4 – Disregarding the organs of the state

In order to clarify somewhat the response to the state prescribed by Christian anarchists, it is helpful to look at specific examples of what, for many of them, Christians cannot collaborate with the state on.

### *4.4.1 – Holding office and voting*

The first and perhaps most obviously forbidden area for Christians concerns the holding of offices of the state. For Christian anarchists, obviously, no true Christian can become a ruler, a member of parliament or a public administrator, because this would make the Christian complicit in state violence and oppression. The only ruler Christian anarchists recognise anyway is God. Christian anarchists also reject the claim that Christian participation in the state machinery can somehow "reform" or "purify" that machine.[118] Quite the contrary: for Chelčický, participation in the government would "contaminate, even vitiate," a Christian's witness.[119] As to the situation whereby a ruler would "perchance, become a Christian," according to Chelčický, "his only means of ruling would then be persuasion, that is, preaching" – but if so, then "he is not a king any more, he becomes a priest."[120]

In addition, in that voting amounts to an endorsement of the state and its electoral procedures, it is also rejected by Christian anarchists. According to Hennacy, "by voting for legislative, judicial, and executive officials, we make these men our arms by which we cast a stone and deny the Sermon on the Mount."[121] Ballou agrees: voting makes us morally responsible for the unchristian

---

[118] Ballou, *Christian Non-Resistance*, chap. 7, para. 16-19; Ballou, *Non-Resistance in Relation to Human Governments*, 6; Ballou, "Non-Resistance," 143.
[119] Wagner, *Petr Chelčický*, 98.
[120] Molnár, *A Study of Peter Chelčický's Life*, 31.
[121] Hennacy, *The Book of Ammon*, xix. On pages 106 and 441, Hennacy writes that to those who ask him how he votes, he replies that he votes "every day" by "practising" his Christian anarchist "ideals."

actions perpetrated by whoever wins that election.[122] Indeed, Hennacy explains that "win or lose, you will have consented, by having voted, to accept the winning candidate's judgement as superior to your own."[123] Taking part in elections thus implies an implicit approval of the election process and of the legitimacy of its outcome – whatever the eventual outcome of that election. For several Christian anarchists, all this leads to a denial of the teaching of Jesus, and therefore Christians cannot take part in state elections.

### 4.4.2 – Paying taxes

Regarding payment of taxes, Christian anarchists hold sometimes slightly different positions. Some believe that Christians should not pay taxes because they fuel the state's unchristian machinery. Others argue that taxes should not be paid *willingly*, but that the state's eventual compulsory collection of them should not be resisted. In the end, most follow Jesus' advice and eventually but reluctantly pay them so as not to cause offence. In any case, among Christians, according to Chelčický, there should be no such taxes: "a Christian cannot tax another Christian."[124]

(In passing, it is worth noting that Tolstoy sometimes keenly defends Henry George's social program, which recommends a single tax on land value. Yet while this may at first seem contradictory, it must be emphasised that Tolstoy only endorses George's proposal, in Maude's words, "by way of a concession to humanity's weakness."[125] If he is at times enthusiastic about George, it is only because his programme is a step in the right direction. Tolstoy's preference, however, is to see a more radical Christian anarchist society come about. Still, his support for George does result in a somewhat ambivalent overall message concerning taxes.)

### 4.4.3 – Conscription and war

On war, the Christian anarchist position has already been discussed. War being so violent and unchristian, Christian anarchists cannot see how a Christian can become a soldier and participate in its horrors. Moreover, as already noted, soldiers are used by the state not only in war but in the repression of their own population. Hence military service, for Christian anarchists, is deeply unchristian. Where it is just an option, it should simply be ignored; but where it is compulsory, it should be opposed.

Tolstoy, who lived at a time when universal military conscription was becoming a norm, was particularly vocal in promoting conscientious objection to military service. In his writings, he reports several cases of it and of the abusive treatment which these objectors received in response to their objection. Tolstoy

---

[122] Ballou, *Christian Non-Resistance*, chap. 1, para. 51-54, and chap. 57, para. 20, 22.
[123] Hence for him, what is "irresponsible" is not refusing to vote, but voting, "for the very act of voting is dodging your responsibility by passing the buck to others." Hennacy, *The Book of Ammon*, 256 (see also 441).
[124] Molnár, *A Study of Peter Chelčický's Life*, 32 (see also 138).
[125] Maude, *The Life of Tolstóy*, 429.

cherished the hope that a wave of conscientious objection might become a tide of public opinion and pave the way for society to adopt Jesus' radical teaching. This is mentioned again in Chapter 6. The point to note here is simply that Christian anarchists called for Christians to refuse to take part in military service.

### 4.4.4 – Other state services

Since they dislike the state so much, predictably, Christian anarchists also refuse to make use of any of its organs. Thus, not only can Christians not work for the police, but for them, they should not make complaints to it or otherwise rely on its services.[126] Similarly, for Christian anarchists, neither can Christians take part in court proceedings, nor can they rely on courts for the adjudication of any disputes. Chelčický furthermore regrets that "a priest who goes [...] himself to court, elevates their shame into honour."[127] Christians cannot seek punishment of others through the judicial system, nor should they adorn secular courts with their presence. Ellul also advocates conscientious objection to things like compulsory vaccination or compulsory schooling – the latter being just a propaganda tool through the national education policy.

Overall, therefore, most Christian anarchists recommend Christian disregard for the organs and services of the state, and refusal to participate in them. Eller is perhaps the only exception in that he says he is "occasionally [...] willing to work through or even use worldly arkys" if "some immediate human good" seems possible by doing so – although he does admit that this is "risky business," because of "the danger of getting caught" in the delusion that the state is a force for good.[128] On the whole, however, most Christian anarchists would rather keep a clear distance between them and the state. Where the state insists on something like payment of taxes, most of them will eventually render Caesar his coin, but where participation in or reliance on the state implies disobedience to God (like in military service), they are calling for Christians to take a stronger stance and thus illustrate their contempt for the state and the primacy they ascribe to God.

## 4.5 – On revolutionary methods

It will be evident by now that however much they criticise the state, Christian anarchists do not favour any overthrow of government. Methods of this kind, for them, follow "the spirit of retaliation, violence, and murder," and end up causing more harm than good.[129] Their response to the state is therefore more

---

[126] Note, however, that Day admits to have called the police when "an armed maniac" tried "to kill" one of their editors, in Day, *The Long Loneliness*, 270. Note also that this is one of the issues where Yoder clearly differs from Christian anarchists: he argues that the police fulfil a role that is acceptable to Christians, although he has reservations as to whether a Christian can ever really be called to serve in the police.
[127] Molnár, *A Study of Peter Chelčický's Life*, 65 (quoting Chelčický).
[128] Eller, *Christian Anarchy*, 14-15.
[129] Garrison, "Declaration of Sentiments Adopted by the Peace Convention," 8.

compassionate, more forgiving, more patient than that of many other revolutionaries – yet they still believe that theirs is the only truly revolutionary method.[130]

### 4.5.1 – No compromise with violence

Christian anarchists therefore make a point of stressing their differences – as well as their similarities – with other revolutionary currents, usually by reiterating their absolute rejection of any compromise with violence or coercion.

Many Christian anarchists thus distinguish their position from (classic) socialist and communist thought.[131] They usually explain that while they genuinely sympathise with the goal of a communist, stateless and classless society, what they strongly disagree with are the coercive means which socialists are willing to adopt to reach that end. For Christian anarchists (as explained in Chapter 1), the end never justifies the means, because "the means become the end" or at the very least "corrupt" or obscure it.[132] Hence a stateless end cannot be reached by using the state as a means to that end. Indeed, just like Bakunin, Tolstoy foresaw the risk of a communist revolution resulting in just another dictatorship.[133] He and other Christian anarchists have therefore repeatedly called for socialists and communists to reflect on the impossibility of reaching their righteous destination by taking the reins of the state or through any other revolution method which compromises with violence.

While on this topic, it is worth noting that if Christian anarchists also sometimes distance themselves from the term "anarchism" and the revolutionary currents behind it, it is usually precisely because of the violent connotations that this word has been known to carry – especially towards the end of the nineteenth century, when anarchism was widely associated with terrorism, regicide and other forms of revolutionary violence. Often, therefore, it is only because they were not (or not yet) familiar with the strong non-violent tradition in anarchist theory that some Christian anarchists rejected the label "anarchism" altogether.[134] The very foundation of Christian anarchism is a rejection of violence, so Christian

---

[130] This is paraphrased from Tolstoy, who wrote: "Mine is the true revolutionary method," in Kennan, "A Visit to Count Tolstoi," 259.

[131] Interestingly, Hennacy suggests that if "Communism [appeals] to so many people," it might be "because we have failed as Christians." Hennacy, *The Book of Ammon*, 182. Berdyaev makes the same point in Berdyaev, *The Realm of the Spirit and the Realm of Caesar*, 150. As to Tolstoy, he writes that "Socialism is unconscious Christianity;" a point Maurin seems to be making as well. Peter Marshall, *Demanding the Impossible: A History of Anarchism* (London: Fontana, 1993), 379 (for Tolstoy's quote); Maurin, *Easy Essays (2003)*, 66.

[132] Day, *Selected Writings*, 272 (for the "means become the end" quote); Segers, "Equality and Christian Anarchism," 219-220 (for the idea that means "corrupt" ends).

[133] On the topic of predictions, note also that in 1949, Hennacy predicted that communism would "fall by its own weight of Bureaucracy and Tyranny of Power." Hennacy, *The Book of Ammon*, 125.

[134] Tolstoy, for instance, changed his mind once he read Eltzbacher's study of anarchism, as explained in David Stephens, "The Non-Violent Anarchism of Leo Tolstoy," in *Government Is Violence: Essays on Anarchism and Pacifism*, by Leo Tolstoy, ed. David Stephens (London: Phoenix, 1990), 177. He still continued to avoid the word "anarchism" to describe his own thinking (probably because of the violent connotations which *his readers* would continue to associate the term with), but he stopped using it dismissively to describe violent revolutionaries.

anarchists are just as quick to denounce anarchist schools that promote violence as they are to denounce other revolutionary currents that seek to attain their goal by taking control of the state.

Christian anarchists also comment on the Zealots, a religious and political sect which was growing in strength during Jesus' time and which sought the violent overthrow of the Roman occupation. Several Christian anarchists stress that Jesus and his followers would have clearly sympathised with the Zealots' criticisms and aspirations (in the same way that they today sympathise with socialism and communism), but that nevertheless, Jesus very clearly distanced himself from these Zealots, precisely over the question of the means to be used for the liberation of the oppressed. As explained in Chapter 1 and 2, it was precisely in his alternative method that, according to Christian anarchists, Jesus was a truly revolutionary messiah. He might have hesitated a few times and he might have contemplated alternative paths to the kingdom of God, but in the end, he willingly took up the cross and demonstrated the revolutionary potential of love and forgiveness. His teaching and his example are clear: evil – even the worst of it – should be responded to with patient love and forgiveness, even at the risk of death.

This is also where Christian anarchism clearly differs from other, more prominent theologies of liberation – theologies which often openly acknowledge their intellectual debts to Marxism. Where liberation theology seeks to overthrow oppressive governments and empower the oppressed through the state, Christian anarchism preaches patient love and forgiveness, despite very real oppression, and point out that this is the only revolutionary method grounded in the New Testament. Moreover, Christian anarchists are critical of liberation theology's dismissive treatment of the cross as a symbol of Jesus' teachings.[135] Myers puts it well, in his interpretation of what Jesus is basically telling other revolutionaries:

> Our nonviolent resistance demands no less of us than does your guerilla war ask of you – to reckon with death. But we ask something more: a heroism of the cross, not the sword. We cannot beat the strong man at his own game. We must attack his very foundations: we must render his presumed lordship over our lives impotent. You consider the cross a sign of defeat. We take it up "as a witness against them," a witness of the revolutionary power of nonviolent resistance. Join us therefore in our struggle to put an end to the spiral of violence and oppression, that Yahweh's reign may truly dawn.[136]

The cross, as discussed in Chapter 2, is not the failure of Jesus' revolution but the very epitome of it, and that is what, from a Christian anarchist perspective, has been misunderstood by other theologies of liberation.

---

[135] Myers, *Binding the Strong Man*, 431, 469-471. On page 471 (original emphasis), Myers writes: "How is it that liberation theologians want the authority of a 'history of Jesus' when it comes to solidarity with the poor, but not at the point of the strategy of the cross? The answer lies in the fact that they regard Jesus' choice of the cross as his abandonment of politics: 'Jesus dies in total *discontinuity* with his life and his cause' (Sobrino, 1978:218). It is ironic that the most indisputably *political* fact of the gospel story is *depoliticized* by liberation theology."
[136] Myers, *Binding the Strong Man*, 431 (verse references removed).

At the same time, Christian anarchists like Ellul and Tolstoy claim to "fully understand the insurrection of the oppressed who see no way out."[137] Their outrage is understandable given the hardship which they feel is imposed upon them. Tolstoy says he "cannot blame the revolutionaries" for using "the same immoral means" as their oppressors – at least the revolutionaries, he says, have "mitigating circumstances on their side."[138] These are: "that their crimes are committed under conditions of greater personal danger" than agents of the state are ever "exposed to;" that they are usually "quite young people to whom it is naturally to go astray;" and that they are anyway only reproducing the methods which they have been taught by the state.[139] Similarly, Ellul calls for Christians to sympathise with the oppressed, even when they adopt violence, though Christians should nevertheless also always question such adoption of violence.[140]

Revolutionary violence has an inherent tendency to backfire: it erodes any public support for the revolutionaries' cause, and it becomes "a convenient pretext" for the state to "intensify" its repression.[141] As noted in Chapter 1, the outcome is not revolutionary change but more violence and repression. Violent revolutionary means only lead to endless violence and counter-violence. Almost every attempt at violent revolution, according to Christian anarchists, has degenerated into bloodbaths and recriminations, and where revolutions did succeed in overthrowing a repressive government, they, too, have led to more repression.[142] Yet, Yoder writes, "If the new people" have "the same techniques, the same willingness to coerce and the same attitude towards authority as the bad guys – then it is not worth changing palace guards."[143] Surely, Tolstoy asks, human beings must be able to devise "better means of improving the conditions of humanity than by killing people whose destruction can be of no more use than the decapitation of that mythical monster on whose neck a new head appeared as soon as one was cut off?"[144]

---

[137] Ellul, *Violence*, 68.
[138] Tolstoy, "I Cannot Be Silent," 405-406.
[139] This is not Tolstoy's exact list. The last mitigating circumstance listed here is only implicit in Tolstoy's text (page 405), and in his own list, Tolstoy mentions two more mitigating circumstance: that "however odious their murder may be, they are still not so coldly, systematically cruel" as those committed by the state; and that "they all quite categorically repudiate all religious teaching and consider that the end justifies the means," whereas state officials (during Tolstoy's time) claim to "all support religion and Christianity." Tolstoy, "I Cannot Be Silent," 406.
[140] Goddard explains that Ellul suggests that "the Christian must be willing to participate in movements using violence," but this must "be a non-conformist participation" which is "always openly questioning the justifications of violence," which must not be seen as "a sign of God's approval" and which must "challenge the movement's idols." Moreover, the Christian must always be "willing to change sides." The Christian also has a role as "a watchman in the world," foreseeing problems and working on trying to resolve them early. Either way, the point is that, as the next Chapter explains, Christians should sympathise with the oppressed and care for them but always keep faith and obedience to God at the forefront of all concerns. Goddard, *Living the Word, Resisting the World*, 186-187.
[141] Tolstoy, "The Kingdom of God Is within You," 215.
[142] For Tolstoy and Ellul, there is no difference between state violence and revolutionary violence – Tolstoy says that "There is as much difference as between cat-shit and dog-shit. But I don't like the smell of either one or the other." Tolstoy, quoted in Marshall, *Demanding the Impossible*, 377. For Ellul's more academic and detailed discussion, see Ellul, *Violence*, 108-118.
[143] Yoder, "Peacemaking Amid Political Revolution," 60.
[144] Tolstoy, "Thou Shalt Not Kill," 197.

## *4.5.2 – Revolution by example*

Lenin is alleged by one Christian anarchist to have said: "I made a mistake. Without doubt the oppressed multitude had to be liberated. But our method only provoked further oppression – and atrocious massacres. It is too late now to alter the past – but what was needed to save Russia were ten Francis of Assisi's."[145] Whether Lenin really did say this, what it suggests is that the true revolution can only come with a new philosophy, a new way of life, and that this alternative can only come about by example, not by force. In a sense, therefore, the revolutions of the past were simply "not revolutionary enough."[146] For Christian anarchists, the true revolution must come by different means – by Christian witness and example.

That Christian anarchist witness and example is discussed in more details in the next Chapter. The point to note here is that this alternative revolutionary method implies that any aspirations of top-down political engineering must be renounced. However appealing it may be, for Christian anarchists, the hope "to make people good by law" is deluded.[147] Eller explains that such "arky faith" is attractive because, "Perfectly confident that our commitments are to the 'good,' we cannot see why it should be anything other than good that our power for good be 'magnified' through the collective solidarities of good arkys," and because "Still completely confident about the justice of our own cause, we dream about the possibility that, judiciously applied to the right spot, the power of even a small pebble from our weak sling will bring down the Goliath of Evil."[148] In practice, however, it does not work, because "arky faith" compromises with violence and coercion, leading to more self-righteous violence and misunderstandings and so on. Christian anarchists therefore believe that those who seek to govern or change society from above are deceiving themselves (an issue which is discussed further in the Conclusion).

Instead, for Christian anarchists, "Real change must come from the bottom up or, better yet, from the inside out."[149] Chelčický argues that to make people better, the only option is to teach them by example – they might then, of their own will, choose to follow that example. "A righteous society," Young

---

[145] Lenin, quoted in Dave Andrews, *Brother Sun and Sister Moons: Engaging a New Dark Age*, available from http://anz.jesusradicals.com/newdarkage.pdf (accessed 17 July 2006), 6. This quotation is said to be found in "Letters on Modern Atheism," but that text appears impossible to trace. Various internet websites also refer this quote to that text, but again without enough publication details to trace it. Other websites claim that these words were actually pronounced by Lenin on his deathbed, to a friend of his. Again, however, there is no way of tracing the original. It is therefore uncertain whether Lenin did write or utter these words – yet they still illustrate the Christian anarchist argument very well.

[146] This expression is paraphrased from Yoder, who, while discussing the Zealots, writes that "Jesus rejected the way of Barabbas, not because it was revolutionary, but because it wasn't revolutionary enough." Yoder, "Peacemaking Amid Political Revolution," 57.

[147] Hennacy, *The Book of Ammon*, 214.

[148] Eller, *Christian Anarchy*, 26-27.

[149] Carl Thomas, quoted in Stephen W. Carson, *Christians in Politics: The Return of the 'Religious Right'*, available from http://www.lewrockwell.com/carson/carson17.html (accessed 21 November 2007), para. 79.

writes, "can only be realized by changing the heart and mind of each individual."[150] Hence, to borrow a famous phrase attributed to Gandhi, "We must be the change we want to see in the world."[151] For Christian anarchists, "There can be no more powerful strategy than that of people who dare to be different."[152] This strategy is discussed in more detail in the next Chapter. The important point to note here is that choosing the road of bottom-up "discipleship" also implies foregoing the (deluded) dream of top-down efficacy.[153] Success is therefore measured not by the "immediate delivery of political outcomes" but "in terms more of the consistent faithfulness" of the witness.[154] The focus is not on the effect of Christian discipleship, but on Christian discipleship itself. That way, as Day writes, "The 'means to the end' begins with each one of us."[155] That is why "the only revolution" that is "worthwhile," for Hennacy, is "the one-man revolution within the heart."[156]

Admittedly, this is not easy, not least since it requires a readiness to die with no guarantee of the martyrdom's efficacy. Yet Jesus shows that it is precisely by such moving examples of personal and non-antagonistic sacrifice that state violence can be gradually unmasked and defeated. Ellul says of Christian martyrs that, over time, "through their implacable meekness and their steady witness they succeed in demolishing the justifications a regime puts forward."[157] For Ballou, when, through "pure Christian examples, [...] a considerable portion of the people have been enlightened and won over to Christian non-resistance, the tide of public sentiment will begin to set with such force [...] that the less enlightened and less conscientious portion will insensibly yield to the current."[158] As the next Chapter shows in more detail, many Christian anarchists thus hope that with time, the violence and deception of the state will be exposed to an increasing number of people who will then also yield to the truth revealed by Christian anarchism and join the church of true Christianity.

Hence for Tolstoy, the real basis of any change is public opinion, and ultimately, public opinion is moved by truth. Tolstoy writes that

> Men bound to one another by deceit, form, as it were, a compact mass. In the compactness of this mass is the evil in the world. The aim of the whole intellectual activity of mankind should be to break through and destroy this aggregate of deceit. Revolutions are attempts to break up this mass by *violence*. Men imagine that if they once disperse it it will cease to exist, and they strike it furiously in order to break it up,– but they only weld the atoms more closely together, for each atom must be filled with an inward power of

---

[150] Roger Young, *A Plea to Christians: Reject the State!* (Strike the Root), available from http://www.strike-the-root.com/columns/Young/young3.html (accessed 21 November 2007), para. 12.
[151] Gandhi, quoted in Andrews, *Plan Be*, 69.
[152] Elliott, *Freedom, Justice and Christian Counter-Culture*, 167.
[153] Bartley, *Faith and Politics after Christendom*, 144-147, 182.
[154] This quote is actually partly a paraphrasing of Bartley, who writes that the church "may come to see success and failure in terms more of the consistent faithfulness or otherwise of its witness than of whether it delivers the immediate political outcomes that the church has often sought historically." Bartley, *Faith and Politics after Christendom*, 221.
[155] Day, *Selected Writings*, 290.
[156] Hennacy, *The Book of Ammon*, 33.
[157] Ellul, *Violence*, 144.
[158] Ballou, *Christian Non-Resistance*, chap. 7, para. 32-33.

its own before the mass can be finally disintegrated. The strength of this bond of union among men rests on a lie, on *deceit*. The strength which can deliver each particle of this mass it *truth*. Truth is communicated to men only by the *deeds of truth*. Only the deeds of truth, lighting the conceptions of every individual man, can destroy this evil attraction and detach men one after another from the mass bound together by it.[159]

Therefore, like other Christian anarchists, Tolstoy places his hopes of revolution on the inspirational, indeed contagious, quality of the Christian example. The true revolution, for him, will not come about through any compromise with political engineering, violence or coercion, but only by a gradual change of public conduct and consciousness spearheaded by courageous Christian anarchist witnesses.

Of course, this relies on Christians leading the way. Hence Christian anarchists call for Christians to fully embrace Jesus' subversive teaching. Their response to the state is not to resist it (at least not violently) but to unmask it, to forgivingly subject themselves to it, to render to it the few things that belong to it – but also to clearly follow God alone and ignore or disobey the state if it demands things which should be rendered to God, if obeying it would entail a disobedience of God. For Christian anarchists, the only truly revolutionary response to the state is not to overthrow it and compose a different government, but to adopt a different – Christian – way of being, to patiently forgive and thereby unmask the state, but at the same time, to live out the stateless alternative "here and now."[160]

Hence what matters for Christian anarchists even more than how Christians respond to the state is how they embody Jesus' teaching in community, because that community is what can set the example for those not convinced by Christianity yet. Therefore, their response to the state is one of indifferent and dismissive submission to most of its demands – provided that these are not incompatible with the will of God. More important than that, however, is their collective witness in striving to embody the true church – and that, in turn, is the topic of the next Chapter.

---

[159] Tolstoy, *What I Believe*, 220 (Tolstoy's emphasis).
[160] Geoffrey Ostergaard and Melville Currell, "Sarvodaya: Indian Anarchism," in *The Gentle Anarchists: A Study of the Leaders of the Sarvodaya Movement for Non-Violent Revolution in India* (Oxford: Clarendon, 1971).

# Chapter 5 – Collective Witness as the True Church

The previous Chapter outlines the main themes of the direct Christian anarchist response to the state. This Chapter explores the indirect – yet perhaps even more important – response to it: the Christian anarchist embodiment of the church as a subversive alternative to the state. In a sense, whereas the previous Chapter discusses the *negative* response to the state's demands, this one discusses the *positive* response of presenting the "true" church as an alternative society.[1]

The main theme is therefore the elaboration of the Christian anarchist vision for society. This vision is ultimately for the whole of humanity, but it is also a vision to be embraced fully by Christians in the present. Since the means for society's transformation cannot be separated from the end, according to Christian anarchists, the transformed society – the true church – must be adopted by Christians as both the means and the end of this transformation.[2] The next Chapter lists some examples of individuals and communities trying to embrace this Christian anarchist vision. This Chapter explores what Christian anarchist thinkers have written about it.

In describing the ideal Christian anarchist community as "church," it should not be forgotten that what is meant is a very different "church" to the institutional "church" described in Chapter 3, where the deep distrust which most Christian anarchists feel towards this official "church" is illustrated. Yet despite the risk of confusing the institutional "church" of Chapter 3 with the subversive "church" of this Chapter, it is precisely in the implicit contrast between the two "churches" that the use of the same word for both finds its rationale: it confirms the width of the chasm that separates what Christian anarchists understand the "church" to have been supposed to be with what has regrettably become of it.

The Chapter has three main sections. The first of these describes the contours of what Christian anarchists sometimes call the "new society within the shell of the old:" the role of repentance as a gateway to the church, the various elements and implications of the church's economy of care and sacrifice, and the way in which the church's organisation is therefore politically subversive. The second section then ponders the difficulties involved in such a mission: how evil

---

[1] Hereafter, "true" church is referred to without quotation marks – it should be obvious that what is meant is what Christian anarchists believe the church should be, as opposed to what it has become (as described in Chapter 3).

[2] There is an undeniably coercive feel to this Christian anarchist language about how Christians "must" behave in community to embody the "true" church. This language, however, stems from Christian anarchists' insistence about following Jesus' teaching with genuineness and authenticity. Indeed, to a large extent, it only mirrors the uncompromising language adopted by Jesus himself on the issue. In any case, even if this language can indeed be described as coercive, it remains radically different to the state coercion which Christian anarchists denounce. Hence although some will no doubt see this as rather ironic, from a Christian anarchist perspective, there is nothing either contradictory or unchristian in criticising state coercion and yet using slightly "coercive" language in this critique.

## 5.1 – "A new society within the shell of the old"

This section demonstrates that for Christian anarchists, converting to Jesus' teaching is subversive because it creates new relationships which render the state superfluous: by caring and sacrificing themselves for their neighbours, converts to the true church deprive the state from its main *raison d'être*. Joining the church is therefore a subversive, political act.

### *5.1.1 – Repenting and joining the church*

To become a member of the true church, as John the Baptist makes clear, we must begin by becoming conscious and repent of "our own sins" – such as our "idolatry" (of money, of the state, and so on), our "apathy towards the poor," and our support for the violent state.[3] For Tolstoy, we must "admit, without self-deception, that the life that we live is wrong."[4] We must "bethink ourselves" and realise that we have not been serving God but idols.[5] We must reconsider our "position and activity" and "not be afraid of the truth."[6] Personal repentance is therefore the first step to the Christian anarchist revolution.

Repentance is a private affair, but then as argued in the previous Chapter, reforming oneself is the only way to eventually reform society. Collective repentance and reform can only come about by the individual repentance and reform of enough members of the community. To Tolstoy's regret, "everybody thinks of changing humanity, and nobody thinks of changing himself."[7] Yet for Christian anarchists, "it is an illusion to think we can change anyone except ourselves."[8] Andrews insists that "Change doesn't begin with others, but with ourselves."[9] In Ballou's words, the "millennium [...] must be *within* men, before it can ever be *around* them."[10] Indeed, Tolstoy argues that "the essence of Christianity lies" precisely "in substituting an inward aim (to

---

[3] Andrews, *Brother Sun and Sister Moons*, 6 (where "idolatry" and "apathy towards the poor" are mentioned); Watson, "The Catholic Worker and Anarchism," 8 (where "our own sins" is borrowed from). (Matthew 3:1-12; Mark 1:1-15; Luke 3:1-20; John 1:19-28.)
[4] Hopton, "Tolstoy, God and Anarchism," 43.
[5] "Bethink yourselves" is how Tolstoy translates the Greek that is more frequently translated as "repent." Tolstoy, "Bethink Yourselves!," 229.
[6] Tolstoï, *What to Do?* , 206, 208.
[7] Tolstoy, "On Anarchy," 70.
[8] Andrews, *Plan Be*, 2.
[9] Andrews, *Brother Sun and Sister Moons*, 16 (emphasis removed); Dave Andrews, *Reweaving the Fabric of Community*, available from http://anz.jesusradicals.com/reweaving.pdf (accessed 17 July 2006), 9.
[10] Ballou, "Non-Resistance," 145 (Ballou's emphasis).

attain which no one else's consent is necessary) in place of external aims (to attain which everyone's consent is necessary)."[11] The essence of Christianity and of its subversion of the state is personal repentance. The only way of reforming society is to first reform ourselves. That is why, as noted in the previous Chapter, the Christian anarchist revolution is a revolution by example.

Becoming conscious of our sins is the gateway to joining Jesus' church, to applying Jesus' teaching and example in our own lives. Jesus himself warns that doing so will not be easy (this is discussed further below), but he nonetheless does clearly and repeatedly say that to be his disciple, we must "follow" him.[12] For Christian anarchists (as explained in Chapter 3), membership of the Christian church is therefore much more about following Jesus' example than about believing in curious dogmas or abiding by church rules.[13] Myers asserts that "theological orthodoxy ('Jesus is Messiah') has no meaning apart from political 'orthopraxy' ('take up the cross')," in other words that Jesus' teaching can only acquire theological meaning through its application in society.[14] Chelčický moreover repeats the New Testament warning that "faith apart from works is dead."[15] Only by following Jesus in practice can faith be brought to life. In short, for Christian anarchists, it is by the "incarnation" of Jesus' teaching and example that membership of the true church is determined.[16] The true church is constituted by those who have repented and chosen to follow Jesus to the cross.

Again, the hope is that by following Jesus, others might be moved to repent and join the church as well. As already noted in previous Chapters, Christian anarchists have faith in the moving power of such Christian witness. Day considered the great saints canonised by the Catholic Church as "her constant companions and daily guides in the imitation of Christ [...], realizing full well that in their own time they were often regarded as eccentrics or dangerous troublemakers."[17] These saints were indeed following Jesus and his subversive gospel, even unto death. That they were canonised seems to suggest that their radical witness was compelling, indeed compelling enough even in persuading others to join the church. As the (here rephrased) saying goes, the seeds of the church were sown by the blood of its martyrs.[18] Yet Day also "regarded sanctity as the ordinary vocation of every Christian."[19] The moving

---

[11] Tolstoy, "The Kingdom of God Is within You," 413.
[12] Matthew 4:19, 8:22, 9:9, 16:24, 19:21; Mark 2:14, 8:34, 10:21; Luke 5:27, 9:23, 9:59, 18:22; John 1:43, 10:27, 12:26, 13:36, 21:22.
[13] Note that Craig seems to disagree with this in that he argues that Jesus was violent but ordered us to be peaceful, so that in that sense, he presumably did not order us to follow him or imitate him, but to do as he said. [Anonymous], *Why I Worship a Violent, Vengeful God*.
[14] Myers, *Binding the Strong Man*, 285 (see also 288).
[15] Molnár, *A Study of Peter Chelčický's Life*, 58 (quoting Chelčický). (James 2:26.)
[16] The notion of "incarnating" Jesus' example is borrowed from Dave Andrews, *Integral Mission, Relief and Development*, available from http://www.daveandrews.com.au/publications.html (accessed 3 December 2006), 8.
[17] Day, *Selected Writings*, xi.
[18] This phrase is attributed to Tertullian, whose precise words were: "the blood of Christians is seed [*semen est sanguis Christianorum*]." Philip Schaff, *Latin Christianity: Its Founder, Tertullian* (Wm. B. Eerdmans), available from http://www.ccel.org/ccel/schaff/anf03.html (accessed 2 January 2009), chap. 50.
[19] Day, *Selected Writings*, xi-xii.

example of the saints – their sacrifice but also their revolutionary impact upon the rest of society, by persuading many to repent and convert to Christianity – is for Christian anarchists this "ordinary vocation of every Christian."

That is why Christian anarchists speak of "change by conversion" rather than "through coercion."[20] The Christian anarchist future of love and forgiveness will only be reached when every human being will have voluntarily repented and converted to the true church. Day therefore speaks of "changing the world one heart at a time."[21] The conversion of non-Christians to Christian anarchism requires the church and its members to witness to the truly revolutionary potential of following Jesus. In Bartley's words, the church must therefore "lead by example."[22] Christians must demonstrate the truth of the Christian anarchist alternative by converting to it and practicing it in their own community.

## 5.1.2 – An economy of care and sacrifice

The true church must therefore exemplify a way of life that is guided by love of God and neighbour above all else. What must distinguish it as a community is how its members genuinely love one another, forgive one another and care for one another. For Hennacy, that is the "supreme test" of what Christians preach.[23] Andrews calls it the "acid test of Christian spirituality."[24]

Perhaps more to the point, the real test is not so much whether Christians love *one another*, but whether they love the outcasts, the people who have been rejected by everyone else. Andrews recalls that Jesus warns that "'Whatever you do to one of the least' – one of those that most of you consider the least – the marginalized, distressed, disabled, and disadvantaged – 'you do it to me.'"[25] Thus "we will *not* be judged on the basis of whether we have subscribed to the right set of doctrines," but "solely on the basis of whether, or not, we have done the right thing by those whom most people consider the least."[26] In other words, it is "the stranger," rather than the Christian fellow, who really "tests the quality of our community life."[27] Maurin therefore claims that "the people in need [...] are the Ambassadors of God."[28] Similarly, for Day, "we love God as much as we love the person we love the least."[29] In the true church, those who suffer the most must be loved and cared for as if they were God.

---

[20] Andrews, *Not Religion, but Love*, 76 (emphasis removed).
[21] Dorothy Day, quoted in *The London Catholic Worker*, issue 13, April 2005, 6.
[22] Bartley, *Faith and Politics after Christendom*, 163, 204.
[23] Hennacy, *The Book of Ammon*, 293.
[24] Andrews is actually quoting David Benner's words here, in Dave Andrews, *Love and Fear*, available from http://www.daveandrews.com.au/publications.html (accessed 3 December 2006), 9.
[25] Andrews, *Plan Be*, 17. (Matthew 25:31-46.)
[26] Andrews, *Not Religion, but Love*, 55 (Andrews' emphasis partly removed).
[27] Andrews, "Heaven on Earth," 95 (emphasis removed).
[28] Maurin writes that "the Greeks used to say that people in need are the ambassadors of the gods. Although you may be called bums and panhandlers you are in fact the Ambassadors of God." Maurin, *Easy Essays (2003)*, 8.
[29] Hennacy reports Day to have said that in Hennacy, *The Book of Ammon*, 346 (where the words are in the past tense).

This moreover implies that wealth should indeed always be shared freely within and by the Christian community: everything – food, clothes, shelter, property – should be shared. For instance, Jesus talks of even giving one's cloak when asked for one's coat – a commandment Day says Maurin "took [...] literally."[30] Several Christian anarchists moreover interpret Jesus' "miraculous" feeding of the thousands in the wilderness as "nothing 'supernatural,'" but as a "triumph of the economics of sharing."[31] They also recall that according to the Book of Acts, the first Christians shared everything – they "had all things in common."[32] That is, *all* things in the Christian community, this passage seems to affirm, should be shared.

Besides, this sharing should be patient and forgiving – it should not be determined by what the receiver does with the gift. To put it in the more colloquial words of a contributor to a conference on Christian anarchism, "I give money to the homeless, whatever crap excuse they give me."[33] Jesus asks his followers to give to anyone who asks, without stipulating any conditions of use – presumably forgiving the receiver for any potential misuse.

Christian anarchists are willing to suffer poverty as a result. Catholic Workers in particular regularly stress the virtues of voluntary poverty. Hennacy argues that it "keeps the radical from becoming bourgeois and selling out."[34] It also demonstrates the "sincerity" of the Christian's intentions.[35] Day adds that it "brings us close to those who Christ loved," and it "means that by taking less ourselves, others can have more."[36] Hence, paradoxically perhaps, voluntary poverty is a way to eradicate poverty. As Maurin says, "nobody would be poor if everybody tried to be the poorest."[37] At the same time, Catholic Workers do not *wish* poverty to befall others: they bemoan the poverty that so many suffer from today, yet they also recommend it as a way to be liberated from the political economy that causes it in the first place. Hence Day's claim: "I condemn poverty and I advocate it."[38] Christian anarchists do not wish poverty to be inflicted upon others, but they nevertheless call for it to be embraced willingly as a way to overcome it.

Christian anarchists (except anarcho-capitalists) also criticise the keeping of property as "private." As mentioned in Chapter 3, they see private property as a major cause of the economic oppression of the masses. For Maurin, it is also unchristian, because for him, "All the land belongs to God,"[39] and therefore "private property is not an absolute right, but a trust, which must be administered for the benefit of God's children."[40] Land is a gift of God, not to be appropriated but shared and laboured by the true church for the benefit of all.

---

[30] Day, *The Long Loneliness*, 179. (Matthew 5:40.)
[31] Myers, *Binding the Strong Man*, 206. (Matthew 14:13-21, 15:32-39; Mark 6:30-44, 8:1-9; Luke: 9:10-17; John 6:1-15.)
[32] Acts 2:44-47, 4:32-35.
[33] Andrew Mandell, "Ellul and the Left" (audio file on compact disc, rec. 5-6 August 2005).
[34] Hennacy, *The Book of Ammon*, 99.
[35] Hennacy, *The Book of Ammon*, 252.
[36] Dorothy Day, "On Voluntary Poverty," *The Digger*, issue 7, May 1986, 8.
[37] Maurin, *Easy Essays (2003)*, 37.
[38] Day, *Selected Writings*, 109.
[39] Maurin, *Easy Essays (2003)*, 167.
[40] Maurin, *Easy Essays (1938)*, 74.

(This resonates strongly with Henry George's political economy, which, as already noted, Tolstoy and Pentecost were keen proponents of.)

Indeed, physical work also features quite prominently among the Christian anarchist prescriptions for the true church. It is crucial for them that we all "earn our bread by the sweat of our brows, in labor."[41] Moreover, such physical labour is not "all pain and drudgery."[42] As Sampson explains, Tolstoy, who frequently eulogises peasant life, believes that labouring the land keeps the worker "in better spirits, healthier, fitter," and "kindlier."[43] Maurin and Day seem to agree. Furthermore, according to Day, Maurin "was vehemently opposed to the wage system" and preferred to speak of the "gift" of labour, for which one would receive, in return, the "'gift' of enough food and clothing."[44] Hence Maurin writes that in Catholic Worker communities, "There is plenty of work to do, but no wages," as "people do not need to work for wages" but "can offer their services as a gift."[45] This makes the wage system redundant, replacing it with a much more personal and loving exchange of gift.

The economy of the true church would therefore be one of personal care and sacrifice for one another. Rather than rely on the state to provide this care through its welfare policies, Christian anarchists would rather see people develop a real sense of care and "personal responsibility" for their neighbours.[46] For Maurin, "what comes from the taxpayer's pocketbook does not come from his heart."[47] Hence Maurin contrasts the "impersonality of state relief" with the "fraternal care" exemplified in personal acts of charity.[48] Besides, personal care helps prevent many of the problems which the welfare state seeks to cure. "Out of these small individual acts" of personal care and sacrifice, Watson therefore notes, "a great revolution takes place that [...] makes the cold and remote state system redundant."[49]

Christian anarchists also address the question of how society would "get on with public affairs," such as "highways, and bridges, and school houses, and education, and alms-houses, and hospitals."[50] According to Hennacy, "Anything that the government does, except make war, all of us could do if we got the idea of doing it, and we could do it better."[51] None of these public works require the government to be completed. In the true church, these would all be done "*voluntarily*."[52] Ballou argues that "all will be eager to contribute their full share of expense and effort to the object," that "instead of the strife, as now, who shall bear the lightest burden, the only strife will be – who shall do most for the

---

[41] Day, *The Long Loneliness*, 227.
[42] Day, *The Long Loneliness*, 227.
[43] Ronald Sampson, "Tolstoy on Power," *Journal of the Conflict Research Society* 1/2 (1977), 69.
[44] Day, *The Long Loneliness*, 178.
[45] Maurin, *Easy Essays (2003)*, 39.
[46] The notion of "personal responsibility" in this context is borrowed from Day, *The Long Loneliness*, 179.
[47] Maurin, *Easy Essays (2003)*, 9.
[48] Segers, "Equality and Christian Anarchism," 214-215.
[49] Watson, "The Catholic Worker and Anarchism," 9-10.
[50] Ballou, *Non-Resistance in Relation to Human Governments*, 19; Ballou, "Non-Resistance," 149.
[51] Hennacy, *The Book of Ammon*, 437.
[52] Ballou, "Non-Resistance," 149 (Ballou's emphasis).

promotion of every good work."[53] Hence in the true church, according to Pentecost, "All things that were for the common good would be done in common by as many as choose to cooperate for that purpose."[54]

For Christian anarchists, therefore, this revolutionary Christian economy can only be built "by *ordinary* people doing *ordinary* things for one another."[55] Tolstoy writes that "Great, true deeds are always simple and modest."[56] For Andrews, "as little people, we can only do little things," but "Great things can happen [...] as a result of the cumulative effect of lots of little people doing lots of the little things we can do."[57] One Christian anarchist notes that this only requires the same "energy, [...] organization and teamwork" which humanity today commits to war.[58] The accumulation of the individual actions of committed followers of Jesus would subvert the state by rendering it obsolete, and replace it by a more personalised economy where even the most abandoned would be lovingly cared for.

### 5.1.3 – Subversive organisation

Building such a Christian community therefore consists in building "a new society within the shell of the old," as Catholic Workers are fond of repeating (thereby borrowing this expression from the Industrial Workers of the World). Like many secular anarchists (anarcho-syndicalists in particular), Christian anarchists will not "wait for a revolutionary situation before developing alternative economic systems,"[59] because it is precisely in the adoption of these new ways of life that the revolution is enacted. Hence both Christian and secular anarchists alike also quote Gustav Landauer's explanation that "The state is not something which can be destroyed by a revolution, but is a condition, a certain relationship between human beings, a mode of human behaviour; we destroy it by contracting other relationships, by behaving differently."[60] In other words, the true church "destroys" the state by creating new relationships. Just by being what Jesus calls it to be, the community of Jesus' followers subverts the state and presents its revolutionary alternative to it.

---

[53] Ballou, *Non-Resistance in Relation to Human Governments*, 20.
[54] Pentecost, *Anarchism*, para. 25.
[55] Andrews, *Not Religion, but Love*, 61 (Andrews' emphasis).
[56] Tolstoï, *What to Do?* , 227.
[57] Andrews, *Plan Be*, 2. In the same vein, Day writes: "if I did not have faith that the works of mercy" of ordinary individuals "do not lighten the sum total of suffering in the world, [...] the problem of evil would indeed be overwhelming." Dorothy Day, "Act of Faith," *The London Catholic Worker*, issue 21, Christmas 2007, 5.
[58] Tom Fox, "The Force of War and the Force of Peace? The Same Force Moving in the Opposite Direction?," *The Mormon Worker*, issue 1, September 2007, available from http://www.themormonworker.org/articles/issue1/volume1_issue1.pdf (accessed 28 February 2008), 1-2.
[59] These words are Kinna's and summarise the view of Ferdinand Pelloutier, who she names as the "founder" of anarcho-syndicalism. Kinna, *Anarchism*, 109.
[60] For instance: Elliott, *Freedom, Justice and Christian Counter-Culture*, 206; Stephens, "The Non-Violent Anarchism of Leo Tolstoy," 18.

The true church is therefore about "developing networks of people,"[61] as Andrews says, "community networks" that "improve our quality of life."[62] This does not mean that there is no "role" for "organisations."[63] It is a common misperception to presume that anarchists reject all forms of organisation – they do not. Jesus himself, some Christian anarchists point out, organised his disciples into groups.[64] The key, however, is for any organisation to be decentralised. Tolstoy for instance recommends "the social organization of agricultural communes," where all members are equal, where cooperation is primordial in any industrial undertaking, where land is shared, and so on.[65] This organisation, however, must be "founded upon mutual agreement," without any centralised planning or coercion.[66] The organisation of the true church must be completely "bottom up," consensual and voluntary.[67] Andrews insists that "there is simply no substitute for our face-to-face, hands-on, grass-roots involvement."[68] This also means that no institutional mechanisms for it can really be prescribed in advance, as if universally applicable. Most of the details can only be agreed upon by the specific community in its specific context, consensually and without coercion – based, of course, on the teachings of Jesus.

The only Christian anarchists who put forward slightly more detailed suggestions for the organisation of their alternative community are the Catholic Workers, who have tested these suggestions in their own communities (the next Chapter chronicles such examples in more detail). The specifics do vary from one Catholic Worker community to another, but most tend to work towards Maurin's "three-point program" of "round-table discussions, houses of hospitality, and farming communes:"[69] the round-table discussions are to encourage thoughtful reflection and dialogue over the issues that affect members of the community; the

---

[61] Andrews, *Brother Sun and Sister Moons*, 10.
[62] Andrews, *Reweaving the Fabric of Community*, 4.
[63] Andrews, "Heaven on Earth," 125.
[64] Elliott argues that Jesus "deliberately set about creating an organization" (page 167) he initially chose "four disciples at the beginning of his ministry" to ensure "that his work was given an embryonic framework;" he later appointed twelve "to positions of responsibility," as "front-line workers for the mission" and for "crowd control;" he "singled out three of these people" as "his particular confidents" (page 168); and he later appointed "thirty-six teams" of two people to "[go] ahead in the towns and rural areas which he [was] proposing to visit in order to prepare the ground for him" (page 169). Thus for Elliott, Jesus did organise his following somewhat. Nevertheless, Elliott is the only core Christian anarchist (as defined in the Introduction) who interprets this to amount to an organisation. Tolstoy barely mentions the thirty-six teams in his version of the Gospel. Yoder briefly notes that the twelve constitute "the formal founding of a new social reality." Myers does go a bit further to speak of Jesus forming a "confederacy, [...] a kind of vanguard 'revolutionary committee,'" but he is after all not a core Christian anarchist (again, as defined in the Introduction). Either way, the point to note is that Jesus was not averse to organisation – though as explained in Chapter 1 and 2, what he expects from such an organisation is not top-down management but servant leadership and the wholehearted embodiment of all the elements of his radical teaching of love and forgiveness (as Andrews and Ballou, for instance, point out). Andrews, *Christi-Anarchy*, 111, 149, 192-193; Ballou, *Christian Non-Resistance*, chap. 2, para. 62; Elliott, *Freedom, Justice and Christian Counter-Culture*, 167-174, 182; Myers, *Binding the Strong Man*, 163-164 (see also 168, 213, 261-264); Tolstoy, "The Gospel in Brief," 182-184; Yoder, *The Politics of Jesus*, 33 (also 39).
[65] Tolstoy, "The End of the Age," 40-42.
[66] Tolstoy, "The End of the Age," 42.
[67] Andrews, *Christi-Anarchy*, 215.
[68] Andrews, "Heaven on Earth," 125.
[69] Maurin, *Easy Essays (2003)*, 36 (capitalisation removed).

houses of hospitality are generally urban houses where society's outcasts are cared for, where shelter, food and company are provided to those in need; and the farming communes, also sometimes referred to as "agronomic universities," are houses in the country where volunteers work the land and live in community. Indeed, all these houses and farms are run by volunteers striving to embrace all the elements of the economy of care and sacrifice outlined in the previous subsection. This three-point programme is the closest to a prescribed plan for the decentralised organisation of the new society in the Christian anarchist literature: elsewhere in that literature, the details of each community's social arrangements are, by and large, implicitly left for each community to agree upon.

According to Christian anarchists, simply living in such a decentralised community is a political statement in itself. That is, the very existence of the true church is, in itself, a political statement. Indeed, Christian anarchists explain that "when Jesus first used" the Greek word which is translated as "church" (εκκλησία or ekklesia), it "was not a religious" but "a political term."[70] The word, they add, actually means "assembly."[71] Bartley maintains that using this word "invoked the idea of people called aside for a purpose – namely, to make political decisions."[72] For Cavanaugh, "In calling itself *ekklesia*, the Church was identifying itself as Israel, the assembly that bears the public presence of God in history."[73] That is, "the Church was not simply another *polis*; it was rather an anticipation of the heavenly city on earth."[74] Therefore, the church's mission was always very political, calling followers away from the state's organisation of community life and towards God's alternative vision for humanity.

Moreover, this church was not expected to withdraw completely from society in the sense of forming a monastic community completely outside it.[75] For Christian anarchists, it was called to live out its alternative *within* society, to embody a subversive "political counter-culture to society and its institutions" and to make this counter-culture visible to the rest of society.[76] The church was to detach itself from the state and yet to present its alternative from within it.

---

[70] Andrews, "Heaven on Earth," 122.
[71] Cavanaugh, "Killing for the Telephone Company," 267; Eller, *Christian Anarchy*, 50 (who adds that it is "a totally anarchic concept"); Tolstoy, "Church and State," 334. (Matthew 16:18, 18:17.)
[72] Bartley, *Faith and Politics after Christendom*, 18.
[73] Cavanaugh, "Killing for the Telephone Company," 267.
[74] Cavanaugh, "Killing for the Telephone Company," 267.
[75] Of course, this particular understanding of monasteries as completely removed from the rest of society is questionable: monasteries played a central role in the fabric of medieval society, and it is only in the modern era that they have been increasingly perceived as spiritual retreats that deliberately cut off all ties with the rest of society. Still, it is as communities far removed from the rest of society that they are cited for instance in Maurin, *Easy Essays (2003)*, 119 (where he speaks of "taking monasticism out of the monasteries"); Tolstoy, *What I Believe*, 154-157. According to Wagner, however, Chelčický favoured a more clearly separated church whose contact with the fallen world would only come in the form of its distant example to non-Christians (but here, it should be noted that Chelčický lived in the Middle Ages, when the state was not as omnipotent and omnipresent as it is today). Wagner, *Petr Chelčický*, 144-147.
[76] Bartley, *Faith and Politics after Christendom*, 164.

For Christian anarchists, therefore, the true church is called to be a subversive political community, "a statement of opposition to the state."[77] Goddard describes it a "revolutionary presence living out God's word within the fallen world."[78] According to Yoder, such a church "constitutes an unavoidable challenge to the powers that be and the beginning of a new set of social alternatives."[79] Its "very existence," for Berkhof, "is itself a proclamation" that "the Powers" have been defeated (as discussed in Chapter 2).[80] For Christian anarchists, the church's existence is a proclamation of God's alternative to the state: just by being itself, this true church both criticises the state and presents an alternative to it. That is why it is such a deeply subversive organisation.

## 5.2 – A difficult mission

At the same time, the church's subversive mission is not an easy one, especially in the personal sacrifices it requires in dealing with evil in the community. This section touches on these difficulties.

### 5.2.1 – Dealing with evil in the community

Many detractors have described the Christian anarchist vision for the church as both too difficult and dangerously unrealistic, particularly regarding the way in which it fails to adequately deal with evil people. Christian anarchists, Tolstoy in particular, rebut these criticisms, and in so doing explain how they expect the true church to deal with evil in the community.

One argument levelled at Christian anarchists is that the way of life of the true church would make it easy for the evil to enslave and oppress the good. Tolstoy remarks, however, that this scenario "is precisely what has long ago happened, and is still happening, in all States" – the evil use the state to oppress the good.[81] The claim that evil people must be restrained by government authority takes "for granted" that "good" people "are now in power," yet for Tolstoy, those who "seek," obtain and "retain" power tend to be moved not by "goodness" but by "pride, cunning and cruelty."[82] With or without the state, Tolstoy moreover argues, some people will oppress others – but at least by abolishing the state, its powerful machinery will not be available to these oppressors anymore.[83] Therefore it is precisely because some people are evil and because they tend to dominate the good that the state should be abolished. Ballou thus reiterates that

---

[77] These words are Bartley's, but he uses them to describe martyrdom rather than the church *per se*. Bartley, *Faith and Politics after Christendom*, 25.
[78] Goddard, *Living the Word, Resisting the World*, 161.
[79] Yoder, *The Politics of Jesus*, 39.
[80] Berkhof, *Christ and the Powers*, 51 (and that chapter more generally).
[81] Tolstoy, "The End of the Age," 34.
[82] Tolstoy, "The Kingdom of God Is within You," 264 (also 270).
[83] Besides, Tolstoy adds that given that those in charge of the state are committing violence and evil, the argument that force should be used to restrain evil can easily be turned against them. Tolstoy, "The Kingdom of God Is within You," 197-198, 267-270, 274.

Christians contribute more "towards keeping the world in order" by following their radical principles than by restraining evil through the state.[84]

Tolstoy also rejects the idea that people "must [...] be guided" by wise government: for him, the very fact that some people "allow themselves to use violence towards human beings, indicates that they are not more, but less wise than those who submit to them."[85] Besides, as already noted, "morality cannot be enforced by law."[86] The very idea that people can be guided by coercive legislation is misguided.

Tolstoy furthermore refuses to concede that "the abolition of the State would involve social chaos."[87] He admits that he does not know exactly what society would look like without a state, but he adds that since the state would have been rendered obsolete by a counter-culture of love and sacrifice, this alternative could not result in more social tensions than those currently resulting from state oppression. A Christian church would be far less prone to riots and social disorder than an unfair society conserved by the state. Besides, he believes that it is "arbitrary" to assert "that the degree of safety and welfare which men enjoy is ensured by State power."[88] It is not necessarily thanks to the state that human beings are able to enjoy some degree of safety and welfare today.

Despite Tolstoy's clever answers, however, the question of how to deal with evil can be phrased in even more challenging terms. That is, what would a Christian anarchist do if an armed maniac attacked them or their family? Would they not use force as a last resort to protect a child being attacked by such a maniac?

In answering this question, some Christian anarchists seem willing to compromise their radical principles. Day, for instance, after citing this question, writes: "How many times have we heard this. Restrain him, of course, but not kill him. Confine him if necessary. But perfect love casts out fear and love overcomes hatred. All this sounds trite but experience is not trite."[89] She then explains that her Catholic Worker community once faced this threat of an armed maniac, and she concedes that they called the police, though they refused to bring charges against him.[90] Berdyaev also seems willing to accept that in such extreme cases, some minimal force might be permissible. Likewise, Ballou grants that "benevolent physical force" is necessary to restrain the truly mad or delirious, though he insists such force must be "uninjurious."[91] Other Christian anarchists, however, are uneasy with such concessions. Tolstoy, for instance, responds to this

---

[84] Ballou, *Non-Resistance in Relation to Human Governments*, 18; Ballou, "Non-Resistance," 148.
[85] Tolstoy, "The Slavery of Our Times," 118.
[86] This is paraphrasing Pentecost, whose exact words are: "Most people think that sobriety and morality can be enforced by law. But they can't." Pentecost, *Anarchism*, para. 23.
[87] Tolstoy, "The Kingdom of God Is within You," 260.
[88] Tolstoy, "The End of the Age," 33-34 (see also 36).
[89] Day, *The Long Loneliness*, 270.
[90] Day, *The Long Loneliness*, 270. Moreover, Hennacy claims that "Dorothy did not know it" when the police was called – implying that she did not personally approve of this course of action. Hennacy, *The Book of Ammon*, 345.
[91] Ballou, *Christian Non-Resistance*, chap. 1, para. 8 (see also para. 22-35).

objection several times across his writings, and offers a more elaborate answer than Day or Berdyaev since the latter merely mention this dilemma in passing.[92]

For a start, Tolstoy remarks that it is generally but mistakenly assumed that the only possible reply to save the child is to kill the assailant. Yet he notes that it is never certain that an evil act would have indeed been committed – but that our own violence would itself be evil and a likely cause of further evil. For Tolstoy, the only type of response available to a Christian faithful to Jesus' teaching would be to "plead with the assailant" or to "interpose his body between the assailant and the victim," but that "he cannot deliberately abandon the law he has received from God."[93] Other Christian anarchists agree: one can plead with the attacker or put one's body between the attacker and the victim. Either way, violence is not the only option.

Moreover, Tolstoy writes, "None of us has ever yet met the imaginary criminal with the imaginary child, but all the horrors which fill the annals of history and of our own times came, and come, from this one thing, namely, that people will believe they really foresee speculative future results of action."[94] People are convinced that violence will lead to the desired solution and thus fill the annals of history with their violent actions, which that one imaginary child continues to legitimise. Furthermore, Tolstoy comments,

> I have never, except in discussions, encountered that fantastic brigand who before my eyes desired to kill or violate a child, but [...] I perpetually did and do see not one but millions of brigands using violence towards children and women and men and old people and all the labourers, in the name of a recognized right to do violence to their fellows.[95]

People, Tolstoy laments, worry about an imaginary – or at least very rare – defenceless child, but not about the real suffering of so many of their neighbours as a result of the acceptance of violence as an appropriate method to respond to real or hypothetical aggression.

Tolstoy does not brush aside the very real torture, rape and murder which can be committed by human beings, especially in warfare. As Chapter 3 makes clear, Tolstoy is aware of these horrors, but where he and other Christian anarchists differ from the majority of political thinkers, and indeed where the source of their originality lies, is in their Christian conviction that to eradicate such horrors, human beings need to stop fighting and start loving and forgiving one another, even at the cost of very real sacrifices and suffering in the short run. That is what Christian anarchists understand Jesus' teaching to be about.

---

[92] Note however that in *What I Believe*, which he wrote soon after his conversion to Christianity (in 1883-4), Tolstoy writes that he "dare not employ any violence whatsoever towards any man whatsoever (*save, say, towards a child to deliver it from an imminent danger*)" (emphasis added). Yet this exception is phrased in a way that does not seem to allow violence to be used against the child's *attacker*, because Tolstoy speaks of violence *towards* the child – though what that means remains unclear. In any case, Tolstoy's many later and much more detailed discussions of this archetypal exception, where he dismisses it, should be seen to supersede this passing comment which is not elaborated further. Tolstoy, *What I Believe*, 215.
[93] Tolstoy, "Letter to Ernest Howard Crosby," 187.
[94] Tolstoy, "Letter to Ernest Howard Crosby," 188.
[95] Leo Tolstoy, "Introduction to a Short Biography of William Lloyd Garrison," in *The Kingdom of God and Peace Essays*, trans. Aylmer Maude (New Delhi: Rupa, 2001), 534.

For them, the suffering resulting from non-resistance might at least lead humanity towards a brighter future. Of course, it is very difficult, especially when talking about one's own child. But as Chapter 1 argues, the use of violence in defence will only aggrieve yet another family – and the cycle of violence thus continues. Therefore, even to protect loved ones from armed maniacs, some Christian anarchists like Tolstoy do not believe violence to be ultimately justified or indeed helpful.

Perhaps the most eloquent and powerful response to this objection, however, comes from Ballou:

> "Well," says the objector, "I should like to know how you would manage matters if the ruffian should actually break into your house with settled intent to rob and murder. Would you shrink back like a coward and see your wife and children slaughtered before your eyes?" I cannot tell how I might act in such a dreadful emergency – how weak and frail I should prove. But I can tell how I ought to act – how I should wish to act. If I am a firm, consistent non-resistant, I should prove myself no coward; for it requires the noblest courage and the highest fortitude to be a true non-resistant. If I am what I ought to be, I should be calm and unruffled by the alarm at my door. I should meet my wretched fellow-man with a spirit, an air, a salutation, and a deportment so Christ-like, so little expected, so confounding, and so morally irresistible that in all probability his weapons of violence and death would fall harmless to his side. I would say, "Friend, why do you come here? Surely not to injure those who wish you nothing but good? This house is one of peace and friendship to all mankind. If you are cold, warm yourself at our fire; if hungry, refresh yourself at our table; if you are weary, sleep in our bed; if you are destitute, poor, and needy, freely take of our goods. Come, let us be friends, that God may keep us all from evil and bless us with his protection." What would be the effect of such treatment as this? Would it not completely overcome the feelings of the invader, so as either to make him retreat inoffensively out of the house, or at least forbear all meditated violence? Would it not be incomparably safer than to rush to the shattered door, half distracted with alarm, grasping some deadly weapon and bearing it aloft, looking fiery wrath and mad defiance at the enemy? How soon would follow the mortal encounter, and how extremely uncertain the outcome? The moment I appeared in such an attitude (just the thing expected), would not the ruffian's coolness and well-trained muscular force be almost sure to seal the fate of my family and myself? But in acting the non-resistant part, should I not be likely, in nine cases out of ten, to escape with perfect safety?[96]

Ballou's answer is so moving in part because it recalls so eloquently that non-resistance is not separable from a broader Christian attitude of love and care: feeding the poor, sheltering the homeless, caring for the afflicted – true love of neighbour and enemy – is likely to prevent anger and violence from arising in the first place. He admits that it is difficult, and that he might fail in doing what Jesus demands, but he rejects the idea that one ought to use violence to protect one's loved ones, because, he argues, a loving and non-resistant attitude is more likely to save us than an aggressive response.

---

[96] Ballou, *Non-Resistance in Relation to Human Governments*, 15-16.

For Christian anarchists, as Chapter 1 argues, any violent response sows the seeds of further violence, and justifies the other side's right to use violence to protect what it regards as its own vital interests. Moreover, in the true Christian church – where no-one would use violence against others, where all would care for, give to and help every single human being – the risk of violence arising would be very low in the first place. Thus the best response to the imaginary criminal wishing to rape or murder the imaginary child is not necessarily to use violence in reply. Several Christian anarchists therefore reject the argument whereby force may be needed to protect one's child or neighbour. For them, there can be no compromise, no exception to Jesus' rule of turning the other cheek.[97] Besides, Tolstoy notes that "no confirmation of such an interpretation can be found anywhere in Christ's teaching."[98] However difficult it might be, a follower of Jesus must try to follow Jesus' commandments.

Christian anarchists rarely explicitly extend this answer to the hypothetical child attacker to interstate relations – no doubt in large part because they are so critical of states in the first place. Yet critics of extreme non-resistance do often extend the question of the child attacker to ask what the non-resistant community would do if the country was attacked. Surely, the argument goes, our nation has to defend itself from potential foreign invasion?

Here again, however, the Christian anarchist answer is negative. For a start, Sampson remarks that, just like with the question concerning the domestic attacker, the hypocritical "implication" behind this question seems to be that we are "basically good" and "would obey" Jesus' advice if others would follow it, too – yet no-one can be "counted on" to take the crucial first step.[99] For Hennacy, however, a foreign attack is probably the result of some prior sin of ours. Our state must have been violent or stolen some territory or resources for another state to wage war against us – perhaps, therefore, we are not as good as we like to think we are. Christian anarchists would certainly seek to publicise some of our own sins which would have contributed to escalating the cycle of violence in the first place. Either way, the only response Hennacy describes to this hypothetical foreign invasion is "to pray for our sins that have brought the attack upon us," and pray for the attacker as well.[100]

Tolstoy, for his part, admits that he does not know what he would do, but that, again, non-resistance offers better hopes for humanity than war. Moreover, he notes that the need to protect ourselves "from neighbouring states" is "what all governments say of one another," yet that the "danger of such attacks" is only caused precisely by the very logic that calls for the raising of armies to protect from hypothetical foreign invasions.[101] It is precisely because

---

[97] Moreover, Brock and Maude explain that in their exchange of letters, Tolstoy clearly disagreed with Ballou on the latter's compromise with force in the case of delirious or mad people, and that for Tolstoy, "The great sin is to compromise in *theory*" (Tolstoy's emphasis) even though the application of the theory would (presumably) be generally compromised by human beings' inherent imperfections. Brock, *Pacifism in Europe to 1914*, 462-464; Brock, *The Roots of War Resistance*, 73; Maude, *The Life of Tolstóy*, 252-253.
[98] Tolstoy, "The Kingdom of God Is within You," 38.
[99] Sampson, "Tolstoy on Power," 68.
[100] Hennacy, *The Book of Ammon*, 433.
[101] Tolstoy, "The Kingdom of God Is within You," 199.

people believe that they their use of force is necessary to protect from foreign evil that they, as foreigners, commit evil abroad – and remain blind to it.

In short, even in the case of a foreign attack, Christian anarchists will not concede that violence should be used in dealing with evil. As noted in Chapter 4, Christians should never fight in war. Indeed, this particular scenario is questionable in a more fundamental way than that of the child attacker, because it somehow conflates the church with the country or assumes that Christians owe allegiance to the state. Such allegiance is rejected, and it is the church, not the country or the state, which is the focus of Christian anarchist prescriptions for Christian community life. In turn, if the question of how to respond to attack or persecution is posed in relation to the church, then Christian anarchists have a lot more to say.

## 5.2.2 – Heroic sacrifices by church members

The question of how the church would deal with evil in many ways brings the argument back to the hypothetical child attacker. There, Ballou was quoted to have claimed that the outcome from not resisting but showing love and care would be positive "*in nine cases out of ten*."[102] It may not work all the time. What if it fails? Ballou admits that the outcome, then, could indeed be death – but he adds:

> Who would not rather pass away thus unstained with blood, into the joys of that Lord, who himself quenched the fiery darts of his malicious murderers with his own vital blood, than to purchase a few days of mortal life by precipitating into eternity a fellow creature, with his millstone of unrepentant crime about his neck? Is it so dreadful a thing for the Christian to be hurried to heaven […]? Is life on earth […] of so much value, that he would murder, rather than be murdered? Oh, let me die the death of the Christian non-resistant, and let my last end by like His![103]

The true Christian, for Ballou, would be willing to embrace death in those few cases in which love and non-resistance would fail. Doing so would only be following Jesus' example – as well as that of "thousands of Christian martyrs."[104] Besides, for Ballou, "to die in the triumph of non-resisting love" is much more "glorious […] than to live wearing the crown of Caesar, bespattered by the blood of the slain."[105]

The point that Ballou illustrates is one made by all Christian anarchists. That is, members of the true church, in dealing with the evil that may face the community, must be ready and willing to make the ultimate sacrifice, to risk death as martyrs to Jesus' teaching. Christian anarchists recall that Jesus himself warns of the ultimate sacrifice involved in following him to the cross. As noted in Chapter 2, for them, that is what he means when he says that he "came

---

[102] Ballou, *Non-Resistance in Relation to Human Governments*, 16 (emphasis added); Ballou, "Non-Resistance," 148 (emphasis added).
[103] Ballou, *Non-Resistance in Relation to Human Governments*, 17.
[104] Ballou, *Christian Non-Resistance in All Its Important Bearings*, 58.
[105] Ballou, "A Catechism of Non-Resistance," 18.

not to send peace, but a sword."[106] Myers therefore asserts (quoting Bonhoeffer) that "When Christ calls a person, He bids them to come and die."[107] For Elliott, "Commitment to the death is the bottom line of [Jesus'] movement," the "immediate future" for which "Jesus never paints a rosy picture."[108] Members of the true church should be prepared to die like Jesus as a testimony to their unwavering faith in him and in his teaching.

Moreover, Jesus warns his followers that they will be persecuted for their faith in his radical teaching, that they will be hated and prosecuted in local councils.[109] Yet these trials are also an opportunity: as Andrews understands Peter to have written, these trials "come [...] so that your faith [...] may be proved genuine."[110] Members of the true church will be persecuted for their radical beliefs, but these are an opportunity to for them to further confirm and witness to these beliefs.

For Christian anarchists, therefore, suffering is unavoidable within the true church.[111] Returning good for evil will always be difficult. Then again, returning evil for evil also entails suffering. As Tolstoy writes, "We might believe that the teaching of Jesus is difficult, terrible, and leads to suffering, were the consequences of the teaching of the world easy, and safe, and agreeable. But in reality the teaching of the world is more difficult to fulfil, more dangerous, more fraught with suffering than that of Jesus."[112] Thus, even though "The disciple of Jesus should be prepared [...] for suffering and death, [...] the disciple of the world" is "exactly in the same position."[113] "The truth is," Ballou writes, that people "can endure almost any thing they choose" – so they might as well choose to follow Jesus' teaching of love and forgiveness.[114]

Moreover, Tolstoy adds that "if we count the martyrs to the world, for every single martyr to Christ we shall find a thousand martyrs of the world, whose sufferings have been a hundredfold greater."[115] Ballou agrees that in the end, the world's path of resistance has led to more suffering and death than that of Christian non-resistance: "where non-resistance demands the sacrifice of one life," he writes, "resistance demands thousands of such sacrifices."[116] Many more lives have been and continue to be lost by practicing resistance than otherwise. Thus, according to Ballou, it is "incomparably safer" to suffer evil "than to resist it by violence."[117]

---

[106] Andrews playfully adapts Jesus' opening words as follows: "Do not imagine that I have come to bring tranquillity. I have not come to bring a gin and tonic, but a gun. For I have come to put people in conflict with each other – even in their own family." Andrews, *Not Religion, but Love*, 199-200. (Matthew 10:34-39.)
[107] Dietrich Bonhoeffer, quoted in Myers, *Binding the Strong Man*, 401.
[108] Elliott, *Freedom, Justice and Christian Counter-Culture*, 171.
[109] For instance: Matthew 10:5-36; Mark 13:9-13; Luke 10:1-7; John 16:33.
[110] Andrews, *The Crux of the Struggle*, 53. (1 Peter 1:3-7.)
[111] Moreover, Day sometimes speaks of the difficulties involved in simply trying to live in community according to Maurin's programme: she speaks of learning "the hard way," but adds that she "never knew any other way." Day, *The Long Loneliness*, 229.
[112] Tolstoy, *What I Believe*, 168 (and that chapter more generally).
[113] Tolstoy, *What I Believe*, 172.
[114] Ballou, *Christian Non-Resistance*, chap. 6, para. 15.
[115] Tolstoy, *What I Believe*, 168.
[116] Ballou, "A Catechism of Non-Resistance," 18.
[117] Ballou, "A Catechism of Non-Resistance," 18.

Either way, there is no doubt that following Jesus requires "courage," "heroism," and "moral bravery."[118] Bartley understands that "People are afraid to make themselves vulnerable."[119] Yet we must "set aside our concern for security," says Andrews.[120] One must be courageous enough to make oneself vulnerable. That is why Ballou writes that "it requires the noblest courage and the highest fortitude to be a true non-resistant."[121] That is also why Allen notes in his foreword to Hennacy's book that "Of all unfair charges we bring against them, the most absurd is that of cowardice."[122] Following Jesus requires no cowardice but heroic courage.

Some even interpret the Eucharist in the context of such courageous sacrifice. Andrews reports that for Carlos Christos, what Jesus means by "Do this in memory of me" is not that we should "merely commemorate" the breaking of bread, but that we "should do likewise," that we should "offer [our] body and blood for the redemption of humanity."[123] For him, "Mass is something to be lived rather than attended," and we must "become *God's sacrament in the world*."[124] Cavanaugh makes a similar point, adding that "we become the body of Christ by consuming it," and that "our assimilation to the body of Christ means that we then become food for the world, to be broken, given away and consumed."[125]

The mission of the church is therefore clearly a difficult one, and requires heroic sacrifices from its members in dealing with evil.[126] Yet "if they suffer with those who suffer," Ellul says, Christians "bear witness before God and man to the consequences of injustice and the proclamation of love."[127] By suffering evil, Christians also unmask it, and this in turn can move others to perhaps repent and join the church as well. Tolstoy says that "It is by those who have suffered, not by those who have inflicted suffering, that the world has been advanced."[128] That is, "The progress of humanity towards good is accomplished not by its tormentors, but by its martyrs."[129] It is this faith in the transformative power of love through suffering even unto death that bears witness to the church's trust in God.

---

[118] Ballou, *Christian Non-Resistance*, chap. 6, para. 21 (for "heroism" and "moral bravery"); Hennacy, *The Book of Ammon*, 50 (for "courage").
[119] Bartley, *Faith and Politics after Christendom*, 214.
[120] Andrews, *Not Religion, but Love*, 44.
[121] Ballou, *Non-Resistance in Relation to Human Governments*, 15.
[122] Steve Allen, "Introduction," in *The Book of Ammon*, by Ammon Hennacy, ed. Jim Missey and Joan Thomas (Baltimore: Fortkamp, 1994), xv.
[123] Carlos Christos, quoted in Andrews, *The Crux of the Struggle*, 42. (Matthew 26:17-30; Mark 14:12-26; Luke 22:7-30.)
[124] Carlos Christos, quoted in Andrews, *The Crux of the Struggle*, 42 (Christos' emphasis).
[125] Cavanaugh, *Torture and Eucharist*, 231-232.
[126] Chelčický notes that this is also why the church should not seek protection by the state, as such protection prevents priests from being harmed and thus from imitating Jesus. Wojciech Iwańczak, "Between Pacifism and Anarchy: Peter Chelčický's Teaching About Society," *Journal of Medieval History* 23/3 (1997), 275-276.
[127] Ellul, *Violence*, 175.
[128] Tolstoy, quoted in Kennan, "A Visit to Count Tolstoi," 259.
[129] Tolstoy, *What I Believe*, 49.

## 5.3 – Trust in God

Faith in the transformative power of the Christian witness and faith in God's mysterious providence are therefore important elements of the true church's enthusiasm for Jesus' teaching. The church is to be a beacon of such faith, confident that with time and patience, it will grow to become the stateless kingdom of God (see the Conclusion) foreseen by Jesus.

### 5.3.1 – A beacon of faith

Clearly, Jesus' demands for the Christian church are radical and difficult. Most people have no faith in their potential application in today's society. They consider it to be too utopian, too unrealistic.[130] Christian anarchists, however, lament this lack of faith.

Chapter 3 discusses the view, held by many church theologians, that non-resistance is impracticable – a view which, for Christian anarchists, is symptomatic of a lack of faith in Jesus. Indeed, the very existence of the state is evidence of humanity's lack of trust in God. For Pentecost (as mentioned in Chapter 3), the state's existence implies "that we have a God who made a lot of laws which are so defective that the universe would go to smash" without it.[131] Moreover, in a way, just as to trust God is an act of faith, to trust the state is also an act of faith – not in love and forgiveness, but in violence and coercion. For Hennacy, therefore, "Most people believe more in the power of evil, for they do not trust in God but put their trust in government, insurance, politicians, […] war, and anything but God."[132]

Christian anarchists, however, would "rather put [their] trust in God than in the gun of a police officer."[133] Jesus repeatedly urges his disciples to trust God, and blames his disciples for having too little faith.[134] His commandments to love enemies, forgive seventy-seven times and not resist evil rely on that faith in God, because for Ellul, the idea that evil can be overcome by love "rests on the conviction that it is God who transforms the heart of man. In other words, it betokens an attitude of utter faith in the action of the Holy Spirit."[135] Ballou also

---

[130] Of course, all anarchists – not just Christian ones – have been accused of utopianism. For a discussion of the general anarchist response to this accusation, see for instance Kinna, *Anarchism*, 86, 97-108.
[131] Pentecost, *Murder by Law*, para. 20.
[132] Hennacy, *The Book of Ammon*, 300.
[133] ter Kuile, "Anarcho Theologie," 16.
[134] Andrews, *Christi-Anarchy*, 169; Andrews, *Love and Fear*, 6; Day, *The Long Loneliness*, 34; Roy Halliday, *Christian Libertarians* (Libertarian Nation Foundation), available from http://www.libertariannation.org/a/f42h2.html (accessed 8 November 2007), para. 17-18.Andrews, *Christi-Anarchy*, 169; Andrews, *Love and Fear*, 6; Day, *The Long Loneliness*, 34; Roy Halliday, *Christian Libertarians* (Libertarian Nation Foundation), available from http://www.libertariannation.org/a/f42h2.html (accessed 8 November 2007), para. 17-18.Andrews, *Christi-Anarchy*, 169; Andrews, *Love and Fear*, 6; Day, *The Long Loneliness*, 34; Roy Halliday, *Christian Libertarians* (Libertarian Nation Foundation), available from http://www.libertariannation.org/a/f42h2.html (accessed 8 November 2007), para. 17-18.For instance : Matthew 5:10-12, 8:23-27; Mark 4:35-41.
[135] Ellul, *Violence*, 13.

recalls that the Bible says that "To him that believeth, all things are possible."[136] Hence Newell writes that "we trust in the power of non-violent love to bring about the conversion and transformation that we seek."[137] Even more than courage, therefore, the true church requires faith – the former then naturally follows the latter. Faith in God gives the church confidence in its witness to the world.

At the same time, this revives the argument, discussed in Chapter 4, that compliance with Jesus' teachings is not to be expected from non-Christians.[138] Given their lack of faith, as Ellul explains, "Christians must freely admit and accept the fact that non-Christians use violence."[139] Of course, such "recourse to violence," for Ellul, "is an admission that faith [...] has been lost."[140] Yet Christians "cannot demand [...] that a non-Christian state should refrain from using violence" or follow the Sermon on the Mount.[141] Christians must accept, however regretfully, that non-Christians have chosen to put their faith in the violent state rather than God – although of course they also know that this choice is evil and doomed, and they must try to convert non-Christians to Jesus' subversive alternative through their witness. Nevertheless, among those who lack faith in God, several Christian anarchists see the state as "a necessary evil" ("necessary" because Jesus' teaching is ignored, but still "evil" and to be overcome nonetheless).[142] According to Chelčický, "The civil law is [...] necessary – as a bitter vinegar, so to speak – for those who transgress the law of love."[143] Chapter 4 explains that for many Christian anarchists, God mysteriously and reluctantly works through the state to hold the world that has rejected him together.

Yet this fallen state of humanity must be redeemed by the church's embodiment of Jesus' teaching and example. As Goddard writes, "the Christian life is to be understood primarily as a form of presence in the fallen world."[144] Hence indifference to the state must be matched by fervour for the true church, and by a hope to subvert the state by broadening the church. Ellul warns his

---

[136] Ballou, *Non-Resistance in Relation to Human Governments*, 11; Ballou, "Non-Resistance," 145. (The exact words from Mark 9:23 are "If thou canst believe, all things are possible to him that believeth.")

[137] Martin Newell, "Works of Mercy and War," *London Catholic Worker*, issue 13, April 2005, 12.

[138] There is something of a tension, here, among Christian anarchists, between those like Ellul who (as Goddard explains) emphasise that Jesus' commandments are for Christians only, and those who agree with Tolstoy that (as Sampson notes) Jesus' teachings are meant to be *universally* applicable – that is, applicable to non-Christians as well. Nevertheless, this tension is largely overcome by the hope, apparently shared by all Christian anarchists, that the church has the potential to grow and encompass the whole of humanity: whether this is seen as an adoption of Christianity by non-Christians or as recognition of the universal truth of Jesus' teaching, the effect is largely same. Goddard, *Living the Word, Resisting the World*, 57; Sampson, *Tolstoy*, 170-171.

[139] Ellul, *Violence*, 131 (also: 158).

[140] Indeed, Ellul writes that "The appeal to and use of violence in Christian action increase in exact proportion to the decrease in faith," noting also that "the use of violence implies total confidence on the part of the user that it is justified and this confidence is a crime against God." Ellul, *Violence*, 149.

[141] Ellul, *Violence*, 159.

[142] Ballou, *Non-Resistance in Relation to Human Governments*, 8; Molnár, *A Study of Peter Chelčický's Life*, 30.

[143] Molnár, *A Study of Peter Chelčický's Life*, 87 (quoting Chelčický).

[144] Goddard, *Living the Word, Resisting the World*, 102.

fellow Christians that "God has put us on this earth not for nothing."[145] Moreover, "Failure by Christians to be faithful to their calling to live and preach the Gospel," for him, "has disastrous consequences," in that it allows the world to carry on perpetrating evil unchallenged.[146] Indeed, for Ellul, "Christians ultimately bear responsibility for our present plight."[147] Violence and suffering persist because Christians have failed to trust God, follow Jesus, and thereby expose the errors of the non-Christian way.

Hence for O'Reilly, as Camus says, "What the world wants of Christians is that Christians should speak out loud and clear."[148] The true church must proclaim loudly and clearly its faith in God and in Jesus' teaching, by witnessing to it both in its own community and in the way it interacts with the world outside it. The true church has a unique calling, and the salvation of humanity depends on its faithfulness to it. Hence the true church must be a beacon of faith in a dark world.

## 5.3.2 – The mysterious growth of a mustard seed

Christian anarchists believe that the collective example set by the community life of the true church can be just as inspirational and contagious as individual examples of personal sacrifices. Andrews writes that "the beauty of love and justice embodied in our communities will encourage all men and all women of goodwill to continue to do good works as well."[149] According to Chelčický, "It was precisely this humble and loving behaviour which effected the conversion of the Gentiles and Jews to faith, because good examples move the unbelievers sometimes more forcibly than preaching and long speeches" on how best to organise society.[150] For Maurin, the true church brings admiration from onlookers and "creates a desire among the admirers to climb on the bandwagon."[151] Indeed, that is also why Christian anarchist subversion "need not be feared" by others: as Tolstoy notes, it "cannot be made coercively binding upon" others, but requires them to adopt it of their own free will.[152]

Christian anarchists like to employ various metaphors to describe the process by which they are expecting the true church to grow. As Andrews and others remark, Jesus himself often uses "organic images to describe how the 'power of the Spirit' [...] operates," how the church is to grow into the stateless kingdom of God.[153] "Like a minute seed," Andrews continues, "the power of the Spirit seems embarrassingly insignificant to begin with, yet grows into a capacity

---

[145] Ellul, *Anarchy and Christianity*, 103.
[146] Goddard, *Living the Word, Resisting the World*, 108.
[147] Goddard, *Living the Word, Resisting the World*, 160.
[148] Albert Camus, quoted in O'Reilly, *Remembering Forgetting*, 28.
[149] Andrews, *Christi-Anarchy*, 126.
[150] Molnár, *A Study of Peter Chelčický's Life*, 59 (quoting Chelčický).
[151] Maurin, *Easy Essays (2003)*, 190.
[152] Tolstoy, "Introduction to a Short Biography of William Lloyd Garrison," 535.
[153] Andrews, *Not Religion, but Love*, 77; Andrews, *Subversive Spirituality, Ecclesial and Civil Disobedience*, 6. The relevant Bible passages are Matthew 13:31-32, 17:20; Mark 4:26-34; Luke 13:18-21, 17:6.

that is of tremendous significance in the end."[154] Hence "despite appearances, the Kingdom [of God] will prevail."[155] However insignificant it might at first appear, the true church has the potential to grow far beyond its current size.

Furthermore, Christian anarchists note that Jesus' parables make clear that *how* the seed grows "is a mystery."[156] Myers writes that the way it grows is "neither obvious nor controllable."[157] Jesus moreover suggests that it "grows strong in an environment that could easily destroy it" – again a warning about the hostile wider environment faced by the true church.[158] In any case, "The vocation of the disciple," as Myers explains, "lies not in trying to provoke the harvest (for that happens 'of itself'), but in tending to the 'sowing.'"[159] The task of Jesus' followers is to sow the seeds and wait patiently for the harvest. The difficulty, of course, is that seeds must "fall into the ground and die if they are to bring fruits."[160] For Andrews, this means that "those of us whose lives constitute those seeds" must "bury ourselves in the life of our community."[161] In a way, however, this metaphor also further clarifies what is meant by describing the martyrs as the seeds of the church: it is indeed out of their blood and sacrifice, their death, that the church can be made to mysteriously flourish.

Moreover, as already noted, the day of the harvest is unknown. We cannot know when the stateless kingdom of the God will be inaugurated, since as Jesus warns and Tolstoy repeats, "of that day and hour knoweth no man, but my Father only."[162] Nonetheless, Tolstoy insists that the growth of the seed is inevitable. According to him (as mentioned in Chapter 4), the true church has "the most powerful thing in the world – Truth" – and the eventual recognition of truth by all human beings is inevitable.[163]

Tolstoy frequently speaks of the inexorable movement of public opinion, which for him is the "fundamental factor" that "has always" decided "everything."[164] He argues that the assimilation of a "new truth" by public opinion "becomes larger and larger like a snowball."[165] Tolstoy furthermore claims that

> Men who accept a new truth when it has reached a certain degree of dissemination always do so suddenly and in a mass. They resemble the ballast with which every ship is laden to keep it steady and enable it to sail properly. Were it not for the ballast the vessel would not be sufficiently

---

[154] Andrews, *Not Religion, but Love*, 78; Andrews, *Subversive Spirituality, Ecclesial and Civil Disobedience*, 6. (Matthew 13:31-32; Mark 4:30-34; Luke 13:18-19.)
[155] Myers, *Binding the Strong Man*, 179 (capitalisation removed).
[156] Andrews, *Not Religion, but Love*, 78. (Mark 4:26-29.)
[157] Myers, *Binding the Strong Man*, 179.
[158] Andrews, *Not Religion, but Love*, 78; Andrews, *Subversive Spirituality, Ecclesial and Civil Disobedience*, 6. (Matthew 13:24-30.)
[159] Myers, *Binding the Strong Man*, 179. (Matthew 13:1-23; Mark 4:1-25; Luke 8:4-15.)
[160] This is paraphrasing Andrews' own paraphrasing of John 12:24, in Andrews, *Not Religion, but Love*, 78; Andrews, *Subversive Spirituality, Ecclesial and Civil Disobedience*, 6.
[161] Andrews, *Not Religion, but Love*, 78 (for the exact wording), 202-203.
[162] Tolstoy, "The Kingdom of God Is within You," 306. (Matthew 24:36.)
[163] Tolstoy, "Address to the Swedish Peace Congress in 1909," 538 (Tolstoy's punctuation removed).
[164] Tolstoy, "The Kingdom of God Is within You," 285.
[165] Tolstoy, "The Kingdom of God Is within You," 277.

immersed in the water and its course would be changed by the slightest modification of surrounding conditions.[166]

The slowness of a shift in public opinion makes it possible for a new truth to be tested before it is adopted by the whole community.

For Tolstoy, however, humanity has now reached one of those tipping points when public opinion must be steered away from the current faith in the state by enough pioneers embodying the required alternative. He writes:

> Men in their present condition are like a swarm of bees hanging from a branch in a cluster. The position of the bees on that branch is temporary and must inevitably be changed. They must bestir themselves and find a new dwelling. Each of the bees knows this and wishes to change its position and that of others, but no one of them is willing to move till the rest do so. […] It would seem that there was no way out of this state for the bees, just as there seems no escape for worldly men who are entangled in the toils of the [current] conception of life. […] Yet as it is enough for one bee to spread her wings, rise up and fly away, and a second, a third, a tenth, and a hundredth, will do the same and the cluster that hung inertly becomes a freely flying swarm of bees; so let but one man understand life as Christianity teaches us to understand it, and begin to live accordingly, and a second, a third, and a hundredth will do the same, till the enchanted circle of social life from which there seemed to be no escape will be destroyed.[167]

Tolstoy thus makes use of many different images and analogies of his own to convey his conviction that the Christian anarchist truth cannot but spread, following the example set by the true church. Hence even the most rationalist of Christian anarchists has faith in the power of the Christian anarchist example to spread and eventually encompass the whole of humankind.

Therefore, whether by faith in Jesus' description of the mysterious growth of the kingdom of God, or by faith in the inevitable recognition by humanity of Jesus' rational teaching, most Christian anarchists believe that the true church is destined to grow through the patient sacrifices of its martyrs (but see Conclusion). Those ready to take up their cross and follow Jesus must therefore build "the new society within the shell of the old," loving and caring for all, courageously forgiving those who commit evil, and above all keeping faith in God (or reason, for Tolstoy) while obeying his commandments. Over time, their communal witness to Jesus' teaching will inevitably subvert the state by moving more and more non-Christians to willingly repent and become members of the true church as well.

Chapter 4 describes the direct response to the state which is prescribed by Christian anarchism, and this Chapter, the indirect response to the state by embodying the true church. Having covered the theoretical response, it is now possible, in the next Chapter, to list the examples which Christian anarchist thinkers cite of individuals and communities who have sought to follow that theory.

---

[166] Tolstoy, "The Kingdom of God Is within You," 277.
[167] Tolstoy, "The Kingdom of God Is within You," 234-235.

# Chapter 6 – Examples of Christian Anarchist Witness

Chapters 4 and 5 describe the two flanks of the response advocated by Christian anarchist thought to the unchristian state's contemporary prominence. To illustrate this theory, Christian anarchists frequently name several examples of communities and charismatic individuals striving to follow this Christian anarchist ideal. They themselves often do their best to live up to it in their own lives. The aim of this Chapter is to point to these examples of Christian anarchist witness.

This book is concerned with Christian anarchist thought rather than practice. A comprehensive discussion of examples of Christian anarchist practice would easily constitute a book on its own. The aim of this short Chapter is therefore much more modest: the various examples can only be cited rather than properly assessed. The footnotes provide details of publications based on which a more thorough analysis of these examples can be pursued.

The reason for nonetheless including this short Chapter in this more theory-driven book is that Christian anarchist thinkers themselves refer to these examples in their articulation of the theory. These examples should therefore be approached as tentative illustrations of elements of the line of thinking outlined in Chapters 1 to 5 rather than as conclusive proof of its vindication. Christian anarchists themselves tend to evoke these examples to draw inspiration from them rather than as empirical evidence of the viability of their interpretation of the Bible. Besides, it could indeed be that, as the Conclusion suggests, Christian anarchism is destined to only ever be adopted in practice at the margins of society, even though it should nevertheless always inform and critique the current state of politics.

The Chapter is divided into two main sections. The first lists what are referred to as "pre-modern" examples of Christian anarchism: the early Christian church, and some of the sects and movements of the Middle Ages and the Reformation. The second main section lists "modern" examples – "modern" in the sense that they have come after the first attempts to articulate, in writing, what amounts to explicitly Christian "anarchist" thought.[1] This division is somewhat

---

[1] The precise dawn of "modernity" is, of course, a matter for debate, and the word "modern" is used here with a clear understanding that to limit it mostly to the late eighteenth century and beyond is highly questionable in the broader context of that debate. As noted in the text, however, the aim is simply to separate examples cited by Christian anarchists as preceding them in the distant past from examples of Christian anarchists themselves and of those communities that have tried to practice their teaching. The exception that upsets this typology is Chelčický and his followers (see below); but in that Chelčický lived at the very early edge of the disputed time frame of "modernity" (late fourteenth, early fifteenth centuries), and in that "anarchism" as a school of thought, and therefore as a term which Chelčický could identify with, was not to come about for another three or four centuries, a case can be made that this exception need not fundamentally undermine the proposed typology. In any case, clearly, the typology is quite fluid, although hopefully also helpful to some extent.

fluid and artificial, but the aim is to set apart those individuals and communities that have been inspired by the writings or leadership of some of the Christian anarchist thinkers identified in the Introduction. This second section therefore mentions Garrison and his followers, Ballou and the Hopedale community, Tolstoy's personal example and Tolstoy's followers in Russia and abroad, Gandhi (for reasons which are explained therein), the Catholic Worker movement, *A Pinch of Salt* and *The Digger*, online communities, and Dave Andrews' community work. The Chapter then concludes by briefly commenting on the incompleteness of many of these examples, thus paving the way for the reflections on Christian anarchist thought and practice that are articulated in the Conclusion.

## 6.1 – Pre-modern examples

Aside from a few marginal heretical movements, Christian anarchists cite two broad sets of examples of communities striving to witness to at least some elements of pure Christian anarchist thought in the relatively distant past: the early Christian church, and many of the Christian sects which mushroomed in Europe in the late Middle Ages and around the time of the Reformation.

### 6.1.1 – Early Christians

As noted in the beginning of Chapter 3, Christian anarchists admire the political organisation of the early Christian church (or church*es*), before it succumbed to the Constantinian temptation. They often cite several Church Fathers, such as Origen, Tertullian, Clement and Lactantius, as men whose writings suggest that the early church interpreted Jesus' teaching in a way that strongly resonates with their own.[2] These writings (which are among the few sources based upon which a picture of the early church or churches can be drawn today) leave the impression that the early Christian community did take Jesus' Sermon on the Mount quite literally and strove to live up to its revolutionary commandments.

The early church, they note, was a community of true love and care for one another. Craig insists that this church was centred "on Hospitality," not "on liturgy."[3] Moreover, as Maurin puts it, "because the poor were fed, clothed and sheltered at a personal sacrifice, the pagans used to say about the Christians 'See how they love each another.'"[4] As noted in Chapter 5, it was precisely this communal attitude of love and sacrifice which set Christians apart and persuaded others to convert and join the church.

Moreover, aside from this positive example of community life, early Christians also drew attention by refusing to worship and obey anyone but God –

---

[2] Other Church Fathers whom they cite include Justin Martyr, Athenagoras, Maximillian, Cyprian, Tatian, and Hippolytus.
[3] [Anonymous], *Ninety-Five Theses in Defense of Patriarchy*, thesis 68.
[4] Maurin, *Easy Essays (2003)*, 110. On the next page, he adds that, by contrast, "because" today "the poor are no longer fed, clothed and sheltered the pagans say about the Christians 'See how they pass the buck.'"

whether pagan deities or human idols claiming divine status, like Caesar. Early Christians, Hennacy writes, thus "refused to place a pinch of incense upon the altar of Caesar."[5] Indeed, Sandlin remarks, they "were savagely persecuted not because they worshipped Jesus Christ, but because they refused to worship the Roman emperor."[6] Their belief in just one God was thus perceived to be "deeply subversive."[7]

Given that they refused to worship the state, they also refused to swear any oath of allegiance to it – thus following Jesus' commandment. Tertullian's writings also imply that they refused "to take the administration of any dignity or power," or to act as judges – again in line with Jesus' demands (as Chapter 4 explains).[8] Naturally, they were particularly passionate about refusing to serve in the military. The early church, Christian anarchists emphasise, was noted for its uncompromising pacifism and its criticism of military service – indeed some blamed the eventual fall of the Roman empire on Christians for this very reason. Hence, as Ellul writes, in many ways, "the first Christian generation was globally hostile to political power and regarded it as bad no matter what its orientation or constitutional structures."[9] Early Christians were therefore "viewed by Roman authorities as subversive to the social order," and the Constantinian temptation was precisely a way to deal with this subversive movement by corrupting its very core.[10]

Before Constantine's clever manoeuvres, the preferred method employed by the Roman state had been (sometimes very brutal) persecution. A different method had to be adopted, however, because not only did persecution not succeed in weakening the church, but the death of its martyrs actually reaffirmed the Christian message, thereby furthering its dissemination. Still, the gruelling ordeals which early Christian martyrs had to endure along the way should not be belittled. They submitted to the state's punishment for refusing to disobey God, but this submission entailed momentous sacrifices. Yet such sacrifices were seen as the heart of what being a Christian was about. According to Cavanaugh, early Christians "built [altars] on the graves of the martyrs" as "centers of Eucharistic celebration," hence "the Eucharist was explicitly connected with martyrdom."[11] Moreover, despite this brutal persecution, early Christians also followed Paul's advice and prayed for and blessed their persecutors. Such "love of enemies," Johnston remarks, was seen as another "particular marker for the early Christian community."[12] Early Christians were persecuted, but they responded to this perception with love and forgiveness.

In short, in line with the argument articulated in Chapters 4 and 5, early Christians loved and cared for each other, and they subjected themselves to

---

[5] Hennacy, *The Book of Ammon*, 61.
[6] P. Andrew Sandlin, *Christianity: Mother of Political Liberty*, available from http://www.lewrockwell.com/orig/sandlin1a.html (accessed 21 November 2007), para. 5.
[7] Bartley, *Faith and Politics after Christendom*, 23.
[8] Tertullian, quoted in [Anonymous], *Early Church Quotes* (Jesus Radicals), available from http://www.jesusradicals.com/library/church_quotes.php (accessed 16 May 2006), para. 28.
[9] Ellul, *Anarchy and Christianity*, 59.
[10] Cavanaugh, *Torture and Eucharist*, 63.
[11] Cavanaugh, *Torture and Eucharist*, 67 and 225 respectively (see also 226).
[12] Johnston, "Love Your Enemies – Even in the Age of Terrorism?," 91.

the state's punishment for any necessary civil disobedience. They had the courage of their conviction. Pacifist Stanley Hauerwas therefore writes that the "very existence [of Christianity] was secured by people who were willing to die rather than conform to the pretentious claims of government."[13] As already noted, the seeds of the church were indeed the blood of its martyrs.

Yet somehow, the movement was corrupted, and the seeds apparently failed to bring the promised harvest. Precisely because Christianity became a considerable "political force," Ellul asserts, Constantine "officially adopted" it "and in so doing trapped the church, which readily let itself be trapped, being largely led at this time by a hierarchy drawn from the aristocracy."[14] As explained in Chapter 3, the church then moderated its radical stance on issues like military service, tempted as it was by the opportunities presented by political power. The dangers presented by this temptation are discussed in the Conclusion. The point to note here is that as Chapter 3 explains, after Constantine, the early church's example of Christian anarchist witness was deeply corrupted. When the Western Roman Empire then fell to barbarian invasions, as Brock explains, "Christian pacifism" – let alone Christian anarchism – "was submerged for nearly a millennium."[15]

### *6.1.2 – The Middle Ages and the Reformation*

Maurin believes that after the fall of Rome, the true Christians that survived "found a refuge in Ireland" – though he is the only Christian anarchist to make this point.[16] For all other Christian anarchists, bar the odd heretical movement, the centuries that followed the fall of Rome were by and large devoid of any recorded example of Christian anarchist witness.[17]

Christian anarchists pick up the thread again around the eleventh and twelfth centuries, when, as Wagner explains, "popular sectarian heresies [...] began to appear with greater frequency."[18] Brock claims that "The pacifist idea was reintroduced by Waldenses," who refused to take oaths and who condemned war and the death penalty.[19] Several Christian anarchists indeed cite this sect as a notable example of radical Christianity. Chelčický is even said by Brock to have been significantly influenced by it. Aside from the Waldenses, the other sect from that period that is cited by Christian anarchists is the Albigenses, who also

---

[13] Stanley Hauerwas, "The Church and Liberal Democracy: The Moral Limits of a Secular Polity," in *A Community of Character: Towards a Constructive Christian Ethic* (University of Notre Dame, 1981), available from http://www.jesusradicals.com/library/hauerwas/Church&LiberalDemocracy.pdf (accessed 16 May 2006), 85.
[14] Ellul, *Anarchy and Christianity*, 94.
[15] Brock, *The Roots of War Resistance*, 13.
[16] Maurin, *Easy Essays (2003)*, 204-206 (for instance).
[17] Among the less significant sects and movements sometimes (but rarely) mentioned as examples of embryonic Christian anarchism, one finds the Carpocratians, the Manicheans, the Montanists (but they all lived around the same time as the early church), and the Paulicians (from the seventh century onwards).
[18] Wagner, *Petr Chelčický*, 25. Among the sects who appeared around that time, which Christian anarchists (rarely) cite and which are not already mentioned in the text, one also finds the Bogomiles and the Cathars.
[19] Brock, *The Roots of War Resistance*, 13.

denounced war and capital punishment and who held the Catholic Church in contempt – as Part I shows, all important themes for several Christian anarchists. Both the Waldenses and the Albigenses were crushed by Catholic persecution, although the Waldenses have managed to adapt and survive in modified forms to this day.

Christian anarchists also refer to monastic movements as examples of attempts to return to the sort of communal life described in Chapter 5.[20] Many of them also admire mendicant friar Francis of Assisi and his followers, noting in passing that with their emphasis on poverty, they were considered "potentially subversive."[21] Andrews also reports, with approval of course, that Francis refused to take up arms during the Crusades. Over time, however, the Franciscan movement was institutionalised and incorporated into the official church, thus losing much of its politically radical edge; and as a result of this institutionalisation, Francis withdrew from it and retired to a hermitage.

The main Christian anarchist example from the fourteenth and fifteenth centuries is Chelčický himself, and to some extent his Bohemian predecessors and followers. Inspired by John Wycliffe and Jan Hus (among others), these Bohemian reformers were responsible for what Molnár describes as the third, separate and forgotten type of continental Reformation along the Calvinist and Lutheran ones. As with other reformers, Chelčický was incensed by the Catholic Church's theology and practice, not least the selling of indulgences, but he differed from other like-minded Czech radicals – most notably the Taborites – because he disagreed with their adoption of violent methods to defend themselves against Catholic armies. Chelčický's followers formed the Unity of Brethren (also known as the Czech or Bohemian Brethren or *Unitas Fratrum*), who distinguished themselves by their strict pacifism, and tried to live in line with the principles described in Chapter 5. The Unity of Brethren and the broader Hussite movement, including the Taborites to some extent, are therefore cited by Christian anarchists as further examples of embryonic Christian anarchist communities striving to live up to the radical political implications of Jesus' teaching. The Taborites, however, were crushed by Catholic armies, and after Chelčický's death, the Unity of Brethren gradually moderated its radical stance on the state.

Most of the seventeenth century examples admired by Christian anarchists emerged in Britain. They often cite the Peasants' Revolt, the Ranters, the Diggers and the Levellers as examples of movements struggling with the radical political implications of Jesus' teaching, and Gerrard Winstanley, who led the Diggers, is often singled out as a courageous radical Christian leader with strong Christian anarchist inclinations. Equally interesting was his contemporary Abiezer Coppe. The Quakers, who were founded in the seventeenth century and continue to thrive today, also stand out for Christian anarchists as a group that courageously embodied some elements of Christian anarchism in its strict pacifism and its consequent civil disobedience to uphold it.

---

[20] For instance, Elliott, Damico and Novak mention the Beghards (also known as the Brethren of the Free Spirit), and Ellul cites the Anchorites – both specific trends within the broader monastic movement.
[21] Bartley, *Faith and Politics after Christendom*, 40.

Probably the most frequently cited movement that arose during the Reformation, however, is the Anabaptist-Mennonite movement. This Protestant denomination emerged in the sixteenth century and continues to have a strong following today. Eller, Yoder and Penner all openly belong to this tradition, and Bartley seems to be speaking from within it, too. Many therefore see this movement, particularly its early martyrs and followers, as exemplifying elements of Christian anarchism. Anabaptism has always affirmed the need to take Jesus' ethical teaching seriously, and has often protested against coercive tendencies in Christianity. Hence it stands against violence and against the swearing of oaths; it is very critical of Constantinian Christianity; and it highlights the importance of presenting to the world a community of Christian love and sacrifice inspired by the witness of the early Christian church. It furthermore stresses that membership of the church must be voluntary – it cannot be meaningfully conferred by automatic infant baptism. Discipleship for Anabaptists therefore implies a "total life of love and as a necessary corollary – nonresistance."[22] Many Anabaptists believe that no Christian can participate in the organs of the state, and thus call for a clearer and total separation of church and state. Given these views, it is no surprise that Kropotkin, one of the famous fathers of anarchism, asserts that there is "a considerable amount of Anarchism" in Anabaptism.[23]

In short, Christian anarchists point to the example of several sects and movements that embodied elements of Christian anarchism before the term "Christian anarchism" was coined. These, however, only embraced *some* of the elements of Christian anarchist thought. Pacifism was usually a strong feature, as was often the call for a clearer separation of the true church from the state, but what was not yet fully developed was an argument that grounded clear and explicit *anarchist* conclusions (say, criticism specifically directed at *the state*, or the longing for an specifically *stateless* society) in Christianity. Brock does argue that these movements' "gospel of revolt and protest, albeit passive, against the existing social order" was usually inspired by a combination of "perfectionism" (or "utopianism") and the consideration of Jesus' example as the "ultimate source of authority."[24] However, they rarely carried their momentum to a full articulation and presentation of Christian *anarchism* in all its implications.

Still, they were often persecuted by state and church authorities. Unfortunately, in face of this persecution, many of these radical sects and movements gradually admitted the use of violence, which, as Ellul adds, "soon led them to reject Christianity itself."[25] Again, therefore, the Christian revolution failed to take hold because its pioneers compromised the purity of their witness. Certainly, these movements all evolved and changed over time. Sociologists of religion have reflected on the process whereby radical sects can develop into more established churches. Some reflections on this phenomenon with a particular focus on Christian anarchism are offered in the Conclusion. What must

---

[22] Penner, *The New Testament, the Christian, and the State*, 31.
[23] Peter Kropotkin, *Modern Science and Anarchism* (The Social Science Club), available from http://dwardmac.pitzer.edu/anarchist_archives/kropotkin/science/toc.html (accessed 7 March 2008), para. 10.
[24] Brock, *The Political and Social Doctrines*, 276.
[25] Ellul, *Violence*, 22.

nonetheless be noted here is that each of these older examples cited by Christian anarchists is imperfect in some way. Nonetheless, in that these movements did strive to courageously embody some of the elements of Christian anarchist thought, and in that they have inspired others to pick up the torch of radical Christianity, they qualify as historical examples which Christian anarchists have considered worth referring to.

## 6.2 – Modern examples

Christian anarchist thinkers also refer to more recent examples of individuals and communities to illustrate their thought. What distinguishes these from older examples is that they are all at least partly inspired by the writings or the leadership of one or several of the people broadly defined in the Introduction as Christian anarchist thinkers.

### *6.2.1 – Garrison and his followers*

As explained in the Introduction, Garrison only can only be described as a Christian anarchist for a brief period of a few years. His Christian anarchism is epitomised by the Declaration of Sentiments which he drafted for a convention in 1838. This Declaration, however, was only signed by twenty seven of the delegates (out of the initial one hundred and sixty).[26] Garrison was proud of his document, but it was not really lived up to either by its signatories or indeed by its composer. Only a few years later, Garrison supported a Presidential candidate in national elections, and a few years after that, he staunchly supported the use of force in the Civil War against the South. His and his followers' battle had always been much more about the abolition of slavery than about the broader Christian perfectionism which he advocated for one Declaration and a few years only. The example provided by him and his followers, therefore, is not one of Christian anarchism, but one of radical and indeed successful campaigning on one particular cause – the abolition of slavery. Thus, even though his Declaration continues to be one of the most eloquent summaries of Christian anarchist thought to ever be penned, Garrison's and his followers' value for Christian anarchism is really limited to that particular document alone.

### *6.2.2 – Ballou and the Hopedale community*

Ballou was a very eloquent speaker and writer on Christian non-resistance, on abolitionism, and on what he called Christian "socialism." He never described himself as an anarchist, even though as proposed by this book, some of his writings certainly contribute to an articulation of Christian anarchist thought. Moreover, what he called "practical Christian socialism" resonates strongly with

---

[26] These numbers are those reported in John L. Thomas, *The Liberator William Lloyd Garrison: A Biography* (Boston: Little, Brown and Company, 1963), 258-259.

the Christian anarchist vision of community outlined in Chapter 5.[27] Ballou tried to implement this vision in a large farm which he purchased with some supporters and lived on for the rest of his life. The history of the Hopedale Community, as it became known, can be found elsewhere. What is relevant to note here that after fourteen years, the radical experiment came to an end, and that only one Christian anarchist (Elliott) refers to it as a typical example of a community "[resisting] violence and [challenging] the right of the [...] state to regulate human behaviour."[28] In truth, Hopedale is just yet another example of a radical Christian community but without a professed or otherwise explicit anarchist identity.

## 6.2.3 – Tolstoy's personal example

Chronologically, the next examples of Christian anarchist witness are provided by Tolstoy and by his followers. Tolstoy himself made serious efforts to live up to what he preached: he stripped his house of luxuries, laboured the land with fellow peasants, made his own (apparently very uncomfortable) shoes, and became a vegetarian. Despite these efforts, he was accused by many of not living up to all the radical implications of his teaching, as seen for instance by the fact that he continued to live in his large country estate. Tolstoy's answer to such critics was to tell them: "Condemn me if you choose, – I do that myself, – but condemn *me*, and not the path which I am following."[29] He added: "My heart is breaking with despair because we have all lost the road; and while I struggle with all my strength to find it and keep in it, you, instead of pitying me when I go astray, cry triumphantly, 'See! He is in the swamp with us!'"[30] Even if he often failed, Tolstoy says, at least he kept on trying.

Tolstoy moreover tirelessly commented on the broader political situation in Russia: he wrote many letters and essays concerning ongoing wars and domestic troubles (including a few letters petitioning the Tsar), criticising the violence of the state and of the revolutionaries and promoting Henry George's programme as a step towards the kingdom of God on earth. Thus, to quote Wenzer, he "increasingly became a symbol of resistance."[31] According to Kentish, "his influence was enormous, both at home and abroad."[32] Woodcock therefore suggests that "his relentless criticism undoubtedly played its part in undermining the foundations of the Romanov empire."[33]

Yet even though they were worried about his following, the authorities dared not imprison him. They censored most of his writings, but their persecution

---

[27] (One major difference is on private property, which Ballou does not disapprove of.) Adin Ballou, *Practical Christian Socialism: A Conversational Exposition of the True System of Human Society* (New York: AMS, 1974).
[28] Elliott, *Freedom, Justice and Christian Counter-Culture*, 147.
[29] Tolstoy, quoted in Kennan, "A Visit to Count Tolstoi," 265 (Tolstoy's emphasis).
[30] Tolstoy, quoted in Kennan, "A Visit to Count Tolstoi," 265.
[31] Kenneth C. Wenzer, "Tolstoy's Georgist Spiritual Political Economy (1897-1910): Anarchism and Land Reform," *American Journal of Economics and Sociology* 56/4 (1997), 643.
[32] Jane Kentish, "Introduction," in *A Confession and Other Religious Writings*, by Leo Tolstoy (London: Penguin, 1987), 9.
[33] George Woodcock, *Anarchism: A History of Libertarian Ideas and Movements* (Harmondsworth: Penguin, 1975), 219.

targeted his followers rather than Tolstoy himself. Tolstoy regretted this, and called for the authorities to persecute him instead. Indeed, the only present he said would "fully satisfy" him on his eightieth birthday would be to be sent to prison.[34] This nearly happened once, but ironically, his aunt prevented it by appealing to the Tsar.

In any case, his influence waned somewhat after 1905, partly because of his continuous criticism of the revolutionaries' violent methods, and partly as a result his excommunication, which Maude claims "produced a tremendous sensation" in Russia.[35] He wrote an open reply to the edict of excommunication and thereafter criticised the church even more bitterly than before, and he continued, until his death in 1910, to write about the problems of his time, promoting conscientious objection and calling for Jesus' teaching to be embraced fully and at once. Tolstoy also famously helped the Doukhobors – a radical Christian sect persecuted by the regime – to emigrate to Canada by handing them the royalties of his last major novel (*Resurrection*). Aside from all this, he also continued to labour the land and to try to live a more humble and Christian life. Thus, even though he was far from perfect, Tolstoy did try to live in accordance with the teaching which he preached.

### 6.2.4 – Tolstoyism and Tolstoyan colonies

The comprehensive history of Tolstoyism, of Tolstoy's broader influence and following at home and abroad, still remains to be written. Given the limited scope of this Chapter, only a few highlights can be noted here. The task is not made any easier by the fact that, as Brock remarks, "Tolstoyism anyhow was a rather nebulous movement."[36] It should also be noted that Tolstoy himself was very uneasy with Tolstoyism: "I am Tolstoy," he said, "but I am not a Tolstoyan."[37] For him, "There is neither a Tolstoyan sect nor a Tolstoyan teaching," but "only one unique teaching, that of truth," so that what Tolstoy is calling for is not for others to follow *him*, but the universal truth which was best articulated by Jesus.[38] Moreover, he criticised Tolstoyan colonies for having few benefits for humanity at large, focused as they were on the inner life of the community rather than the whole of humanity.

Nonetheless, Tolstoy quickly gathered followers at home and abroad. In Russia, many of these came from what Brock calls "'penitent' landowners" and upper classes, but also from political agitators and uneducated peasants.[39] He was respected among fellow Russian progressives and anarchists, even though they disagreed with him on important issues. His country home "became a place of pilgrimage" for radical thinkers (from both Russia and abroad).[40]

---

[34] Maude, *The Life of Tolstóy*, 451.
[35] Maude, *The Life of Tolstóy*, 411.
[36] Brock, *The Roots of War Resistance*, 73-74.
[37] Tolstoy, quoted in Brock, *The Roots of War Resistance*, 73.
[38] Tolstoy, quoted in E. B. Greenwood, *Tolstoy: The Comprehensive Vision* (London: Methuen, 1975), 148.
[39] Brock, *Pacifism in Europe to 1914*, 464-465.
[40] Marshall, *Demanding the Impossible*, 381.

Unsurprisingly, therefore, Tolstoyism was described by the Russian church as a "well-defined and harmful sect."[41] Several Tolstoyan colonies were set up across the country. However, Tolstoyism in Russia did not survive the Bolshevik revolution. Tolstoyans were severely persecuted and all but wiped out by Stalin. The Soviet attitude to Tolstoy's work was to applaud his literary talent but bemoan as foolish and dangerous, and therefore harshly suppress, his social teaching. As a result, one struggles to find any traces of Tolstoyism in Russia today.

Abroad, Tolstoy had a following in Hungary thanks largely to Eugen Heinrich Schmitt, whom he regularly corresponded with. After he read *The Kingdom of God Is within You*, Schmitt was won over by Tolstoy, and he thereafter proudly called himself an anarchist. He became a political activist in Hungary and, for a few years, an important figure among the Social Democrats and their rural political base, endowing their political programme with a distinctively anarchist character.[42] His influence in that party only lasted a few years, however, after which, according to Brock, his Tolstoyism "took on a more cloistered character."[43] He later "[espoused] a syncretic religion in which Jesus figured as only one [...] of a long line of religious thinkers,"[44] and he even appealed to patriotism at times – both evidence of his steering away from pure Tolstoyism. Nonetheless, as Brock and Aleksov report, by then, a few small centres of Tolstoyism or sects at least partly inspired by it (such as the Nazarenes) had been founded in Hungary; yet eventually, they, too, fell apart. Gradually, Schmitt's Tolstoyan influence waned, until he finally moved back to Berlin and was quickly forgotten in Hungary. Nonetheless, as Brock suggests, even though Tolstoyism ultimately "proved a failure in Hungary" as a whole, at least, "the nonviolence preached by Schmitt very likely spared the countryside unproductive bloodshed."[45]

Another country in which Tolstoy inspired a few radicals was the Netherlands, where Tolstoyism had a particular influence on Felix Ortt and J. K. van der Veer, and the Dutch Reformed Church. Ortt published a short (still not translated) book called "Christian Anarchism" in which, according to André de Raaij, he describes love as "the unifying principle of the universe" and calls for people to follow their conscience – both very Tolstoyan themes.[46] Ortt also promoted conscientious objection to military service. Tolstoy's views on what

---

[41] Maude, *The Life of Tolstóy*, 372.
[42] Peter Brock, "Tolstoyism and the Hungarian Peasant," *Slavonic and Eastern European Review* 58/3 (1980), 350-357. Indeed, Brock argues (on page 357) that Schmitt provides the only example of a follower of Tolstoy attempting "to inject the Tolstoyan idea into the programme of a political party and to use the politically organized peasantry of his country as the instrument for bringing a new, non-violent world order into being."
[43] Brock, "Tolstoyism and the Hungarian Peasant," 356.
[44] Brock, "Tolstoyism and the Hungarian Peasant," 357.
[45] Brock, "Tolstoyism and the Hungarian Peasant," 368-369.
[46] André de Raaij, "On Ortt, Dutch Christian Anarchist, in English, on the Net" (email to me, 16 April 2007); André de Raaij, *Parallels or Influence: The Dutch Christian Anarchist Movement in 1907, and the Landauer Connection*, available from http://www.geocities.com/christianarchy/haifa.html (accessed 31 October 2003), para. 7.

Nettlau calls "agrarian collectivism" were also popular among Dutch radicals.[47] Yet Tolstoy was not the only influence: Dutch radicals were also inspired by thinkers such as Henry George, for instance. They founded several small colonies, each of which adopted different elements of Tolstoyism and faced different problems, but few of which, in the end, can truly be characterised as genuinely embodying the pure Christian anarchist ideal.

Tolstoyan colonies also sprang up elsewhere in Europe.[48] The Purleigh colony in England, where Tolstoy's views were quite popular, is one such example. Among the people who joined it were Maude (Tolstoy's friend and translator) and his family, and Chertkov (a close associate of Tolstoy in his later years). The colony, however, ended in disaster, suffering as it did from bitter disagreements as "discussion of minor everyday matters tended to escalate into a discussion of principles."[49] For Maude, Purleigh's failure was due to the impossibility of "trying to combine a gospel of poverty, self-abnegation, and brotherhood, with an autocratic administration of large affairs and the irresponsible power of one man."[50] The other Tolstoyan colonies across Europe suffered similar fates to Purleigh's: as Woodcock notes, all seem to have "failed in a relatively short period, either from the personal incompatibility of the participants or from the lack of practical agricultural experience."[51]

Beyond Europe, Tolstoy also influenced a few thinkers in the United States and in Asia. As already noted, he corresponded (and disagreed with) Ballou. Crosby was also inspired by Tolstoy and became a keen promoter of his ideas. Woodcock however suggests that perhaps Tolstoy's most lasting impact in the United States is through the Catholic Worker movement.[52] There is little evidence that Day or Maurin were influenced by Tolstoy's Christian anarchist writings, but Hennacy, perhaps the third most famous Catholic Worker, openly and repeatedly claims he was. Tolstoy also corresponded with, and was visited by, intellectuals from Asia. Yet as Fueloep-Miller argues, these relations "were disrupted by differences," for instance on "the divine authority of the Veda," on "Confucian 'principles of good government'" and on "the role and value of patriotism."[53]

In any case, Tolstoyism as a broadly defined – if perhaps nebulous – movement did not survive the two World Wars. What became of Tolstoyism in Russia has already been noted. Tolstoy's writings were also banned by Hitler and Mussolini, for instance, as they realised, according to Maude, that his teaching

---

[47] de Raaij, *Parallels or Influence*, para. 11; Max Nettlau, *A Short History of Anarchism* (London: Freedom, 1996), 237.
[48] In Portugal, for instance, António Gonçalves Correia, an anarchist inspired by Tolstoy, founded two (short-lived because persecuted) Tolstoyan colonies, as explained in Alberto Franco, *A Revolução É a Minha Namorada: Memória De António Gonçalves Correia, Anarquista Alentejano* (Castro Verde: Câmara Municipal de Castro Verde, n.d.).
[49] M. J. de K. Holman, "The Purleigh Colony: Tolstoyan Togetherness in the Late 1890s," in *New Essays on Tolstoy*, ed. Malcolm Jones (Cambridge: Cambridge University Press, 1978), 209.
[50] Maude, *The Life of Tolstóy*, 378-381 (the quote is from the last of these pages).
[51] Woodcock, *Anarchism*, 218.
[52] Woodcock, *Anarchism*, 218.
[53] Rene Fueloep-Miller, "Tolstoy the Apostolic Crusader," *Russian Review* 19/2 (1960), 119.

was "dangerous to a dictatorship relying on physical force."[54] Moreover, among pacifists and conscientious objectors, Brock explains that "few [...] have been prepared to follow Tolstoy to his final conclusion and repudiate not only the state in all its aspects but the use of even noninjurious forms of force."[55]

Thus Tolstoy's ideas inspired many, but they failed in many colonies, were suppressed by authoritarian regimes, and were rejected as too extreme by pacifists and other political radicals. Nevertheless, even with their failures and imperfections, Tolstoy himself and the many colonies he inspired both provide examples of attempts to live up to Tolstoy's brand of Christian anarchism. As already noted, the comprehensive study of these examples, and of their relation to Tolstoy's thought, still remains to be written. In any case, only rarely are they cited by other Christian anarchists as exemplary attempts to apply Christian anarchist theory in practice.

In the end, it may well be that, as several commentators have suggested, Tolstoyism's "lasting legacy" for humanity (so far) has been largely as "a major influence in bringing into being a new pacifism, more universal in its outreach [...] than previous religious pacifism."[56] Brock maintains that the importance of Tolstoy's contribution was in bringing the idea of non-violence out of the Christian tradition and into "a common language with the rest of mankind."[57] Thus universalised through Tolstoy, Jesus' teaching on means and ends has inspired many figures in the pacifist movement, and has contributed to the broader convergence of anarchism and pacifism. Perhaps Tolstoy's most significant impact to date, however, has taken place through the actions of one of the most famous of the twentieth century advocates of non-violence – "Mahatma" Gandhi.

### 6.2.5 – Gandhi: a leader by example

Gandhi openly acknowledged that Tolstoy's *The Kingdom of God Is within You* "deeply impressed" him and converted him to non-violence for good.[58] Even though he disagreed with some of Tolstoy's "not accurately stated" ideas, he described him as "that great teacher whom I have long looked upon as one of my guides," as "one of the clearest thinkers in the western world."[59] The two briefly corresponded just before Tolstoy's death, and Gandhi's second ashram in South Africa was called "Tolstoy Farm."[60]

---

[54] Aylmer Maude, "Introduction," in *The Kingdom of God and Peace Essays*, by Leo Tolstoy, trans. Aylmer Maude (New Delhi: Rupa, 2001), vii.
[55] Brock, *Pacifism in Europe to 1914*, 468.
[56] Christian Bartolf, "Tolstoy's Legacy for Mankind: A Manifesto for Nonviolence," paper presented at *Second International Conference on Tolstoy and World Literature*, Yasnaya Polyana and Tula, 12-28 August 2000, available from http:://www.fredsakademiet.dk/library/tolstoj/tolstoy.htm (accessed 5 November 2006); Brock, *Pacifism in Europe to 1914*, 470 (for the latter quote).
[57] Brock, *Pacifism in Europe to 1914*, 469.
[58] Gandhi, quoted in Stephens, "The Non-Violent Anarchism of Leo Tolstoy," 18.
[59] M. K. Gandhi, "Introduction," in *Recollections and Essays*, by Leo Tolstoy, trans. Aylmer Maude (London: Oxford University Press, 1937), 413-415.
[60] Janko Lavrin, "Tolstoy and Gandhi," *Russian Review* 19/2 (1960), 132; Stephens, "The Non-Violent Anarchism of Leo Tolstoy," 176.

Gandhi's famous campaigns of non-violent resistance against the British in India need not be summarised here. What should be noted is that many Christian anarchists praise Gandhi as an example of someone who courageously applied a method that has very strong similarities with Jesus'. Of course, they accept that it is "ironic" that it had to take "a non-Christian to teach us such a valuable lesson on Christianity's true way,"[61] that "Christians have a Hindu to thank for 'putting the cross back into politics.'"[62] Yet according to Andrews, Gandhi "suggested that if Christ could only be unchained from the shackles of Christianity, he could become 'The Way,' not just for Christians, but for the whole world."[63] For Andrews, apart from Gandhi, "no-one has ever enunciated a more Christ-like set of principles for conducting a campaign of nonviolent resistance to political oppression."[64]

At the same time, Gandhi's campaign was one of *resistance* – even if of a non-violent type. He famously said that if the choice is "between cowardice and violence," he would "advise violence."[65] Moreover, Gandhi did not reject patriotism, and certainly did not follow Tolstoy's anarchist conclusions. Clearly, therefore, Gandhi is a very imperfect illustration of Jesus' way, and not really an example of Christian anarchism. Despite this, however, Christian anarchists have drawn inspiration from him.[66] Catholic Workers in particular claim to combine "the spirit of Christ and the method of Gandhi."[67] They admire his consistency of means and ends, his courage and his willingness to suffer in campaigning against political oppression. As is noted below, Catholic Worker actions certainly bear strong similarities with Gandhi's.

Before describing the example presented by the Catholic Worker movement, however, it should be noted that Gandhi has inspired many famous "dissidents" aside from Christian anarchists. Martin Luther King, for instance, adapted Gandhi's methods for the Civil Rights campaign in the United States, thereby bringing these methods back within the wider frame of Christianity. Other famous admirers and followers of Gandhian non-violence include Nelson Mandela, Desmond Tutu, Lanza del Vasto, Lech Walesa and Aung San Suu Kyi. In turn, these dissidents are all esteemed by Christian anarchists despite their imperfections (from a Christian anarchist point of view). In the end, however, they are examples of what Chapter 4 describes as a drifting away from Jesus' teaching into more confrontational political activism. Nevertheless, for their courage and their general (but here again, not always consistent) rejection of

---

[61] Charlie, "The Love of Jesus," 5.
[62] Andrews, *The Crux of the Struggle*, 51 (partly quoting an apparently anonymous foreword to an edited book on Gandhi).
[63] Andrews, *Christi-Anarchy*, 95; Andrews, *Not Religion, but Love*, 22.
[64] Andrews, *Subversive Spirituality, Ecclesial and Civil Disobedience*, 24 (the principles are listed on that and the preceding page).
[65] Gandhi, quoted in Hennacy, *The Book of Ammon*, 425-426; Lavrin, "Tolstoy and Gandhi," 137.
[66] Note that Ellul, however, takes exception to this admiration, arguing that Gandhi is not an example of Jesus' way since his method aimed "to establish the oppressive power of the Indian state," and that Gandhi's success was also partly due to his campaign having targeted "a people shaped by centuries of concern for holiness and the spiritual." Ellul, *Anarchy and Christianity*, 100 (for the first quote); Ellul, *Violence*, 14-15 (for the second quote).
[67] [Anonymous], "Conversation between Scott Albrecht and Ven. Gikan Ito. 29/02/04," *London Catholic Worker*, April 2004, 4.

violence, they are sometimes cited by Christian anarchists as examples worth drawing inspiration from.

## 6.2.6 – The Catholic Worker movement

The Catholic Worker movement has always keenly protested against social injustices. In doing so, it has often campaigned alongside other protest movements. In the United States, in the early days of the *Catholic Worker* newspaper, its members supported workers' strikes, contributed to picket lines, and thus drew attention to various contemporary injustices. Catholic Workers were staunch pacifist during the Second World War. Later on, they were at the forefront of the anti-nuclear and the anti-Vietnam war movements. During the Cold War, one of Hennacy's impacts on the Catholic Worker movement was to make its protests more confrontational. Before him, Catholic Workers had not engaged in direct civil disobedience. After Hennacy, however, an increasing number of Catholic Workers participated for example in "Ploughshares action" (such as hammering military planes), inspired by the Biblical prophecy of "turning swords into ploughshares."[68] Although they are not Catholic Workers themselves, the Berrigan brothers – famous priests and Ploughshares activists in the United States – have been closely associated with the movement, and there is clearly mutual admiration and mutual inspiration between them.

Outside the United States and more recently, Catholic Worker Ciaron O'Reilly has been engaged in civil disobedience, Ploughshares actions and symbolic acts of "liturgy" in Australia, Ireland and the United Kingdom, including the pouring of symbolic blood in boardrooms of military corporations, rites of "exorcism" of public Ministries, and "disarming" (hammering) military equipment.[69] In England, the *London Catholic Worker* has been published since 2001, reporting similar acts of public liturgy and protest by its members about various issues, such as the Iraq War or the deportation of refugees. One of its main figures, Catholic priest Martin Newell, has been arrested several times and jailed twice, and his actions and beliefs have been reported as far as *The Times*.

Aside from these acts of protests, of course, Catholic Workers have set up a number of houses of hospitality and farming communes, mainly, but not only, in the United States – where the movement was founded and has always been strongest. In her autobiography, Day reports the mushrooming of such communities. Hennacy also tells of his frequent visits to radical communities, Catholic Worker or other, across the country. Today, there are over one hundred and seventy Catholic Workers communities in the United States and Canada.[70] In

---

[68] The "Ploughshares" movement's name is a reference to Isaiah 2:4 and Micah 4:3 (the wording is very similar, but the following excerpt is from Isaiah): "And he shall judge among the nations, and shall rebuke many people: and they shall beat their swords into plowshares, and their spears into pruninghooks: nation shall not lift up sword against nation, neither shall they learn war anymore."
[69] O'Reilly, *Remembering Forgetting*. (The book is an autobiographical diary of his actions between 1993 and 2000.)
[70] The information is taken from [Anonymous], *List of States with Catholic Worker Communities* (The Catholic Worker Movement), available from
http://www.catholicworker.org/communities/commstates.cfm (accessed 12 March 2008). Note that Mormons have very recently been inspired by the *Catholic Worker* to get together and produce an

the United Kingdom, Catholic Worker houses have been set up in London, Liverpool, Glasgow and Oxford. There are also Catholic Worker houses in the Netherlands (Amsterdam), Belgium (Ghent), Germany (Hamburg, Dortmund), Sweden (Angered), Mexico (Coatepec) and New Zealand (Christchurch, Lyttleton).[71] Each Catholic Worker community is different, but all strive to provide hospitality to the afflicted and to generally embody the life of love and care eulogised by its founders.

In short, the Catholic Worker movement continues to try to embody the type of Christian anarchism advocated by Day, Maurin and Hennacy, combining a community life of love, care and hard work with participation in protests on, and if need be civil disobedience against, the burning issues of the day. The Catholic Worker movement is therefore cited by other Christian anarchists as a moving example of Christian anarchism in practice.

### 6.2.7 – A Pinch of Salt and The Digger and Christian Anarchist

The same methods of non-violent protest were supported by *A Pinch of Salt*, the Christian anarchist newspaper that was published in the late 1980s in England. Its fourteen issues include reports denouncing nuclear energy and weapons, the arms trade, torture, United States involvement in Central and South America, and the extremes of free market capitalism, as well as reports about animal rights and gay rights, and in support of famous individuals like Israeli whistleblower Mordechai Vanunu or Sri Lankan illegal immigrant Viraj Mendis. Ploughshares actions figure prominently, as do other similar acts of "liturgy" like public vigils, "reclaim the city" services, or the writing, in charcoal, of messages of "repentance" on the walls of the Ministry of Defence on Ash Wednesday. The main person and editor behind *Pinch* was Stephen Hancock, and the newspaper's publication stopped soon after he was arrested for "cleansing the temple of war" (the Ministry of "'Defence'").[72]

The aim of *Pinch*, according to Hancock, was "To pitch the tent of Justice, to get involved in the thick of it, and to reflect, and learn, and act again."[73] *Pinch* never aimed to found the sort of organised community of care and hospitality that is so central to the *Catholic Worker* (which is not to say that *Pinch* contributors did not admire or promote it in other contexts). Hence the example provided by *Pinch* in the late 1980s, and cited by several Christian anarchists since, is predominantly one of reporting injustices and engaging in liturgical

---

equivalent paper for their denomination, as explained in Cory Bushman, "The Mormon Worker," *The Mormon Worker*, issue 1, September 2007, available from http://www.themormonworker.org/articles/issue1/volume1_issue1.pdf (accessed 28 February 2008), 1.

[71] [Anonymous], *List of States with Catholic Worker Communities*; Martin Newell, "Hosting Refugees: A Conversation," *The London Catholic Worker*, issue 19, Summer 2007, 9.

[72] Hancock's actions are reported in [Anonymous], "The Cleansing of the Temple – Burglars for Peace," *A Pinch of Salt*, issue 13, Summer 1989, 10; [Anonymous], "Swords into Ploughshares," *A Pinch of Salt*, issue 12, March 1989, 7; Stephen Hancock, "'No Rearmament Plan'," *A Pinch of Salt*, issue 13, Summer 1989, 11.

[73] Stephen Hancock [?], "Third Birthday Polemic," *A Pinch of Salt*, issue 11, Autumn/Winter 1988, 8.

protests against them, rather than one of community life of the type described in Chapter 5.

Very much the same thing can be said of *The Digger and Christian Anarchist*, a very similar newspaper to *Pinch* that was produced by Kenny Hone in Canada around the same time. The editors of *Pinch* and *The Digger* exchanged letters and reprinted one another's writings in their respective newspapers. It does seem, however, that *Pinch* had a considerably larger readership than *The Digger*, perhaps partly because its presentation was more attractive and combined criticism of the state with humour, sarcasm, and colourful drawings and images.[74] Either way, both newspapers folded in the early 1990s.

*Pinch* has recently been revived by Keith Hebden, and although the presentation is inevitably different, the thematic content so far appears quite similar to that of its previous incarnation, reporting on Ploughshares actions, London's Catholic Workers, and advertising the Camp for Climate Change – thus reflecting the different social context. Issue sixteen also includes a report on the first two conferences on Christian anarchism ever held in the United Kingdom, following the example set by the Jesus Radicals, an online community founded in the United States.

## *6.2.8 – Online communities*

The Jesus Radicals is essentially an online community around a website that promotes Christian anarchism. Based in the United States, it has now branched out to the United Kingdom, Australia and New Zealand. The website includes an impressive discussion forum, a list of recommended reading, short essays by members, and regular advertising for the latest conference on Christian anarchism. Its very existence attests to a growth of interest in Christian anarchism, but again, there seems to be no evidence of organised community life of the style described in Chapter 5. As a website, it is inevitably confined mostly to discussions of contemporary issues from a Christian anarchist standpoint – it is difficult for a website to embody the community life prescribed by Christian anarchist thought. At the same time, it does form an *online* "community" of people with a mutual interest in Christian anarchism. Moreover, Jesus Radicals conferences do bring together thinkers, practitioners, and those curious about Christian anarchism (the 2009 conference was attended by some 250 participants), thus providing some of the basic ingredients on the back on which a "real" community could take shape.

While on the subject of online communities and resources, the "Christian Anarchists" group on Facebook should probably be mentioned, as should *The Mormon Worker* and the Yahoo group "The Lost Religion of Jesus."[75]

---

[74] Hancock regularly reported the number of copies he made of each issue. According to these figures, at its height, *Pinch* reached 1000 copies per issue, and Hancock explains in issue 10 (page 20) that he usually managed to distribute 900 or more of these copies. By contrast, according to a letter sent by Hone to Hancock (which was part of the *Pinch* files which Hebden lent me), Hone only usually printed only around 100-150 copies of *The Digger*.
[75] Note that this is not an exhaustive list: plenty of online communities can be found discussing Christian anarchist ideas or sometimes even claiming Christian anarchism as their central concern (for

The first provides photos, a discussion forum, links to several other websites, and the possibility to learn more about its several hundreds of members through typical Facebook tools and applications; the second publishes *The Mormon Worker* (with many articles on current tensions in the Middle East) but also allows readers to post comments on individual articles; and the third provides a (relatively dormant) mailing list for people interested in Christian anarchism. Only the Facebook group, however, compares quite well with the vibrant online community of the Jesus Radicals. Finally, perhaps worth a passing mention is the *Academics and Students Interested in Religious Anarchism* mailing list, an online forum born out of a series of conference panels on religious anarchism in 2008.

### 6.2.9 – Andrews' community work

The final main example of contemporary efforts to put Christian anarchist theory to practice is provided by Australian Christian anarchist Dave Andrews, whose writings often combine more theoretical reflections with numerous moving examples of people and communities taking the risk to courageously embrace Jesus' teaching of love, care and forgiveness. Andrews himself appears to be heavily engaged in his local community in Brisbane, participating in countless local initiatives to care for the afflicted, to foster a real sense of community, and to protest about (local to global) injustices. He is also actively promoting "web-based networks" through which people can be moved to pledge to try to follow Jesus' example in their own lives – an example of which is the *Plan Be* website, forum and community. Thus, although the community in which Andrews participates cannot really be labelled "Christian anarchist" in that such a label does not appear to be explicitly adopted by most of its members, Andrews nonetheless provides an example of an individual Christian anarchist trying his utmost to practice what he preaches in his local community and to convert people from different walks of life to Jesus' teaching along the way.

## 6.3 – Incomplete examples

The examples cited in this Chapter are all either mentioned by Christian anarchists or directly inspired by them.[76] All the pre-modern examples cited by

---

instance: Akeldama on http://www.akeldama09.blogspot.com/). The examples cited here are therefore only indicative of the types of online communities embracing elements of Christian anarchism. Still on the subject of the internet, it is also worth citing the newsletters titled *Religious Anarchism* and edited by Bas Moreel, which report on anarchist trends in various religions and in branches of Christianity.

[76] Of the main Christian anarchist thinkers identified in the Introduction, nothing has been said of the examples provided by Pentecost, Berdyaev, Ellul, Eller, Elliott, Cavanaugh, Bartley and the Christian anarcho-capitalists. The reason for this is simple: none of them really provide examples of the type discussed in this Chapter – certainly none is cited by other Christian anarchists as doing so – and none seems to have gathered a following that openly acknowledges to be directly inspired by them (except perhaps Ellul, who appears to be a very important Christian anarchist thinker in the eyes of the Jesus Radicals). This is not to say that they have not tried to live up to what they preach, but simply that if and when they have done so, this has apparently not been noted and praised by other Christian anarchists.

Christian anarchists are reported; but of the modern examples, only those directly inspired by Christian anarchist thinkers are. This is not to say that the numerous other individuals and communities who are cited in the Christian anarchist literature as modern examples of radicals striving to follow Jesus are not worth seeking inspiration from, but simply that they cannot really be described as examples of attempts to exemplify Christian *anarchist* thought.[77] They neither adopt that label, nor claim inspiration from its main authors.

In any case, it will be evident by now that most of the examples cited in this Chapter are, in some way or other, imperfect or incomplete illustrations of Christian anarchism. Although they might all agree on the Christian anarchist criticism of the state outlined in Part I, few embrace fully both of the two flanks of the response advocated by Christian anarchist thought as articulated in Chapters 4 and 5. Of all the communities mentioned above, the ones that most fully embody all the main themes from these Chapters would seem to be: the early church, inasmuch as the idyllic picture which Christian anarchists draw of its life can be seen as accurate; some of the sects and movements of the late Middle Ages and early modern period, even though many fairly quickly moved away from the purer motives which animated them at first; and arguably the Catholic Worker movement, in that among modern examples, it is the one that most fully embraces both the Christian critique of the state and a committed attempt to subvert it by building an alternative society.

It is too early to see if the Catholic Worker witness will succeed in sparking a Christian anarchist revolution (and the potential importance and impact of its apparent subtle drift away from Paul's counsel of subjection would require a study of its own). As already noted, however, the Christian anarchist seeds of the early church were spoilt after a few centuries. Those of the radical communities of the late Middle Ages and early modern period mentioned above also seem to have failed to grow to their promised potential. Thus, both sets of pre-modern examples seem to have ultimately failed to usher the kingdom of God on earth. To reflect on why this may be so is one of the intentions of the Conclusion.

---

[77] Indeed, if the criteria are kept broad enough, many more could be added, since as Allen writes, "It is remarkable how many heroes of our cultural and moral tradition were committed to the revolutionary ideal of social development achieved by interior commitment rather than exterior coercion." Allen, "Introduction," xvii.

# Conclusion – The Prophetic Role of Christian Anarchism

The main themes of Christian anarchism's critique of the state and response to its prominence are articulated and illustrated in Parts I and II. Given that Christian anarchist writings had never been synthesised (that is, weaved into one single and relatively comprehensive book) before, the bulk of the present book has had to concentrate on doing just that. As a result, the present study has thus far been more descriptive than reflective. Now that the main themes of Christian anarchist thought have been synthesised, however, a few reflections on its contemporary relevance can be put forward. More exhaustive critical reflections remain a subject of future scholarship, but such future study will now be able to build upon the synthesising work offered by the present book.

This Conclusion nevertheless does provide the space to begin reflecting on questions concerning the past, present and potential future role of Christian anarchist thought, and on its understanding of history. For instance, how do Christian anarchists explain the apparent failure – so far at least – of the stateless kingdom of God to come about on earth? Indeed, do they expect the whole of humanity to ever embrace the full anarchist implications of Jesus' teaching? How do they expect history to unfold? How should Christian anarchists locate themselves in a society that does not seem to pay attention to their message – how should they conceive of their role? How does Christian anarchist thought relate to the broader Christian and anarchist traditions? What is Christian anarchist thought's unique contribution to political thought? Indeed, is "Christian anarchism" the best term to name this position? Some of these questions have been touched upon in previous Chapters. The aim of this Conclusion is not to close them, but to reflect on them further, and thus to consider the role and original contribution of Christian anarchist thought.

This Conclusion is divided into four main sections. The first reflects on the name and definition of "Christian anarchists" and "Christian anarchism." The second elaborates the Christian anarchist understanding of the kingdom of God by discussing the extent to which its advent should be "hastened," the mysterious manner of its unfolding through history, and the temptation to manage the course of history through human agency. The third section then establishes a theological framework to situate Christian anarchists as the contemporary equivalent of the prophets of the past, and stresses the importance of a clear separation between church and state. The final section then teases out Christian anarchism's unique contribution to Christianity, to political thought, and to contemporary society.

## "Christian anarchists" and "Christian anarchism"

The expression "Christian anarchist" is used throughout the book to refer to thinkers and activists brought together by one defining characteristic: the derivation of "anarchism" from "Christianity." Indeed, this characteristic can be seen as the very definition of "Christian anarchism" adopted here. Its proponents may begin from a very different understanding of "Christianity," ranging for instance from Day's and Maurin's respect for liturgy and for important figures in traditional theology, to Tolstoy's somewhat crude rationalism and constant return to Jesus' teaching as summarised in the Sermon on the Mount. They may also reach different types of "anarchist" conclusions, from Tolstoy's critique of state violence and deception, to Ellul's and Eller's denunciation of devotion to the state as idolatry, to the Catholic Workers' practical work aiming to build a stateless society. But what unites them all is their reaching of explicitly "anarchist" conclusions based on their understanding of "Christianity." The specific lines of argument that lead each of them along this general path are what this book elaborates in greater detail.

Moreover, rarely is any Christian anarchist argument studied in the main body of this book not made by at least a couple of the Christian anarchists identified in the Introduction. The precise composition of the group of thinkers making this or that particular argument varies, and they each have their unique way of deriving their own anarchist conclusions from their own take on Christianity, but only very few of the Christian anarchist lines of argument outlined in Chapters 1 to 6 have not been developed by several Christian anarchists (often independently from one another). Collectively, therefore, this book finds them to be voicing a fairly coherent, rich and comprehensive set of arguments in defence of Christian anarchism. Of course, each thinker brings a slightly different emphasis, a different specialisation to the general theory. Moreover, there is no doubt that an even more comprehensive outline of Christian anarchism could be produced by the weaving into it of relevant threads from precursors of Christian anarchism praised in Chapter 6, for instance, or from more contemporary radical Christian political thinkers. Nonetheless, this book already shows that the Christian anarchist school of thought is both very diverse and fairly coherent at the same time, even before the possible inclusion of additional thinkers.

A question arises, however, as to whether the term "Christian anarchism" is really the best term to describe this school of thought, because of an etymological quirk spotted by Eller. "An-archy," a word derived from the Greek, is usually explained by political theorists to literally mean "without government" or "no rule." Yet while to understand the prefix "an-" to mean "no" or "without" is correct, the meaning of the Greek "arky" is not confined to "government," "rule" or "state." As Eller explains, "The '-archy' root [which he thereafter spells 'arky'] is a common Greek word that means 'priority,' 'primacy,' 'primordial,' 'principal,' 'prince,' and the like."[1] Indeed, he notes that "'pri-' is simply the Latin equivalent of the Greek 'arky.'"[2] Therefore "anarchy"

---

[1] Eller, *Christian Anarchy*, 1.
[2] Eller, *Christian Anarchy*, 1.

does mean "no government," "no rule" or "no leader" in the sense of "no prince" or "no principality." Yet Eller also remarks that "in Colossians 1:18 Paul actually identifies Jesus as 'the beginning,' 'the prime', 'THE ARKY.'"[3] Christian "anarchism," however, does not reject *Jesus* as the arky – quite the contrary. Moreover, the "hier-" in "hierarchy" comes from the Greek "hieros," which means "sacred." Hence etymologically, "hierarchy" means something like "sacred principle," "sacred government," or "sacred rule" – something that, in a sense, Christian anarchists are keen promoters of.

All this implies that the term "Christian anarchism," if one wants to be etymologically pedantic, is somewhat inadequate: Christian anarchists do not reject Jesus as the arky, and what they are calling for is for human beings to govern themselves by the rule of God. Eller suggests that the "goal" of Christian anarchism is indeed "'theonomy' – the rule, the ordering, the arky of *God*."[4] It is precisely because of their "theonomy," because they consider Jesus as "the arky," that Christian anarchists reject the state.

If a word should be added to "theonomy" to underscore this rejection of the state, perhaps a more appropriate one than "anarchism" would be "acratism," from the Greek word "cratos" which means "state." Yet even this would be problematic in that "cratos" derives from the notion of "holding power," which is why Jesus is also referred to in the Orthodox tradition as "the pantocrator" – that is, "the holder of all power." Besides, since, for Christian anarchists, "acratism" is really the flip side of their "theonomy," the expression "acratic theonomy" or "theonomic acraty" would really be pleonasm, a redundancy of terms.

It may be that Eller's simple suggestion of "theonomy" is the best one. Likewise, however, the term "Christianity" should also really be enough, since Christian anarchists' anarchism stems from their understanding of Christianity – hence the reference in the Introduction to "Christian (anarchism)." When it comes to such playful attempts to find the best name, there are also those who refer to it as "Christianarchy." In a sense, this word is ideal in that it can imply that the only true arky is Christian (Christian/archy). Unfortunately, however, it can equally plausibly be read as preserving the problems and ambiguities of the term "anarchy" (Christi/anarchy).

Anyway, despite all these considerations, given the common understanding of the meanings of "Christianity" (as an apolitical religion at best, a religion supportive of the state at worst) and "anarchism" (as the rejection of the state), it may well be that the term "Christian anarchism" continues to best identify the essence of what this perspective is about, in that this name immediately prepares for a radical and political interpretation of Jesus' teaching and example. It immediately prepares for a perspective that derives "anarchism" from "Christianity." Therefore even if this short discussion suggests that, strictly speaking, the term is not etymologically adequate, "Christian anarchism" probably remains the best way to name this interpretation of Christianity, because

---

[3] Eller, *Christian Anarchy*, 1 (Eller's upper-case).
[4] Eller, *Christian Anarchy*, 3 (Eller's emphasis). Eller's discussion of theonomy seems to imply that "arky" and "nomos" are synonyms – which they are not, or at least not exactly even though their meanings are not wholly dissimilar.

it immediately declares that for its advocates, the rejection of the state and the growth of a stateless society are inevitable political implications of Christianity.

## The kingdom of God in history

Many Christian anarchists identify their vision of a stateless society with the kingdom of God foreseen by Jesus. They expect this kingdom to become a future reality here on earth. Tolstoy in particular repeats several times that if all human beings were to fulfil Jesus' anarchist teaching, then God's kingdom would indeed "come upon earth."[5] Hence to follow Jesus is to tread the path that leads to the future replacement of human kingdoms by the stateless kingdom of God. Indeed, the Christian anarchist mission is to "anticipate and represent" that kingdom today.[6] The hope cherished by several Christian anarchists is that doing so might perhaps thereby "hasten" its coming.[7]

### "Hastening" God's kingdom

However, from the pure Christian anarchist perspective outlined in this book, there is a great danger in trying to precipitate the advent of the kingdom of God: the temptation to adopt violent means towards that end. Numerous millenarian sects and movements have fallen into this trap and thereby betrayed the essence of Jesus' teaching. Indeed, one could argue that many utopian visions for society – be they religious or secular – have degenerated into violent and brutal movements precisely because of their (usually honest albeit deluded) hope that the adoption of some coercion might help precipitate the advent of their (usually well-intended) utopia. The problem, as Christian anarchism makes a point of emphasising, lies not in the utopian end, but in the coercive means to this end.

As noted in Chapter 4, it is also here that one finds perhaps one of the clearest differences between Christian anarchism and more famous theologies of liberation, in that the latter more willingly advocate the adoption of coercive means to liberate the oppressed. In his comparison of Christian anarchists and pacifists with liberation theologians, Wogaman comments that the latter are "Least of all [...] impressed by the insistence" by the former "that Christians should not attempt to manage the course of history," because "That is precisely what liberation theologians have set out to do!"[8] In other words, liberation theologians are usually assuming that the advent of the kingdom of God can and should be managed by human beings, whereas (most) Christian anarchist thinkers, although hoping to anticipate and represent God's kingdom through their witness, ultimately rely on God's mysterious providence rather than human management to see that the kingdom does indeed grow to its full potential.

---

[5] Leo Tolstoy, "What's to Be Done?," in *Recollections and Essays*, trans. Aylmer Maude (London: Oxford University Press, 1937), 394.
[6] Jurgen Moltmann, quoted in Andrews, "Heaven on Earth," 88.
[7] The notion of "hastening" is borrowed from 2 Peter 3:12, and repeated for instance by Redford, *Jesus Is an Anarchist*, 59-60.
[8] Wogaman, *Christian Perspectives on Politics*, 100.

Admittedly, as noted in Chapter 4 and 6, there does seem to be a tendency for strict, Christian anarchist non-resistance to drift towards non-violent resistance and sometimes further into increasingly confrontational forms of resistance. A detailed examination of this tendency falls outside the immediate scope of this book. Driving that tendency, however, seems to be an increasing (and understandable) exasperation and loss of patience with what is seen as the oppressive status quo – indeed an attempt to therefore somehow precipitate, through human intervention, the fall of the state and the advent the kingdom of God on earth. That impatient exasperation with oppression, in some form or other, is present in the more confrontational variants of Christian anarchism just as it is present in liberation theology, and informs, in both, the will to accelerate humanity's promised emancipation from evil.

Bartley seems to uncover the root of the problem when he suggests that the adoption of violence by Christians to "hasten" the kingdom of God depends "a great deal on how they believe God achieves his purposes, and how they interpret Jesus' teaching on the Kingdom of God."[9] To put things crudely, if you believe that God is waiting for human beings to manage a transition to his kingdom, then coercion quickly becomes appropriate. This is not so, however, if you believe that Jesus' teaching implies a letting go of any delusion about the efficacy of political management; that God wants us to witness to Jesus' teaching of patient and sacrificial love and forgiveness in our own lives and communities; that the kingdom of God can only be hastened by the *willing* conversion of fellow human beings in response to such witness; and that God calls us to keep faith in his oversight of the mysterious advent of his kingdom. The latter is obviously what this book has identified as the "purest" (or strictest) Christian anarchist position.

Christian anarchist thought argues that in his teaching and example, Jesus rejects the temptation of political engineering and instead resigns himself to the cross. He does not call us to manage the course of history, but to surrender fully to God's commandments and to keep faith in God and in the growth of his kingdom. Thus, even though Christian anarchist thinkers certainly do passionately long for the advent of the stateless kingdom of God, they insist that the only way of "hastening" it consists in patiently loving and forgiving evil, thus *surrendering* the conventional tools for the steering of history, while at the same time keeping faith in God's admittedly mysterious providence (this theme is discussed in more detail further below).

It is the loss of such Christian patience and faith that is at the root of the decision "to build the kingdom on earth with [human] hands," to supplant God's providence by human management.[10] Tolstoy remarks that "a great part of the evil of the world is due to our wishing to see the realisation of what we are striving at, but *are not yet ready for*."[11] It is tempting to lose patience and try to prod things forward a little faster, especially in the face of very real injustice. Yet just as Jesus rejected the temptation of political engineering, his followers must do so, too. They must trust God and Jesus' methods instead. This does not mean

---

[9] Bartley, *Faith and Politics after Christendom*, 200.
[10] Ellul, *Violence*, 150 (note that here, Ellul says this concerning faith, not so much patience).
[11] Tolstoy, quoted in Maude, *Tolstoy and His Problems*, 62 (Tolstoy's emphasis).

that Christians must sit back and passively observe God's providence of history from afar. As mentioned above (especially in Chapter 5), Christians are called to anticipate and represent God's kingdom, to follow the method taught and exemplified by Jesus. Indeed, they are called to try to present God's kingdom on earth through their own example – but they are told to remain patient and forgiving with the world's apparent deafness to it. They are called to keep faith that in the end, the stateless kingdom of God will indeed come.

## *History's mysterious unfolding*

There is therefore a clear sense, among several Christian anarchists, of gradual progress towards God's kingdom. Ballou and Tolstoy, in particular, frequently speak of such progress. Elliott likewise warns that "The development of the Kingdom depends [...] on the members of the Kingdom *gradually* extending its claims over all systems and structures, transforming them in that process."[12] Just like for Tolstoy and Ballou, for Elliott, the kingdom of God is a "present reality" as soon as one decides "to live under the rule of God, rather than the rule of others," and this kingdom gradually spreads by the decision by an increasing number of others to do the same thing.[13] In short, when writing about the kingdom of God, Elliott, Ballou and Tolstoy all seem to expect a gradual progress of humanity towards it.

Ellul and Eller take a very different view: both expect some sort of momentous divine intervention to usher the kingdom. Eller devotes an entire chapter to this issue. He argues that there are "two completely different understandings of how human history is directed" and of "moral progress."[14] He classes one such understanding as "arky faith" because it believes that "social good becomes actual as those arkys we perceive to be good either displace the established arkys of evil or convert them to good," and he explains that such a view implies "gradualism," gradual "learning" and "progress," even "triumphalism."[15] The other view, he says, "will make no use of the arkys" because it identifies Jesus Christ as "The Arky," as a result of which it sees human history through the lens of "death and resurrection."[16]

That is, rather than a story of gradual progress, Eller sees history as a gradual "deterioration and fall to the low point of Good Friday," at which point "God intervenes" to usher his kingdom.[17] Eller cites numerous passages in the Bible that narrate a similar "death-and-resurrection pattern."[18] Several of these are from the Book of Revelation, which indeed portrays the rise to political power of the Antichrist and his eventual defeat after a spectacular intervention from heaven. For Eller, this confirms that Christians must have faith not in the gradual progress of humanity towards the kingdom of God, but "in the grace of a God of

---

[12] Elliott, *Freedom, Justice and Christian Counter-Culture*, 117 (emphasis added).
[13] Elliott, *Freedom, Justice and Christian Counter-Culture*, 69.
[14] Eller, *Christian Anarchy*, 221.
[15] Eller, *Christian Anarchy*, 221-222 (emphasis removed).
[16] Eller, *Christian Anarchy*, 222-223 (emphasis removed). On page 1, he explains that it is Paul who describes Jesus as "The Arky" in Colossians 1:18.
[17] Eller, *Christian Anarchy*, 223-224.
[18] Eller, *Christian Anarchy*, 224-229.

resurrection capability."[19] Still, Eller nevertheless maintains that this does not mean that efforts at moral progress have "no significance" at all, but simply that Christians must distance themselves from any "moral triumphalism" and brace themselves for the very worst before the long-awaited advent of God's kingdom.[20]

Ellul takes a similar view. "The Bible," he writes, "tells us that it is God alone [...] who will institute the kingdom at the end of time."[21] For Ellul, "history is not a progress towards the kingdom of God," and the kingdom will only materialise "via another rupture."[22] Like Eller, therefore, Ellul is keen to dissociate himself from the "illusion" that "kindness and virtue will always triumph" so that with each trial, humanity progresses by yet another step towards the promised land.[23] Clearly, then, both Eller and Ellul disagree with the view of history trumpeted by Elliott, Ballou and Tolstoy. What all share, however, is a longing for the kingdom of God, a confidence that it will one day come about (whether progressively or through some spectacular rupture), and an understanding that Christians ought to try to present an image of this kingdom to the pagan world that surrounds them.

While on the topic of the kingdom of God, brief mention should be made of Berdyaev's and Cavanaugh's idiosyncratic perceptions of it. Berdyaev repeatedly speaks of two realms – of Caesar and of the Spirit – which he believes to be clearly separate and governed by different forces. He insists on this dualism and indeed accuses Tolstoy precisely of being "fundamentally monistic."[24] One of his main aims is to criticise those who believe that a "perfect, harmonious" society will ever materialise in the "realm of Caesar," because according to him, "Only the Kingdom of God, the realm of the Spirit, can be perfect and harmonious."[25] It may well be that his stance is a reaction to the brutality that tends to be justified by those who seek to usher God's kingdom in the realm of Caesar.[26] Yet Berdyaev also speaks of a "final monism," which he says will only "be confirmed in the Kingdom of God."[27] Of this kingdom, he says that it will be

---

[19] Eller, *Christian Anarchy*, 230.
[20] (The precise expression Eller uses here is "moral triumph.") Eller, *Christian Anarchy*, 231-232.
[21] Ellul, *Violence*, 76.
[22] Goddard, *Living the Word, Resisting the World*, 89, 99. (Goddard describes it as an *other* rupture in history because the Fall was the first such rupture.)
[23] Ellul, *Violence*, 88.
[24] Berdyaev, "The Voice of Conscience from Another World," 17. As mentioned in the Introduction, Tolstoy's take on religion was very rationalistic (arguably deistic) and very sceptical of supernatural phenomena (although his understanding of the relation between the finite and the infinite confuses matters somewhat), and it is on the basis of this that Berdyaev can accuse him of such "monism." Berdyaev is also critical (on page 12) of Tolstoy's faith that the kingdom can come through humanity's gradual adoption of Jesus' teaching.
[25] Berdyaev, *The Realm of the Spirit and the Realm of Caesar*, 177. On the basis of this clear dualism, Berdyaev believes that the state will remain a necessity in the realm of Caesar, as explained in Berdyaev, *The Realm of the Spirit and the Realm of Caesar*, 72; David Nicholls, *Deity and Domination: Images of God and the State in the Nineteenth and Twentieth Centuries* (London: Routledge, 1989), 125.
[26] His book often reads as a deliberate response to Soviet communism, which is an obvious example of the adoption of violent means to precipitate the advent of a better society. Berdyaev, *The Realm of the Spirit and the Realm of Caesar*.
[27] Berdyaev, *The Realm of the Spirit and the Realm of Caesar*, 42.

"the creation of a new world," of "this world transfigured," and that it can thus "be envisaged only eschatologically."[28] In other words, the specifics of this kingdom cannot be foreseen, and it will look fundamentally different to the realm of Caesar, but Berdyaev still envisages an eschatological transformation of the hitherto separate realms of Caesar and the Spirit. He may refuse to expect God's kingdom *on earth*, but then he expects earth to be transformed at the end point of history.

Cavanaugh, for his part, criticises at length the clear separation of the spiritual and material planes. Moreover, he argues that "in the Eucharist the Kingdom [of God] irrupts into time and 'confuses' the spiritual and the temporal."[29] He writes that the Eucharist results in such "confusion" because it "anticipates the future Kingdom, re-members Jesus' conflict with the powers of this world, and brings both future and past dimensions of Christ into the present in the form of a visible body."[30] Hence "Eucharistic celebrations," for Cavanaugh, "are the link between heavenly and earthly times."[31] In other words, the kingdom of God, for him, is a mysterious phenomenon very different to our current reality, yet one that irrupts into this reality at the liturgical moment of the Eucharist.

What is clear from all this is that Christian anarchists (broadly defined) take very different views on the nature of the kingdom of God, on the manner of its advent, and on the broader relationship between the material and the spiritual. They all look forward to this kingdom, but they also often remain uncertain about its specifics, and they usually stress that they do not know *when* it will come. What unites most of them, however, is their refusal to succumb to the temptation of trying to hasten it through common political means.

## *The temptation of normal political action*

For most Christian anarchist thinkers, it is crucial to dissociate Christianity from any delusions of political efficacy (as noted in Chapter 4). Jesus' way, for them, is not about political effectiveness, but about surrendering to God. The temptation to mould society through political power is the very temptation that Jesus rejects in the wilderness (see Chapter 2), because it implies worship of the devil and a lack of faith in God. Jesus' way is political not because it prescribes the adoption by the state of this or that policy, but because it subverts the very legitimacy of political power by criticising its methods and by exemplifying a way of life that makes the state and the customary channels of political action superfluous.

Ellul therefore insists that Christians today must not seek to find and apply a "Christian 'solution'" to political problems.[32] For him, it is an "illusion" to think that "our problems can actually be solved through politics."[33] God's kingdom cannot be reached by "'Christianising' society" from the top down, by

---

[28] Berdyaev, "Personality, Religion, and Existential Anarchism," 164 (for the first two quotes); Berdyaev, *The Realm of the Spirit and the Realm of Caesar*, 178 (for the last quote).
[29] Cavanaugh, *Torture and Eucharist*, 206.
[30] Cavanaugh, *Torture and Eucharist*, 251.
[31] Cavanaugh, *Torture and Eucharist*, 224.
[32] Ellul, *Violence*, 24.
[33] Wogaman, *Christian Perspectives on Politics*, 59.

using the state to somehow incite the development of Christian values.[34] Yet even from the bottom up, Jesus' way of the cross is not to be seen merely as the magic solution to political problems, as the ultimate tool to manage the course of history.

One of the clearest discussions of the Christian rejection of the temptation to "manage history" can be found in Yoder's *Politics of Jesus*.[35] Yoder claims that most Christians "are obsessed with the [...] direction of history" and "moved by a deep desire to make things move in the right direction."[36] Yet just like Christian anarchists, Yoder suggests that "Christ's teaching on meekness" and "servanthood" raises questions about "whether it is our business at all to guide our actions by the course we wish history to take."[37] Instead of guiding their actions thus, Yoder argues (based on Revelation) that Christians must rely more on Jesus both to understand the movement of history and to seek guidance for how to act within it: Jesus, he says, "is to be looked at as the mover of history and as the standard by which Christians must learn how they are to look at the moving of history."[38] That standard, for Yoder, is the suffering of the cross.

Yoder argues that Jesus faced a clear choice between the "effectiveness" of "the crown" and "obedience" through "the cross."[39] His choice of the cross, for Yoder, demonstrates a "commitment to such a degree of faithfulness to the character of divine love that he was willing for its sake to sacrifice 'effectiveness.'"[40] To choose the cross rather than the crown is a demonstration of faith in God and in the nature of love.

Furthermore, Yoder maintains that the cross is "not adequately" understood if it is seen "as a peculiarly efficacious technique [...] for getting one's way."[41] According to Yoder, "The point is not that one can attain all of one's legitimate ends without using violent means. It is rather that our readiness to renounce legitimate ends whenever they cannot be attained by legitimate means itself constitutes our participation in the triumphant suffering of the Lamb."[42] Following Jesus and taking up one's cross is not about "results," but

---

[34] Goddard, *Living the Word, Resisting the World*, 112.
[35] Yoder, *The Politics of Jesus*, 230.
[36] Yoder, *The Politics of Jesus*, 228. On that page and the next two, he adds that Christians' concern often "has to do with looking for the right 'handle' by which one can 'get a hold on' the course of history and move it in the right direction," and that this attempt to manage history "involves at least three distinguishable assumptions:" that "the relationship of cause and effect is visible, understandable, and manageable;" that "we are adequately informed to be able to set for ourselves and for all society the goal towards which we seek to move it;" and that "effectiveness in moving towards these goals which have been set is itself a moral yardstick." Yoder then proceeds to criticise each of these assumptions.
[37] Yoder, *The Politics of Jesus*, 230.
[38] Yoder, *The Politics of Jesus*, 233.
[39] Yoder, *The Politics of Jesus*, 233-234.
[40] Yoder, *The Politics of Jesus*, 234.
[41] Yoder, *The Politics of Jesus*, 237.
[42] Yoder, *The Politics of Jesus*, 237. Yoder therefore argues (on pages 238-239) that the debate among Christians should not be on "the theoretical issue of whether evil may be done for the sake of good," because "really the deeper question is the axiom that underlies the question, namely that it is a high good to make history move in the right direction."

about "obedience" and "faithfulness."[43] It is not to be seen as a useful method to provoke an effect on something else, but as a sign of confidence in God. Thus, as Myers notes, Yoder highlights that Jesus' teaching "has little to say concerning *ends*, or the criterion of efficacy."[44] It concentrates "upon historical means," and leaves "the historical 'fruits' [...] in the hands of God."[45]

Moreover, again just like Christian anarchists, Yoder admits that we cannot fully understand "*How* God acts."[46] Yet he also adds that "the crucified Jesus" provides a "key to understanding what God is about," because "in Jesus we have a clue to which kind of causation, which kinds of community-building, which kinds of conflict management, go with the grain of the cosmos."[47] In Jesus, God provides a clue as to how he steers the course of history. Hence according to Yoder, it is only by following Jesus to the cross and thereby renouncing any attempts to manage history that Christians (paradoxically) come close to participating in God's steering of history.

Chelčický is aware that this resignation of political effectiveness will be criticised by those who seek to hasten God's kingdom through political means. He is "certain that all who would be true Christians will always be reviled, rebuked and despised by those who seek an earthly kingdom."[48] Despite this, however, they "must distance themselves from hope for physical redemption."[49] They must not seek top-down political reform but work on "the regeneration of [their] own life" through faith.[50] Furthermore, even if the world around them is not moved by their witness, these true Christians must be "a colony of heaven," a beacon of faith striving to present "an image of the Kingdom of God" to the dark world that surrounds and often ignores them.[51]

The important difference is between anticipating and precipitating the kingdom: Christians are to anticipate it in their own lives and communities, but not seek to precipitate it – lest they become impatient and step upon the slippery slope to increasingly confrontational activism.[52] What is important is not the future but the here and now, not the eventual dawning of the Christian anarchist utopia but witnessing to its potential today. Therefore, even if their witness does not seem efficacious in hastening God's kingdom, Christians must continue to strive to follow Jesus in their own life and community, and not be tempted to force others to do the same as well. Their witness *might* move others to convert to

---

[43] Yoder, *The Politics of Jesus*, 238.
[44] Myers, *Binding the Strong Man*, 461 (Myers' emphasis).
[45] Myers, *Binding the Strong Man*, 349.
[46] Yoder, *The Politics of Jesus*, 245.
[47] Yoder, *The Politics of Jesus*, 246.
[48] Wagner, *Petr Chelčický*, 134.
[49] Wagner, *Petr Chelčický*, 146.
[50] Wagner, *Petr Chelčický*, 156.
[51] Molnár, *A Study of Peter Chelčický's Life*, 8.
[52] Obviously, what is being said here builds upon the thinking of several Christian anarchist thinkers, but may well be contested by several Christian anarchist activists, especially those who favour the adoption of more confrontational tactics. Christian anarchists (and pacifists) do not all speak the same voice on this issue. Hence the view articulated in this section of the Conclusion is not a summary that all Christian anarchists would subscribe to, but a set of reflections building on the insights from Christian anarchist thought as described in this book. As already noted, this tension is one worth devoting a whole study to in the future.

Jesus' way – but, equally, it might not. It might precipitate the kingdom – but, equally, it might not. They must assess their own actions not against the extent to which they have succeeded in hastening the kingdom, but solely on the extent to which they have strived to anticipate and represent the kingdom by following Jesus' teaching and example in their own lives.[53]

It is perhaps also here that another explanation for the corruption of the church around the time of Constantine, and of many of the radical Christian sects and movements of the Middle Ages (see Chapters 3 and 6), is to be found. That is, these pre-modern examples of (at least partial or embryonic) Christian anarchism succumbed to the temptation to precipitate the advent of God's kingdom through political action. They apparently saw political power or the adoption of violent means as an opportunity to hasten the kingdom of God's advent on earth. It seems they thought that by moving away from the persecuted and seemingly politically ineffective edge of society, they might have a better chance of doing God's work. In doing so, however, they demonstrated a loss of faith in God and a disobedience of Jesus' counsel of patience, love and forgiveness. Even if they were motivated by an understandable desire to change society for the better, they succumbed to the temptation which Jesus rejected. Where they once worshiped God, keeping faith in his steering of history, they now worshipped human agency, expecting it to deliver what God alone can deliver.

Eller discusses at length this temptation to "worship" (etymologically: "the considering worthy of") the state and similar forms of human agency. He insists that "The threat of the arkys is not so much their *existence* as it is our granting that existence reality and weight – our giving ourselves to them, attaching importance to them, putting faith in them, making idols of them."[54] As explained in Chapter 4, he argues that in response to the tax question, Jesus "makes the distinction between the one, ultimate, absolute choice and all lesser, relative choices," that the lesson from this episode is "to absolutize God alone and let the state and all other arkys be the human relativities they are."[55] Next to God, the state is not to be granted any worth. For Eller, Jesus' way "deprives arkys of their pathos" and "starves them out" in doing so.[56] In other words, Jesus refuses to be passionate about the state, and teaches indifferent dismissal of it, because what is important – indeed absolutely important – is obedience to God, not the deluded grandeur of idolatrous human pretensions. Thus Christians must not succumb to the temptation to take human agency seriously, for instance by ascribing value to the state.

It is in this sense and this sense only that Christianity is indeed "apolitical:" it is indifferent to the petty politics of human management. Yet

---

[53] Even Tolstoy and Ballou, identified above as expecting some sort of gradual progress towards the kingdom of God, generally stress that what matters over and above visible social and historical progress is personal effort towards applying Jesus' teaching in one's own life.

[54] Eller, *Christian Anarchy*, 12.

[55] Eller, *Christian Anarchy*, 82, 83.

[56] Rather than an exact quotation, this is actually paraphrasing Eller's quotation of Karl Barth, which reads as follows: "Deprive them of their PATHOS, and they will be starved out; but stir up revolution against them, and their PATHOS is provided fresh fodder." Eller, *Christian Anarchy*, 125 (Barth's upper-case).

precisely because human beings worship the state so highly, Christianity's implications are very political and subversive. In calling to worship God as the one and only master, Jesus is draining the state of any power and legitimacy. In this sense, true Christianity's indifference to the state destroys it. This might also be one of the reasons why Jesus' crucifixion not only unmasks the state's violent nature and idolatrous pretensions, but also defeats it – it drains it of its legitimacy, defeating it from within. Where Christianity is adopted, it renders the state obsolete. The state continues to exist, but it is already defeated by Jesus' crucifixion. For followers of Jesus, the state becomes irrelevant. That is why any obedience or disobedience to it is accidental and secondary to the only priority of obeying God. To repeat, Jesus' followers are called to anticipate and represent the kingdom of God, but they must guard against the temptation to worship political action to precipitate it.

Thus, the main peril of politics is this temptation to steer the course of history. Yet there is also another peril – one which all anarchists are aware of. That is, the danger with any bottom-up organisation is that it can easily degenerate into a much more coercive, top-down structure of the kind that anarchists loathe. As Chapter 6 shows, many a commune has degenerated in that way, following a crisis, for instance, or the influence of some charismatic but somewhat controlling leader. There is a tendency in organic communities to seek to define and fix the community's organisation more rigidly, usually out of a desire to safeguard its essential core. Often, however, this later leads to coercion against those whose behaviour drifts away from the agreed rules. This tendency is examined in the next section, where it is also suggested that Jesus' teaching acts as a permanent reminder of this risk. If indeed so, then the only way to safeguard the essence of a Christian anarchist community is again to always fall back to Jesus' teaching, not human rules, when addressing whatever new situation the community may be faced with.

## Relentless prophecy at the margins

In order to elaborate on this tendency of communities to rigidify and become more coercive, and on the prophetic role of Jesus' political teaching in response to it, it is helpful to digress briefly into insights derived from Christian theology. What follows is therefore not a position articulated in the Christian anarchist literature, but a set of somewhat heuristic reflections, inspired by broader Christian theology, on the dynamic nature of political institutions and on the role of Christian anarchism in that context.

### *Love, justice, and social ontology*

This digression begins by summarising and at times paraphrasing heavily the relevant arguments made in an article, co-authored with Joseph Milne, which reflects on the ontological ground and eschatological calling of love, justice, and social and political institutions.[57] The significance of it for Christian anarchist thought is teased out further below.

In this article, following theologian Paul Tillich, love is described as a "the moving power of life," as a primordial force that reunites the separated, and justice, as giving form to this reunion.[58] Given this book's limited scope, these insights cannot be fully examined and justified here.[59] The point is that from this ontological perspective, "love is the principle of justice."[60] Love and justice are ontologically united in that justice is driven by love and gives form to it. Moreover, and importantly for the present book, love and justice work together towards the full actualisation of being, but they remain in tension within their ontological unity. Furthermore, any attempt to define justice – for instance by trying to encapsulate it in laws that prejudge future concrete situation – amounts to a move that is untrue to the ontological essence of justice. Any such definition of "justice" almost immediately loses touch with love – and indeed thereby immediately begins losing touch with justice itself – because love continues its conquest of the separated, and thus continuously transforms justice anew. Justice, from Tillich's perspective, is therefore essentially dynamic.[61] Whenever attempts are made to fix or define it, justice begins losing touch with its ontological ground, and, over time, the ageing definition of justice gradually becomes increasingly more unjust.

These reflections are enriched by Paul Ricoeur's on the relation between the Golden Rule and the commandment to love our enemies. Ricoeur argues that there is a tension between the two in that the "hyperethical" commandment to love our enemies "develops a logic of superabundance" which "at first glance […] opposes itself to the logic of equivalence" and "reciprocity" embodied in the Golden Rule – the same logic of equivalence which is also present in most contemporary discourses on justice.[62] Ricoeur, however, then argues that

> the commandment of love does not abolish the golden rule but instead reinterprets it in terms of generosity, and thereby makes not just possible but necessary an application of the commandment whereby, owing to its hyperethical status, it does not accede to the ethical sphere except at the price of paradoxical and extreme forms of behavior, those forms which are in fact recommended in the wake of the new commandment.[63]

---

[57] The passages closely paraphrased or copied from that article in this subsection are so numerous (they together amount to most of the subsection) that I have chosen not to indicate them with quotation marks. For the more detailed original, see Alexandre J. M. E. Christoyannopoulos and Joseph Milne, "Love, Justice, and Social Eschatology," *The Heythrop Journal* 48/6 (2007). I am obviously very grateful to Joseph Milne for his huge input and collaboration in producing that article.

[58] Paul Tillich, *Love, Power, and Justice: Ontological Analyses and Ethical Applications* (London: Oxford University Press, 1954), 25.

[59] For their detailed exposition, see Tillich, *Love, Power, and Justice*. Here, some of Tillich's insights are simply taken as helpful starting points for an interesting perspective on political institutions and Christian anarchist thought.

[60] Tillich, *Love, Power, and Justice*, 57.

[61] He uses the term "creative." Tillich, *Love, Power, and Justice*, 64.

[62] Paul Ricoeur, "Love and Justice," in *Paul Ricoeur: The Hermeneutics of Action*, ed. Richard Kearney, trans. David Pellauer (London: Sage, 1996), 33-34.

[63] Ricoeur, "Love and Justice," 35.

The commandment to love our enemies fulfils the Golden Rule by reinterpreting it "in terms of generosity," resulting in ethical recommendations that are radical and "paradoxical." Examples of such ethical suggestions, Ricoeur continues, "are in fact recommended [by Jesus] in the wake of the new commandment."[64] These recommendations are none other than Jesus' instructions in the Sermon on the Mount – the very Bible passage which Chapter 1 identifies as the essential inspiration for Christian anarchist thought.[65] Thus, for Ricoeur, Jesus' commandments in the Sermon on the Mount are informed by love's radical reinterpretation of ethics and of the logic of equivalence. (Interestingly, Ricoeur also notes that "those unique and extreme forms of commitment" were "taken up by St Francis, Gandhi, and Martin Luther King" – all noted in Chapter 6 as examples also praised by Christian anarchists.[66])

Ricoeur then argues that "Without the corrective of the commandment to love, the golden rule would be constantly drawn in the direction of a utilitarian maxim whose formula is [...]: I give so *that* you will give."[67] That is, without love, justice would be caught in a utilitarian logic of equivalence and reciprocity. Therefore, the "hyperethical" commandment to love does not criticise the logic of equivalence of the Golden Rule so much as its perverse, self-interested interpretation.[68] Put in broader terms, love is not critical of distributive or reciprocal justice *per se*, but of its selfish interpretation. Without love, justice tends to be defined by cold calculations based on rigid rules on equivalence and reciprocity. When love informs justice, however, it drives justice to its limits, where it is enveloped by love's logic of superabundance and leads to revolutionary forms of behaviour. Indeed, from this perspective, the Golden Rule is truly just only when informed by love – not when it is interpreted as cold, calculative, self-interested reciprocity.

Hence Ricoeur reaches a conclusion similar to Tillich's: justice, he says, is "the necessary medium of love; precisely because love is hypermoral, it enters the practical and ethical sphere only under the aegis of justice."[69] At the same time, love remains "hyperethical," that is, beyond, just ahead of ethics itself. It enters ethics in the form of justice, and yet works for justice to transform itself anew. In sum, from Tillich's and Ricoeur's perspective, love drives towards the reunion of the separated, and justice holds the reunited together by giving form to the reunion. Love, however, carries on working for broader reunion of the still separated. Thus love constantly calls justice to adopt new forms, to push itself to its limits and transform itself anew, because ageing formulations of justice tend to become inadequate to new situations.

These theological reflections on love and justice are relevant here because they have a bearing on the nature and purpose of political institutions, a prime example of which is, of course, the state. Ontologically speaking, social and political institutions can be said to embody or articulate a community's vision

---

[64] Ricoeur, "Love and Justice," 35.
[65] Note that Ricoeur quotes Jesus' commandments according to Luke rather than Matthew. Ricoeur, "Love and Justice," 35.
[66] Ricoeur, "Love and Justice," 35.
[67] Ricoeur, "Love and Justice," 35-36 (Ricoeur's emphasis).
[68] Ricoeur, "Love and Justice," 36.
[69] Ricoeur, "Love and Justice," 36-37.

of justice. They are instituted by the coming together of society, and they set down the form which justice is expected to take in that society. Yet since justice is continuously transformed by love, any institution that is not open to continuously transforming itself anew by reinterpreting its formulation of justice tends to become increasingly unjust. When political and religious institutions try to seize, legislate and defend a fixed definition of social justice, they fail to remain open to love's continuous reinterpretation of justice. Instead, they tend to decline into juridicalism, into producing rigid regulations enforced by violent means. They thus become ever more unjust in the dynamic present.

Indeed, and more to the point for Christian anarchism, the very process by which the state draws legislation is already caught up in the logic that leads to legal rigidity and fixity, because what is just in a concrete situation cannot be defined *a priori* by some positive universal law. Tillich indeed declares that "there are no principles which could be applied mechanically and which would guarantee that justice is done."[70] The highest level of justice, of "transforming or creative justice," is based on the understanding that "intrinsic justice is dynamic" and "as such," therefore, "it cannot be defined in definite terms."[71] For that reason, fixed legislation that is believed to inform all concrete situations *ex ante* is ultimately unjust. True justice informs and reforms itself in every new situation. By contrast, by setting down rules, any positive law, though it may have been informed by justice at its root, immediately begins to lose touch with justice since justice continues to be transformed by love. Over time, therefore, positive legislation becomes an ever more distant approximation of true justice. To the extent that the state is the paradigmatic producer of positive laws which it then proceeds to police using violent means, then from this ontological perspective, it is unjust and indeed destined to eventually be supplanted by a new formulation of justice transformed and reinterpreted by love.

It is here that the prophetic element of Christian anarchist thought and practice becomes apparent. Reformers, philosophers and prophets have always animated politics. Every society was formed by visionaries, and within them there have always been thinkers calling for further political reform to fulfil an even higher degree of justice. These ideals constantly call humankind forward – the challenge is to actualise them. Love calls for reform, but political institutions sometimes fail to take up the challenge and freeze into juridicalism. For a society's political institution to avoid degenerating into such juridicalism, for that society to be open to continuous reinterpretation of its formulation of justice, it must always pay attention to its radicals and prophets, because the vision which these prophets are striving to articulate (as explained below, both in their critique and in their practice, and both individually and collectively) may well be the transformed vision of justice which love is calling society towards. To remain just, social and political institutions must pay attention to the radicals who seek to reinterpret and transform justice in terms of love and generosity.

The temptation to codify and fix once and for all any formulation of justice is a dangerous temptation. One of its perils is the justification it immediately presents for the adoption of violence to try to enforce compliance to

---

[70] Tillich, *Love, Power, and Justice*, 56.
[71] Tillich, *Love, Power, and Justice*, 64.

this formulation. As explained in Chapter 3, from a Christian anarchist perspective, precisely such a fate befell the established church once it allied itself with the state. Secular ideologies, however, are equally prone to a similar adoption of violence to defend their fixed vision of justice. Yet this danger is also one eventually faced by all organic, alternative communities. One day, the temptation will arise to try to preserve the community's essence by freezing it into rules, conformity to which then becomes a test of one's commitment to the community's formulation of social justice. Thus, the dangerous temptation of trying to freeze a formulation of justice for posterity is a danger faced by all human communities – including Christian anarchist ones. All radical communities must guard against this temptation if they are to really preserve their prophetic edge.

## Christian anarchists as prophets

Nevertheless, and perhaps somewhat paradoxically, it may be that Christian anarchist thought points to the one vision which by definition does not allow itself to be frozen into juridicalism, because it is grounded in the logic of superabundance articulated in Jesus' teaching and example. That teaching and example is the only acceptable manifesto for community life, the only set of rules, which Christian anarchist thought admits. Because Christian anarchists refuse to consider any human rules worthy next to God's commandments, they will always seek inspiration from the latter when facing new and challenging situations. If so, then their actions will always be inspired by love's logic of superabundance and thus avoid the risk of freezing into increasingly violent juridicalism.

Jesus' teaching and example are the paradigmatic illustration of love's logic of superabundance. Even though Christian anarchists take Jesus' commandments literally, as rules to be followed, these commandments escape the dangers of violent juridicalism because they are firmly grounded in love. These rules challenge us to love and forgive rather than to posit what is just and demand compliance to it by others. They put the emphasis on us, calling us to go beyond demanding justice by responding with love and generosity in the face of injustice. They cannot degenerate into increasingly unjust rules because they continuously call us beyond the limits of justice – transforming and reinterpreting justice in the process. They do not posit definitions of justice, but call us to be informed by love in responding to each new situation we may be faced with. Hence as long as their witness is informed by Jesus' teaching and example, Christian anarchists prophetically articulate the reinterpretation of justice by love's logic of superabundance. Even a literal reading of Jesus' commandments, far from a sign of juridicalism, escapes such juridicalism by bearing witness to love's dynamic and "hyperethical status."[72]

Therefore, as long as Christian anarchists are informed by Jesus' teaching and example, they act as prophets to society. Their critique of the state and response to it calls humanity forward, inciting it to reconsider its institutions

---

[72] Ricoeur, "Love and Justice," 35.

and continuously reform them anew. Where the state (as formulator of positive law) embodies the backward-looking tendency towards juridicalism, Christian anarchism embodies the forward-looking logic of superabundance. The tendency of the state *qua* state to freeze and become unjust is countered by the tendency of Christian anarchist prophets *qua* prophets to reinterpret justice through the eyes of Christian love.

Moreover, Christian anarchists embody the role of the prophet both in their critique of society's violence and idolatry and in their attempts to live out their understanding of Christianity in community. That is, in both their teaching and their example, and as long as they continue to be informed by Jesus' own teaching and example, Christian anarchists act as the prophets of old. Both their verbal critique and their individual and communal examples articulate love's permanent call for political communities to reinterpret their formulation of justice and thereby transform their institutions anew.

Furthermore, as has already been hinted at, this prophetic role for Christian anarchists applies not just to the wider society, but to Christian anarchists' own communities, too. Only if Christian anarchists are grounded in Jesus' teaching and example will their own critique and example remain prophetically inspired. If they attempt to preserve their radicality by positing new rules, then their grounding in love is lost. They must guard against the temptation to replace God's commandments by human ones. There can be no rigid, positive legislation. As mentioned in Chapters 4 and 5, it is by example that Christian anarchists lead the way forward, not by positing legislation requiring others to behave in a specific way. To remain Christian and prophetic, the Christian anarchist witness must only ever be informed by Jesus' teaching and example. Any formulation of justice must be continuously open to reinterpretation.

Here, it is interesting to explore another implication of the above ontological perspective for the present discussion. Implied in it is a different perspective on the essence of the state than is assumed by most Christian anarchist thinkers – indeed by most anarchists and even most social and political thinkers. In Part I, this book unquestioningly describes the state as the monopoly over the legitimised use of violence over a given territory. From the ontological perspective elaborated above, however, the state can be seen as an articulation of a society's definition of justice, as the form which love's conquest of the separated takes in a particular time and place. Still, to the extent that the state freezes this form of justice and seeks to protect it using any means necessary, it immediately tends to become unjust. Yet such an ontological view of political "institutions" is quite different to today's predominant understanding of the state. From this ontological perspective, institutions arise organically, but in that they are prone to immediately tend to rigidify, they never really remain informed by justice for long unless they continuously transform themselves anew.

Thus, while political institutions may arise from the productive tensions between love and justice, as soon as they posit laws which they commit themselves to protect, they become unloving and unjust. If the state is such a rigidification of justice, then it always tends to be unjust, to fall short of the demands of creative justice. Since love continuously transforms justice anew, any attempt to capture justice in positive legislation will fail. On the other hand, if a political "institution" is fluid, organic, and never claims to capture justice but continuously rearticulates and reinterprets justice anew in terms of generosity, then it can be said to be informed by love. It is when it becomes a human organisation which pretends to manage history, to fix justice through positive laws, and to protect these laws using violence and coercion, that a political institution not only ceases to be informed by love, but indeed thereby becomes gradually ever more unjust.

The Christian anarchist critique of the state obviously has rigidified political institutions in mind. It is not critical of the sort of fluid and organic "institutions" informed and transformed by love which the above ontological perspective refers to. Indeed, if anything, political "institutions" grounded in love are precisely the sorts of political community eulogised by Christian anarchists. Some radical Christian and Christian anarchist communities even provide perhaps some of the better examples of such political "institutions." They are informed not by human pretensions to manage society, but by personal repentance and by love of God and neighbour as taught and exemplified by Jesus. Theoretically, therefore, the best example of a social and political "institution" which is always informed and transformed by love is the "true" church of Chapter 5.

In other words, in response to the state's inherent tendency to juridicalism, the true church must embody the role of the prophet critiquing society's lethargy and presenting to it an alternative political institution informed by love. The church is called to continuously reinterpret justice in terms of love and generosity, to continuously awaken society out of machine-like juridicalism by articulating what the Christian logic of superabundance calls for in each new context. At the same time, any such community of true Christians must also guard against the temptation to freeze its own prescriptions into positive laws – lest it degenerate just like every other religious and political institution has tended to. The true church must guard against all juridicalism – whether by the state or by the church. To do so, it must never define *a priori* what justice requires in each emerging situation, but always return to Jesus' teaching and example as a source of inspiration to inform its reinterpretation of justice in this new situation and to thereby fulfil its prophetic role.

One of the markers of modernity has been the rise to near omnipresence and omnipotence of the state – a state which (according to Chapter 3) tends to be violent, deceptive, exploitative and idolatrous, and therefore unchristian. The response which this calls for from the church, from the community of faithful followers of Jesus' teaching and example, is to act as a critic of the state and as a witness to its alternative. In other words, the Christian response called for by the rise of the state is the response advocated by Christian anarchist thought. This response, unsurprisingly, has largely been articulated precisely in this modern context, during this increase in the power of the state. Within this context, Christian anarchists may well act as the prophets of the past. It may be that in a very different future in which the state may have been humbled, Christian anarchism's focus on the state will have become redundant, and Christian prophets, inspired by Jesus' teaching and example, will articulate a very different set of prophecies in response to that different context. But in today's context of the all-powerful state, Christian anarchism may well be providing the sort of reinterpretation of justice in terms of love and generosity which humanity needs to avoid the dangers of violent juridicalism by the state.

At the same time, Christian anarchists cannot force others to adopt their views. Here again, they act as prophets, this time in that they are asking us to look at ourselves, to look at Jesus, to repent, and to live differently. They do not act as the (real or metaphorical)[73] kings who try to manage society by government decree, but as the prophets who denounce and expose the pitfalls of such human government. As prophets, they call us to repent and to anoint Jesus as the sole king, to focus on our own behaviour rather than that of others, and to subvert earthly kingdoms by anticipating and representing the kingdom of God. (Thus, if there is one way in which Christian anarchists can be said to see Jesus as "the Christ," it is in his role as the messianic "king" of God's alternative kingdom.) In sum, in more ways than one, Christian anarchists seem to embody a prophetic role.

Of course, Christian anarchists are not the only prophets of the modern era. Liberals, communists, anarchists and democrats have also been acting as prophets of the modern era, as have many other radicals and critics of the *status quo*. Christian anarchists, however, highlight the religious dimension of social injustice. They call us back to God's covenant. They unmask the state as a jealous god who seeks to usurp God's authority. They expose the delusion – and its consequences – of seeking political solutions to injustice and suffering, they decry the arrogance of human pretensions to God's throne, and instead they point humanity back towards God's covenants. Moreover, their prophetic critique is firmly and explicitly rooted in love – as articulated in Jesus' teaching and example. More than other prophets, therefore, their prophecy stems from the ontological ground of political institutions: their critique most fully embodies love's contemporary reinterpretation of justice.

Prophecy in this sense thus pulls society back to the love that originally informed it. It encourages society to reflect on how far it has ventured away from that source. In its pure form, Christian anarchism acts in such a prophetic manner today. The potential tendency even among Christian anarchists to move away from this pure position has been noted several times already. The ontological perspective outlined above indeed suggest that this tendency manifests itself naturally in any human community – even the most radical tends to drift away from the pure and prophetic vision that originally informed it. If anything, however, this only further underscores the importance of the pure prophetic critique rooted in the ontological source of human community. Christian anarchist thought in its "purest" (or strictest) form articulates that prophecy in the modern era.

## Distinguishing church and state

Just like with the prophets of the past, however, it seems that the message articulated by today's prophets is falling on deaf ears. The true church is ignored while the state continues to be worshiped instead of God.

---

[73] "Metaphorical" because even democracy crowns a collective human agent – the demos – as "king."

As discussed above, the Bible suggests that God tolerates humanity's idolatry for the powers that be, and that he somehow works through them to preserve some order. Thus, among those who have rejected God and elevated human agency to divine status, at its best, the state might maintain some sort of justice – an imperfect justice of a calculative, reciprocal, utilitarian kind. Ricoeur suggests that "Perhaps the mystery of the state is indeed to limit evil without curing it, to conse humankind without saving it."[74] But that last section of his statement is important: the state will not save us, and however forgivable it might be, it remains an aberration from the will of God. It might conserve humanity, but it tends to violence and juridicalism. It might administer some sort of justice and social care, but it does so out of the taxpayers' pockets rather than out of their heart. The very existence of the state betrays a failure to love our neighbour, a shameful delegation of our responsibility towards fellow human beings. This might somehow conserve humanity, but it is not enough to save it. Salvation will not be attained through politics, but through the cross – not through an idolatrous veneration of and delegation to political engineering, but through the love and sacrifice which God expects from the church of true Christians.

There may be some parallels between the law of the Old Testament and the law of the state (when at its best).[75] From a Christian anarchist perspective, however righteous the former is and the latter can sometimes (but rarely) be, both are insufficient for the salvation of humankind.[76] Nevertheless, where love is lacking, they can help preserve an imperfect order. Thus as mentioned in Chapter 4, Chelčický, for instance, accepts that "The civil law is [...] necessary – as a bitter vinegar, so to speak – for those who transgress the law of love."[77] Yet as Molnár explains, he also believes that "To him who obeys God the state becomes a superfluity, for the fullness of the law is love."[78] Chelčický may be confusing the Old Testament law with civil law, but the point is that love exceeds and fulfils both.

Love fulfils the law because it goes beyond it. For example (as explained in Chapter 1), love does not seek justice in an eye for an eye, but fulfils *lex talionis* by carrying its intent further in the same direction. Similarly, Christianity fulfils the purpose of the state, but it does so by calling us beyond it. Christian anarchism reaches back to the original intentions of social and political institutions and fulfils them by exceeding them. Hence in a (perhaps paradoxical) way, Christian anarchism does not so much destroy the state as it fulfils it.

---

[74] Paul Ricoeur, "State and Violence," in *History and Truth*, trans. Charles A. Kelbley (Evanston: Northwestern University Press, 1965), 238-239.

[75] This analogy may well be rather dubious and ultimately untenable, not least since Old Testament law arguably warns against the very serious idolatry which the state is often guilty of. Besides, the former is said to be handed down by God, while the latter often prides itself in being a human construction. There are also countless types of state law, compared to the one main body of Old Testament law (at least as canonised in the traditional Christian Bible). Yet as the following paragraphs suggest, from a Christian anarchist perspective, both are imperfect (albeit in different ways), and only truly fulfilled by love.

[76] This statement holds true whether one expects this salvation to be some mysterious eschatological transformation of the material and spiritual through some divine intervention (Berdyaev, Eller, Ellul) or some sort of very rational kingdom of peace and love on earth (Tolstoy).

[77] Molnár, *A Study of Peter Chelčický's Life*, 87 (quoting Chelčický).

[78] Molnár, *A Study of Peter Chelčický's Life*, 32.

Jesus' teaching and example fulfil God's intentions for human society. As long as it is inspired by them, the Christian church will act as a prophet in its contemporary society. Implied in this prophetic role, however, is the likelihood that the church is to continuously remain a small and radical sect at the edge of society. Since its mission is to strive to articulate love's continuous call for reform and transformation, it can never settle for a particular institution's formulation of justice. It must continue to reinterpret it in terms of love and generosity, it must always be calling humanity further forward, and thus it must probably always find itself at the radical margin of the political spectrum.

It is therefore not surprising that several Christian anarchists insist that the church must remain clearly separate from the state. This is not to say that the church must withdraw from *society:* as already noted, it must be a radical voice within it, calling it to transform itself anew. But the church must be separate from the *state*. It must tolerate the state, but unmask its true nature, name its sins and imperfections. The church must not be subsumed into the state, but an alternative to it.

For Ellul, the church "is not to instruct the political power how to govern," but "prophetically to discern the signs of the times, warn of the consequences of political power's action or inaction, and oppose and resist all the political power's attempts to overstep its limits and sacralise itself."[79] The most "serious threat," for Ellul, is "the modern state's pretensions to be worthy of the religious devotion and worship of its people and to be able to solve all society's problems."[80] The church must therefore also avoid the post-Constantinian trap of granting the state the religious status which would warrant such devotion. Political power must remain secular, separate from the church.

That church and state should be kept separate does not mean that religion and politics can or should be, too. This book is arguing precisely that Christianity carries with it important political implications. Besides, in its quest for worship and power, the state has been said to be seeking quasi-divine or religious authority. This very contest between church and state illustrates the unavoidable overlap between religion and politics. Thus from a Christian anarchist perspective, while the true church must be separated from the state, religion cannot be separated from politics.

For Christian anarchists, the church must embrace the radical political implications of Jesus' teaching and example. Especially since the 1960s, for instance, Christian churches have indeed been increasingly involved in pacifist and liberation movements and in similar prophetic criticisms of axioms of modern society. From a Christian anarchist perspective, these are steps in the right direction, but they are not quite radical enough, and the Christian church must go much further. It must fully embody the role of the prophet and denounce all the sins of society, even at the risk of being counted as too radical by the rest of society. In today's context, this means going as far as denouncing the state and exposing its many sins. Even if it is not heard, always small, or even persecuted, the true church must be the voice which comments on society from a Christian perspective and continuously reinterprets the formulations of its social and

---

[79] Goddard, *Living the Word, Resisting the World*, 291.
[80] Goddard, *Living the Word, Resisting the World*, 292.

political "institutions" in terms of love and generosity. It must denounce the sins of contemporary society, respond to them with love and forgiveness, and anticipate and represent the kingdom of God on earth. That, for Christian anarchists, should be the Christian church's radical contribution to the wider society.

## Christian anarchism's original contribution

By spelling out such a critique of the state and response to it, the Christian anarchist contribution to political thought is original in several ways: it articulates an emphatically *Christian* political theory (in the broadest sense of a theory or perspective that is concerned with political issues), though an uncommon one at that; it enriches the anarchist tradition, though based on grounds which many anarchists are likely to be uncomfortable with; and it contributes to the debate on means and ends with a stubborn refusal to compromise with violence or coercion.

Christian anarchist thought's grounding in Christianity is foreign to modern theories of politics and the state. Here, it is helpful to draw from Cavanaugh's work on the parallels and contrasts between political thought (more specifically, social contract theory) and Christianity. He argues that both Christianity and political thought are based on a founding myth on the origins of social division, and that based on this myth, both advocate the "enactment of a social body" to overcome social strife and bring about peace.[81] These two myths and consequent social bodies for salvation, however, are very different.

Cavanaugh contends that the Christian myth begins with "the natural unity of the human race," a unity which finds itself disrupted "by Adam and Eve's attempted usurpation of God's position."[82] The restoration of this unity, according to Christian soteriology, must take place "through participation in Christ's Body," the heart of which, for Cavanaugh, is the Eucharist.[83] By contrast, what Cavanaugh calls the "state story" (following social contract theory) begins with a "state of nature" which assumes "the essential individuality of the human race" and a natural starting point of war of all against all.[84] Based on this different ontological myth, "salvation from the violence of conflicting individuals" again "comes through the enactment of a social body," but in this case this happens by coming together to form a social contract "to protect person and property."[85]

---

[81] Cavanaugh, "The City," 182.
[82] Cavanaugh, "The City," 183-184.
[83] Cavanaugh, "The City," 184.
[84] Cavanaugh, "The City," 186. Cavanaugh's description of political thought (pages 186-190) is based on a very succinct synopsis of the social contract theories of Hobbes, Locke, and (perhaps to a lesser extent) Rousseau. One of his main points, however, is to stress that while in the Christian story human beings were *separated*, in the state story, they have always been *separate*. This, he sees as a fundamental ontological difference between the two stories, in that one speaks of a disrupted unity, but the other of a primordial disunity. For a discussion of this argument in light of the ontological perspective on love and justice elaborated above, see Christoyannopoulos and Milne, "Love, Justice, and Social Eschatology," 986-989.
[85] Cavanaugh, "The City," 187-188. Cavanaugh emphasises (on page 186) the theological shift which this represents from "a theology of participation" to "a theology of will," something which, again, is

Hence both the Christian story and social contract theory begin by an ontological myth to explain social disunity and propose a road to salvation that depends on the enactment of a social body.

What Cavanaugh then explains, however, is that "the Church is perhaps the primary thing from which the modern state is meant to save us. The modern secular state, after all, is founded precisely, the story goes, on the need to keep peace between contentious religious factions."[86] Indeed, the "Wars of Religion" of the sixteenth and seventeenth century are often cited are prime examples of the sort of religious conflict and violence which the secular state is here to save us from. Cavanaugh therefore argues that the process of "secularization" must be seen as "the substitution of one *mythos* of salvation for another."[87] The two contrasting stories of salvation are not just incompatible, but also competing with one another.

It is in this context that Cavanaugh goes on to argue, as explained in Chapter 3, that to call the wars out of which the modern liberal state emerged "Wars of Religion" is "an anachronism, for what was at issue in these wars was the very creation of religion as a set of privately held beliefs without direct political relevance."[88] For him, these wars were actually "the *birthpangs* of the State, in which the overlapping jurisdictions, allegiances, and customs of the medieval order were flattened and circumscribed into the new creation of the sovereign state [...], a centralizing power with a monopoly on violence within a defined territory."[89] The state relied on a myth to legitimise its increasing omnipotence through this monopoly, a myth that also deliberately confined religion to the private and subjective sphere, away from modern politics.

Like other Christian anarchists, however, Cavanaugh contends that "The state has promised peace but has brought violence."[90] Moreover, he notes that this new "sovereign is a jealous god," for whom "any association which interferes with the direct relationship between sovereign and individual becomes suspect."[91] Just like other Christian anarchists, therefore, Cavanaugh notices that Caesar has a tendency to seek to displace God, to sit in his throne, and to use violence and deception to protect this status.

The Christian story is an alternative to the state's ontological mythology and soteriology. Cavanaugh speaks of "eucharistic anarchism," and explains that "in the making of the Body of Christ, Christians participate in a practice which envisions a proper 'anarchy' [...] in that it challenges the false order of the state."[92] According to Cavanaugh, "The Eucharist defuses both the false theology and the false anthropology" of the state story, and instead "overcomes" our "separateness [...] precisely by participation in Christ's

---

commented on further in Christoyannopoulos and Milne, "Love, Justice, and Social Eschatology," 986-989.
[86] Cavanaugh, "The City," 188.
[87] Cavanaugh, "The City," 190.
[88] Cavanaugh, "A Fire Strong Enough to Consume the House," 398.
[89] Cavanaugh, "The City," 191 (Cavanaugh's emphasis).
[90] Cavanaugh, "The City," 194.
[91] Cavanaugh, "The City," 191.
[92] Cavanaugh, "The City," 194.

Body."[93] Christians must therefore stop acknowledging the state's salvation myth and instead recover and proclaim their own. Christianity, he says, "provides resources for resistance" against the state's deceptive ontological myth and path to salvation.[94]

Cavanaugh's focus on the Eucharist is his own. No other Christian anarchist speaks of it in as much detail or indeed as an "anarchic" liturgy in those terms. Yet Cavanaugh's voice adds to the broader chorus of Christian anarchist thinkers, and highlights the same sort of themes (idolatry, violence, the church as an alternative to the state, and so on). His particular contribution is this contrast which he draws between Christianity and social contract theory as based on completely different founding myths, and therefore as proposing very different paths to salvation. He makes it clear that Christianity provides an alternative to this dominant tradition in political thought. Of course, social contract theory is not the only school of thought in political theory. Yet it is a central school within it, and it helps Cavanaugh illustrate this contrast between the ontological assumptions of Christianity and political thought. This contrast might not be as clear for other traditions within political thought, but the basic point about Christianity's ontology and soteriology remains: Christianity provides an anarchist alternative to modern, secular political thought.

Hence the Christian anarchist version of the political implications of Christianity is unique. No other Christian theory about politics is so critical of the state. Christian anarchism does share a lot with Christian pacifism, but it goes further, especially by carrying this pacifism forward as implying a critique of the violent state. Christian anarchism also shares a lot with liberation theology, especially its insistence that Christianity does have very real political implications. But Christian anarchism is critical of liberation theology's emphasis on human agency, of its compromise with violence, and of its lack of New Testament references compared to Christian anarchism. In short, while related to at least two important trends within Christian political thinking, Christian anarchism is more radical than both, and thus provides a unique contribution to Christian political thought.

Christian anarchist thought is also a unique form of anarchist thought. The main difficulty for other anarchists will be that Christian anarchism is adamantly Christian. Worse (from a secular anarchist perspective), many of its thinkers advocate anarchism to Christians only, and accept that the state may have some sort of (though highly imperfect) ordering role for non-Christians. Then again, they insist that worship of the state is idolatry, and that the state tends to be violent, deceptive, exploitative, and generally stands against Jesus' teaching and example. Moreover, the hope they do entertain is that non-Christians might convert to Christianity and thus to Christian anarchism. Even in Tolstoy's rationalised version of Christianity, the salvation of humanity will only come by the conversion of non-Christians to the full implications of Jesus' rational teaching. Hence even though Christian anarchists advocate anarchism only to Christians, they advocate Christianity, and therefore anarchism, to all.

---

[93] Cavanaugh, "The City," 195.
[94] Cavanaugh, "The City," 198.

Still, Christian anarchism remains based on Jesus' *commandments*. Jesus is taken as an authority, God as the absolute authority. It is because they preach total obedience to God that Christian anarchists preach total dismissal of the state. For these reasons, many anarchists will probably be very uncomfortable with the thinking behind Christian anarchism. Yet the essential Christian anarchist point – that Christianity calls for a form of anarchism – remains a basis for dialogue and collaboration between secular and Christian anarchists. That being said, Christian anarchism is certainly a peculiar type of anarchism.

In sum, Christian anarchist thought belongs to both the Christian and the anarchist traditions. It is a unique political theology, and a unique political theory. As such, it has a unique contribution to make to debates within both the Christian tradition and the anarchist school of thought. One particular topic which is debated in both, and on which Christian anarchism has much to offer, is the question of the means of social and political change – especially with regards to the usefulness (but also the origins) of violence or coercion. Moreover, on this topic, even though all Christian anarchists reject the use of violence, they each have a slightly different point to make.

Tolstoy, for example, universalises the debate over means and ends by couching Jesus' teaching and example in the language of reason. Eller's view is more tolerant of state violence and more focused on a critique of the pretensions of human agency as idolatry. Andrews adds a personal touch by recounting numerous moving anecdotes of individual and collective instances of non-violence and non-resistance. Many in the Catholic Worker movement advocate a more confrontational stance to oppression, though they still insist on never using violence towards another human being. In other words, these and other voices within the Christian anarchist tradition each have a slightly different emphasis on this rejection of violence, so that taken together, Christian anarchists have a rich set of arguments to offer on this particular question for both political theology and political thought.

Christian anarchists can be accused of assuming perhaps too literal a reading of the Bible (as a set of moral recommendations for life in society) and too narrow a view of the state (as the legitimised monopoly over the use of violence). These assumptions, however, are quite typical of the modern mindset (perhaps especially so of Protestant theology and social contract theory). Such views of the Bible and the state may well be discredited in the future by more sophisticated perspectives, but for the moment, both are dominant among Christians, political thinkers, and educated citizens. In this context, the Christian anarchist interpretation of the political implications of Christianity will remain potent and in resonance with prevalent ways of thinking about the Bible and about the state.

A related attribute which many Christian anarchists can be criticised for is their almost complete and deliberate bypassing of traditional dogmas and practices in interpreting Jesus' teaching and examples. Here, however, these Christian anarchists argue (as explained in Chapter 3) that the historical legacy of the tradition and of the church hierarchy that keeps it alive shows that it cannot be trusted to articulate the truly radical political implications of what Jesus preached. That being said, the Christian anarchist commentary on the Gospel need not necessarily rule out all traditional dogmas and rituals – though it may invite a serious reinterpretation of some of these. The Christian anarchist emphasis on Jesus' teaching and example over and above other aspects of the Christian tradition may be excessive, but then its contribution to Christian thinking is precisely to refuse to turn the spotlight off the radical political implications of Jesus' teaching. These political implications are not the only truth or the only purpose there is to Christianity, but what Christian anarchists do is remind us of these challenging verses, refusing to allow us to forget them and their radical implications.

Christian anarchism teases out the revolutionary political implications of Christianity, and in so doing acts as a invitation to reflect, both individually and collectively, on a range of issues of importance today – such as the omnipotence of the modern state, the wisdom of adopting violent means to reach however laudable ends, the usual methods for dealing with criminals in society, for tackling poverty and famine, and so on. It also reminds us of the moving power of love, forgiveness, and sacrifice. More generally, Christian anarchism invites us to reflect on the most appropriate way for human beings to approximate social justice, to interact and live with one another in society.

Christian anarchists call Christians in particular to gather the courage to exemplify even the most radical political implications of Jesus' teaching and example, and to hopefully thereby convert others not by coercion, but by example. Several of them hope that in the process, Christians might perhaps lead a revolution more radical than any of the revolutions of the past – more radical because of the focus on means rather than ends. For this, however, Christian anarchists stress the absolute choice that each of us must make on whether to worship and obey God or human agency. In sum, both in their teaching and in their example, Christian anarchists try to act as prophets, cautioning humanity about its sins, encouraging it to follow God, and reminding it of the revolutionary potential of love, forgiveness, and sacrifice – that is, of following Jesus all the way to the cross.

# Epilogue

The aim of my doctoral thesis – and by extension, this book – was to pull together and portray as fairly coherent and sound the various publications I have come across which argue that Christianity logically implies anarchism. Doing so has meant presenting fairly different lines of argument as one, as part of one general and generic thesis. It has also meant having to give special consideration to the seemingly more challenging passages discussed in Chapter 4. That Chapter, some of Chapter 1, the discussion of Jesus' crucifixion in Chapter 2, much of Chapter 5 as well as the Conclusion have arguably resulted in the book as a whole placing a perhaps disproportionate focus on the peculiar idea of turning the other cheek to evil in the very process of seeking to overcome it, of subverting the state by nevertheless indifferently submitting to it, of transforming society through love and paradoxical sacrifice. This unexpected method is, I would suggest, one of the aspects of Christian anarchism that make it particularly original as a radical political perspective – one that clearly even if paradoxically still seeks a very different political order.

Having said that, it should perhaps be stressed, in closing, that not all Christian anarchists give as much importance to that particular aspect of Jesus' teaching and example – indeed several are very critical of the passivity and compliance that such an interpretation of Christianity seems to preach. For these Christian anarchists, there is a very important role to be played confronting political powers and refusing to be complicit in their evil. I do not wish to claim either one of these perspectives as the true "Christian anarchist" one – to exclude from the label "Christian anarchist" a whole set of people who associate themselves with that radical political label but take issue with some of the thinking presented in this book. What this book puts forward is a varied set of reflections and exegeses that, in my view, all enrich the overarching argument that Christianity today implies a form of anarchism. The emphasis placed by some who identify as Christian anarchists on subversion through indifferent submission is not one adhered to by all Christian anarchists, but the same applies to other lines of argument in this book. Few are the arguments fully, wholeheartedly and explicitly adhered to by all Christian anarchists. Yet however diverse, all those voices nevertheless still conglomerate into a generic albeit internally diverse position that can be labelled "Christian anarchist."

In any case, all Christian anarchists – whether preaching submission *à la* Romans 13 or not – see it as one of the responsibilities of Christians, inspired by the teaching and example of the one who they claim to follow, not to shy away from denouncing as both unchristian and wrong, in word and deed, the political and economic injustices plaguing the modern world. Even if when push came to shove, Jesus willingly took on the cross, he had also made it his mission to denounce his contemporaries for losing sight and moving away from the way of life called for by God. It is because in fulfilling his mission he engaged in activities that clearly posed a challenge to his contemporary authorities that these eventually resolved to confront him, and thus that his commitment to love and sacrifice was tested to its most difficult limit. Similarly, even if when push comes to shove, it may be that followers of Jesus today ought to forgivingly submit to the state's dealing with them (provided they are not disobeying God or doing other than what Jesus counsels in the process), that need not tone down their vocation to denounce that same state for its numerous and at times monstrous excesses. It is only if and when the state comes knocking on their door that the weighty dilemma of the cross presents itself. In the meantime, Jesus' followers are still called to wrestle against the principalities and powers, against the spirit and ideologies of unjust social, political and economic institutions.

Jesus calls humanity back to God's vision of a stateless kingdom of peace, love and justice, a kingdom where swords have been beaten into ploughshares, where people are neighbours to one another and where justice prevails. He warns of the high demands placed by the cross, but he also confronts society, deplores its waywardness and calls it forward. His message is important, so it is crucial that is it not misunderstood. But relatively minor disagreements or differences in emphases should not obscure the bigger picture. Jesus challenges humanity to follow him. That requires honesty, forthrightness and courage, but also an unwavering dedication to love. Each concrete situation brings with it a challenge specific to its circumstances. When rising to it enthused and informed by Jesus' teaching and example, human society follows the path to the Christian anarchist kingdom of God.

# Bibliography

[Anonymous]. *The Aims and Means of the Catholic Worker*. Available from http://www.catholicworker.org/aimsandmeanstext.cfm?Number=5 (accessed 2 February 2007).

[Anonymous]. *Anabaptist Network: Core Convictions*. January 2006. Available from http://www.anabaptistnetwork/coreconvictions (accessed 2 February 2007).

[Anonymous]. "The Body of Christ..." *A Pinch of Salt*, issue 5, December 1986, 2.

[Anonymous]. "Book Reviews." *A Pinch of Salt*, issue 14, March 1990, 9.

[Anonymous]. "Canadian Christian Anarchism." *A Pinch of Salt*, issue 3, Pentecost 1986, 11-12.

[Anonymous]. *Catholic Priest Jailed after an Anti-War Service Outside Mod*. Ekklesia, 2007. Available from http://www.ekklesia.co.uk/node/5200 (accessed 3 May 2007).

[Anonymous]. "Christian Anarchism." Unpublished pamphlet. Peterborough: The Digger and Christian Anarchist.

[Anonymous]. *Christian Anarchism*. Labor Law Talk. Available from http://dictionary.laborlawtalk.com/Christian_anarchism (accessed 31 October 2007).

[Anonymous]. "A Christian Anarchist Trainspotter's Guide to Christian Anarchist Books [?]." *A Pinch of Salt*, issue 14, March 1990, 9.

[Anonymous]. *Christianity and State Archive*. Available from http://www.lewrockwell.com/orig2/christianity-arch.html (accessed 21 November 2007).

[Anonymous]. *The Christmas Conspiracy*. Vine and Fig Tree. Available from http://thechristmasconspiracy.com (accessed 10 April 2007).

[Anonymous]. "Cleansing of the Temple." *A Pinch of Salt*, issue 1, September 1985, 12-13.

[Anonymous]. "The Cleansing of the Temple – Burglars for Peace." *A Pinch of Salt*, issue 13, Summer 1989, 10.

[Anonymous]. "Conversation between Scott Albrecht and Ven. Gikan Ito. 29/02/04." *London Catholic Worker*, April 2004, 4-6.

[Anonymous]. *Early Church Quotes*. Jesus Radicals. Available from http://www.jesusradicals.com/library/church_quotes.php (accessed 16 May 2006).

[Anonymous]. "Editorial." *The Raven: anarchist quarterly 25* 7/1 (Spring 1994): 1-2.

[Anonymous]. "From an Old Christian Anarchist Manuscript." *The Digger and Christian Anarchist*, issue 36, April 1990, 7.

[Anonymous]. *God Sends Evil: Why Calvinists Are Anarchists*. Vine and Fig Tree. Available from http://members.aol.com/Patriarchy/predestination/sendevil.htm (accessed 9 November 2005).

[Anonymous]. "He Has Scattered the Proud..." *A Pinch of Salt*, issue 5, December 1986, 2.

[Anonymous]. "In God's Name." *The Economist*, issue 385, 3 November 2007, 3-5.

[Anonymous]. "The Jesuit Reductions." *The Digger and Christian Anarchist*, issue 16, February 1987, 8.

[Anonymous]. "L. C. W. News." *The London Catholic Worker*, issue 17, Christmas 2006, 17.

[Anonymous]. "Letter." *A Pinch of Salt*, issue 8, October 1987, 10.

[Anonymous]. *List of States with Catholic Worker Communities*. The Catholic Worker Movement. Available from http://www.catholicworker.org/communities/commstates.cfm (accessed 12 March 2008).

# Bibliography

[Anonymous]. *Multi-Denominational Statements*. Jesus Radicals. Available from http://www.jesusradicals.com/library/taxes/wartaxes.html (accessed 5 November 2006).

[Anonymous]. *Ninety-Five Theses in Defense of Patriarchy*. Vine and Fig Tree. Available from http://members.aol.com/VF95Theses/thesis.htm (accessed 20 April 2007).

[Anonymous]. "Non-Violent Revolution in India." *A Pinch of Salt*, issue 5, December 1986, 12.

[Anonymous]. "O Come All Ye Faithful." *The Economist*, issue 385, 3 November 2007, 6-10.

[Anonymous]. *Personalism: A Brief Account*. Available from http://www.philosophy.ucf.edu/pers.html (accessed 11 March 2005).

[Anonymous]. "The Power of Non-Violence." *London Catholic Worker*, issue 12, January 2005, 2-3.

[Anonymous]. *Praying through Romans 13*. Vine and Fig Tree. Available from http://members.aol.com/TestOath/Romans13.htm (accessed 9 November 2005).

[Anonymous]. *The Predestined Pencil*. Vine and Fig Tree. Available from http://members.aol.com/Patriarchy/predestination/pencil.htm (accessed 9 November 2005).

[Anonymous]. *Religion and Mythology*. Libertarian Nation Foundation. Available from http://www.libertariannation.org/b/religion.org (accessed 21 November 2007).

[Anonymous]. *The Rigorous Intuition Board*. 4 November 2006. Available from http://p216.ezboard.com/Regarding-praxeologynetanarchistjesuspdf/frigorousintuitionfrm10.ShowMessage?topicID=6754.topic (accessed 20 April 2007).

[Anonymous]. *Roots of the Catholic Worker Movement: Emmanuel Mounier and Personalism*. Casa Juan Diego. Available from http://www.cjd.org/paper/roots/remman.html (accessed 11 March 2005).

[Anonymous]. "Satyagraha – Soul Force." *The Digger*, issue 7, May 1986, 3.

[Anonymous]. *Seventeen Commitments*. Vine and Fig Tree. Available from http://members.aol.com/KEVIN4VFT/17.htm (accessed 25 April 2008).

[Anonymous]. *Sheltered from the Wicked World: Stories and Pictures from Hopedale's Past*. Available from http://www.geocities.com/daninhopedale (accessed 9 March 2008).

[Anonymous]. "The Strategy of Plowshares." *A Pinch of Salt*, issue 13, Summer 1989, 8-9.

[Anonymous]. "Swords into Ploughshares." *A Pinch of Salt*, issue 12, March 1989, 6-7.

[Anonymous]. "Towards an Anarchic Church?" *A Pinch of Salt*, issue 2, March 1986, 7.

[Anonymous]. *Vine and Fig Tree's Web Pages*. Vine and Fig Tree. Available from http://vftonline.org/VFTfiles/Directory/9b_author.htm (accessed 25 April 2008).

[Anonymous]. "A Vote for the State Means..." *A Pinch of Salt*, issue 12, March 1989, 9.

[Anonymous]. "Waging Peace: A Ten Year Experiment with Nonviolent Resistance (Book Review)." *A Pinch of Salt*, issue 13, Summer 1989, 14.

[Anonymous]. *What Is Personalism?* Vine and Fig Tree. Available from http://members.aol.com/Patriarchy/definitions/personalism.htm (accessed 9 November 2005).

[Anonymous]. *Why I Worship a Violent, Vengeful God Who Orders Me to Be Loving and Non-Violent*. Vine and Fig Tree. Available from http://members.aol.com/Patriarchy/predestination/Jesus.htm (accessed 4 November 2005).

[Anonymous]. "Wild Boar Commits Plowshare Action." *A Pinch of Salt*, issue 7, Summer 1987, 16.

[Anonymous]. "The World Turned Upside Down." *A Pinch of Salt*, issue 3, Pentecost 1986, 10.

[Anonymous]. "Yesterday, Tomorrow and Today Is Anarchist." *A Pinch of Salt*, issue 1, September 1985, 5.
A. I. R. "A True Theosophist." *Lucifer* 1 (September 1887): 55-63.
Abraham, Elizabeth. "Christian Anarchy." *A Pinch of Salt*, issue 4, August 1986, 12.
Abraham, J. H. "The Religious Ideas and Social Philosophy of Tolstoy." *International Journal of Ethics* 40/1 (October 1929): 105-120.
Adams, Maurice. "The Ethics of Tolstoy and Nietzsche." *International Journal of Ethics* 11/1 (October 1900): 82-105.
Albrecht, Scott. "The Early Christians and War." *The London Catholic Worker*, issue 21, Christmas 2007, 6-9.
———. "The Politics of Liturgy." *The London Catholic Worker*, issue 14, Advent 2005, 4.
Aleksov, Bojan. "Religious Dissenters and Anarchists in Turn of the Century Hungary." In *Religious Anarchism: New Perspectives*, edited by Alexandre J. M. E. Christoyannopoulos, 47-68. Newcastle upon Tyne: Cambridge Scholars Publishing, 2009.
Alexis-Baker, Andy. "Footwashing Sermon" (audio file on compact disc, recorded 5-6 August 2005). Chicago: Jesus Radicals, 2005.
Alexis-Baker, Nekeisha. "The Church as Resistance to Racism and Nation: A Christian, Anarchist Perspective." In *Religious Anarchism: New Perspectives*, edited by Alexandre J. M. E. Christoyannopoulos, 166-200. Newcastle upon Tyne: Cambridge Scholars Publishing, 2009.
———. "Embracing God and Rejecting Masters: On Christianity, Anarchism and the State." Unpublished article sent by email by its author to me on 17 November 2005.
———. "Embracing God, Rejecting Masters." *Christianarchy* 1/1 (September 2005): 2.
Alexis-Manners, Nekeisha. *Deconstructing Romans 13: Verse 1-2*. Available from http://www.jesusradicals.com/essays/theology/Romans13.htm (accessed 28 October 2005).
Allen, Steve. "Introduction." In *The Book of Ammon*, by Ammon Hennacy, edited by Jim Missey and Joan Thomas, xv-xvii. Baltimore: Fortkamp, 1994.
Andrews, Dave. *Brother Sun and Sister Moons: Engaging a New Dark Age*. 2002. Available from http://anz.jesusradicals.com/newdarkage.pdf (accessed 17 July 2006).
———. *Christi-Anarchy: Discovering a Radical Spirituality of Compassion*. Oxford: Lion, 1999.
———. *The Crux of the Struggle*. 2001. Available from http://www.daveandrews.com.au/publications.html (accessed 3 December 2006).
———. "Heaven on Earth: Trinity, Community and Society." Unpublished draft book sent by email by its author to me on 8 November 2006, later edited and eventually published as *A Divine Society: The Trinity, Community, and Society* (West End: Frank Communications, 2008).
———. *Integral Mission, Relief and Development*. Available from http://www.daveandrews.com.au/publications.html (accessed 3 December 2006).
———. *Love and Fear*. Available from http://www.daveandrews.com.au/publications.html (accessed 3 December 2006).
———. *Not Religion, but Love: Practicing a Radical Spirituality of Compassion*. Cleveland: Pilgrim, 2001.
———. *Plan Be: Be the Change You Want to See in the World*. Milton Keynes: Authentic, 2008.
———. *Reweaving the Fabric of Community*. Available from http://anz.jesusradicals.com/reweaving.pdf (accessed 17 July 2006).
———. *A Spiritual Framework for Ethical Reflection*. Available from http://www.daveandrews.com.au/publications.html (accessed 3 December 2006).

———. *Subversive Spirituality, Ecclesial and Civil Disobedience: A Survey of Biblical Politics as Incarnated in Jesus and Interpreted by Paul*. Available from http://anz.jesusradicals.com/subspirit.pdf (accessed 17 July 2006).

———. *The Urgent Need for a Global Ethic*. Available from http://www.daveandrews.com.au/publications.html (accessed 3 December 2006).

Armytage, W. H. G. "J. C. Kenworthy and the Tolstoyan Communities in England." *American Journal of Economics and Sociology* 16/4 (July 1957): 391-404.

Asad, Talal. *Formations of the Secular: Christianity, Islam, Modernity*. Stanford: Stanford University Press, 2003.

Augustine, Aurelius. *The Sermon on the Mount Expounded, and the Harmony of the Evangelist*. Translated by William Findlay and S. D. F. Salmond. Edited by Marcus Dods, *The Works of Aurelius Augustine, Bishop of Hippo*. Edinburgh: T. and T. Clark, 1873.

Avrich, Paul. "Russian Anarchists and the Civil War." *Russian Review* 27/3 (July 1968): 296-306.

———, ed. *The Anarchists in the Russian Revolution*. Edited by Heinz Lubasz, *Documents of Revolution*. London: Thames and Hudson, 1973.

Baker, Andrew. *Anarchism Is the Only Political Option for Christians*. Available from http://www.jesusradicals.com/essays/theology/anarchism.html (accessed 16 May 2006).

———. *Christi-Anarchy: Discovering a Radical Spirituality of Compassion by David Andrews (Book Review)*. Available from http://www.jesusradicals.com/essays/reviews/christi-anarchy.html (accessed 8 November 2007).

Baker, Andy. *Nonviolent Action in the Temple*. Available from http://www.jesusradicals.com/essays/theology/temple.html (accessed 16 May 2006).

Ballou, Adin. "A Catechism of Non-Resistance." In *The Kingdom of God and Peace Essays*, by Leo Tolstoy, translated by Aylmer Maude, 14-19. New Delhi: Rupa, 2001.

———. *Christian Non-Resistance*. Friends of Adin Ballou. Available from http://www.adinballou.org/cnr.shtml (accessed 12 February 2007).

———. *Christian Non-Resistance in All Its Important Bearings*. Second edition. Oberlin: www.nonresistance.org, 2006. Available from http://www.nonresistance.org/literature.html (accessed 28 March 2007).

———. *Non-Resistance in Relation to Human Governments*. www.nonresistance.org, 1839. Available from http://www.nonresistance.org/literature.html (accessed 28 March 2007).

———. "Non-Resistance: A Basis for Christian Anarchism." In *Patterns of Anarchy: A Collection of Writings on the Anarchist Tradition*, edited by Leonard I. Krimerman and Lewis Perry, 140-149. Garden City: Anchor, 1966.

———. *Practical Christian Socialism: A Conversational Exposition of the True System of Human Society*. New York: AMS, 1974.

Ballou, Adin, and William S. Heywood. *History of the Hopedale Community: From Its Inception to Its Virtual Submergence in the Hopedale Parish*. Philadelphia: Porcupine, 1977.

Banks, Gordon. "Christian Anarchy [?]." *A Pinch of Salt*, issue 10, Summer 1988, 14-15.

Barclay, Harold B. "Islam, Muslim Societies and Anarchy." *Anarchist Studies* 10/1 (2002): 105-118.

Barnhart, Robert K., ed., *Dictionary of Etymology*. Edinburgh: Chambers, 1988.

Barr, Jason. *Radical Hope: Anarchy, Christianity, and the Prophetic Imagination*. 2008. Available from http://propheticheretic.files.wordpress.com/2008/03/radical-hope-anarchy-christianity-and-the-prophetic-imagination.pdf (accessed 11 March 2008).

Barrow, Simon. *Rethinking Religion in an Open Society*. Ekklesia. Available from http://www.ekklesia.co.uk/research/070201 (accessed 17 January 2008).

Bartley, Jonathan. *Easter and Anarchy*. The Guardian, 2009. Available from http://www.guardian.co.uk/commentisfree/belief/2009/apr/07/religion-christianity-easter-disestablishment (accessed 8 April 2009).

———. *Faith and Politics after Christendom: The Church as a Movement for Anarchy*, After Christendom. Milton Keynes: Paternoster, 2006.

Bartolf, Christian. "Tolstoy's Legacy for Mankind: A Manifesto for Nonviolence." Paper presented at *Second International Conference on Tolstoy and World Literature*, Yasnaya Polyana and Tula, 12-28 August 2000. Available from http:://www.fredsakademiet.dk/library/tolstoj/tolstoy.htm (accessed 5 November 2006).

Bayley, John. *Leo Tolstoy, Writers and Their Work*. Plymouth: Northcote House, 1997.

Berdyaev, Nicolas. "Personality, Religion, and Existential Anarchism." In *Patterns of Anarchy: A Collection of Writings on the Anarchist Tradition*, edited by Leonard I. Krimerman and Lewis Perry, 150-164. Garden City: Anchor, 1966.

———. *The Realm of Spirit and the Realm of Caesar*. Translated by Donald A. Lowrie. London: Victor Gollancz, 1952.

———. "The Voice of Conscience from Another World: An Introduction." In *Essays from Tula*, by Leo Tolstoy, translated by Free Age Press, 9-18. London: Sheppard, 1948.

Berkhof, Hendrik. *Christ and the Powers*. Translated by John Howard Yoder. Scottdale: Herald, 1977.

Berrigan, Daniel. "Foreward." In *Remembering Forgetting: A Journey of Non-Violent Resistance to the War in East Timor*, by Ciaron O'Reilly, xi-xii. Sydney: Otford, 2001.

Berrigan, Philip. *Jesus the Anarchist*. Jonah House. Available from http://www.jonahhouse.org/Anita_Roddick.htm (accessed 10 April 2007).

Berrigan, S. J., William Sloane Coffin, Jr., Morton Kelsey, Virginia Mollenkott, James B. Nelson, Robert Raines, and Walter Wink. "The Gift of Sexuality." *A Pinch of Salt*, issue 6, Easter 1987, 6-7.

Birch, Simon. *Religion, Politics and Liberty*. Libertarian Alliance, 1991. Available from http://www.libertarian.co.uk/lapubs/relin003.pdf (accessed 21 November 2007).

Blavatsky, H. P. "Leo Tolstoi and His Unecclesiastical Christianity." *Lucifer* 7 (September 1890): 9-15.

Bowman, Archibald A. "The Elements and Character of Tolstoy's Weltanschauung." *International Journal of Ethics* 23/1 (October 1912): 59-76.

Bradford, George. "Nature, Flesh, Spirit: Against Christianity." *The Fifth Estate*, Summer 1984, 9-10.

Brock, Peter. *Pacifism in Europe to 1914*. Vol. 1, *A History of Pacifism*. Princeton: Princeton University Press, 1972.

———. *The Political and Social Doctrines of the Unity of Czech Brethren in the Fifteenth and Early Sixteenth Centuries*. The Hague: Mouton and Co., 1957.

———. *The Roots of War Resistance: Pacifism from the Early Church to Tolstoy*. New York: Fellowship of Reconciliation, 1981.

———. "Tolstoyism and the Hungarian Peasant." *Slavonic and Eastern European Review* 58/3 (July 1980): 345-369.

Brown, Jason. "Cooperation: A Common Principle of Mormonism and Anarchism." *The Mormon Worker*, issue 2, January 2008. Available from http://www.themormonworker.org/articles/issue2/cooperation_a_common_principle_of_mormonism_and_anarchism.php (accessed 2 May 2008).

———. "The Zion/Babylon Dualism in Mormonism and Anarchism." *The Mormon Worker*, issue 3, March 2008, 4-5. Available from http://www.themormonworker.org/articles/issue3/volume_1_issue_3.pdf (accessed 2 May 2008).

# Bibliography

Bushman, Cory. "A Brief History of Peasant Tolstoyans." *The Mormon Worker*, issue 2, January 2008. Available from http://www.themormonworker.org/articles/issue2/a_brief_history_of_peasant_tolstoyants.php (accessed 2 May 2008).

———. "The Mormon Worker." *The Mormon Worker*, issue 1, September 2007, 1. Available from http://www.themormonworker.org/articles/issue1/volume1_issue1.pdf (accessed 28 February 2008).

Bushman, Tyler. "Borders from an Eternal Perspective." *The Mormon Worker*, issue 2, January 2008. Available from http://www.themormonworker.org/articles/issue2/borders_from_an_eternal_perspective.php (accessed 2 May 2008).

———. "Revolutionary Charity." *The Mormon Worker*, issue 1, September 2007, 16. Available from http://www.themormonworker.org/articles/issue1/volume1_issue1.pdf (accessed 28 February 2008).

Camara, Dom Helder. "Violence, Non-Violence and the Christian." *London Catholic Worker*, issue 13, April 2005, 6.

Carson, Stephen W. *Biblical Anarchism*. 7 June 2001. Available from http://www.lewrockwell.com/orig/carson2.html (accessed 8 November 2007).

———. *Christians in Politics: The Return of the 'Religious Right'*. 30 October 2003. Available from http://www.lewrockwell.com/carson/carson17.html (accessed 21 November 2007).

———. *Separation of Church and Nation*. 2002. Available from http://www.lewrockwell.com/orig/carson6.html (accessed 21 November 2007).

Carter, Timothy. "Commentary: The Irony of Romans 13:1-8." *Third Way*, issue 28, May 2005, 21.

Casanova, José. *Public Religions in the Modern World*. Chicago: University of Chicago Press, 1994.

———. "Religion and Politics: Global Affairs." Paper presented at *Ph.D. course on Religion and Politics*, Copenhagen, 22 October 2007

———. "Religion, European Secular Identities, and European Integration." In *Religion in an Expanding Europe*, edited by Timothy A. Byrnes and Peter J. Katzenstein, 65-92. Cambridge: Cambridge University Press, 2006.

———. "Rethinking Secularization: A Global Comparative Perspective." *The Hedgehog Review* 8/1-2 (Spring and Summer 2006): 7-22.

Cavanaugh, William T. "The City: Beyond Secular Parodies." In *Radical Orthodoxy: A New Theology*, edited by John Milbank, Catherine Pickstock and Graham Ward, 182-200. London: Routledge, 1999.

———. "A Fire Strong Enough to Consume the House: The Wars of Religion and the Rise of the State." *Modern Theology* 11/4 (October 1995): 397-420.

———. "Killing for the Telephone Company: Why the Nation-State Is Not the Keeper of the Common Good." *Modern Theology* 20/2 (April 2004): 243-274.

———. *Torture and Eucharist: Theology, Politics, and the Body of Christ*. Oxford: Blackwell, 1998.

———. "The World in a Wafer: A Geography of the Eucharist as Resistance to Globalization." *Modern Theology* 15/2 (April 1999): 181-196.

Chan, Andy. "Violence, Nonviolence, and the Concept of Revolution in Anarchist Thought." *Anarchist Studies* 12/2 (2004): 103-123.

Charlie. "The Love of Jesus." *A Pinch of Salt*, issue 5, December 1986, 5.

Christian, R. F., ed. *Tolstoy's Diaries*. 2 vols. Vol. 1. New York: Scribner, 1985.

———, ed. *Tolstoy's Letters*. Vol. 1. London: Athlone, 1978.

Christoyannopoulos, Alexandre. "Religious Anarchism Panel: A Call for Papers." *A Pinch of Salt*, issue 16, December 2007, 5.
———. "Tolstoy the Peculiar Christian Anarchist." *A Pinch of Salt*, issue 15, December 2007, 6-7.
———. "Tolstoy the Peculiar Christian Anarchist." Paper presented at *God Save the Queen: Anarchism and Christianity Today*, All Hallows Church, Leeds, 2-4 June 2006. Available from http://uk.jesusradicals.com/Tolstoy%20the%20Christian%20anarchist%20-%20draft%201.pdf (accessed 4 June 2006).
Christoyannopoulos, Alexandre J. M. E. "Christian Anarchism: A Revolutionary Reading of the Bible." In *New Perspectives on Anarchism*, edited by Nathan Jun and Shane Wahl, 135-152. Lanham: Rowman & Littlefield, 2009.
———. "Leo Tolstoy on the State: A Detailed Picture of Tolstoy's Denunciation of State Violence and Deception." *Anarchist Studies* 16/1 (2008): 20-47.
———. "Responding to the State: Christian Anarchists on Romans 13, Rendering to Caesar, and Civil Disobedience." In *Religious Anarchism: New Perspectives*, edited by Alexandre J. M. E. Christoyannopoulos, 106-144. Newcastle upon Tyne: Cambridge Scholars Publishing, 2009.
———. "Turning the Other Cheek to Terrorism: Reflections on the Contemporary Significance of Leo Tolstoy's Exegesis of the Sermon on the Mount." *Politics and Religion* 1/1 (April 2008): 27-54.
Christoyannopoulos, Alexandre J. M. E., and Joseph Milne. "Love, Justice, and Social Eschatology." *The Heythrop Journal* 48/6 (November 2007): 972-991.
Clairborne, Shane, and Chris Haw. *Appendix 3: Subordination and Revolution: What About Romans 13?* Zondervan, 2008. Available from http://www.jesusforpresident.org/download/Web_Appendix_3.pdf (accessed 4 August 2009).
———. *Jesus for President: Politics for Ordinary Radicals*. Grand Rapids: Zondervan, 2008.
Cohn, Jesse. *Messianic Troublemakers: The Past and Present Jewish Anarchism*. Available from http://www.zeek.net/politics_0504.shtml (accessed 14 February 2006).
Cohn, Norman. *The Pursuit of the Millennium: Revolutionary Millenarians and Mystical Anarchists of the Middle Ages*. London: Paladin, 1970.
Coles, Robert. "Introduction." In *The Long Loneliness: The Autobiography of the Legendary Catholic Social Activist*, by Dorothy Day, 1-6. New York: HarperSanFrancisco, 1952.
Cornell, Tom. "Air Raid Drills and the New York Catholic Worker." *The Catholic Worker*, issue 73, May 2006, 1, 6.
———. *My Dorothy Day*. Casa Juan Diego. Available from http://www.cjd.org/paper/dday.html (accessed 14 February 2007).
Coy, Patrick G. "The One-Person Revolution of Ammon Hennacy." In *A Revolution of the Heart: Essays on the Catholic Worker*, edited by Patrick G. Coy, 134-173. Philadelphia: Temple University Press, 1988.
———, ed. *A Revolution of the Heart: Essays on the Catholic Worker*. Philadelphia: Temple University Press, 1988.
Craig, Kevin. *About the Author*. Vine and Fig Tree. Available from http://libertyundergod.org/author.htm (accessed 25 April 2008).
Cranfield, C. E. B. "The Christian's Political Responsibility According to the New Testament." *Scottish Journal of Theology* 15/2 (June 1962): 176-192.
Creskey, Jim. *A Most Unusual Saint*. The Tablet, 2000. Available from http://www.thetablet.co.uk/articles/6828 (accessed 14 February 2007).

Crosby, Ernest Howard. *Tolstoy and His Message*. BoondocksNet Edition, 2000. Available from http:www.broondocksnet.com/editions/tolstoy/index.html (accessed 18 August 2003).

Crowder, George. *Classical Anarchism: The Political Thought of Godwin, Proudhon, Bakunin and Kropotkin*. Oxford: Clarendon, 1991.

Damico, Linda H. *The Anarchist Dimension of Liberation Theology*. New York: Peter Lang, 1987.

Dart, Ron. *Christian Anarchy: An Aberration of Sorts*. Clarion, 2006. Available from http://clarionjournal.typepad.com/clarion_journal_of_spirit/2006/06/christian_anarc.html (accessed 10 April 2007).

———. *A. James Reimer and Anabaptist Anarchism: A Prophet to His People*. Clarion, 2006. Available from http://clarionjournal.typepad.com/clarion_journal_of_spirit/2006/06/a_james_reimer_.html (accessed 10 April 2007).

———. *Stanley Hauerwas and Noam Chomsky: Anarchist Affinities*. Clarion, 2006. Available from http://clarionjournal.typepad.com/clarion_journal_of_spirit/2006/06/stanley_hauerwa.html (accessed 10 April 2007).

Davie, Anna. "Setting Prisoners Free: A Workshop on an Anarchist Christian Response to Imprisonment." Paper presented at *God Save the Queen: Anarchism and Christianity Today*, All Hallows Church, Leeds, 2-4 June 2006. Available from http://uk.jesusradicals.com/Setting_the_Prisoners_Fre.pdf (accessed 4 June 2006).

Davies, Jim. *Christian Anarchist: An Oxymoron?* Strike the Root, 9 August 2005. Available from http://www.strike-the-root.com/52/davies/davies1.html (accessed 21 November 2007).

Davis, Richard. "From Patriotism to Peace." *Scoop*, 25 October 2001. Available from http://www.scoop.co.nz/stories/HL0110/S00134.htm (accessed 4 April 2008).

———. *Slaver or Saviour?* Available from http://www.rad.net.nz/267.0.html (accessed 4 April 2008).

Davis, Richard A. "Love, Hate, and Kierkegaard's Christian Politics of Indifference." In *Religious Anarchism: New Perspectives*, edited by Alexandre J. M. E. Christoyannopoulos, 82-105. Newcastle upon Tyne: Cambridge Scholars Publishing, 2009.

Day, Dorothy. "Act of Faith." *The London Catholic Worker*, issue 21, Christmas 2007, 5.

———. "Deliver Us from Fear." *The Catholic Worker*, issue 73, May 2006, 1, 5.

———. *Farming Communes*. The Catholic Worker, 1944. Available from http://www.catholicworker.org/dorothyday/reprint.cfm?TextID=149 (accessed 11 April 2005).

———. "Foreword." In *The Book of Ammon*, by Ammon Hennacy, edited by Jim Missey and Joan Thomas, ix-xiv. Baltimore: Fortkamp, 1994.

———. "The Green Revolution." In *Patterns of Anarchy: A Collection of Writings on the Anarchist Tradition*, edited by Leonard I. Krimerman and Lewis Perry, 372-378. Garden City: Anchor, 1966.

———. "Introduction." In *Easy Essays*, by Peter Maurin, i-vii. Washington: Rose Hill, 2003.

———. *Loaves and Fishes*. London: Victor Gollancz, 1963.

———. *The Long Loneliness: The Autobiography of the Legendary Catholic Social Activist*. New York: HarperSanFrancisco, 1952.

———. *On Pilgrimage*. Edinburgh: T. and T. Clark, 1999.

———. "On Voluntary Poverty." *The Digger*, issue 7, May 1986, 8.

———. *Peter's Program*. The Catholic Worker, 1955. Available from http://www.catholicworker.org/dorothyday/reprint.cfm?TextID=176 (accessed 11 April 2005).

———. *Peter Maurin: Apostle to the World*. Maryknoll: Orbis, 2004.
———. *Selected Writings: By Little and by Little*. Edited by Robert Ellsberg. Maryknoll: Orbis, 2005.
de Raaij, André. *A Brief Look at the Life of Felix Ortt, Prominent Dutch Christian Anarchist*. portrettengalerij, 2007. Available from http://portrettengalerij.blogspot.com (accessed 10 April 2007).
———. "The International Fraternity Which Never Was: Dutch Christian Anarchism between Optimism and near-Defeat, 1893-1906." In *Religious Anarchism: New Perspectives*, edited by Alexandre J. M. E. Christoyannopoulos, 69-80. Newcastle upon Tyne: Cambridge Scholars Publishing, 2009.
———. *Mysticism and Action: Christian Anarchism as a Paradigm*. Available from http://www.geocities.com/christianarchy/bergenmyst.htm (accessed 31 October 2003).
———. "On Ortt, Dutch Christian Anarchist, in English, on the Net" (email to me, 16 April 2007).
———. "On Reading Tolstoy" (email to me, 22 April 2007).
———. *Parallels or Influence: The Dutch Christian Anarchist Movement in 1907, and the Landauer Connection*. Available from http://www.geocities.com/christianarchy/haifa.html (accessed 31 October 2003).
Deming, Barbara. "On Anger." *A Pinch of Salt*, issue 1, September 1985, 10-11.
Dick. "Pure Quakerism and Ploughshares." *A Pinch of Salt*, issue 8, October 1987, 11.
Dietrich, Jeff. "Catholic Worker Celebrates." *A Pinch of Salt*, issue 10, Summer 1988, 4.
Douglass, Jim. "Civil Disobedience as Prayer." *A Pinch of Salt*, issue 3, Pentecost 1986, 8-9.
Downes, Lawrence. "Editorial Observer: From the Bowery to Guantánamo with Dorothy Day." *The New York Times*, 8 December 2005, 38.
Duane, Michael. "Church, State and Freedom." *The Raven: anarchist quarterly 25* 7/1 (Spring 1994): 82-95.
Dudley, Jeremy. "Another Letter." *A Pinch of Salt*, issue 9, Spring 1988, 19.
Dupré, Louis. *Passage to Modernity: An Essay in the Hermeneutics of Nature and Culture*. New Haven: Yale University Press, 1993.
Earp, Charley. "Christianity and Anarchism" (audio file on compact disc, recorded 5-6 August 2005). Chicago: Jesus Radicals, 2005.
Edmonds, Rosemary. "Introduction." In *Resurrection*, by Leo Tolstoy, translated by Rosemary Edmonds, 5-16. London: Penguin, 1966.
Egan, Eileen. *Dorothy Day and the Permanent Revolution*. Erie: Pax Christi U.S.A., 1983.
———. "Dorothy Day: Pilgrim of Peace." In *A Revolution of the Heart: Essays on the Catholic Worker*, edited by Patrick G. Coy, 69-114. Philadelphia: Temple University Press, 1988.
———. "Foreword." In *Easy Essays*, by Peter Maurin, viii-xii. Washington: Rose Hill, 2003.
Eikhenbaum, B. M. "On Tolstoy's Crises." In *Tolstoy: A Collection of Critical Essays*, edited by Ralph E. Matlaw, translated by Ralph E. Matlaw, 52-55. Englewood Cliffs: Prentice-Hall, 1967.
Eller, Vernard. *Christian Anarchy: Jesus' Primacy over the Powers*. Eugene: Wipf and Stock, 1987.
Elliott, Michael C. *Anarchism: An Annotated Bibliography*. 2005. Available from http://anz.jesusradicals.com/elliott.doc (accessed 17 July 2006).
———. *Freedom, Justice and Christian Counter-Culture*. London: SCM, 1990.
Ellis, Marc H. *Peter Maurin: Prophet in the Twentieth Century*. Washington: Rose Hill, 2003.

———. "Peter Maurin: To Bring the Social Order to Christ." In *A Revolution of the Heart: Essays on the Catholic Worker*, edited by Patrick G. Coy, 15-46. Philadelphia: Temple University Press, 1988.

Ellsberg, Robert. "Preface to the Anniversary Edition." In *Selected Writings: By Little and by Little*, by Dorothy Day, xi-xii. Maryknoll: Orbis, 2005.

Ellul, Jacques. "Anarchism and Christianity." In *Jesus and Marx: From Gospel to Ideology*, translated by Joyce Main Hanks, 153-177. Grand Rapids: William B. Eerdmans, 1998.

———. *Anarchy and Christianity*. Translated by George W. Bromiley. Grand Rapids: William B. Eerdmans, 1991.

———. *Apocalypse: The Book of Revelation*. Translated by George W. Schreiner. New York: Seabury, 1977.

———. *The Judgement of Jonah*. Translated by Geoffrey W. Bromiley. Grand Rapids: William B. Eerdmans, 1971.

———. *La Subversion Du Christianisme*. Paris: Seuil, 1984.

———. *The Meaning of the City*. Translated by Dennis Pardee. [Grand Rapids?]: William B. Eerdmans, 1993.

———. *The Political Illusion*. Translated by Konrad Kellen. New York: Vintage, 1967.

———. *The Politics of God and the Politics of Man*. Translated by Geoffrey W. Bromiley. Grand Rapids: William B. Eerdmans, 1972.

———. *Violence: Reflections from a Christian Perspective*. Translated by Cecilia Gaul Kings. London: SCM, 1970.

Faure, Sébastien. "Twelve Proofs of the Non-Existence of God." *The Raven: anarchist quarterly 25* 7/1 (Spring 1994): 37-67.

Fiscella, Anthony. "Imagining an Islamic Anarchism: A New Field of Study Is Ploughed." In *Religious Anarchism: New Perspectives*, edited by Alexandre J. M. E. Christoyannopoulos, 280-317. Newcastle upon Tyne: Cambridge Scholars Publishing, 2009.

Flew, Antony. "Tolstoi and the Meaning of Life." *Ethics: An International Journal of Social, Political, and Legal Philosophy* 73/2 (January 1963): 110-118.

Fontana, Retta. *Citizen Jesus*. Strike the Root, 5 June 2006. Available from http://www.strike-the-root.com/61/fontana/fontana3.html (accessed 21 November 2007).

Fowler, R. B. . "The Anarchist Tradition of Political Thought." *The Western Political Quarterly* 25/4 (December 1972): 738-752.

Fox, Tom. "The Force of War and the Force of Peace? The Same Force Moving in the Opposite Direction?" *The Mormon Worker*, issue 1, September 2007, 1-2. Available from http://www.themormonworker.org/articles/issue1/volume1_issue1.pdf (accessed 28 February 2008).

Franco, Alberto. *A Revolução É a Minha Namorada: Memória De António Gonçalves Correia, Anarquista Alentejano*. Castro Verde: Câmara Municipal de Castro Verde, n.d.

Fueloep-Miller, Rene. "Tolstoy the Apostolic Crusader." *Russian Review* 19/2 (April 1960): 99-121.

Gallie, W. B. "Tolstoy: From 'War and Peace' to 'the Kingdom of God Is within You'." In *Philosophers of Peace and War: Kant, Clausewitz, Marx, Engels and Tolstoy*, 100-132. London: Cambridge University Press, 1978.

Gandhi, M. K. "Introduction." In *Recollections and Essays*, by Leo Tolstoy, translated by Aylmer Maude, 413-415. Vol. 21, *Tolstóy Centenary Edition*. London: Oxford University Press, 1937.

Garrison, William Lloyd. "Declaration of Sentiments Adopted by the Peace Convention." In *The Kingdom of God and Peace Essays*, by Leo Tolstoy, translated by Aylmer Maude, 5-10. New Delhi: Rupa, 2001.

Gay, Kathlyn, and Martin K. Gay, eds., *Encyclopedia of Political Anarchy*. Oxford: ABC-CLIO, 1999.

Gneuhs, Geoffrey B. "Peter Maurin's Personalist Democracy." In *A Revolution of the Heart: Essays on the Catholic Worker*, edited by Patrick G. Coy, 47-68. Philadelphia: Temple University Press, 1988.

Goddard, Andrew. *Living the Word, Resisting the World: The Life and Thought of Jacques Ellul*. Edited by David F. Wright, Trevor A. Hart, Anthony N. S. Lane, Anthony C. Thiselton and Kevin J. Vanhoozer, *Paternoster Theological Monographs*. Milton Keynes: Paternoster, 2002.

Goodchild, Chris. "Christian Anarchism." Unpublished pamphlet distributed by London Catholic Workers at the London Anarchist Bookfair in October 2003.

Gordon. "Contempt of Court." *A Pinch of Salt*, issue 4, August 1986, 14.

Gordon, Uri. "Αναρχία: What Did the Greeks Actually Say?" *Anarchist Studies* 14/1 (2006): 84-91.

Grant, R. M. *A Short History of the Interpretation of the Bible*. London: Adam and Charles Black, 1965.

Gray, Phillip W. "Peace, Peace, but There Is No Peace: A Critique of Christian Pacifist Communitarianism." *Politics and Religion* 1/3 (December 2008): 411-435.

Greenwood, E. B. "Tolstoy and Religion." In *New Essays on Tolstoy*, edited by Malcolm Jones, 149-174. Cambridge: Cambridge University Press, 1978.

———. *Tolstoy: The Comprehensive Vision*. London: Methuen, 1975.

Gregg, Richard B. *The Power of Nonviolence*. Abridged edition. Lusaka: M. M. Temple, 1960.

Guseinov, A. A. "Faith, God, and Nonviolence in the Teachings of Lev Tolstoy." *Russian Studies in Philosophy* 38/2 (Fall 1999): 89-103.

Gustafson, Richard F. *Leo Tolstoy: Resident and Stranger: A Study in Fiction and Theology*. Princeton: Princeton University Press, 1986.

Gutierrez, Gustavo. "Liberation Theology." In *Ideals and Ideologies: A Reader*, edited by Terence Ball and Richard Dagger, translated by Sister Caridad Inda and John Eagleson, 409-416. New York: Longman, 1999.

Halliday, Roy. *Christian Libertarians*. Libertarian Nation Foundation. Available from http://www.libertariannation.org/a/f42h2.html (accessed 8 November 2007).

Hamilton, Richard. "Anger: An Anarchist Perspective." *The Digger and Christian Anarchist*, issue 36, April 1990, 9.

Hancock [?], Stephen. "Christian Anarchy – Give It a Go." *A Pinch of Salt*, issue 9, Spring 1988, 3.

———. "Christian Anarchy: Jesus' Primacy over the Powers (Book Review)." *A Pinch of Salt*, issue 8, October 1987, 13.

———. "Easter." *A Pinch of Salt*, issue 2, March 1986, 2.

———. "Interview with Dan Berrigan." *A Pinch of Salt*, issue 11, Autumn/Winter 1988, 10-11.

———. "Letters." *The Digger and Christian Anarchist*, issue 12, October 1986, 3.

———. "On Trying to Love Police People." *A Pinch of Salt*, issue 4, August 1986, 13.

———. "The Politics of Jesus (Book Review)." *A Pinch of Salt*, issue 6, Easter 1987, 12, 14.

———. "Third Birthday Polemic." *A Pinch of Salt*, issue 11, Autumn/Winter 1988, 8.

———. "Transfiguration Plowshares Begin Fourth Disarmament of Missouri Missile Site." *A Pinch of Salt*, issue 8, October 1987, 4.

Hancock, Stephen. "'No Rearmament Plan'." *A Pinch of Salt*, issue 13, Summer 1989, 11.

Hastings, James, ed., *Dictionary of the Bible*. Edinburgh: T. & T. Clark, 1909.

Hauerwas, Stanley. "The Church and Liberal Democracy: The Moral Limits of a Secular Polity." In *A Community of Character: Towards a Constructive Christian Ethic*, 72-86: University of Notre Dame, 1981. Available from

http://www.jesusradicals.com/library/hauerwas/Church&LiberalDemocracy.pdf (accessed 16 May 2006).
Haynes, Jeffrey. *An Introduction to International Relations and Religion*. Harrow: Pearson, 2007.
Haywood, Peter. "If Truth Were Known." *A Pinch of Salt*, issue 5, December 1986, 11.
Hebden, Keith. "Binding the Strongman: A Political Reading of Mark's Gospel (Book Review)." *The London Catholic Worker*, issue 17, Christmas 2006, 4.
———. "Building a Dalit World in the Shell of the Old: Conversations between Dalit Indigenous Practice and Western Anarchist Thought." In *Religious Anarchism: New Perspectives*, edited by Alexandre J. M. E. Christoyannopoulos, 145-165. Newcastle upon Tyne: Cambridge Scholars Publishing, 2009.
———. "Editorial: A Pinch of Salt to Shake the Empire." *A Pinch of Salt*, issue 15, December 2007, 2.
———. "A Subversive Gospel." *The London Catholic Worker*, issue 20, Autumn 2007, 14.
———. "The Subversive Gospel: Christianity and Anarchism Conference 2007." *A Pinch of Salt*, issue 16, December 2007, 6.
Helms, Robert. *Hugh Owen Pentecost (1848-1907): A Biographical Sketch*. Dead Anarchists. Available from http://www.deadanarchists.org/Pentecost/PentecostBio.html (accessed 12 November 2007).
Hennacy, Ammon. *The Book of Ammon*. Edited by Jim Missey and Joan Thomas. Second edition. Baltimore: Fortkamp, 1994.
———. "Can a Christian Be an Anarchist?" In *Patterns of Anarchy: A Collection of Writings on the Anarchist Tradition*, edited by Leonard I. Krimerman and Lewis Perry, 48-52. Garden City: Anchor, 1966.
———. "The One-Man Revolution." In *Patterns of Anarchy: A Collection of Writings on the Anarchist Tradition*, edited by Leonard I. Krimerman and Lewis Perry, 364-371. Garden City: Anchor, 1966.
Heppenstall, Annie. "Anarchy and the Old Testament." Paper presented at *God Save the Queen: Anarchism and Christianity Today*, All Hallows Church, Leeds, 2-4 June 2006. Available from http://uk.jesusradicals.com/otanarchy.pdf (accessed 4 June 2006).
Herman, A. L. "Satyagraha: A New Indian Word for Some Old Ways of Western Thinking." *Philosophy East and West* 19/2 (April 1969): 123-142.
Heywood, Andrew. *Political Ideologies: An Introduction*. Second edition. London: Macmillan, 1998.
Holben, Lawrence. *All the Way to Heaven: A Theological Reflection on Dorothy Day, Peter Maurin and the Catholic Worker*. Marion: Rose Hill, 1997.
Holladay, Martin. "Spears into Pruning Hooks." *A Pinch of Salt*, issue 4, August 1986, 7.
Holman, M. J. de K. "The Purleigh Colony: Tolstoyan Togetherness in the Late 1890s." In *New Essays on Tolstoy*, edited by Malcolm Jones, 194-222. Cambridge: Cambridge University Press, 1978.
Hone [?], Kenny. "The Church of Satan." *A Pinch of Salt*, issue 14, March 1990, 8.
———. "Editorial." *The Digger and Christian Anarchist*, issue 12, October 1986, 1.
———. "From Me to You." *The Digger*, issue 7, May 1986, 2.
———. "The Gift." *A Pinch of Salt*, issue 3, Pentecost 1986, 12.
———. "Reply to Thornton Kimes." *The Digger and Christian Anarchist*, issue 13, November 1986, 7.
Hone, K. C. "Who Were the Diggers?" *A Pinch of Salt*, issue 15, December 2007, 9.
Hone, Kenneth C. "Gerrard Winstanley and the Diggers." Peterboro: Peterboro Anarchist Agency, 1984.
Hopton, Terry. "Tolstoy, God and Anarchism." *Anarchist Studies* 8 (2000): 27-52.

Hovey, Craig. "Making Caesar Tell the Truth and Telling the Truth to Caesar: Christian Witness as Fearless Speech and Radical Protest." Paper presented at *Faith's Public Role: Politics and Theology*, Cambridge, 7 April 2005. Available from http://www.st-edmunds.cam.ac.uk/vhi/fis/fpr/hovey.pdf (accessed 20 May 2005).

Hunt, James D. *Adin Ballou, Tolstoy, and Gandhi*. 2002. Available from http://www.adinballou.org/BallouTolstoyGandhi.shtml (accessed 6 March 2008).

Imminent Anarchy Press. "The Greatest Violence Is Committed by the State: Reassessing the Works of Tolstoy." *Peace News*, 28 October 1983, 10-11.

Iwańczak, Wojciech. "Between Pacifism and Anarchy: Peter Chelčický's Teaching About Society." *Journal of Medieval History* 23/3 (1997): 271-283.

Jackson, Ben. "God's Left Wing." *A Pinch of Salt*, issue 1, September 1985, 8-9.

James. "Lifestyle and Survival." *A Pinch of Salt*, issue 8, October 1987, 7-8.

Jamie. "The World Turned Upside Down." *A Pinch of Salt*, issue 5, December 1986, 12-13.

Jarvis, Eddie. "Fascist Skeletons – in Catholic Cupboards." *The London Catholic Worker*, issue 21, Christmas 2007, 10-12.

Jeremy. "Letter." *A Pinch of Salt*, issue 4, August 1986, 11.

Johnston, Laurie. "Love Your Enemies – Even in the Age of Terrorism?" *Political Theology* 6/1 (2005): 87-106.

Kellerman, Bill, and Bill McCormick. "Anarchy and Christianity: An Exchange." *The Fifth Estate*, Summer 1984, 8, 22.

Kennan, George. "A Visit to Count Tolstoi." *The Century Magazine* 34/2 (June 1887): 252-265.

Kentish, Jane. "Introduction." In *A Confession and Other Religious Writings*, by Leo Tolstoy, 7-15. London: Penguin, 1987.

Kinjo-Bushman, Kristen. "Peter Chelčický." *The Mormon Worker*, issue 3, March 2008, 10, 18. Available from http://www.themormonworker.org/articles/issue3/volume_1_issue_3.pdf (accessed 2 May 2008).

Kinna, Ruth. *Anarchism: A Beginner's Guide*. Oxford: Oneworld, 2005.

Kirk, Daniel, ed. *Quotations from Chairman Jesus*. New York: Bantam, 1971.

Klejment, Anne. "War Resistance and Property Destruction: The Catonsville Nine Draft Board Raid and Catholic Worker Pacifism." In *A Revolution of the Heart: Essays on the Catholic Worker*, edited by Patrick G. Coy, 272-309. Philadelphia: Temple University Press, 1988.

Kofmel, Erich. "Comparative Political Theology." Paper presented at *Fourth General Conference of the European Consortium for Political Research*, University of Pisa, Italy, 6 September 2007. Available from http://www.essex.ac.uk/ecpr/events/generalconference/pisa/papers/PP1206.pdf (accessed 28 October 2007).

Kopel, David B. *Evolving Christian Attitudes Towards Personal and National Self-Defense*. Social Science Research Network, 2007. Available from http://ssrn.com/abstract=1028849 (accessed 8 April 2008).

Krimerman, Leonard I., and Lewis Perry, eds. *Patterns of Anarchy: A Collection of Writings on the Anarchist Tradition*. Garden City: Anchor, 1966.

Kropotkin, Peter. *'Anarchism'*. Encyclopaedia Britannica, 1910. Available from http://dwardmac.pitzer.edu/Anarchist_Archives/Kropotkin/britanniaanarchy.html (accessed 26 April 2007).

———. *Modern Science and Anarchism*. The Social Science Club 1903. Available from http://dwardmac.pitzer.edu/anarchist_archives/kropotkin/science/toc.html (accessed 7 March 2008).

Küng, Hans. *Christianity: Its Essence and History*. Translated by John Bowden. London: SCM, 1995.

Langley, Scott. "End the Death Penalty Now!" *The Catholic Worker*, issue 73, May 2006, 3.
Lavrin, Janko. "Tolstoy and Gandhi." *Russian Review* 19/2 (April 1960): 132-139.
Lawrence, Andrew. "Power Politics and Love." *A Pinch of Salt*, issue 12, March 1989, 8-9.
Lee, V. *Tolstoi as Prophet: Notes on the Psychology of Asceticism*. Brentano's, 1909. Available from http://dwardmac.pitzer.edu/Anarchist_archives/lee/tolstoi.html (accessed 8 August 2007).
Lord [?], Kenny. "Synthesis." *The Digger and Christian Anarchist*, issue 21, October 1987, 2-3.
Louise. "Religion Screws You Up." *A Pinch of Salt*, issue 8, October 1987, 10.
Lumsden, Peter. "Only the Atheist Can Understand Religion." *The Raven: anarchist quarterly 25* 7/1 (Spring 1994): 26-28.
Lyttelton, Edith. "Introduction to a Confession and What I Believe." In *A Confession and the Gospel in Brief*, by Leo Tolstoy, translated by Aylmer Maude, vii-xiv. Vol. 11, *Tolstóy Centenary Edition*. London: Oxford University Press, 1933.
Maas, A. J. *Resurrection of Jesus Christ*. Robert Appleton, 1911. Available from http://www.newadvent.org/cathen/12789a.htm (accessed 1 October 2007).
Madson, Joshua. "Means and Ends in a Post 9/11 World." *The Mormon Worker*, issue 2, January 2008. Available from http://www.themormonworker.org/articles/issue2/means_and_ends_in_a_post_9_11_world.php (accessed 2 May 2008).
Mandell, Andrew. "Ellul and the Left" (audio file on compact disc, recorded 5-6 August 2005). Chicago: Jesus Radicals, 2005.
Marshall, Chris. "Following Christ in Life: The Anabaptist-Mennonite Tradition." *Reality* 7/37 (2000): 19-26.
Marshall, Peter. *Demanding the Impossible: A History of Anarchism*. London: Fontana, 1993.
Martin, David. *A General Theory of Secularization*. New York: Harper and Bow, 1978.
Mathews, Don. *A Catholic Looks at the State*. 29 March 2002. Available from http://www.lewrockwell.com/orig/mathews5.html (accessed 21 November 2007).
Maude, Aylmer. "Editor's Note." In *Recollections and Essays*, by Leo Tolstoy, translated by Aylmer Maude, xi-xxxv. Vol. 21, *Tolstóy Centenary Edition*. London: Oxford University Press, 1937.
———. "Editor's Note." In *A Confession and the Gospel in Brief*, by Leo Tolstoy, translated by Aylmer Maude, xv-xxiv. Vol. 11, *Tolstóy Centenary Edition*. London: Oxford University Press, 1933.
———. "Introduction." In *The Kingdom of God and Peace Essays*, by Leo Tolstoy, translated by Aylmer Maude, vii-xii. New Delhi: Rupa, 2001.
———. *The Life of Tolstóy*. 2 vols, *Tolstóy Centenary Edition*. London: Oxford University Press, 1930.
———. *The Life of Tolstóy: Later Years*. Vol. 2, *Tolstóy Centenary Edition*. London: Oxford University Press, 1930.
———. *Tolstoy and His Problems*. London: Grand Richards, 1901.
Maurin, Peter. *Easy Essays*. Washington: Rose Hill, 2003.
———. *Easy Essays*. London: Sheed and Ward, 1938.
———. "What the Catholic Worker Believes." *The London Catholic Worker*, issue 15, Lent 2006, 5.
McKenna, Jarrod. "Be Purple! And Other Unhelpful Commands." In *Plan Be: Be the Change You Want to See in the World*, by Dave Andrews, 85-93. Milton Keynes: Authentic, 2008.
McLellan, David. *Unto Caesar: The Political Relevance of Christianity*. London: University of Notre Dame Press, 1993.

———. "Unto Caesar: The Political Relevance of Christianity." In *Religion in Public Life*, edited by Dan Cohn-Sherbok and David McLellan, 110-121. New York: St. Martin's, 1992.

———, ed. *Political Christianity: A Reader*. London: SPCK, 1997.

McMaken, Ryan. *Taking Stock: Christianity and the State*. 1 April 2002. Available from http://www.lewrockwell.com/mcmaken/mcmaken57.html (accessed 21 November 2007).

Medzhibovskaya, Inessa. "Tolstoi's Response to Terror and Revolutionary Violence." *Kritika* 9/3 (Summer 2008): 505-531.

Meggitt [?], Justin. "Anarchism and the New Testament: Some Reflections." *A Pinch of Salt*, issue 10, Summer 1988, 10-12.

———. "Jesus and Marx: From Gospel to Ideology (Book Review)." *A Pinch of Salt*, issue 12, March 1989, 17.

Meggitt, Justin. "One of Three Letters." *A Pinch of Salt*, issue 9, Spring 1988, 7.

Merrill, Walter M. *Against Wind and Tide: A Biography of Wm. Lloyd Garrison*. Cambridge: Harvard University Press, 1963.

Michell, John. "Jeremiah O'Callaghans Fight against Usury." *The Digger*, issue 7, May 1986, 5-6.

Milbank, John. *Theology and Social Theory: Beyond Secular Reason*. Oxford: Blackwell, 1990.

Miller, B. Jaye. "Anarchism and French Catholicism in Esprit." *Journal of the History of Ideas* 37/1 (January-March 1976): 163-174.

Molnár, Enrico C. S. *A Study of Peter Chelčický's Life and a Translation from Czech of Part One of His Net of Faith*. Edited by Tom Lock. Oberlin: www.nonresistance.org, 2006. Available from http://www.nonresistance.org/literature.html (accessed 28 March 2007).

Moreel, Bas. *Religious Anarchism and Criticism of Religion*. Available from http://www.geocities.com/christianarchy/basmoreel7.htm (accessed 29 March 2005).

———. *Religious Anarchism Newsletters*. Available from http://www.geocities.com/christianarchy/basindex.htm (accessed 29 March 2005).

———. *Religious Anarchism No 1 – June 2001*. Available from http://www.geocities.com/christianarchy/basmoreel1.htm (accessed 31 March 2005).

———. *Russian Orthodox Anarchism in the Twenty-First Century: Radio Omsk Interview on Christian Anarchism*. Available from http://www.geocities.com/christianarchy/prawoslaw.htm (accessed 29 March 2005).

Morgachev, Dmitri Yegorovich. "Extract from 'Yasnaya Polyana'." *A Pinch of Salt*, issue 13, Summer 1989, 6.

Morris, Brian. *Tolstoy and Anarchism*. Spunk Library. Available from http://www.spunk.org/library/pubs/freedom/raven/sp001746.html (accessed 29 July 2003).

Mounier, Emmanuel. *Communisme, Anarchie Et Personnalisme*. City of publication unknown: Seuil, 1966.

Mumford, David. "The Bible and Anarchy." *A Pinch of Salt*, issue 14, March 1990, 8.

Myers, Ched. *Binding the Strong Man: A Political Reading of Mark's Story of Jesus*. Maryknoll: Orbis, 1988.

Nafzinger, Tim. "Marks of a Resistance Church." *London Catholic Worker*, issue 13, April 2005, 8-9.

Nettlau, Max. *A Short History of Anarchism*. London: Freedom, 1996.

Newell, Martin. "Advent: Preparing to Welcome the Christ into Our World." *The London Catholic Worker*, issue 17, Christmas 2006, 12-13.

———. "Hosting Refugees: A Conversation." *The London Catholic Worker*, issue 19, Summer 2007, 2, 9-13.

———. "Obituary: Peter Lumsdaine: An Unusual Disciple." *The London Catholic Worker*, issue 21, Christmas 2007, 4-5.

———. "'We Looked for Peace, but Behold Terror' (Jer 14:19)." *The London Catholic Worker*, issue 15, Lent 2006, 12-15.

———. "Works of Mercy and War." *London Catholic Worker*, issue 13, April 2005, 10-12.

Nicholls, David. *Deity and Domination: Images of God and the State in the Nineteenth and Twentieth Centuries*. London: Routledge, 1989.

Niebuhr, H. Richard. "The Churches of the Disinherited." In *Theology and Sociology: A Reader*, edited by Robin Gill, 69-78. London: Cassell, 1996.

Novak, D. "The Place of Anarchism in the History of Political Thought." *The Review of Politics* 20/3 (July 1958): 307-329.

O'Reilly, Ciaron. "The Anarchist Implications of Christian Discipleship." *A Pinch of Salt*, issue 6, Easter 1987, 8-11.

———. "The Anarchist Implications of Christian Discipleship." *Social Alternatives* 2/3 (February 1982): 9-12.

———. "An Experiment in Truth!" *The London Catholic Worker*, issue 1, July 2001, 1.

———. "Nonviolence at Boggo Road Gaol." *A Pinch of Salt*, issue 10, Summer 1988, 8-9.

———. *Open Letter: London Anarchist Bookfair Banning the Catholic Worker Workshop*. Indymedia, 2001. Available from http://www.indymedia.org.uk/en/2001/10/13500.html (accessed 15 October 2003).

———. *Remembering Forgetting: A Journey of Non-Violent Resistance to the War in East Timor*. Sydney: Otford, 2001.

Ostergaard, Geoffrey. *Resisting the Nation State: The Pacifist and Anarchist Tradition*. Peace Pledge Union. Available from http://www.ppu.org.uk/e_publications/dd-trad1.html (accessed 8 August 2007).

Ostergaard, Geoffrey, and Melville Currell. "Sarvodaya: Indian Anarchism." In *The Gentle Anarchists: A Study of the Leaders of the Sarvodaya Movement for Non-Violent Revolution in India*, 32-45. Oxford: Clarendon, 1971.

Pattillo, Matthew. *Violence, Anarchy and Scripture: Jacques Ellul and René Girard*. Available from http://www.preachingpeace.org/documents/Patillo_Ellul_Girard.pdf (accessed 17 March 2009).

Penner, Archie. *The New Testament, the Christian, and the State*, Mennonite Reprint Series. Hagerstown: James Lowry/Deutsche Buchhandlung, 2000.

Pentecost, Hugh O. *Anarchism*. Available from http://www.deadanarchists.org/Pentecost/anarchism.html (accessed 22 November 2007).

———. *The Crime of Owning Vacant Land*. Available from http://www.deadanarchists.org/Pentecost/vacantland.html (accessed 22 November 2007).

———. *First Anniversary Address*. Available from http://www.deadanarchists.org/Pentecost/anniversary.html (accessed 22 November 2007).

———. *A Gigantic Poorhouse*. Available from http://www.deadanarchists.org/Pentecost/poorhouse.html (accessed 22 November 2007).

———. *Murder by Law*. Available from http://www.deadanarchists.org/Pentecost/murder.html (accessed 22 November 2007).

———. *The Sins of the Government*. Available from http://www.deadanarchists.org/Pentecost/sins.html (accessed 22 November 2007).

Perry, Lewis. "Versions of Anarchism in the Antislavery Movement." *American Quarterly* 20/4 (Winter 1968): 768-782.

Phipson, Evacustes A. "A Happier Social Order." *A Pinch of Salt*, issue 14, March 1990, 10.
Pick, Peter. "A Theology of Revolutions: Abiezer Coppe and the Uses of Tradition." In *Religious Anarchism: New Perspectives*, edited by Alexandre J. M. E. Christoyannopoulos, 30-46. Newcastle upon Tyne: Cambridge Scholars Publishing, 2009.
Pieper, Josef. *The End of Time: A Meditation on the Philosophy of History*. Translated by Michael Bullock. San Francisco: Ignatius, 1999.
Pignatta, Valerio. *Dio L'anarchico: Movimenti Rivoluzionari Religiosi Nell'inghilterra Del Seicento*. Milano: Arcipelago Edizioni, 1997.
Rapp, John A. "Anarchism or Nihilism: The Buddhist-Influenced Thought of Wu Nengzi." In *Religious Anarchism: New Perspectives*, edited by Alexandre J. M. E. Christoyannopoulos, 202-225. Newcastle upon Tyne: Cambridge Scholars Publishing, 2009.
———. "Daoism and Anarchism Reconsidered." *Anarchist Studies* 6/2 (1998): 123-152.
Reagan, Jim. "The Sweet Fruit of the Spirit." *The Catholic Worker*, issue 73, May 2006, 8.
Redfearn, David. *Tolstoy: Principles for a New World Order*. London: Shepheard-Walwyn, 1992.
Redford, James. *Jesus Is an Anarchist*. SSRN, 4 May 2009 2009. Available from http://ssrn.com/abstract=1337761 (accessed 13 September 2009).
———. *Jesus Is an Anarchist: A Free-Market, Libertarian Anarchist, That Is – Otherwise What Is Called an Anarcho-Capitalist*. 1 June 2006. Available from http://praxeology.net/anarchist-jesus.pdf (accessed 14 August 2006).
Reichert, William O. "The Philosophical Anarchism of Adin Ballou." *The Huntington Library Quarterly* 27/4 (August 1964): 357-374.
Ricoeur, Paul. "Love and Justice." In *Paul Ricoeur: The Hermeneutics of Action*, edited by Richard Kearney, translated by David Pellauer, 23-39. London: Sage, 1996.
———. "State and Violence." In *History and Truth*, translated by Charles A. Kelbley, 234-246, *Northwestern University Studies in Phenomenology and Existential Philosophy*. Evanston: Northwestern University Press, 1965.
Ringma, Charles. "Foreword." In *Christi-Anarchy: Discovering a Radical Spirituality of Compassion*, 9-12. Oxford: Lion, 1999.
Roberts, Nancy L. "Dorothy Day: Editor and Advocacy Journalist." In *A Revolution of the Heart: Essays on the Catholic Worker*, edited by Patrick G. Coy, 115-133. Philadelphia: Temple University Press, 1988.
Rockwell, Llewellyn H., Jr. *Church and State*. 10 May 2000. Available from http://www.lewrockwell.com/churchandstate.html (accessed 21 November 2007).
———. *The Ten Commandments Question*. 30 August 2003. Available from http://www.lewrockwell.com/rockwell/commandments.html (accessed 21 November 2007).
———. *What Moral Rules Bind the State?* 25 May 2002. Available from http://www.lewrockwell.com/rockwell/moralrules.html (accessed 21 November 2007).
Roger. "Christianarchy." *A Pinch of Salt*, issue 2, March 1986, 13.
Rosenberg, Randall S. "The Catholic Imagination and Modernity: William Cavanaugh's Theopolitical Imagination and Charles Taylor's Social Imagination." *The Heythrop Journal* 48/6 (November 2007): 911-931.
Rowland, Chris. "Liberation Theology and Politics." In *Religion in Public Life*, edited by Dan Cohn-Sherbok and David McLellan, 74-90. New York: St. Martin's, 1992.
Sampson, R. V. *Tolstoy: The Discovery of Peace*. London: Heinemann, 1973.
Sampson, Ronald. "Christian Soldiers?" *A Pinch of Salt*, issue 14, March 1990, 10.
———. "Tolstoy on Power." *Journal of the Conflict Research Society* 1/2 (November 1977): 66-74.

Sandlin, P. Andrew. *Christianity: Mother of Political Liberty*. 17 August 2000. Available from http://www.lewrockwell.com/orig/sandlin1a.html (accessed 21 November 2007).

———. *War, the Bible and the State*. 1 September 2000. Available from http://www.lewrockwell.com/orig/sandlin2.html (accessed 21 November 2007).

Schaff, Philip. *Latin Christianity: Its Founder, Tertullian*. Wm. B. Eerdmans, 2005. Available from http://www.ccel.org/ccel/schaff/anf03.html (accessed 2 January 2009).

Scott, Peter, and William T. Cavanaugh, eds. *The Blackwell Companion to Political Theology*. Oxford: Blackwell, 2004.

Segers, Mary C. "Equality and Christian Anarchism: The Political and Social Ideas of the Catholic Worker Movement." *Review of Politics* 40/2 (1978): 196-230.

Sibley, Mulford Q. "The Political Theories of Modern Religious Pacifism." *The American Political Science Review* 37/3 (June 1943): 439-454.

Slonim, Marc. "Four Western Writers on Tolstoy." *Russian Review* 19/2 (April 1960): 187-204.

Smith, George H. *Christianity and Liberty*. Libertarian Alliance, 1998. Available from http://www.libertarian.co.uk/lapubs/relin/relin008.pdf (accessed 21 November 2007).

Spann, Edward K. *Hopedale: From Commune to Company Town 1840-1920* Columbus: Ohio State University Press, 1992.

Spence, G. W. "Suicide and Sacrifice in Tolstoy's Ethics." *Russian Review* 22/2 (April 1963): 157-167.

———. "Tolstoy's Dualism." *Russian Review* 20/3 (July 1961): 217-231.

———. *Tolstoy the Ascetic*. Edinburgh: Oliver and Boyd, 1967.

Stanoyevich, Milivoy S. "Tolstoy's Theory of Social Reform. Ii." *The American Journal of Sociology* 31/6 (May 1926): 744-762.

Stassen, Glen H. *The Fourteen Triads of the Sermon on the Mount*. Fuller, 2008. Available from http://documents.fuller.edu/sot/faculty/stassen/cp_content/homepage/homepage.htm (accessed 31 December 2008).

———. *Living the Sermon on the Mount: A Practical Hope for Grace and Deliverance*. San Francisco: Josey-Bass, 2006.

Stassen, Glen H., and David P. Gushee. *Kingdom Ethics: Following Jesus in the Contemporary Context*. Madison: Intervarsity, 2003.

Stephens, David. "The Non-Violent Anarchism of Leo Tolstoy." In *Government Is Violence: Essays on Anarchism and Pacifism*, by Leo Tolstoy, edited by David Stephens, 7-19. London: Phoenix, 1990.

Stepun, Fedor. "The Religious Tragedy of Tolstoy." *Russian Review* 19/2 (April 1960): 157-170.

Storkey, Alan. *Jesus and Politics: Confronting the Powers*. Grand Rapids: Baker, 2005.

Struve, Gleb. "Tolstoy in Soviet Criticism." *Russian Review* 19/2 (April 1960): 171-186.

Tarleton, George. *Birth of a Christian Anarchist*. Pennington: Pendragon, 1993.

Tennant, Michael. *Christianarchy?* Strike the Root, 4 May 2005. Available from http://www.strike-the-root.com/51/tennant/tennant5.html (accessed 21 November 2007).

———. *Government as Idolatry*. Strike the Root, 14 July 2005. Available from http://www.strike-the-root.com/3/tennant/tennant1.html (accessed 21 November 2007).

ter Kuile, Frits. "Anarcho Theologie." *A Pinch of Salt*, issue 12, March 1989, 16.

Thomas, Joan. "Afterword: The Price of Courage." In *The Book of Ammon*, by Ammon Hennacy, edited by Jim Missey and Joan Thomas, 481-491. Baltimore: Fortkamp, 1994.

Thomas, John L. *The Liberator William Lloyd Garrison: A Biography*. Boston: Little, Brown and Company, 1963.
Thomas, Matthew. "Commonwealth." *The Mormon Worker*, issue 3, March 2008, 10, 15-18. Available from http://www.themormonworker.org/articles/issue3/volume_1_issue_3.pdf (accessed 2 May 2008).
Tillich, Paul. *Love, Power, and Justice: Ontological Analyses and Ethical Applications*. London: Oxford University Press, 1954.
Tilly, Charles. "War Making and State Making as Organized Crime." In *Bringing the State Back In*, edited by Peter Evans, Dietrich Rueschemeyer and Theda Skocpol, 169-186. Cambridge: Cambridge University Press, 1985.
Tolstoï, Lyof N. *What to Do?* London: Walter Scott.
Tolstoy, Alexandra. "Tolstoy and the Russian Peasant." *Russian Review* 19/2 (April 1960): 150-156.
Tolstoy, Leo. "Address to the Swedish Peace Congress in 1909." In *The Kingdom of God and Peace Essays*, translated by Aylmer Maude, 537-544. New Delhi: Rupa, 2001.
———. "An Appeal to Social Reformers." In *Government Is Violence: Essays on Anarchism and Pacifism*, edited by David Stephens, translated by Vladimir Tchertkoff, 53-66. London: Phoenix, 1990.
———. "An Appeal to the Clergy." In *On Life and Essays on Religion*, translated by Aylmer Maude, 282-308. Vol. 12, *Tolstóy Centenary Edition*. London: Oxford University Press, 1934.
———. "The Beginning of the End." In *Tolstoy's Writings on Civil Disobedience and Non-Violence*, translated by Aylmer Maude, 9-17. New York: Bergman, 1967.
———. "Bethink Yourselves!" In *Recollections and Essays*, translated by Aylmer Maude, 204-271. Vol. 21, *Tolstóy Centenary Edition*. London: Oxford University Press, 1937.
———. "Carthago Delenda Est." In *Tolstoy's Writings on Civil Disobedience and Non-Violence*, translated by Aylmer Maude, 95-103. New York: Bergman, 1967.
———. "Christianity and Patriotism." In *The Kingdom of God and Peace Essays*, translated by Aylmer Maude, 422-500. New Delhi: Rupa, 2001.
———. "Church and State." In *On Life and Essays on Religion*, translated by Aylmer Maude, 331-345. Vol. 12, *Tolstóy Centenary Edition*. London: Oxford University Press, 1934.
———. "Conclusion of a Criticism of Dogmatic Theology." In *A Confession and the Gospel in Brief*, translated by Aylmer Maude, 85-93. Vol. 11, *Tolstóy Centenary Edition*. London: Oxford University Press, 1933.
———. "A Confession." In *A Confession and Other Religious Writings*, translated by Jane Kentish, 17-80. London: Penguin, 1987.
———. "The End of the Age: An Essay on the Approaching Revolution." In *Government Is Violence: Essays on Anarchism and Pacifism*, edited by David Stephens, translated by Vladimir Tchertkoff, 21-52. London: Phoenix, 1990.
———. "Gandhi Letters." In *Recollections and Essays*, translated by Aylmer Maude, 433-439. Vol. 21, *Tolstóy Centenary Edition*. London: Oxford University Press, 1937.
———. "The Gospel in Brief." In *A Confession and the Gospel in Brief*, translated by Aylmer Maude, 113-302. Vol. 11, *Tolstóy Centenary Edition*. London: Oxford University Press, 1933.
———. "How to Read the Gospels and What Is Essential in Them." In *On Life and Essays on Religion*, translated by Aylmer Maude, 205-208. Vol. 12, *Tolstóy Centenary Edition*. London: Oxford University Press, 1934.
———. "I Cannot Be Silent." In *Recollections and Essays*, translated by Aylmer Maude, 395-412. Vol. 21, *Tolstóy Centenary Edition*. London: Oxford University Press, 1937.

———. *The Inevitable Revolution*. Translated by Ronald Sampson. London: Housmans, 1975.

———. "Introduction to a Short Biography of William Lloyd Garrison." In *The Kingdom of God and Peace Essays*, translated by Aylmer Maude, 530-536. New Delhi: Rupa, 2001.

———. "Introduction to an Examination of the Gospels." In *A Confession and the Gospel in Brief*, translated by Aylmer Maude, 95-109. Vol. 11, *Tolstóy Centenary Edition*. London: Oxford University Press, 1933.

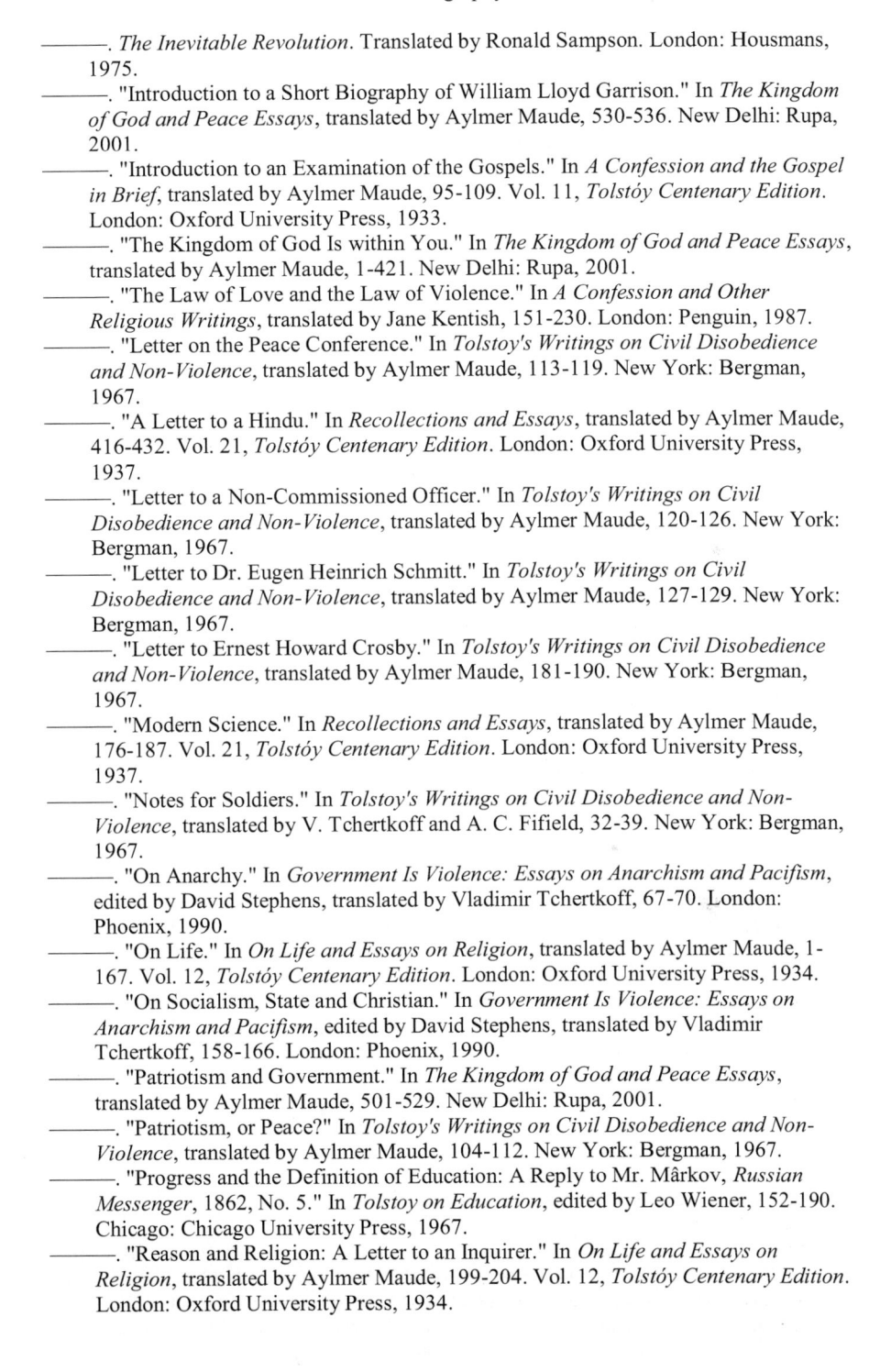

———. "The Kingdom of God Is within You." In *The Kingdom of God and Peace Essays*, translated by Aylmer Maude, 1-421. New Delhi: Rupa, 2001.

———. "The Law of Love and the Law of Violence." In *A Confession and Other Religious Writings*, translated by Jane Kentish, 151-230. London: Penguin, 1987.

———. "Letter on the Peace Conference." In *Tolstoy's Writings on Civil Disobedience and Non-Violence*, translated by Aylmer Maude, 113-119. New York: Bergman, 1967.

———. "A Letter to a Hindu." In *Recollections and Essays*, translated by Aylmer Maude, 416-432. Vol. 21, *Tolstóy Centenary Edition*. London: Oxford University Press, 1937.

———. "Letter to a Non-Commissioned Officer." In *Tolstoy's Writings on Civil Disobedience and Non-Violence*, translated by Aylmer Maude, 120-126. New York: Bergman, 1967.

———. "Letter to Dr. Eugen Heinrich Schmitt." In *Tolstoy's Writings on Civil Disobedience and Non-Violence*, translated by Aylmer Maude, 127-129. New York: Bergman, 1967.

———. "Letter to Ernest Howard Crosby." In *Tolstoy's Writings on Civil Disobedience and Non-Violence*, translated by Aylmer Maude, 181-190. New York: Bergman, 1967.

———. "Modern Science." In *Recollections and Essays*, translated by Aylmer Maude, 176-187. Vol. 21, *Tolstóy Centenary Edition*. London: Oxford University Press, 1937.

———. "Notes for Soldiers." In *Tolstoy's Writings on Civil Disobedience and Non-Violence*, translated by V. Tchertkoff and A. C. Fifield, 32-39. New York: Bergman, 1967.

———. "On Anarchy." In *Government Is Violence: Essays on Anarchism and Pacifism*, edited by David Stephens, translated by Vladimir Tchertkoff, 67-70. London: Phoenix, 1990.

———. "On Life." In *On Life and Essays on Religion*, translated by Aylmer Maude, 1-167. Vol. 12, *Tolstóy Centenary Edition*. London: Oxford University Press, 1934.

———. "On Socialism, State and Christian." In *Government Is Violence: Essays on Anarchism and Pacifism*, edited by David Stephens, translated by Vladimir Tchertkoff, 158-166. London: Phoenix, 1990.

———. "Patriotism and Government." In *The Kingdom of God and Peace Essays*, translated by Aylmer Maude, 501-529. New Delhi: Rupa, 2001.

———. "Patriotism, or Peace?" In *Tolstoy's Writings on Civil Disobedience and Non-Violence*, translated by Aylmer Maude, 104-112. New York: Bergman, 1967.

———. "Progress and the Definition of Education: A Reply to Mr. Mârkov, *Russian Messenger*, 1862, No. 5." In *Tolstoy on Education*, edited by Leo Wiener, 152-190. Chicago: Chicago University Press, 1967.

———. "Reason and Religion: A Letter to an Inquirer." In *On Life and Essays on Religion*, translated by Aylmer Maude, 199-204. Vol. 12, *Tolstóy Centenary Edition*. London: Oxford University Press, 1934.

———. "Religion and Morality." In *On Life and Essays on Religion*, translated by Aylmer Maude, 168-198. Vol. 12, *Tolstóy Centenary Edition*. London: Oxford University Press, 1934.

———. "A Reply to the Synod's Edict of Excommunication, and to Letters Received by Me Concerning It." In *On Life and Essays on Religion*, translated by Aylmer Maude, 214-225. Vol. 12, *Tolstóy Centenary Edition*. London: Oxford University Press, 1934.

———. "The Restoration of Hell." In *On Life and Essays on Religion*, translated by Aylmer Maude, 309-330. Vol. 12, *Tolstóy Centenary Edition*. London: Oxford University Press, 1934.

———. *Resurrection*. Translated by Rosemary Edmonds. London: Penguin, 1966.

———. "The Slavery of Our Times." In *Essays from Tula*, translated by Free Age Press, 65-136. London: Sheppard, 1948.

———. "The Teaching of Jesus." In *On Life and Essays on Religion*, translated by Aylmer Maude, 346-409. Vol. 12, *Tolstóy Centenary Edition*. London: Oxford University Press, 1934.

———. "Thou Shalt Not Kill." In *Recollections and Essays*, translated by Aylmer Maude, 195-203. Vol. 21, *Tolstóy Centenary Edition*. London: Oxford University Press, 1937.

———. "What's to Be Done?" In *Recollections and Essays*, translated by Aylmer Maude, 384-394. Vol. 21, *Tolstóy Centenary Edition*. London: Oxford University Press, 1937.

———. *What I Believe <My Religion>*. Translated by Fyvie Mayo? London: C. W. Daniel, [1902?].

———. "What Is Religion, and Wherein Lies Its Essence?" In *On Life and Essays on Religion*, translated by Aylmer Maude, 226-281. Vol. 12, *Tolstóy Centenary Edition*. London: Oxford University Press, 1934.

Troeltsch, Ernst. "Churches and Sects." In *Theology and Sociology: A Reader*, edited by Robin Gill, 56-68. London: Cassell, 1996.

Troyat, Henri. *Tolstoy*. Translated by Nancy Amphoux. Garden City: Doubleday, 1967.

Urban, Wilbur B. "Tolstoy and the Russian Sphinx." *International Journal of Ethics* 28/2 (January 1918): 220-239.

Van Dyke, Michael T. "Kenneth Rexroth's Integrative Vision: Anarchism, Poetry, and the Religious Experience in Post-World War II San Francisco." In *Religious Anarchism: New Perspectives*, edited by Alexandre J. M. E. Christoyannopoulos, 223-247. Newcastle upon Tyne: Cambridge Scholars Publishing, 2009.

Van Wagenen, William. "War and the State." *The Mormon Worker*, issue 1, September 2007, 8-10. Available from http://www.themormonworker.org/articles/issue1/volume1_issue1.pdf (accessed 28 February 2008).

Vanwagenen, William. "An Introduction to Mormon Anarchism." *The Mormon Worker*, issue 1, September 2007, 1-7. Available from http://www.themormonworker.org/articles/issue1/volume1_issue1.pdf (accessed 28 February 2008).

Veneuse, Mohamed Jean. "To Be Condemned to a Clinic: The Birth of the Anarca-Islamic Clinic." In *Religious Anarchism: New Perspectives*, edited by Alexandre J. M. E. Christoyannopoulos, 249-279. Newcastle upon Tyne: Cambridge Scholars Publishing, 2009.

Vincent, Andrew. *Modern Political Ideologies*. Second edition. Oxford: Blackwell, 1995.

Vincent, John J. "Christian Discipleship and Politics." In *Religion in Public Life*, edited by Dan Cohn-Sherbok and David McLellan, 38-50. New York: St. Martin's, 1992.

Wagner, Murray L. *Petr Chelčický: A Radical Separatist in Hussite Bohemia*, Studies in Anabaptist and Mennonite History. Scottdale: Herald, 1983.

Walford, George. "Through Religion to Anarchism." *The Raven: anarchist quarterly 25* 7/1 (Spring 1994): 29-36.

Walter, Nicolas. "Anarchism and Religion." *The Raven: anarchist quarterly 25* 7/1 (Spring 1994): 3-9.

Ward, Colin. "Anarchist Entry for a Theological Dictionary." *The Raven: anarchist quarterly 25* 7/1 (Spring 1994): 19-25.

Watson, Simon. "The Catholic Worker and Anarchism." *The London Catholic Worker*, issue 15, Lent 2006, 8-11.

Watts, Greg. "Following Jesus in Love and Anarchy." *The Times*, 29 February 2008. Available from http://www.timesonline.co.uk/tol/comment/faith/article3461731.ece (accessed 29 February 2008).

Weber, Max. "Prophets and the Routinisation of Charisma." In *Theology and Sociology: A Reader*, edited by Robin Gill, 36-45. London: Cassell, 1996.

Wellington, Stephen. "Fascist Roots of Corporate America (and the Bush Family)." *The Mormon Worker*, issue 3, March 2008, 5-7. Available from http://www.themormonworker.org/articles/issue3/volume_1_issue_3.pdf (accessed 2 May 2008).

Wenzer, Kenneth C. *An Anthology of Tolstoy's Spiritual Economics*. Vol. 2, *The Henry George Centennial Trilogy*. Rochester: University of Rochester Press, 1997.

———. "Tolstoy's Georgist Spiritual Political Economy (1897-1910): Anarchism and Land Reform." *American Journal of Economics and Sociology* 56/4 (October 1997): 639-667.

Westerlund, David, ed. *Questioning the Secular State: The Worldwide Resurgence of Religion in Politics*. London: Hurst, 1996.

White, Mark, and Angela Jones. "Christian Radicalism in the United States: The Catholic Worker Tradition." *Social Alternatives* 7/3 (September 1988): 39-43.

Wilson, A. N. *Tolstoy: A Biography*. New York: Norton, 1988.

Wink, Walter. *Engaging the Powers: Discernment and Resistance in a World of Domination*. Minneapolis: Fortress, 1992.

———. *Jesus' Third Way*. Philadelphia: New Society, 1987.

———. *Naming the Powers: The Language of Power in the New Testament*. Philadelphia: Fortress, 1984.

———. *Unmasking the Powers: The Invisible Forces That Determine Human Existence*. Philadelphia: Fortress, 1986.

Wogaman, J. Philip. *Christian Perspectives on Politics*. Revised and expanded edition. Louisville: Westminster John Knox, 2000.

Wood, George. "The Kingdom of God." *A Pinch of Salt*, issue 12, March 1989, 14.

Woodcock, George. *Anarchism: A History of Libertarian Ideas and Movements*. Harmondsworth: Penguin, 1975.

———, ed. *The Anarchist Reader*. Glasgow: Collins, 1977.

Yoder, John Howard. *The Christian Witness to the State*. Scottdale: Herald, 1992.

———. "The Limits of Obedience to Caesar: The Shape of the Problem." Unpublished Study Conference Paper. Elkhart: Associate Mennonite Biblical Seminary, June 1978. Available from http://www.jesusradicals.com/library/yoder/limitsofobedience.pdf (accessed 16 May 2006).

———. "Peacemaking Amid Political Revolution." Elkhart: Associate Mennonite Biblical Seminary, [1970?]. Available from http://www.jesusradicals.com/library/yoder/peacemakingamidrevolution.pdf (accessed 16 May 2006).

———. "The Political Axioms of the Sermon on the Mount." In *The Original Revolution: Essays on Christian Pacifism*, 34-54. Scottdale: Herald, 1998.

———. *The Politics of Jesus: Vicit Agnus Noster*. Second edition. Grand Rapids: William B. Eerdmans, 1994.
———. "The Theological Basis of the Christian Witness to the State." Elkhart: Associate Mennonite Biblical Seminary, 1955. Available from http://www.jesusradicals.com/library/yoder/witnesstostate.pdf (accessed 16 May 2006).
———. "Translator's Preface." In *Christ and the Powers*, by Hendrik Berkhof, translated by John Howard Yoder, 5-7. Scottdale: Herald, 1977.
———. "The Wider Setting of Liberation Theology." *The Review of Politics* 52 (Spring 1990): 285-296.
York, Tripp. *Living on Hope While Living in Babylon: The Christian Anarchists of the Twentieth Century*. Cambridge: Lutterworth, 2009.
Young, Roger. *Christianity and Anarchism: A Match Made in Heaven*. Strike the Root, 9 August 2005. Available from http://www.strike-the-root.com/52/young/young1.html (accessed 8 November 2007).
———. *A Plea to Christians: Reject the State!* Strike the Root, 25 February 2002. Available from http://www.strike-the-root.com/columns/Young/young3.html (accessed 21 November 2007).
Zwick, Mark, and Louise Zwick. "Introduction: Dorothy Day and the Catholic Worker Movement." In *On Pilgrimage*, by Dorothy Day, 1-64. Edinburgh: T. and T. Clark, 1999.

# Index

N.B.: The following words occur too frequently in this book to justify their inclusion in this index: anarchism; Christ; Christian; example; God; human; Jesus; politics; power; state; teaching; thinker.

Academics and Students Interested in Religious Anarchism, 212
Acts, 126, 153, 178
Adam, 140, 141, 235
agriculture, 181, 206
Albigense, 199
Aleksov, Bojan, 205
Alexis-Baker, Andy, 22
Alexis-Baker, Nekeisha, 5, 22, 71, 74, 75, 109, 156
allegiance, 20, 53, 54, 55, 71, 75, 119, 126, 151, 156, 159, 188, 198, 236
Allen, Steve, 190, 213
altar, 54, 56, 109, 110, 158, 198
Ambrose, 109, 134
Amsterdam (Netherlands), 210
Anabaptism, 16, 201
Anarchist Academics, viii
Anarchist Studies, 113
Anarchist Studies Network, viii
anarcho-capitalism, 9, 24, 25, 84, 121, 124, 158, 160, 178, 212
anarcho-syndicalism, 180
Anchorite, 200
Andrews, Dave, **17–18**, 22, 30, 36, 41, 55, 57, 58, 59, 60, 65, 66, 68, 70, 71, 74, 79, 80, 81, 82, 84, 94, 98, 109, 110, 111, 112, 113, 134, 138, 142, 143, 175, 177, 180, 181, 189, 190, 193, 194, 197, 200, 208, 212, 238
Angered (Sweden), 210
Antichrist, 103, 113, 144, 219
apocrypha, 12
Aquinas, Thomas, 19
arm, 34, 91, 120, 151, 158, 167, 184, 186, 200, 210
army, 44, 47, 49, 70, 108, 109, 111, 114, 120, 121, 127, 187, 200
arrest, 67, 76, 86, 87–**90**, 90, 91, 92, 97, 104, 106, 158, 209, 210
Ash Wednesday, 210
Asia, 206
Athanasius, 109

Athenagoras, 197
atonement, 84, 140
Augustine of Hippo, 2, 30, 109, 128, 129, 130, 134, 136
Australia, 17, 20, 209, 211, 212
authoritarian, 76, 82, 207
authority, 5, 6, 11, 24, 33, 54, 60, 67, 69, 72, 74, 75, 77, 78, 82, 83, 84, 90, 91, 92, 93, 94, 95, 97, 98, 99, 102, 103, 107, 113, 114, 118, 119, 125, 126, 127, 132, 134, 135, 137, 142, 143, 145, 147, 148, 149, 150, 151, 152, 153, 154, 155, 156, 157, 158, 162, 169, 170, 183, 198, 201, 203, 206, 232, 234, 238, 240
Babylon, 103
Bakunin, Mikhail A., 5, 16, 20, 21, 26, 168
Ballou, Adin, 12, 21, 27, 34, 37, 38, 41, 42, 44, 45, 46, 48, 49, 53, 61, 62, 64, 76, 79, 83, 86, 88, 89, 92, 126, 131, 132, 133, 153, 156, 165, 172, 175, 179, 181, 183, 184, 186, 187, 188, 189, 190, 191, 197, 202, 203, 206, 219, 220, 224
baptism, 108, 201
Baptism, 23
Barabbas, 90, 171
Barr, Jason, 72, 117
Barth, Karl, 224
Bartley, Jonathan, 24, 35, 36, 95, 108, 109, 110, 172, 177, 182, 183, 190, 201, 212, 218
beast, 102, 156
Beatitudes, 58, **59–60**, 65
Beelzebub, 137
Beghards (Brethren of the Free Spirit), 200
Belgium, 210
belief, 2, 7, 43, 50, 51, 100, 101, 103, 105, 110, 115, 131, 137, 138, 139, 141, 143, 189, 192, 193, 198, 209, 236

Benedict XV, 45
Benner, David, 177
Berdyaev, Nicolas, 19, 21, 23, 38, 39, 44, 110, 126, 168, 184, 185, 212, 220, 221, 233
Berkhof, Hendrik, 93, 94, 96, 99, 183
Berkman, Alexander, 20
Berlin (Germany), 205
Berrigan brothers, 14, 209
Bible, 5, 10, 12, 13, 14, 15, 16, 17, 18, 19, 23, 25, 26, 27, 28, 32, 36, 49, 55, 56, 66, 67, 69, 70, 73, 86, 92, 94, 104, 107, 109, 129, 130, 133, 137, 139, 140, 165, 192, 193, 196, 209, 219, 220, 227, 233, 238
bishop, 115
blood, 5, 45, 89, 94, 103, 104, 134, 170, 176, 188, 190, 194, 199, 205, 209
Bloy, Léon, 19
Bohemia, 200
Bolshevik, 205
Bonhoeffer, Dietrich, 189
Bornkamm, Günther, 63
bread, 122, 179, 190
Brisbane (Australia), 18, 212
Britain, 21, 24, 25, 200, 208
Brock, Peter, 46, 187, 199, 201, 204, 205, 207
Buddhism, 4
Caesar, 2, 3, 13, 16, 23, 54, 67, 79, 92, 110, 135, 147, 154, 157, 158, 160, 161, 167, 188, 198, 220, 221, 236
Caiaphas, 90
Cain, 72
Calabria, 122
Calvin, John, 112
Calvinism, 16, 200
Camp for Climate Change, 211
Camus, Albert, 193
Canada, 21, 28, 204, 209, 211
Canterbury (United Kingdom), vii
Capernaum, 78, 160
capitalism, 3, 210
care, vii, 54, 73, 133, 142, 156, 157, 170, 174, 177, 179, 180, 182, 186, 187, 188, 197, 198, 210, 212, 233
Carson, Stephen W., 68, 70, 71, 72
Carter, Timothy, 150
Catholic Worker, **18–20**, 21, 22, 25, 55, 139, 143, 144, 164, 178, 179, 180, 181, 184, 197, 206, 208, **209–10**, 210, 211, 213, 215, 238

Catholicism, 12, 18, 19, 20, 24, 143, 144, 176, 200
Cavanaugh, William T., 2, 14, 22, 24, 114, 115, 182, 190, 198, 212, 220, 221, 235, 236, 237
Central America, 210
chaos, 4, 43, 46, 93, 156, 184
charity, 51, 112, 179
Chelčický, Peter, 9, 12, 21, 26, 44, 50, 51, 53, 68, 70, 72, 88, 95, 101, 109, 110, 111, 126, 133, 135, 136, 137, 142, 144, 152, 153, 155, 165, 166, 167, 171, 176, 182, 190, 192, 193, 196, 199, 200, 223, 233
Chertkov, Vladimir, 206
Chesterton, G. K., 144
Christchurch (New Zealand), 210
Christendom, 107, **108–13**
Christos, Carlos, 190
Chronicles, 73
church, 2, 3, 4, 11, 13, 15, 18, 19, 20, 24, 26, 31, 54, 56, 59, 60, 63, 81, 86, 99, 105, 106, **107–45**, 148, 149, 157, 172, 173, **174–95**, 196, 197, 198, 199, 200, 201, 204, 205, 213, 214, 224, 229, 231, 232, 233, 234, 236, 237, 238
Church Fathers, 112, 128, 197
citizen, 43, 45, 55, 56, 66, 76, 108, 122, 125, 159, 238
city, 52, 72, 123, 182, 210
Civil Rights campaign, 208
Civil War, 23, 202
civilian, 33
Clement, 197
clergy, 54, 109, 130, 138, 144
Coatepec (Mexico), 210
coercion, 5, 9, 36, 39, 40, 43, 45, 56, 57, 65, 67, 79, 83, 86, 92, 98, 105, 111, 112, 114, 120, 124, 126, 134, 135, 168, 170, 171, 173, 174, 177, 181, 184, 191, 193, 201, 213, 217, 218, 225, 231, 235, 238, 239
coin, 158, 159, 160, 167
Cold War, 209
Colossians, 93, 95, 216, 219
commune, 19, 181, 209, 225
communism, 17, 18, 44, 168, 169, 220, 232
community, 8, 11, 13, 17, 18, 22, 25, 30, 31, 33, 59, 65, 66, 69, 72, 81, 82, 83, 96, 99, 108, 110, 140, 147, 150, 154, 173, 174, 175, 177, 178, 179,

180, 181, 182, 183, 184, 187, 188, 189, 193, 194, 195, 196, 197, 198, 200, 201, 202, 203, 204, 209, 210, 211, 212, 213, 218, 223, 225, 227, 229, 230, 231, 232
compulsion, 46, 81, 116, 120, 166, 167
Confucius, 206
conscientious objection, 166, 167, 204, 205, 207
conscription, 118, 120, 127, 148, 166
conservativism, 84, 157
Constantine, 3, 107, 112, 113, 115, 136, 148, 197, 198, 199, 201, 224, 234
conversion, 14, 20, 177, 185, 192, 193, 218, 237
Coppe, Abiezer, 9, 200
Corinthians, 93, 152, 156
Cornelius, Geoffrey, viii
Correia, António Gonçalves, 206
Council of Nicaea, 109, 110
country, 14, 50, 121, 159, 182, 187, 188, 203, 204, 205, 209
Craig, Kevin, 25, 63, 64, 70, 72, 82, 95, 106, 176, 197
Creation, 51
Crosby, Ernest, 56, 57, 76, 85, 90, 206
cross, 76, 77, 83, 91, 93, 95, 96, 97, 98, 99, 100, 101, 103, 104, 105, 111, 131, 133, 134, 142, 162, 169, 176, 188, 195, 208, 218, 222, 223, 233, 239, 240, 241
crucifixion, 67, 87, 93–**100**, 100, 106, 155, 225, 240
Crusades, 112, 200
Cyprian, 197
Czech, 26, 200
Damico, Linda H., 76, 200
Dark Ages, 112
daughter, 70, 105
David, 71
Day, Dorothy, 6, 9, 14, 19, 20, 60, 65, 66, 85, 101, 139, 143, 144, 145, 159, 163, 167, 172, 176, 177, 178, 179, 180, 184, 185, 189, 206, 209, 210, 215
de Raaij, André, 205
death, 19, 43, 63, 67, 91, 99, 102, 106, 111, 119, 135, 137, 141, 153, 158, 169, 171, 176, 186, 188, 189, 190, 194, 198, 199, 200, 204, 207, 219
Decalogue, 158

deception, 30, 54, 99, 107, 113, 114, 115, **117–21**, 136, 139, 141, 143, 145, 172, 175, 215, 236
defence, vii, 25, 28, 40, 41, 53, 62, 63, 87, 88, 89, 90, 92, 95, 104, 107, 120, 136, 150, 156, 157, 159, 166, 185, 186, 187, 200, 215, 228, 229
deism, 100, 220
del Vasto, Lanza, 208
democracy, 71, 117, 118, 149, 162, 232
demon, 38, 42, 52, 70, 78, 86, 94, 95, 126, 163
Deuteronomy, 72
Devellennes, Charles, viii
devil, 75, 77, 92, 102, 137, 138, 139, 221
dictatorship, 70, 117, 136, 144, 149, 168, 207
Digger, 200
Digger and Christian Anarchist, 9, 21, 197, 211
disarm, 88, 95, 96, 98, 99, 209
disobedience, 13, 20, 50, 54, 69, 103, 147, 149, 150, 151, 152, 155, 156, 161–**65**, 167, 173, 198, 199, 200, 209, 210, 224, 225, 241
disorder, 4, 184
dissent, 34, 105, 108, 110, 112
doctrine, 38, 65, 107, 115, 124, 127, 129, 137, 140, 143, 159, 177
dogma, 12, 18, 23, 107, 130, 136–**44**, 145, 176, 238
Dortmund (Germany), 210
Doukhobor, 204
Dutch Reformed Church, 205
Earp, Charley, 74
earth, 3, 4, 5, 37, 48, 50, 52, 53, 61, 65, 75, 76, 77, 82, 92, 93, 94, 95, 101, 102, 103, 104, 111, 134, 152, 160, 182, 188, 193, 203, 213, 214, 217, 218, 221, 223, 224, 232, 233, 235
Ecclesiastes, 72
economy, 4, 37, 57, 60, 71, 83, 84, 86, 107, 109, 113, 114, 117, 121, 123, **121–25**, 153, 174, **177–80**, 180, 182, 240
Edict of Milan, 108, 110
Edwards, Brian, viii
ekklesia, 182
Ekklesia, 24
election, 9, 77, 110, 117, 118, 121, 148, 165, 202

Eller, Vernard, 9, **16–17**, 21, 22, 24, 27, 48, 63, 70, 71, 77, 92, 100, 101, 109, 148, 151, 152, 154, 155, 156, 157, 158, 159, 160, 161, 162, 163, 164, 165, 167, 171, 201, 212, 215, 216, 219, 220, 224, 233, 238
Elliott, Michael C., 17, 32, 33, 34, 35, 62, 64, 71, 75, 76, 83, 85, 87, 91, 96, 103, 143, 149, 181, 189, 200, 203, 212, 219, 220
Ellsberg, Robert, 19
Ellul, Jacques, 3, 4, 5, 10, 14, **16**, 21, 22, 24, 38, 39, 40, 41, 43, 44, 57, 68, 69, 70, 72, 73, 75, 82, 88, 89, 91, 92, 94, 95, 100, 101, 102, 103, 104, 125, 126, 142, 148, 149, 151, 152, 155, 158, 159, 160, 162, 163, 167, 170, 172, 190, 191, 192, 198, 199, 200, 201, 208, 212, 215, 219, 220, 221, 233, 234
Emmaus, 96
emperor, 108, 109, 111, 198
empire, 76, 91, 92, 109, 110, 111, 112, 128, 150, 152, 156, 198, 199, 203
end, 97, 98, 217
ends, 38, 39, 42, 52, 87, 136, 168, 170, 172, 174, 207, 208, 217, 219, 222, 235, 238, 239
enemy, 31, 33, 34, 39, 41, **49–52**, 54, 55, 62, 79, 81, 97, 103, 121, 129, 134, 137, 144, 151, 155, 158, 162, 186, 191, 198, 226, 227
England, vii, 20, 21, 206, 209, 210
English, 9, 12, 26
Enlightenment, 3, 112, 132
Ephesians, 93, 94
equality, 6, 33, 57, 119, 181
ethics, 30, 93, 101, 109, 145, 201, 226, 227, 229
eucharist, 24, 139, 140, 190, 198, 221, 235, 236, 237
Europe, 2, 112, 115, 122, 127, 197, 206
European Consortium of Political Research, viii
Eve, 235
evil, 31, 32–**47**, 47, 48, 49, 50, 51, 52, 53, 54, 55, 57, 58, 61, 62, 66, 68, 75, 76, 80, 81, 87, 88, 92, 94, 98, 99, 107, 122, 128, 129, 130, 132, 133, 134, 138, 141, 144, 148, 149, 151, 152, 153, 154, 155, 158, 161, 162, 163, 164, 169, 171, 172, 174, 180, 183–**88**, 188, 189, 190, 191, 192, 193, 195, 218, 219, 222, 233, 240
excommunication, 204
exegesis, 8, 10, 12, 13, 15, 16, 27, 28, 30, 31, 32, 53, 57, 67, 72, 77, 78, 81, 101, 102, 105, 130, 134, 147, 149, 150, 151, 155, 161, 240
exemplify, 66, 71, 93, 96, 106, 147, 177, 179, 201, 213, 219, 221, 231, 239
Exodus, 44, 69, 72, 74
exploitation, 55, 85, 107, 113, 114, 115, 121–**25**, 127, 145, 231, 237
Ezekiel, 73
Facebook, 211
faith, 5, 9, 10, 26, 43, 48, 51, 70, 71, 77, 84, 97, 108, 110, 111, 125, 126, 131, 136, 139, 140, 142, 143, 152, 157, 159, 161, 170, 171, 172, 175, 176, 180, 185, 189, 190, 191, 192, 193, 195, 218, 219, 220, 221, 222, 223, 224, 231
fall, 4, 30, 44, 51, 53, 75, 76, 81, 87, 88, 94, 103, 110, 111, 112, 125, 131, 134, 141, 153, 168, 175, 182, 183, 186, 192, 194, 198, 199, 217, 218, 219, 220, 225, 230, 232
family, 40, 72, 86, 105, 119, 168, 184, 186, 189, 206
farm, 19, 181, 182, 203, 207, 209
Fasching, Darrell J., 10
father, 49, 50, 51, 54, 69, 79, 93, 105, 137, 153, 194, 201
feminism, 11
Ferrer, Francisco, 19
flesh, 94, 104
force, 5, 20, 33, 37, 39, 40, 41, 43, 44, 46, 49, 54, 55, 84, 86, 92, 93, 99, 102, 106, 109, 110, 111, 114, 118, 120, 123, 124, 125, 126, 128, 129, 133, 135, 136, 139, 148, 151, 153, 154, 167, 171, 172, 183, 184, 186, 187, 188, 199, 202, 207, 220, 223, 226, 228, 232
Forest, Fanny L., viii
forgive, 31, 36, 41, 42, 48, 51, 53, 57, 66, 67, 78, 79, 81, 84, 88, 92, 93, 97, 98, 99, 100, 103, 106, 127, 137, 143, 151, 154, 155, 156, 157, 162, 163, 168, 169, 173, 177, 178, 181, 185, 189, 191, 195, 198, 212, 218, 219, 224, 229, 233, 235, 239, 241
France, 16, 19, 44

Francis of Assisi, 171, 200, 227
Franco, Francisco, 44, 136
free market, 24, 25, 210
freedom, 4, 5, 17, 38, 53, 72, 74, 102, 117, 118, 121, 123, 137, 145, 156, 160, 178, 186, 192, 193, 195
Fueloep-Miller, Rene, 206
fundamentalism, 66
Gandhi, Mohandes K., 38, 42, 134, 142, 164, 172, 197, 207, 208, 227
Garden of Eden, 72
Garrison, William Lloyd, 22, 23, 40, 197, 202
Genesis, 72
Genghis Khan, 116
Gentile, 82, 83, 193
George, Henry, 166, 179, 203, 206
Germany, 54, 210
Gethsemane, 140
Ghent (Belgium), 210
Gideon, 69
gift, 56, 141, 143, 178, 179
Glasgow (United Kingdom), 210
Goddard, Andrew, 125, 170, 183, 192, 220
Godwin, William, 19, 20
Golden Rule, 31, 55, 226, 227
Goldman, Emma, 20
Gonçalves, Tânia, vii
Gonya, Paul, 79
Good Friday, 219
Good Samaritan, 50
gospel, 1, 3, 12, 13, 15, 17, 27, 30, 32, 35, 45, 49, 53, 54, 57, 60, 64, 67, 76, 77, 78, 79, 81, 82, 84, 87, 88, 91, 100, 101, 102, 104, 105, 106, 109, 110, 127, 128, 129, 133, 134, 137, 139, 140, 158, 164, 169, 176, 181, 193, 201, 206, 238
government, 9, 11, 18, 20, 23, 27, 43, 44, 45, 46, 47, 55, 68, 69, 70, 71, 73, 76, 77, 82, 97, 103, 113, 114, 116, 117, 118, 120, 121, 122, 126, 145, 149, 152, 154, 156, 164, 165, 167, 169, 170, 173, 179, 183, 184, 187, 191, 199, 206, 215, 232
Greek, 32, 34, 56, 58, 59, 82, 93, 94, 129, 158, 159, 164, 175, 177, 182, 215, 216
Gregg, Richard, 40
Guérin, Daniel, 21
Guseinov, A. A., 46
Gushee, David P., 57

Hamburg (Germany), 210
Hancock, Stephen, 21, 162, 210, 211
hate, 36, 38, 41, 49, 50, 52, 56, 62, 69, 81, 89, 98, 105, 126, 132, 158, 162, 184, 189
Hauerwas, Stanley, 199
heaven, 49, 51, 52, 53, 61, 94, 95, 102, 182, 188, 219, 221, 223
Hebden, Keith, 150, 211
Hebrews, 36
Hegel, G. W. F., 1, 124
hell, 56, 101, 137, 138
Hengel, Martin, 158
Hennacy, Ammon, 5, 20, 36, 37, 38, 43, 45, 46, 55, 66, 79, 80, 85, 86, 88, 89, 117, 136, 138, 142, 143, 144, 149, 158, 159, 163, 164, 165, 168, 172, 177, 178, 179, 184, 187, 190, 191, 198, 206, 209, 210
Heppenstall, Annie, 69, 71, 72, 73, 74
heresy, 70, 110, 111, 112, 125, 137, 142, 197, 199
Herod Antipas, 74, 157
Herzen, Alexander, 116
hierarchy, 1, 57, 74, 82, 199, 216, 238
Hinduism, 208
Hippolytus, 197
history, 2, 4, 6, 13, 32, 37, 73, 74, 86, 87, 88, 93, 99, 101, 107, **108–13**, 134, 139, 140, 144, 150, 169, 172, 182, 185, 202, 203, 204, 214, 220, 222, 224, **217–25**, 231, 238
Hitler, Adolf, 206
Hobbes, Thomas, 43, 235
Holocaust, 112
holy, 70, 208
Holy Ghost, 139
Holy Roman Church, 109
Holy Roman Empire, 112
Holy Spirit, 191
Holy Week, 140
Hone, Kenneth C., 21, 211
Hopedale community, 197, 203
Hopton, Terry, 54, 123
hospitality, 19, 181, 197, 209, 210
human nature, 41, 122, 145
Hungary, 205
Hus, Jan, 200
hypnotism, 114, 118, 119, 120, 121, 138, 139, 140, 142, 143, 145
hypocrisy, 48, 51, 55, 85, 114, 120, 129, 143, 145, 157, 187

ideal, 43, 49, 66, 143, 144, 145, 165, 196, 206, 213, 228
ideology, 5, 18, 84, 86, 94, 136, 142, 155, 229
idolatry, 69, 70, 71, 107, 108, 111, 113, 115, 125–27, 142, 158, 170, 175, 198, 215, 224, 225, 230, 231, 233, 237, 238
imitation, 51, 71, 176, 190
India, 42, 66, 127, 208
indifference, 134, 147, 155, 159, 173, 192, 224, 240
individual, 1, 8, 10, 11, 13, 42, 43, 44, 45, 46, 54, 100, 118, 119, 131, 132, 158, 172, 173, 174, 175, 179, 180, 193, 195, 196, 197, 202, 210, 212, 213, 228, 230, 235, 236, 238, 239
Industrial Workers of the World, 19, 180
industry, 9, 25, 70, 123, 181
inequality, 114
injustice, 19, 37, 40, 41, 49, 57, 60, 70, 87, 91, 97, 98, 100, 108, 117, 120, 122, 124, 134, 145, 152, 154, 155, 157, 164, 190, 209, 210, 212, 218, 229, 230, 232, 240
Inquisition, 112
institution, 13, 20, 44, 46, 52, 59, 69, 81, 82, 84, 94, 95, 96, 108, 111, 114, 119, 122, 143, 144, 153, 174, 181, 182, 200, 220, 225, 226, 227, 228, 229, 230, 231, 232, 233, 234, 235
international, vii, 46, 120, 122, 127
interpretation, 2, 3, 6, 11, 12, 13, 15, 17, 27, 30, 31, 32, 35, 37, 48, 49, 50, 59, 60, 63, 64, 65, 66, 67, 69, 72, 73, 77, 78, 79, 80, 81, 84, 92, 94, 99, 100, 101, 105, 106, 110, 127, 128, 129, 130, 131, 132, 133, 134, 135, 137, 138, 140, 143, 145, 147, 149, 150, 151, 153, 155, 156, 157, 160, 164, 169, 178, 181, 187, 190, 196, 197, 216, 218, 227, 238, 240
Iraq War, 209
Ireland, 20, 199, 209
Isaiah, 48, 74, 209
Israel, 60, 68, 69, 70, 71, 72, 73, 97, 152, 159, 182, 210
James, 53, 81, 82, 83, 176
Jeremias, Joachim, 76
Jerusalem, 52, 76, 83, 97
Jesus Radicals, 22, 24, 211, 212

Jew, 36, 49, 50, 60, 64, 70, 73, 74, 76, 90, 92, 93, 95, 96, 97, 112, 158, 159, 193
Jewish, 49
John, 53, 58, 63, 74, 80, 82, 83, 85, 87, 90, 92, 97, 140, 164, 175, 176, 178, 189, 194
John Chrysostom, 125
John the Baptist, 74, 133, 175
Johnston, Laurie, 52, 79, 129, 198
Joseph, 149
Joshua, 69
Judaism, 62
judge, 4, 10, 31, 47, 48, 49, 55, 56, 57, 67, 69, 78, 80, 81, 95, 103, 105, 106, 110, 119, 125, 126, 129, 131, 133, 144, 153, 166, 177, 198, 209
justice, viii, 4, 17, 35, 37, 40, 41, 45, 48, 49, 60, 64, 81, 87, 91, 99, 117, 122, 126, 128, 129, 134, 135, 149, 152, 154, 171, 193, 210, **225–29**, 229, 230, 231, 232, 233, 234, 235, 239, 241
Justin Martyr, 197
Kent (United Kingdom), vii
Kentish, Jane, 203
king, 52, 68, 69, 70, 71, 72, 73, 76, 82, 91, 92, 93, 96, 97, 126, 134, 135, 152, 153, 156, 160, 164, 165, 232
King, Martin Luther, 208, 227
kingdom, 15, 23, 47, 50, 54, 60, 61, 65, 74, 75, 82, 92, 96, 97, 99, 108, 111, 142, 169, 191, 193, 194, 195, 203, 205, 207, 213, 214, 220, 224, **217–25**, 232, 233, 235, 241
Kinna, Ruth, vii, 6, 113, 114, 180
Kropotkin, Peter, 16, 19, 20, 21, 201
Küng, Hans, 30
labour, 19, 47, 95, 121, 122, 123, 124, 136, 178, 179, 185, 203, 204
Lactantius, 197
land, 9, 69, 70, 109, 121, 122, 123, 124, 159, 166, 178, 179, 181, 182, 203, 204, 220
Landauer, Gustav, 180
Latin, 215
Latin America, 3, 112
law, 31, 32, 33, 34, 35, 36, 37, 38, 39, 40, 42, 43, 44, 46, 48, 53, 54, 55, 56, 65, **61–65**, 65, 66, 68, 69, 70, 72, 79, 80, 81, 90, 91, 95, 99, 109, 110, 111, 112, 114, 116, 118, 119, 121, 122, 124, 125, 126, 127, 128, 130, 132,

133, 138, 139, 150, 152, 153, 156, 157, 159, 161, 162, 163, 164, 171, 184, 185, 191, 192, 210, 226, 228, 230, 231, 233
Lawrence, Andrew, 76, 82
leader, 27, 59, 63, 69, 71, 73, 76, 77, 82, 83, 97, 140, 142, 153, 181, 197, 200, 202, 216, 225
legislation, 45, 46, 49, 65, 68, 114, 115, 116, 125, 127, 165, 184, 228, 230
Lenin, Vladimir I., 171
Leveller, 200
Leviathan, 46
Leviticus, 72
Lew Rockwell, 25
Lewin, David, viii
lex talionis, **35–37**, 37, 38, 40, 64, 66, 233
liberalism, 2, 6, 71, 115, 157, 232, 236
liberation theology, 3, 7, 8, 10, 21, 27, 72, 169, 217, 218, 234, 237
Libertarian Nation Foundation, 25
libertarianism, 18, 25, 84
Lichtenberg, 122
lie, 41, 75, 138, 158, 173
life, 12, 14, 17, 18, 19, 30, 33, 35, 43, 51, 59, 63, 65, 66, 67, 68, 74, 77, 87, 97, 100, 102, 106, 110, 118, 123, 124, 127, 132, 133, 135, 139, 140, 141, 142, 144, 145, 147, 156, 158, 169, 171, 175, 176, 177, 179, 180, 181, 182, 183, 188, 189, 192, 193, 194, 195, 197, 200, 201, 203, 204, 210, 211, 212, 213, 221, 223, 224, 226, 229, 238, 240
liturgy, 19, 139, 140, 143, 163, 197, 209, 210, 215, 221, 237
Liverpool (United Kingdom), 210
Locke, John, 43, 235
London (United Kingdom), 209, 210, 211
Lord's Prayer, 79
Lost Religion of Jesus, 211
love, vii, viii, 5, 18, 19, 20, 30, 31, 36, 37, 41, 42, 43, 45, 46, 47, 49, 50, 51, 52, 53, 55, 57, 60, 63, 64, 65, 66, 79, 81, 83, 85, 92, 97, 98, 99, 100, 105, 106, 111, 121, 126, 127, 129, 134, 138, 142, 145, 151, 154, 155, 156, 157, 161, 162, 164, 169, 177, 178, 179, 180, 181, 184, 185, 186, 188, 189, 190, 191, 192, 193, 195, 197, 198, 201, 205, 210, 212, 218, 222, 224, **225–29**, 229, 230, 231, 232, 233, 234, 235, 239, 240, 241
Luke, 30, 50, 53, 59, 63, 74, 75, 78, 80, 81, 83, 84, 87, 88, 89, 90, 96, 97, 99, 104, 105, 110, 125, 137, 157, 162, 175, 176, 178, 189, 190, 193, 194, 227
Luther, Martin, 137
Lutheranism, 200
Lyttleton (New Zealand), 210
Magnificat, 74
Malatesta, Errico, 20, 21
Mammon, 125, 142, 159
Mandela, Nelson, 208
Mark, 27, 53, 58, 74, 78, 82, 83, 84, 87, 90, 97, 99, 101, 105, 140, 147, 148, 155, 157, 158, 160, 164, 175, 176, 178, 189, 190, 191, 192, 193, 194
martyr, 97, 98, 108, 131, 134, 153, 172, 176, 183, 188, 189, 190, 194, 195, 198, 199, 201
Marxism, 8, 23, 27, 164, 169
Mary, 74, 149
master, 5, 19, 53, 62, 71, 123, 125, 126, 137, 153, 156, 157, 159, 160, 225
Matthew, 30, 32, 48, 49, 53, 54, 55, 56, 58, 59, 60, 61, 63, 68, 74, 75, 77, 78, 80, 82, 83, 87, 90, 97, 99, 104, 105, 125, 128, 137, 140, 147, 157, 160, 161, 163, 164, 175, 176, 177, 178, 182, 189, 190, 191, 193, 194, 227
Maude, Aylmer, 46, 68, 78, 140, 164, 166, 187, 204, 206
Maurin, Peter, 19, 20, 65, 66, 86, 112, 124, 143, 144, 168, 177, 178, 179, 181, 189, 193, 197, 199, 206, 210, 215
Maximillian, 197
McLellan, David, vii, 5
means, 32, 34, 35, 36, 38, 40, 42, 52, 72, 76, 87, 113, 116, 118, 122, 126, 136, 162, 164, 168, 169, 170, 171, 172, 174, 207, 208, 217, 220, 221, 222, 223, 224, 228, 230, 235, 238, 239
Mei, Todd, viii
Mendis, Viraj, 210
Mennonitism, 27, 28, 201
Merton, Thomas, 52
messiah, 74, 76, 77, 78, 93, 96, 97, 106, 169, 176, 232
Metz, Johann Baptist, 2
Mexico, 210

Micah, 209
Middle Ages, 2, 112, 115, 182, 196, 197, **199–202**, 213, 224
Middle East, 33, 212
military, 33, 34, 54, 57, 69, 70, 71, 78, 92, 94, 102, 108, 117, 119, 120, 127, 133, 136, 148, 166, 167, 198, 199, 205, 209
millennium, 7, 110, 131, 175, 199, 217
Milne, Joseph, vii, 225, 226
ministry, 62, 63, 67, 74, 75, 76, 77, 78, 97, 181
Ministry of Defence, 210
miracle, 14, 67, 77, 78, 101, 110, 139, 160, 178
Miranda, José Porfirio, 74
mission, 74, 76, 99, 106, 135, 174, 181, 182, 183, 190, 217, 234, 240
modern, 2, 9, 12, 13, 16, 20, 21, 70, 84, 107, 112, 113, 114, 115, 124, 182, 196, 212, 213, 224, 231, 232, 234, 235, 236, 237, 238, 239, 240
Molnár, Enrico C. S., 109, 110, 200, 233
monarchy, 5, 70, 71, 73, 74, 76, 102, 115
monastery, 110, 163, 182, 200
money, 83, 84, 86, 91, 95, 112, 117, 121, 124, 125, 158, 159, 160, 175, 178
Moore, Peter, vii
morality, 15, 30, 38, 40, 49, 55, 62, 63, 65, 68, 77, 78, 93, 96, 99, 114, 117, 118, 119, 126, 130, 139, 140, 141, 152, 165, 170, 184, 186, 190, 213, 219, 220, 222, 227, 238
Moreel, Bas, 22, 212
Mormon Worker, 22, 211
Mormonism, 22, 209
Moses, 62, 63, 64, 68, 69, 71, 72, 80, 126, 128, 132, 133, 139
mother, 19, 54, 105, 125
Mounier, Emmanuel, 19
movement, 7, 8, 9, 18–**20**, 21, 24, 26, 55, 70, 101, 108, 110, 139, 143, 163, 164, 170, 189, 194, 196, 197, 198, 199, 200, 201, 204, 206, 207, 208, 209, 210, 213, 217, 222, 224, 234, 238
Mumford, David, 72, 73, 83, 91
murder, 44, 45, 47, 50, 57, 116, 118, 121, 122, 129, 167, 170, 185, 186, 187, 188

Mussolini, Benito, 206
Myers, Ched, 20, 24, 27, 71, 77, 78, 83, 84, 85, 86, 90, 91, 95, 97, 99, 101, 105, 134, 140, 159, 169, 176, 181, 189, 194, 223
myth, 2, 109, 170, 235, 236, 237
nation, 19, 25, 45, 49, 50, 52, 69, 70, 71, 90, 96, 102, 105, 114, 115, 120, 121, 122, 126, 133, 167, 187, 202, 209
Nazarene, 205
Nazareth, 74
Nazism, 2
neighbour, 5, 49, 50, 63, 64, 68, 126, 129, 133, 164, 175, 177, 179, 185, 186, 187, 231, 233, 241
Netherlands, 22, 205, 206, 210
Nettlau, Max, 206
New Testament, 3, 12, 13, 30, 53, 61, 64, 67, 68, 73, 77, 86, 87, 100, 101, 102, 104, 133, 135, 139, 147, 148, 156, 157, 159, 169, 176, 237
New Zealand, 210, 211
Newell, Martin, 87, 192, 209
Nicene creed, 109, 140
Nimrod, 72
non-resistance, 11, 27, 30, 31, **32–47**, **32–47**, 47, 48, 49, 52, 54, 55, 62, 64, 66, 67, 68, 81, 83, 87, 88, 89, 92, 97, 99, 100, 106, 107, 115, 127, 130, 131, 132, **130–35**, 151, 154, 163, 164, 165, 166, 172, 173, 186, 187, 188, 189, 190, 191, 201, 202, 218, 238
non-violence, 11, 15, 34, 35, 36, 38, 41, 46, 60, 77, 83, 90, 106, 110, 130, 134, 142, 162, 163, 164, 165, 168, 169, 192, 205, 207, 208, 210, 218, 238
O'Reilly, Ciaron, 1, 20, 110, 193, 209
oath, 31, 52, 53, 54, 55, 62, 64, 118, 126, 128, 156, 198, 199, 201
obedience, 39, 40, 43, 53, 54, 62, 69, 76, 102, 116, 119, 121, 125, 126, 131, 140, 147, 151, 153, 155, 156, 159, 161–**65**, 170, 173, 187, 195, 197, 222, 223, 224, 225, 233, 238, 239
Old Testament, 5, 12, 13, 16, 35, 36, 48, 49, 50, 61, 63, 64, 67, **68–73**, 77, 106, 132, 133, 139, 152, 233
ontology, 37, **225–29**, 230, 231, 232, 235, 236, 237

order, 1, 24, 36, 43, 46, 53, 54, 63, 69, 77, 78, 82, 83, 84, 99, 106, 118, 121, 124, 132, 133, 148, 149, 152, 153, 155, 156, 176, 184, 198, 201, 205, 216, 233, 236, 237, 240
Origen, 197
orthodox, 8, 54, 62, 129, 130, 137, 145, 176
Orthodox, 216
Ortt, Felix, 205
Osservatore Romano, 19
outlaw, 50, 55, 58, 88, 133
Oxford (United Kingdom), 210
Pacific, 22
pacifism, 7, 8, 10, 11, 27, 31, 32, 34, 35, 40, 46, 49, 56, 103, 164, 198, 199, 200, 201, 207, 209, 217, 223, 234, 237
pagan, 68, 71, 82, 111, 154, 155, 156, 197, 198, 220
Palestine, 76
parable, 50, 105, 194
paradise, 101
Passover, 89, 104
patience, vii, 48, 51, 60, 103, 132, 143, 150, 154, 157, 163, 164, 168, 169, 173, 178, 191, 194, 195, 218, 219, 223, 224
patriotism, 49, 50, 52, 114, 120, 205, 206, 208
Paul, 27, 48, 81, 93, 94, 95, 96, 102, 126, 128, 135, 141, 147, 148, 149, 150, 151, 152, 153, 154, 155, 156, 198, 213, 216, 219
Paulician, 199
peace, 36, 41, 42, 57, 60, 65, 87, 88, 93, 104, 120, 121, 134, 138, 149, 154, 176, 186, 189, 233, 235, 236, 241
peasant, 19, 119, 179, 203, 204, 205
Peasants' Revolt, 200
Penner, Archie, 28, 30, 35, 36, 49, 86, 89, 90, 103, 108, 109, 110, 112, 148, 152, 159, 201
Pentecost, Hugh O., 23, 60, 77, 90, 116, 117, 122, 125, 134, 140, 179, 180, 184, 191, 212
Perón, Juan Domingo, 136
persecution, 3, 4, 49, 81, 99, 103, 108, 110, 134, 137, 150, 151, 152, 154, 155, 162, 188, 189, 198, 200, 201, 203, 204, 205, 206, 224, 234
personalism, 18, 19

Peter, 3, 53, 76, 77, 87, 88, 89, 97, 102, 126, 137, 143, 148, 156, 160, 189, 217
Pharisee, 58, 61, 63, 64, 80, 97, 105, 128, 137, 157
Philemon, 156
Philistine, 69
philosophy, 14, 23, 65, 110, 124, 150, 171, 228
Pilate, 90, 91, 92, 135
Pinch of Salt, 21, 44, 45, 61, 66, 67, 76, 90, 98, 126, 144, 150, 162, 197, 210, 211
Ploughshares, 21, 209, 210, 211, 241
police, 28, 43, 46, 49, 102, 125, 167, 184, 191, 228
Political Science Association, viii
pope, 18, 19, 45, 109, 111, 137, 143, 144
poverty, 3, 60, 102, 107, 122, 123, 136, 140, 145, 162, 169, 175, 178, 186, 197, 200, 206, 239
practice, 2, 3, 8, 13, 17, 18, 20, 24, 26, 31, 33, 37, 43, 46, 47, 58, 63, 65, 66, 68, 79, 83, 84, 97, 99, 106, 107, 122, 131, 132, 134, 140, 144, 171, 176, 177, 189, 191, 196, 197, 200, 202, 206, 207, 210, 212, 215, 227, 228, 236, 238
prayer, 19, 49, 59, 68, 69, 79, 83, 88, 93, 131, 135, 138, 144, 163, 187, 198
priest, 23, 69, 70, 84, 87, 91, 92, 128, 137, 142, 143, 144, 165, 167, 190, 209
prison, 20, 45, 46, 56, 68, 74, 79, 86, 90, 119, 121, 122, 163, 203
propaganda, 57, 85, 102, 167
property, 9, 24, 25, 47, 121, 122, 159, 178, 203, 235
prophecy, 13, 14, 55, 61, 63, 64, 73, 89, 97, 100, 105, 112, 124, 139, 143, 209, 214, **225–35**, 239
protest, 20, 33, 84, 85, 161, 164, 201, 209, 210, 211, 212
Protestant, 12, 16, 66, 201, 238
Proudhon, Pierre-Joseph, 16, 19, 20, 21, 23, 26
punishment, 36, 44, 45, 48, 56, 69, 79, 81, 91, 92, 93, 96, 98, 99, 105, 116, 129, 132, 134, 135, 140, 149
Purleigh colony (United Kingdom), 206
Quaker, 200

radical, 1, 7, 9, 10, 12, 19, 25, 31, 34, 35, 62, 63, 64, 65, 66, 73, 74, 75, 77, 79, 92, 97, 102, 106, 107, 108, 112, 124, 130, 134, 135, 136, 139, 140, 142, 143, 145, 162, 166, 167, 174, 176, 178, 181, 184, 189, 191, 199, 200, 201, 202, 203, 204, 205, 207, 209, 213, 215, 216, 224, 227, 228, 229, 230, 231, 232, 234, 235, 237, 238, 239, 240
Radical Orthodoxy, 24
Ranter, 200
rape, 185, 187
rationality, 2, 9, 12, 14, 15, 77, 78, 100, 114, 139, 141, 195, 215, 220, 233, 237
Redford, James, 25, 55, 74, 75, 82, 84, 85, 103, 121, 124, 149, 150, 151, 156, 158
reform, 26, 109, 111, 118, 165, 175, 176, 200, 223, 228, 230, 234
Reformation, 112, 114, 115, 196, 197, **199–202**
reinterpretation, 37, 50, 61, 62, 63, 64, 65, 77, 97, 106, 107, **128–35**, 136, 143, 226, 227, 228, 229, 230, 231, 232, 234, 239
religion, vii, viii, 2, 4, 6, 7, 10, 14, 22, 60, 63, 66, 68, 78, 83, 84, 86, 87, 90, 91, 93, 96, 103, 104, 108, 110, 111, 125, 128, 130, 138, 139, 141, 143, 154, 157, 169, 170, 182, 201, 205, 207, 212, 216, 217, 220, 228, 231, 232, 234, 236
Religious Anarchism newsletter, 22, 212
Renaissance, 114
repentance, 33, 135, 174, 175–77, 188, 190, 195, 210, 231, 232
Research on Anarchism mailing list, viii
resistance, 3, 31, 48, 49, 55, 62, 96, 99, 112, 121, **130–35**, 148, 152, 155, 157, 162, 164, 169, 189, 203, 208, 218, 234, 237
resurrection, 67, **100–101**, 101, 139, 204, 219
Revelation, 3, 67, 104, 105, 156, 157, 219, 222
revolt, 34, 82, 84, 91, 201
revolution, 4, 9, 11, 15, 17, 19, 34, 39, 44, 60, 63, 66, 74, 90, 91, 92, 97, 101, 110, 136, 139, 142, 143, 144, 145, 148, 151, 154, 157, **167–73**,

175, 176, 177, 179, 180, 181, 183, 197, 201, 203, 204, 205, 213, 224, 227, 239
Ricoeur, Paul, 226, 227, 233
Rimbaud, Arthur, 95
ritual, 18, 68, 69, 103, 107, **139–43**, 239
Romans, 3, 9, 13, 16, 48, 81, 93, 126, 135, 147, 148, 149, 150, 151, 152, 153, 154, 155, 156, 157, 160, 240
Rome, 34, 60, 74, 76, 81, 90, 91, 95, 97, 102, 103, 108, 109, 110, 111, 128, 133, 137, 147, 149, 150, 154, 155, 156, 158, 159, 169, 198, 199
Rossbach, Stefan, vii
Rothbard, Murray, 24, 84
Rousseau, Jean-Jacques, 43, 235
rule, 4, 5, 30, 43, 50, 55, 64, 65, 69, 70, 71, 73, 74, 76, 82, 93, 94, 96, 99, 113, 114, 116, 117, 125, 127, 131, 135, 142, 148, 149, 151, 152, 153, 155, 162, 165, 176, 187, 215, 216, 219, 225, 227, 228, 229, 230, 239
rural, 181, 205
Russia, 14, 23, 171, 197, 203, 204, 206
Russian, 164
Sabbath, 58, 62, 63, 162
sacrament, 9, 139, 140, 190
sacrifice, 17, 41, 42, 62, 68, 69, 84, 95, 97, 98, 99, 111, 133, 151, 155, 157, 162, 172, 174, 175, 177, 179, 182, 183, 184, 185, 188, 189, 190, 193, 194, 195, 197, 198, 201, 218, 222, 233, 239, 240, 241
saint, 19, 103, 108, 134, 176
salt, 61
salvation, 77, 98, 131, 137, 138, 140, 141, 145, 171, 185, 186, 193, 233, 235, 236, 237
Sampson, Ronald V., 54, 110, 179, 187, 192
Samuel, 67, **68–71**, 72, 73, 94, 106, 111, 125, 152, 153
Sandlin, P. Andrew, 198
Sanhedrin, 90, 95
Satan, 38, 41, 75, 76, 77, 92, 95, 106, 144
Saul, 71, 152
Schillabeer, James, viii
Schmitt, Carl, 2
Schmitt, Eugen Heinrich, 122, 205
science, 77, 116, 124, 164
scripture, 12, 30, 50, 69, 73, 84, 85, 87, 89, 99, 104, 106, 133, 135, 139, 140

Second World War, 209
sect, 4, 7, 110, 112, 154, 169, 196, 197, 199, 201, 204, 205, 213, 217, 224, 234
secular, 1, 2, 5, 6, 8, 24, 111, 145, 156, 167, 217, 229, 234, 236, 237
secular anarchism, 4, 6, 7, 8, 9, 18, 20, 21, 25, 27, 136, 180, 237, 238
Sermon on the Mount, 13, 15, 16, 20, 27, 28, **30–66**, 67, 80, 81, 87, 88, 98, 104, 105, 106, 107, 126, 127, 128–**30**, 131, 134, 135, 139, 140, 141, 142, 151, 156, 158, 165, 192, 197, 215, 227
Sermon on the Plain, 30
service, 14, 47, 48, 53, 62, 67, 70, 75, 76, 78, 80, **82–83**, 83, 86, 87, 92, 106, 108, 116, 118, 122, 125, 126, 138, 151, 152, 153, 154, 157, 159, 160, 162, 165, 166, 167, 175, 179, 181, 198, 199, 205, 210, 222
sexuality, 95
Simon, 160
sin, 36, 43, 56, 70, 79, 80, 84, 85, 92, 111, 125, 131, 135, 137, 140, 141, 152, 153, 154, 155, 175, 176, 187, 234, 239
slavery, 22, 35, 45, 70, 71, 102, 116, 118, 121, 122, 123, 124, 145, 156, 183, 202
Social Democrat, 205
socialism, 19, 23, 25, 54, 145, 168, 169, 202
society, 1, 7, 16, 24, 31, 33, 35, 37, 39, 46, 47, 55, 60, 65, 70, 73, 76, 81, 82, 87, 93, 102, 105, 106, 107, 111, 118, 119, 121, 124, 125, 126, 144, 145, 147, 154, 161, 162, 166, 167, 168, 171, 174, 175, 176, 177, 179, 180, 182, 184, 191, 193, 195, 196, 201, 213, 214, 215, 217, 220, 221, 222, 224, 228, 229, 230, 231, 232, 234, 238, 239, 240, 241
Society for the Study of Theology, viii
soldier, 33, 54, 55, 70, 87, 88, 108, 111, 118, 119, 120, 133, 143, 166
Solomon, 71
son, 12, 48, 50, 51, 53, 70, 97, 101, 105
Sotiropoulos, George, viii
South, 202
South Africa, 207
South America, 210
Soviet, 205, 220

spirit, 23, 69, 79, 86, 91, 92, 94, 95, 124, 129, 132, 147, 156, 157, 167, 177, 179, 182, 186, 193, 208, 220, 221, 233
Stalin, Joseph, 25, 205
Stassen, Glen H., 57
Stepun, Fedor, 14
Stevenson, Robert Louis, 65
strategy, 33, 34, 35, 62, 76, 95, 130, 163, 169, 172
Strike the Root, 25
structure, 1, 15, 24, 45, 69, 74, 93, 118, 198, 219, 225
submission, 16, 42, 56, 91, 92, 96, 102, 121, 123, 140, 143, 147, 148, 149, 150, 151, 155, 156, 157, 161, 162, 164, 173, 184, 198, 240, 241
subversion, 16, 18, 19, 33, 34, 65, 75, 78, 84, 91, 93, 95, 96, 98, 99, 106, 108, 109, 111, 117, 129, 135, 136, 138, 139, 140, 141, 143, 147, 150, 154, 156, 157, 159, 162, 173, 174, 175, 176, 180, 182, 183, 192, 193, 195, 198, 200, 213, 221, 225, 232, 240
suffering, 39, 41, 42, 48, 51, 60, 61, 82, 83, 87, 96, 97, 98, 99, 124, 137, 143, 151, 156, 157, 177, 178, 180, 185, 186, 189, 190, 193, 206, 208, 222, 232
suppress, 62, 110, 205, 207
Suu Kyi, Aung San, 208
Sweden, 210
sword, 41, 51, 87, 88, 89, 90, 103, 104, 118, 134, 148, 156, 169, 189, 209, 241
Sylvester I, 109, 111
symbol, 78, 83, 84, 85, 86, 97, 99, 100, 102, 103, 108, 111, 162, 169, 203, 209
synagogue, 74, 85
syndicate, 44
system, 1, 18, 24, 25, 33, 34, 37, 44, 48, 49, 55, 69, 71, 78, 81, 84, 91, 113, 114, 118, 119, 120, 123, 132, 157, 159, 167, 170, 179, 180, 219
Taborite, 200
Taoism, 4
Tarleton, George, 25, 26
Tatian, 197
tax, 53, 67, 68, 91, 104, 109, 117, 122, 123, 124, 147, 148, 156, 157, 158,

159, 160, **157–61**, 161, 163, 166, 167, 179, 224, 233
Telford, William, 105
temple, 53, 58, 67, 84, **83–87**, 90, 91, 92, 97, 104, 105, 147, 163, 210
temptation, 40, 57, 67, 75, 76, 77, 78, 87, 88, 92, 102, 109, 111, 117, 123, 125, 126, 141, 157, 197, 198, 199, 214, 217, 218, 221, 222, 223, 224, 225, 228, 230, 231
Ten Commandments, 44, 65
Tennant, Michael, 68, 69, 71, 153, 155
terror, 20, 37, 41, 79, 148, 152, 168
Tertullian, 176, 197, 198
theology, vii, viii, 1, 2, 3, 4, 7, 8, 10, 12, 16, 18, 21, 23, 24, 27, 37, 51, 56, 61, 72, 91, 92, 100, 101, 109, 127, 128, 129, 130, 131, 132, 133, 134, 135, 136, 140, 141, 142, 143, 148, 149, 152, 157, 169, 176, 191, 200, 214, 215, 217, 218, 225, 226, 227, 235, 236, 237, 238
theory, 1, 2, 3, 7, 8, 9, 18, 24, 25, 27, 43, 46, 47, 65, 66, 84, 106, 107, 117, 124, 127, 134, 154, 168, 187, 195, 196, 207, 212, 215, 222, 231, 235, 237, 238
Thoreau, Henry David, 164
threat, 19, 39, 52, 63, 74, 90, 91, 93, 97, 99, 109, 111, 116, 132, 133, 136, 158, 159, 184, 224, 234
throne, 52, 92, 102, 109, 110, 125, 160, 232, 236
Tillich, Paul, 226, 227, 228
Tilly, Charles, 115
Tolstoy, Leo N., 4, 9, 10, 12, **14–15**, 16, 19, 20, 21, 22, 23, 24, 26, 27, 30, 31, 35, 37, 38, 39, 40, 42, 43, 46, 47, 48, 49, 50, 52, 53, 54, 55, 57, 59, 60, 62, 63, 64, 65, 66, 67, 68, 77, 78, 81, 85, 86, 87, 88, 90, 100, 101, 105, 109, 110, 111, 113, 114, 116, 117, 118, 119, 120, 121, 122, 123, 124, 125, 126, 127, 128, 129, 130, 131, 132, 133, 134, 136, 137, 138, 139, 140, 141, 142, 143, 144, 145, 149, 151, 154, 159, 163, 164, 166, 168, 170, 172, 173, 175, 179, 180, 181, 183, 184, 185, 186, 187, 189, 190, 192, 193, 194, 195, 197, **203–4**, 204, 205, 206, 207, 208, 215, 217, 218, 219, 220, 224, 233, 237, 238
Tolstoyism, 204, 205, 206, 207
torah, 63
torture, 118, 185, 210
trade, 85, 145, 210
tradition, 4, 7, 8, 10, 12, 15, 16, 18, 20, 21, 22, 30, 36, 63, 67, 71, 73, 93, 100, 116, 129, 138, 140, 143, 149, 168, 201, 207, 213, 214, 215, 216, 233, 235, 237, 238
Treaty of Westphalia, 115
trial, 20, 49, 67, 87, 88, 89, 92, **90–93**, 95, 97, 106, 135, 189, 220
Trinity, 140
truth, 4, 5, 11, 13, 16, 38, 41, 42, 46, 48, 50, 51, 54, 64, 71, 77, 78, 79, 83, 85, 87, 92, 94, 95, 97, 99, 103, 107, 108, 110, 111, 112, 113, 119, 121, 124, 126, 127, 131, 134, 135, 137, 138, 139, 140, 141, 142, 143, 144, 145, 150, 151, 154, 157, 161, 165, 168, 171, 172, 173, 175, 177, 189, 192, 194, 195, **174–95**, 197, 199, 201, 203, 204, 208, 216, 223, 225, 226, 228, 231, 232, 233, 234, 239, 240
Tsar, 118, 119, 203, 204
Tutu, Desmond, 208
tyranny, 39, 82, 94, 96, 144, 149, 154, 155, 168
United Kingdom, 20, 209, 210, 211
United States of America, 16, 18, 19, 20, 22, 23, 24, 25, 27, 44, 45, 66, 117, 206, 208, 209, 210, 211
Unity of Brethren, 200
universal, 4, 37, 39, 76, 102, 113, 120, 124, 154, 166, 181, 192, 204, 207, 228, 238
urban, 182
usury, 121, 124
utopia, 65, 96, 132, 155, 191, 201, 217, 223
van der Veer, J. K., 205
Vanunu, Mordechai, 210
Vatican, 19
Veda, 206
Vietnam War, 209
Vine and Fig Tree, 25
violence, 4, 15, 24, 32, 33, 34, 35, 36, 37–**43**, 43, 44, 45, 46, 47, 52, 54, 55, 57, 58, 59, 65, 66, 67, 69, 76, 79, 85, 86, 87, 88, 89, 90, 92, 94, 95, 96, 98, 99, 100, **104–6**, 107, 108, 111, 112, 113, 114, 115–**17**, 117, 118, 119, 120, 121, 123, 124, 126, 127, 133, 134, 135, 140, 142, 143, 145, 148,

154, 157, 162, 163, 164, 165, 166, 167, **168–70**, 171, 172, 173, 175, 176, 183, 184, 185, 186, 187, 188, 189, 191, 192, 193, 200, 201, 203, 204, 208, 209, 215, 217, 218, 220, 222, 224, 225, 228, 229, 230, 231, 233, 235, 236, 237, 238, 239
Vonnegut, Kurt, 65
vote, 80, 117, 165, 166
wage, 123, 124, 179
Wagner, Murray L., 110, 182, 199
Waldense, 199
Walesa, Lech, 208
Walter, Nicolas, 4, 74
war, 4, 37, 41, 44, 45, 46, 49, 50, 52, 57, 60, 68, 69, 79, 86, 88, 92, 95, 103, 109, 111, 115, 120, 121, 122, 127, 129, 131, 133, 134, 156, 158, 159, 166, 169, 179, 180, 187, 188, 191, 199, 203, 209, 210, 235, 236
Ward, Colin, 4, 21
Wars of Religion, 114, 115, 236
Washington (United States of America), 25
Watson, Simon, 179
wealth, 121, 122, 136, 178
Webbe, Gale, 98
Wenzer, Kenneth C., 203

West, 2, 120, 207
Wilhelm, Kaiser, 54
Williams, Duane, viii
Wink, Walter, 14, 20, 21, 24, 27, 32, 33, 34, 35, 41, 51, 52, 85, 94, 95, 98, 103, 163, 164
Winstanley, Gerrard, 9, 21, 200
witness, 13, 18, 32, 97, 100, 103, 108, 113, 128, 138, 149, 161, 162, 163, 165, 169, 171, 172, 173, 176, 177, 189, 190, 191, 192, 193, 195, 196, 197, 199, 201, 203, 213, 217, 218, 223, 229, 230, 231
Wogaman, J. Philip, 98, 217
Woodcock, George, 203, 206
World Wars, 206
worship, 75, 76, 85, 102, 125, 126, 134, 142, 151, 160, 197, 198, 221, 224, 225, 232, 234, 237, 239
Wycliffe, John, 200
Yahoo, 211
Yoder, John Howard, 2, 14, 20, 21, 22, 24, 27, 36, 39, 40, 51, 56, 61, 63, 64, 68, 73, 74, 75, 83, 85, 89, 91, 93, 96, 97, 99, 103, 151, 153, 157, 167, 170, 171, 181, 183, 201, 222, 223
Young, Roger, 171
Zealot, 76, 91, 158, 169, 171